WOODCARVING
TOOLS, MATERIALS & EQUIPMENT

WOODCARVING
TOOLS, MATERIALS & EQUIPMENT

Chris Pye

Guild of Master Craftsman Publications Ltd

First published 1994 by
Guild of Master Craftsman Publications Ltd,
166 High Street, Lewes,
East Sussex BN7 1XU

© Christopher J. Pye 1994
Line drawings © Christopher J. Pye, 1994
ISBN 0 946819 49 1

Designed by Fineline Studios
Typeset in Goudy Old Style
Printed and bound in Great Britain by
Eyre & Spottiswoode Ltd

Photo Credits
I would like to thank the following for their kind
permission to use their photographs:
Dennis Abdy of Henry Taylor (Tools) Ltd: Figs. 2.17,
2.18, 5.20; George Candlin of Spencer Franklin
Engineering: Fig.6.46; Tony Masero: photograph
opposite of Gino Masero's hands; Jonathan Simms of
Tilgear: Figs. 4.44, 4.47, 4.49, 4.50, 4.80, 4.83, 4.85,
4.86; Startrite Machine Tool Company: 4.43, 4.78.
Colour pages: 'Wide-spreading oak trees' etc. by
Ken Day; 'Life-size skull in yew wood' etc. by
Amir Boerstamam
All other photographs by Chris Pye,
© Christopher J. Pye, 1994.

Note: BCE (meaning 'Before Common Era') is used with dates otherwise
identified as BC.
CE (meaning 'Common Era') is used with dates otherwise identified as AD.

Gino Masero's hands

CONTENTS

FOREWORD

I first met Chris Pye in 1974 shortly after I had moved from London to Sussex. In my newly acquired rural workshop, sited among blossoming apple trees, we took stock of one another across a carving bench, and became friends. I was on the verge of possible retirement, while Chris was in the early stages of his career, but it has always seemed remarkable how a common interest in woodcarving can quickly bridge any age gap.

Although having an irrepressible sense of humour, he struck me as being a thoughtful and studious person, an adept carver and with the ability to express himself well on craft matters – a rare combination.

Since those days in the early 1970s he has taught carving and developed into a designer–craftsman of some stature. This has been borne out by the creation of a very successful carving and woodturning business in the south west of England, which thrived despite the recession.

As a woodcarving instructor myself, over the years I have made a point of reading through many craft books and periodicals on the subject but only at intervals did I find something of major interest that I could pass on to students. There seemed to be a certain lack of vital information published, and to some degree it troubled me.

To be taught by a caring expert is the best possible way of learning a craft and Chris Pye is foremost in this, being blessed with friendliness as well as approachability, and a genuine interest in his students, talented and otherwise. For the amateur, who for one good reason or another has to go it alone, it can be conceded that with some ability, carving is not too onerous in the initial stage (after all, our palaeolithic ancestors did not do too badly carving bone and ivory figurines). But major and minor problems can soon arise, often leading to frustration and despair. Setbacks tend to occur when the student, naturally, wants to progress towards more ambitious work. Apart from the inevitable problems that stem from lack of technique, the most serious difficulties, I have found arise from trying to carve with blunt tools, or even damaged ones. So it was a most welcome and splendid surprise when Chris sent to me the outline of his book on carving tools, materials and a whole range of equipment that traditional and modern carvers require for their work.

Even at the initial stage I was happily aware of a very closely researched and comprehensive source book, packed with information, and with sketches and photos galore. I believe that it is a most useful work, and can only anticipate that it will be widely read, so increasing student potential, as well as obtaining for them the maximum enjoyment that a truly great craft can offer.

Gino Masero
December 1993

ACKNOWLEDGEMENTS

When I cast my mind, like a net, over all the people and events that have, in whatever way, contributed to this book, I soon realized that my gratitude must extend more widely than I have room to record. In fact there seems no end to those who have influenced me.

For example I would include the makers of every carving I have ever gazed at, their patrons and toolmakers. Then there are those who have taught me, whose workshops I have visited, and who have shared their experience with me. And the authors of books and articles I have read, some long dead but whose thoughts I have taken as my own. And I have the tools of long-dead carvers whose names appear as watery shadows on the handles of many of my carving tools, but of whom I know little or nothing at all. And students I remember, but whose names I have forgotten, who made me think about what I was telling them and why I was saying it – and who caused me to write the original sheets on which this book is based. I want to acknowledge the influence of all these, and my debt to them.

But I really have only the space here to throw my net at selected parts of the water, to personally thank those who have more immediately helped me to write this book – with sincere apologies to those I have missed.

Foremost among these must come the indefatigable Gino Masero, who oversaw my initial attempts at sharpening, and witnessed the first time I laid a cutting edge into a piece of limewood. His spirited friendship is a source of great joy and, deservedly, I dedicate this book to him – an inadequate gesture of appreciation.

Then in the genesis of the book itself I am particularly grateful to the editor, Liz Inman, whose continuous encouragement and enthusiasm has really made the book possible.

In its preparation I took up the time of many people, who freely gave me information, ideas and advice about tools and materials, and sometimes the tools and equipment themselves to try out. I would like to thank: Tony Walker from Robert Sorby Ltd; Bill Tilbrook from Tilgear; John Tiranti from Alec Tiranti Ltd; Barry Martin from Henry Taylor Tools Ltd; Tony Iles of Ashley Iles (Edge Tools) Ltd; Charles Sterling of Bristol Design; Peter Peck of Record Tools and Glynn Bilson of HTF Tools. In this context I would also like to thank Ray Gonzalez for the idea of marking gouge handles with numbers corresponding to particular circle arcs.

Coming closer to home, and actually writing this book, I would catch, as it were in a quick gather of the net, some of the many people who so generously gave their time to read through different parts and made helpful corrections and suggestions – for which I am really grateful: Stephen Parr, Tony Walker, Candy Harrison and Ken Day. I would very much like to thank Gino Masero again for his stoical efforts in this respect, as well as for the use of his drawings of the tilting portable bench. My good friend Phil Hutchins who, having no interest in carving whatsoever, took the role of an objective reader – his effort on my behalf can only be described as heroic. I am also very grateful to Phyllis van de Hoek who made life a lot easier by tirelessly photocopying the drawings.

And in my net, saving the loveliest catch till last, my wife Karin Vogel, who has put up with such a lot as I wrestled with several learning curves and who has given me untold and unstinting support in the background. I sincerely wish to thank her for her help and patience.

INTRODUCTION

In the 1980s I wrote a set of handouts on carving tools and sharpening for students in the adult education evening class which I was teaching. I wrote them to fill in a shortcoming I found in woodcarving books at the time. Years on, I still feel students are inadequately supplied with basic information on tools and sharpening, and that is why I have enlarged these notes into book form.

Most carvers in this country are individuals carving in their leisure time, and most of these will have learned about carving and carving tools from books – the apprentice system having long been unavailable. On the whole, books about carving seem to treat the subjects of sharpening and handling carving tools in a perfunctory way – as a chapter to be got through in order to begin carving something, anything, quickly.

There is an assumption that competence in sharpening and handling tools grows naturally with experience of carving, but this is far from the case with the majority of beginners. Quite often they are only able to spend intermittent hours at their craft, and a great deal of frustration – if not despair – arises in students as a result of their inability to care for, sharpen and use their tools properly, and to work comfortably with their chosen material. This frustration affects the way they carve, as well as the final carving itself.

There are other consequences too, including the greatly increased use of sandpaper, not for abstractly bringing out the grain but as an expedient. Then there is the growth in sales of pre-sharpened tools and the increased marketing of electrical sharpening systems, which, to be used properly, still rely on beginners acquiring experience.

Some of the carvers who have learned from the type of books referred to above end up writing books themselves, and repeat a pattern that downgrades and minimizes carving-tool skills, which are in fact an essential foundation for good carving.

It is not that the information cannot be written down, or that there is no information to be had. If the scanty bits about carving tools, equipment and sharpening – in books, magazines and manufacturers' leaflets – are added up, there seems to be plenty to read. But the information is becoming superficial, incomplete and without due emphasis on its importance. Students continually appear with badly sharpened tools, and are frustrated with their work and progress, even though they have lots of carving books. There is something missing: an attitude or approach.

This book is my attempt to describe, as completely as possible, what tools and equipment are available to the woodcarver – particularly specific carving tools and equipment – together with the fundamental skills of how to care for them, sharpen them, and use them to a high standard. By concentrating on tools first, I am acknowledging a fundamental truth about woodcarving: the tools and the carving are inseparable – as inseparable as the hands and mind.

These techniques and approaches to sharpening woodcarving tools represent a long tradition, but have only been around for a long time *because they work*. If they did not they would have been dropped long ago. This does not mean that they cannot be bettered, but I feel it is a mistake to drop them for something less effective.

Fig 1.1 (Above) A medieval Green Man from southern Germany. Fewer tools, and of less variety, were in use at this time; perhaps this in itself gives the design its robustness and energy.

Fig 1.2 Carving tools have been called 'extensions of the carver's hands'. They transmit the carver's vision into the wood.

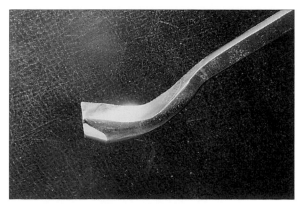

Fig 1.3 A detail of 'The Banquet at Simon's' by Riemenschneider (1490–92). Uncomplicated but effective tool cuts to the edge of Mary's hood are typical of this carver. The hair is carved with fluidity, and falls like liquid.

I have presented several sorts of information in this book: some practical information and advice which is vitally and immediately useful, especially for beginners; some reference information which will be lying in wait for a particular need, filling gaps as experience increases; and some information that is intended to be just interesting, enlarging the general pool of knowledge for all levels of carvers.

It must be pointed out that in this book there is a degree of opinion – descriptions of *my* way of doing or seeing things. I make no apologies for this. Carvers do vary in their approach and about what they think is important; they have their own habits, which work for them, and ultimately each individual must arrive at his or her own conclusions.

For example, I have had to make some decisions about what to call things – I might call a spade a 'spade', but others have different names. I have tried to set down clearly what is meant by a particular technical term, and, where there are common alternatives, to make sure these are mentioned.

This book is self-contained, but it does not contain carving projects as such. Carving itself will be the subject of a future book, a sort of Part 2. This book, however, contains enough concrete information on how, when and where woodcarving tools are used, qualities of wood, and how these factors relate, to enable someone either to start or to improve their carving.

As more and more people are taking up carving – and for many being in a workshop, or handling any tools, is a new experience – I have felt it necessary to emphasize *safety* as an important aspect of carving. Please pay attention to such details.

Each chapter starts with a set of *aims* for that chapter. Besides outlining what I hope to communicate, these sections are also an introduction to more general concepts, ideas and attitudes. I believe that the attitudes and mental states behind what we do are as important as the actions themselves, and it is guidance on attitudes that I wish to put across, as much as technical, practical information. As a consequence, I sincerely hope for nothing more than that this book results in a more satisfying *experience* of woodcarving for the reader, and, of course more satisfying carvings.

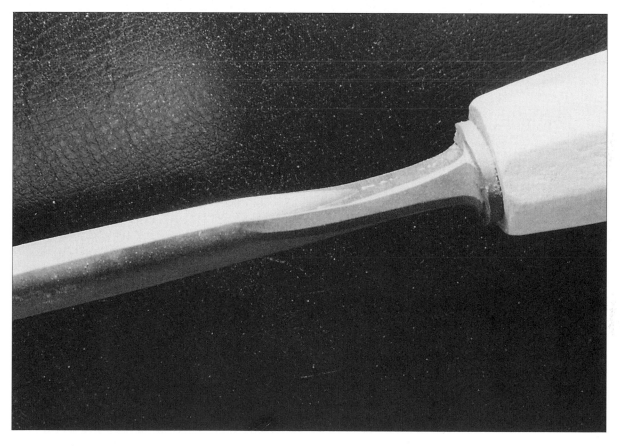

Fig 1.4 Finely made carving tools have an elegance and purposeful beauty all of their own.

WOODCARVING TOOLS

Aims

To help sort out the wide variety of shapes that are found among woodcarving tools and describe their purposes

To describe what a woodcarving tool consists of, and how it 'works'

To show how to assess the quality of a carving tool in order to know exactly what is being bought

To show how the shapes of carving tools relate to their function

To advise on the care of woodcarving tools

To promote, through understanding, a degree of confidence in the use of woodcarving tools

Each of the aims will be considered in a little more detail in turn.

Sorting out the wide variety of shapes found among woodcarving tools and describing their purposes

The vast choice of chisels and gouges is often one of the first things to bewilder a newcomer to carving – indeed, one manufacturer has the ability to make over 2000 different shapes and sizes. A degree of confusion may also arise in some woodcarvers who, although they have been carving for some time, started with a few randomly bought tools, and in beginners who have been given a boxed set of tools and are looking to expand their range. All of these people, and others, may be unsure as to whether the specific tools they need are available, or whether a particular tool might meet their requirements.

There is a system for finding what you need.

What a woodcarving tool consists of, and how it 'works'

It is a cliché that, when someone joins the army, before they can even think of firing their brand-new rifle, they are made to take it apart – then 'politely' asked to put it back together again. Then to take it apart . . . This is not as meaningless as it might at first appear; it establishes a deep familiarity with the weapon at an early stage, a confidence which may prove life-saving. The key points here are that if you have an intimate

knowledge of the tools on which your skill is based, are thoroughly familiar with them, unafraid of them, and even feel free to alter their shape if you want – all this adds enormously to your confidence as a carver. And through confidence comes competence.

Assessing the quality of a carving tool, and knowing exactly what is being bought

It is very important to appreciate a good carving tool when you see one; and just as important to avoid one of inferior quality. There are some tools on the market which are so badly made as to be worse than useless. There are others of excellent steel but badly shaped – these, with a little attention can be greatly improved: both in how they feel and how they work. There are also perfect tools which a carver will almost venerate. We will look at factors which decide this.

How the shapes of carving tools relate to their function

You may only need one or two tools for a certain job, or you may need a small range to start woodcarving seriously. You may be tempted by sets, special offers or old woodcarving gouges in shops. Knowing what a particular tool can do will help you buy only those that you need; and so avoid ending up with tools that are rarely, or never, used.

The care of woodcarving tools

I have some woodcarving tools which are well over 100 years old; they have the names of several previous owners stamped on the handles. It is sobering to think that you never really *own* a woodcarving tool – you only have custody and care of it. Eventually it will pass on to someone else who will use it and, hopefully, also take care of it and use it to create many beautiful works.

If you want a more prosaic reason for looking after your woodcarving tools they represent quite an investment – of money and time – and are a major contributor to job satisfaction.

Promoting a degree of confidence in the use of woodcarving tools

When all these points are assimilated, along with those in the following chapter on sharpening, a feeling and understanding for your woodcarving tools will be established which will underpin both the quality of your work and your enjoyment of carving. And this applies whether you will be carving full time or just need one tool for a particular purpose.

TYPES OF WOODCARVING TOOL

Finding your way around

If you had wanted a tool for carving wood before the Industrial Revolution, you would have needed a willing blacksmith to make you one. And not just any smith, but a metalsmith with the fairly specialized knowledge to make these unusual tools.

In the past, tools were far more precious than they appear to us today, both in terms of what they cost and their comparative scarcity. Having gone to some trouble and expense to have tools made, their owners did not consider them disposable; they would be passed down from master to apprentice, or be kept within a family. They were valued as a key to earning a living in a way that is not easy for us to appreciate. Combining tools with a marketable skill, like carving, ensured a place in what was a harsh world; and

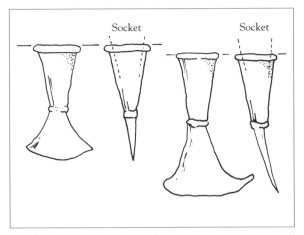

Fig 2.2 These small, socketed chisels were found near Cardiff and are now in the National Museum of Wales. They took a skilled Bronze Age smith time and trouble to make.

Fig 2.3 Panelwork at Abbey Dore Church which has been vigorously executed with a few simple tools.

Fig 2.1 This expressive Tudor head in Abbey Dore Church, Herefordshire, shows the simple, decisive tool marks of a skilled worker in oak.

proficiency in a craft, even if it would never make you wealthy, was very important when there was little in the way of financial lifelines. It is interesting to note that the term 'craft' has its roots in the Anglo-Saxon word for strength in skill.

Pre-industrial carvers would have particular tools made: some for general work and others for special commissions. In this way an assorted collection of tools would be built up relatively slowly over a lifetime. Eventually these tools would be passed on. Such carvers would have thought they were entering a magical cave, full of priceless treasures, if they could see the variety, consistency and availability of today's woodcarving tools.

Transported into our replete tool shops, carvers from the pre-industrial past would certainly be able to pick out familiar carving tools, as well as having an understanding of what the more recently developed ones are for. This would probably be true of any carver from the 4,600 years since the date of one of the earliest surviving woodcarvings – the so-called 'Sheikh-el-Beled', an Egyptian carving in acacia wood dating from the fifth dynasty. The reason is that the carving and shaping of 'wood' has involved – and always will involve – overcoming the same problems inherent in the material. The tools used then would still be appropriate today.

Carvers of the past would have been taught by true masters of the craft. They in turn would carefully impart trade secrets, guarded knowledge, to their apprentices and pupils. The proliferation of written information about carving is a very recent phenomenon. It is only since World War II that, in Britain at least, the whole tradition of bestowed carving expertise has virtually died out – the last flowering of an innovative 'school' of carving design was that of Art Nouveau, up to World War I.

This means that anyone who decides to take up carving today rarely has the chance of intimate access to another carver – someone who will show them the way of the tools, what types there are, and how to sharpen and use them to accomplish an intention. The newcomer can

Fig 2.4 A dry Egyptian tomb kept this woodcarving of a nobleman from deteriorating, although it has split from shrinkage. Made about 3000 BCE, its great presence and workmanship speak of a well-established craft.

Fig 2.5 An outer door in Berkeley Castle, Gloucestershire – the clear, but quite subtle, carving speaks of a long tradition.

Fig 2.6 Riemenschneider's virtuosity placed great demands on the tools. A wide range of sophisticated shapes were needed to get into the deep recesses of this angel, part of the limewood 'Elevation of the Magdelane', Bayerisches Nationalmuseum, Munich.

be left in the same magical cave of choice, not knowing how to find his or her way around it.

The Industrial Revolution, with its commercial competition, brought together the ability and capacity to manufacture a large variety of tools relatively easily. There was the need to satisfy both a large and growing number of Victorian trade carvers as well as, for the first time, leisured 'gentlemen and lady carvers'. Woodcarving tools were still made with a large degree of hands-on skill but the numbers and variety of shapes became enormous. From about the 1880s a regular illustrated list was needed; it was published in the tool-making heart of the country and became known as the 'Sheffield List'.

The Sheffield List

The Sheffield List (*see* following page) was a numerical description of the carving tools being made at the time. It soon became a recognized, standard system of nomenclature across Britain. It is still trade practice to use such a catalogue, either as a whole or with some small variations. To some extent a similar system, or version of it, is followed in other countries.

This numbering system, which will be described here, will enable you to recognize quite easily 'what's what' within the diverse range of carving tools available. Although this is particularly true of the tools made in Britain, the Sheffield listing is generally only accepted as a guide – individual tools made by different manufacturers may vary, especially in some of the more specialized shapes. A firm may also add another number to specify an additional attribute of the tool such as the overall length of blade – whether larger or smaller. For example, a firm may list a longer 'workman's' or 'professional' size of tool next to an 'amateur's' size. This presumably dates from the expectation that 'ladies' and 'gentlemen' would use more refined and delicate tools for their hobby.

Continental systems arrange tool shapes in clusters, one residing within another; essentially this is the same as the system where the shapes are spread across the page. Many people find the spread-out chart easier to follow.

Numerical description

When you pick up a carving tool look for a number, normally stamped on the shank just beyond the handle (*see* Figs 2.8, 2.9). Associated with this number will be the manufacturer's name, and/or the logo, and sometimes the place of manufacture as well. All specialist woodcarving-tool manufacturers in Britain put such details on, as do those of repute abroad. In fact this is a good first check on the quality of a tool: if the tool has no stamp on it then either it is individually hand made or the maker did not think it worth acknowledging. The number will also appear in the manufacturer's catalogue and it is worth having a few of these on file to compare sizes and shapes. A list of sources is included in the Reference Section (*see* page 345).

This numbering system is essentially a shorthand description of a particular woodcarving tool.

THE BASIC NUMBERING SYSTEM	
Number	**Shape**
01 (1)	Straight, flat chisels
02 (2)	Straight, corner chisels (skew chisels)
03 (3)–11	Straight gouges
12–20	Long bent gouges (swan neck)
21	Short bent chisels
22	Right short bent corner chisels
23	Left short bent corner chisels
24–32	Short bent gouges
33–38	Back bent gouges
39	Straight
40	Long bent } 60°(medium) parting tools
43	Short bent
41	Straight
42	Long bent } 30° (deep) parting tools
44	Short bent
45	Straight } 90° (shallow) parting tools
46	Long bent

The appearance of any carving tool is a combination of three factors:

- The **width** of the blade;
- The shape of the blade in **cross-section**;
- The shape of the blade along its length (i.e. the **longitudinal section**).

It is the variation in these three elements that creates the variety of woodcarving tools.

An important term to introduce is **sweep** – referring to the curvature of a gouge that is part of a circle. More will be said on this later (*see* page 20).

The basic numerical list (the Sheffield List) concerns two of the factors: the cross-section of the

THE SHEFFIELD LIST OF WOOD

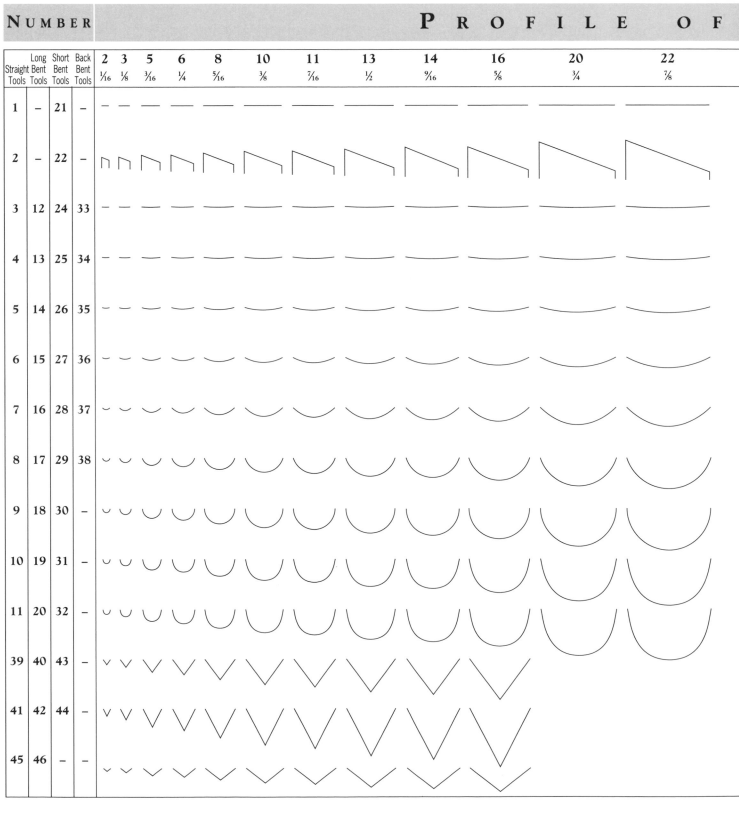

NUMBER				PROFILE OF

Straight Tools	Long Bent Tools	Short Bent Tools	Back Bent Tools	2 1/16	3 1/8	5 3/16	6 1/4	8 5/16	10 3/8	11 7/16	13 1/2	14 9/16	16 5/8	20 3/4	22 7/8
1	–	21	–												
2	–	22	–												
3	12	24	33												
4	13	25	34												
5	14	26	35												
6	15	27	36												
7	16	28	37												
8	17	29	38												
9	18	30	–												
10	19	31	–												
11	20	32	–												
39	40	43	–												
41	42	44	–												
45	46	–	–												

CARVING TOOL SHAPES & PROFILES

C U T T I N G   E D G E

26	30	32	36	38	MM
1	1⅛	1¼	1⅜	1½	Ins

Fig 2.7 This chart shows the cutting edge profiles of carving tools, drawn full size. Placing a gouge, for example, lightly over the appropriate curve will give you both its size and number. Tools up to 2in (50mm) are also available. This system has been used in Britain for well over 100 years; a continental system stacks the tool profiles, but I have found the layout presented here the most useful to work with.

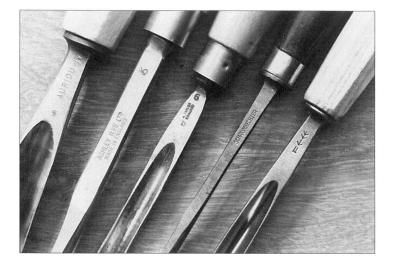

Fig 2.8 **The shanks of a selection of modern tools, stamped with the names and logos of the manufacturers, as well as a tool number.**

Fig 2.9 **If important details are on the ferrule and handle, this information may get lost if the handle ever needs replacing.**

blade and the shape along its length. The width is usually given separately in inches (or parts of an inch) or millimetres.

The various names, terminology and shapes of carving tools will be looked at in greater detail in the section on the parts of a woodcarving tool (*see* page 12). After these numbers come assorted tools, including fishtails (a series from 50 onwards in the original list but often now given a prefix number).

The range of straight gouges has equivalents in shape and size in the ranges of bent gouges. So, for example, the curvature across the blade of a ½in

(13mm) no. 3 straight gouge should be exactly the same as that of a ½in (13mm) no. 12 long bent gouge, a ½in (13mm) no. 24 short bent gouge, and a ½in (13mm) no. 33 back bent gouge.

Note that where you might – according to the list – expect nos 39–41 to be back bent gouges, these numbers refer to parting tools. The reason for this is that these deeper shapes of gouge do not work as well as back bent tools. (See also the section on shapes and

Fig 2.10 **Any curvature across the blade is available in different longitudinal shapes, for different purposes.**

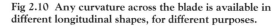

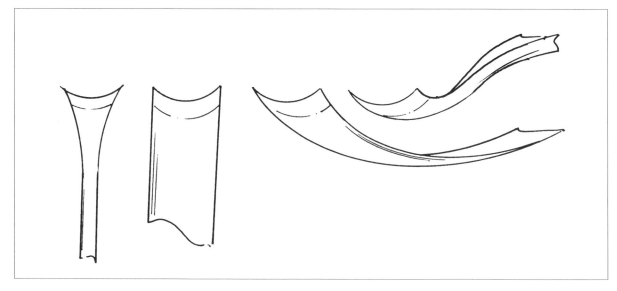

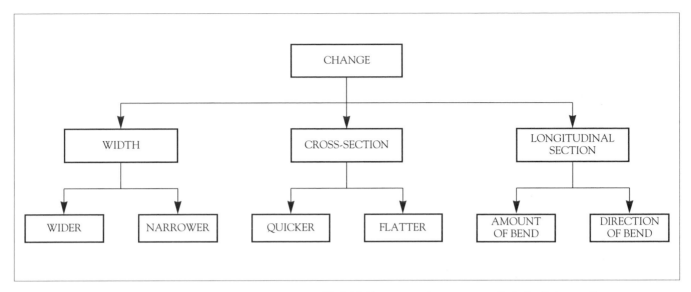

Fig 2.11 You can work your way quite logically to exactly the tool you need for a particular job.

function in this chapter, page 79.)

Bear in mind that you do not need this list to start carving – so do not worry about memorizing these numbers at the outset. The main use of the listing is for reference; it has a practical application when selecting and buying carving tools.

There is often more than one name for a particular style of carving tool, sometimes several. These names will be noted in the text in appropriate places.

Using the numbering systems

A beginner can start off with any carving tool, making the most use out of it and discovering its limitations. What normally happens is that as carving progresses, the beginner realizes the carving tool is no longer suitable – its useful limit has been reached for the work in hand. A change to a different carving tool is needed to continue. There are usually only three changes to be made (*see* Fig 2.11):

■ To the width
■ To the cross-section (or sweep)
■ To the shape along its length (longitudinal section).

The following examples show how this might work out in practice, using the numbering system.

◆ **The tool is the right width and shape along its length but the sweep of the cross-section is not the curvature you want.**

Fig 2.12 These tools all specify the same Sheffield List number (01) and differ only in the specification of the width.

Here you can move up or down the numbering system to increase or decrease the amount of curvature.

◆ **The tool is the right width and sweep but the shape along its length does not suit the work.**

In this case the listing enables you to keep the sweep and width you have been using, but in some bent or fishtail form.

◆ **The tool is the right sweep and shape along its length, but the width is too narrow or not wide enough.**

You may have to estimate this by trial and error because, as will be discussed below, it is not just a matter of going to the next width – the curvature actually changes as well. A carver often knows by experience which tool is needed to continue cutting a curve, or may well impel the tool to do the work. You can find the tool you want, but under a different number. Refer to the Sheffield List (*see* Fig 2.7) where the profiles of carving tools are shown full size.

Remember that a degree of hand-forging creates some slight differences. A good idea, especially for such work as mouldings, is to work out the similarity of sweep for your own tools and mark a corresponding numbering system on to the handles. More will be said about this later (*see* page 22).

PARTS OF A WOODCARVING TOOL

Various terms are used to describe the different parts of woodcarving tools. The following describes a 'typical' carving tool (*see* Fig 2.13).

The steel **blade** of a woodcarving tool is fitted to a wooden handle by its **tang** – it is normally quite straightforward to separate them. Sometimes the word 'blade' refers to all the tool except the handle, sometimes to the immediate part with the cutting edge, depending on context.

The handle itself may have a metal **ferrule** at the

tang end. Another, heavier, ferrule is sometimes fitted to the other end limiting damage to the handle when it is struck with a mallet.

Between the blade proper and the tang may be a shaped lump of metal: the **shoulder** or **bolster**. This prevents the tang being forced into the wooden handle and splitting it.

Blades are either flat (**chisels**) or curved in cross-section (**gouges**). A flat chisel has two bevels and each side looks the same, but a gouge will have a concave surface and a convex one. The concave side is known as the **inside**, **face**, **hollow**, **channel** or **mouth** of the gouge. The other, convex, surface is the **outside**, **reverse** or **back**.

The terms '**in cannel**' and '**out cannel**' refer to the inner and outer faces of *any* carving tool which has them – without specifying an actual tool (*see* Fig 2.14). Cannel comes through 'cannelure' – from the French for a channel – and is used in architectural contexts to mean a flute. It is also related to the word 'channel', and 'canal', the watercourse. The root of all these words is the Latin *canālis*, a pipe or duct. Although useful words, they are more often used by toolmakers than carvers.

From the shoulder is the **shank**: which leads into the various shapes of blade.

At the working end of the tool, a **bevel** diminishes the thickness of the steel into the cutting **edge**. There

Fig 2.13 The parts of a typical carving gouge.

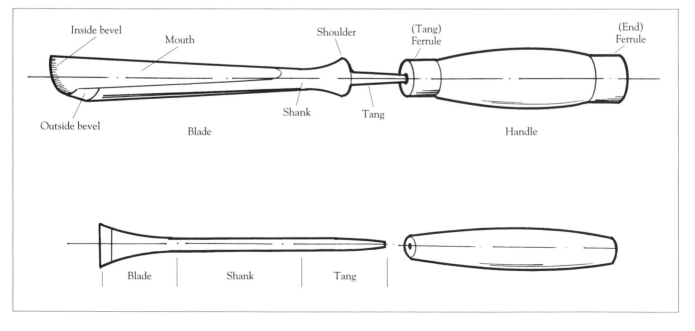

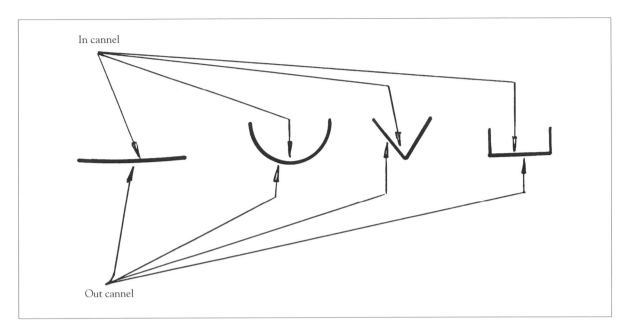

Fig 2.14 'Cannel' is a useful term referring to the inner and outer faces of a carving tool.

In cannel

Out cannel

Fig 2.15 Five similar gouges from different manufacturers, each finishing the tool in a different way – how do you know what the steel is like underneath?

may also be a bevel on the inside of the gouge – in other words there may be an **inner bevel** and an **outer bevel**. The corner where the bevel meets the full thickness of the blade is known as the **heel**.

We will now look in detail at the various parts of a woodcarving blade – first at the quality of its steel, then how the parts fit together.

Blades

QUALITY OF STEEL

The steel used in woodcarving tools needs to be what is known as high-carbon. It is often an alloy with small amounts of other metals and must be of appropriate quality (purity) to keep its cutting edge. If you put high-carbon steel to a fast grinding wheel, an intense, bright shower of sparks will be produced (*see* Fig 2.16). Anything that produces dull sparks, in small quantities, will be a low-carbon 'mild' steel and useless for carving. Manufacturers keep the makeup and sources of their steels to themselves.

High-speed steel (HSS), which is becoming popular for woodturning, has a superior edge-holding ability to high-carbon steel. In turning, the wood is cut at a high speed, concentrating both heat and wear on one small spot – under these conditions carbon steel softens and dulls more quickly. However, HSS is much more difficult to work and forge into the various

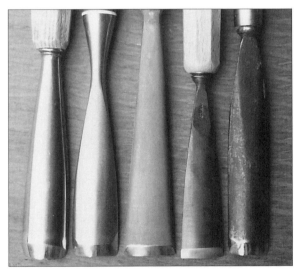

shapes that carvers need. Turning tools, which are comparatively simple shapes to make, are fashioned by grinding or cutting away excess metal from a round or square blank. For this reason HSS is unlikely to become available in the same way to carvers, unless some better way of working it is developed. Modern methods of 'sintering' – fusing the HSS under pressure into a single shape – may produce tools in the future.

To make a carving tool, a blank of high-carbon steel is heated in a forge and shaped on swage blocks –

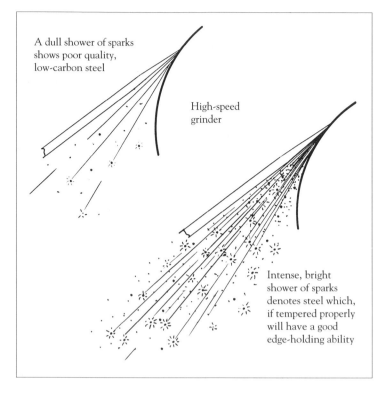

A dull shower of sparks shows poor quality, low-carbon steel

High-speed grinder

Intense, bright shower of sparks denotes steel which, if tempered properly will have a good edge-holding ability

Fig 2.16 The spark test for carving-tool quality of steel.

Fig 2.17 Tool-making today may still involve a large amount of hand forging.

Fig 2.18 Both the forging and final shaping need a high degree of skill, taking many years to learn.

creating the tang, shoulder, shank and blade. There are different ways of doing this: from crude, mechanical 'drop forging' to the more sensitive, hands-on 'hammer forging' – which is a highly skilled craft like smithing, requiring sensitivity and judgement to shape the blade consistently and correctly (*see* Figs 2.17, 2.18). Hammer forging creates a finer, stronger grain structure within the metal and is regarded as the superior method, used by the best toolmakers.

After the forging or shaping process, the blade is subjected to heat treatment, achieving the optimum hardness and tensile strength for the job it has to do. Only the cutting blade itself, and not necessarily all of that, is hardened. A greater or lesser part of the metal towards the handle (including the shank, shoulder and tang) is made softer and less brittle; this gives these parts more resilience.

These three factors:

■ The steel
■ The forging
■ The heat treatment,

establish the quality of a carving-tool blade. They determine both the shape and its cutting ability; and variations in any one of these factors can produce a superior or inferior tool.

Woodcarvers love to debate tools: who makes the best; which tools exhibit what qualities; how the steel, forging or tempering in each type of tool compares; the edge-holding properties of the 'old' versus the 'new' and so on. There is no consensus of opinion.

It is worth going a little further into this discussion about what it is in a blade that makes a good tool so that you can make as best, or at least as reasonable, a choice as possible.

Steel technology and research – as well as the ability to produce the appropriate quality of steel consistently – have developed a long way since the height of the Industrial Revolution. Modern steel can be considered superior for these reasons alone.

Victorian tools are much valued because it is really only from this period onwards that working tools (i.e. those tools with real working life left in them) have come down to us. As you might expect, these tools are quite often considerably worn by years of good use (*see* Fig 2.19) – taking the cutting edge back into a part of the blade which may be softer. The steel is the same throughout the tool but the heat treatment differs; the remaining part of the blade may have less hard, but more resilient, steel. If you have any of these tools in this shorter condition, keeping their edges badly, you can resurrect them by re-tempering. The method is explained in Chapter 5 (*see* page 235).

It is not just for the quality of steel alone that these tools are justifiably prized. The best makers of tools today shape and forge in very similar ways to the past. But you can often see, when you look at an old woodcarving tool, a considerable difference from some of its modern counterparts (*see* Fig 2.20). It is as if the older tools used thinner metal to get the same strength of structure, and it may be the quality of the steel that allowed this. There is also a matter of individual care: perhaps more time was taken in the shaping, giving to the older tools a consistently higher quality – the blade being better formed and finished off. But this, again, is arguable for some modern tools are beautifully made, and some old ones are far from perfect.

The final process, known as hardening and tempering – when the steel is rendered into the appropriate hardness for carving – is even more contentious. Suffice to say here that a large tool which takes a heavy pounding from a mallet, say a 1in (25mm) gouge, requires a different treatment from one which is used for delicate and precise cutting. It needs to be a little less brittle and able to absorb the stresses of impact without cracking the steel.

Different sizes and shapes of tools need to be heat-treated differently; not only because of the use to which they will be put, but also because of the variations in the quality of steel which can happen despite the intentions of the manufacturers. To

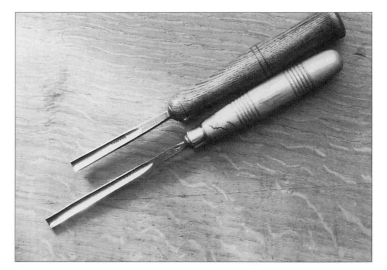

Fig 2.19 The old tool at the top would originally have been as long as the one beneath. The reduction in length represents many years of carving and sharpening.

produce a large volume of tools economically in a modern factory – compared with comparatively smaller numbers using cheaper labour in the past – means that the tools get an 'average' heat treatment *en masse*. They are not treated individually, according to how they will be used. On the other hand there is probably much more care and consistency today than there has ever been, with heat treatment being computer-aided. Modern tools may get more of an 'average' treatment, but it can be a very good one in terms of quality and consistency. There are also definite differences between the tools which

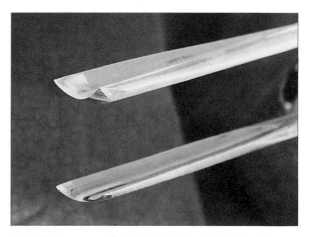

Fig 2.20 Some manufacturers today make their tools (as on the left) of much thicker metal than older ones (right).

Fig 2.21 The maker of the gouge above chooses to leave the tool black on the outside from the quenching, but polished inside. The maker of the bottom gouge chooses to leave the tempering colours visible.

manufacturers produce, as well as between tools within a manufacturer's range.

In the past there were also methods of quenching the hot tools, such as lead dipping, which (for economic and other reasons) are not used today. Such different methods may have given an improved crystal grain structure to the blade and allowed for the refined thickness in the walls that was mentioned above.

So far all this, with its reference to a historical background, is quite debatable. And the person whose only wish is to get on with carving something, might justifiably ask: where does all this lead us and how am I to decide which are the best quality carving tools? Here is my view.

If you compare the tools made by specialist woodcarving toolmakers – those firms which have been working within the tradition of making woodcarving tools for many years (some over 100 years) – there is, in fact not so much to choose between them. We are talking here of quality tools

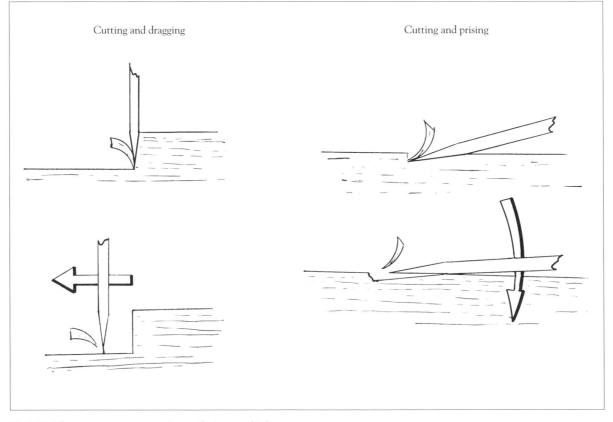

Fig 2.22 There are two poor carving techniques which quickly blunt cutting edges – avoid them.

from reputable manufacturers. There are also woodcarving tools – often from abroad but not just from abroad – which are much cheaper than the equivalent ones sold in the UK. These *look* like bargains, but beware; this cheapness has as much to do with poor quality steel and inadequate manufacturing techniques as with cheap labour and the rate of currency exchange.

There are factors, often not taken into account, affecting the ability of a tool to hold its sharpness other than those concerning the type of steel and the forging or tempering of the blade. Three of these factors are considered below.

◆ The cutting technique.

One primary reason why even top quality tools become blunt quickly is not the nature of the steel or tempering, but because of poor carving technique. For example, the habit of scraping the edge of the tool across the wood after cutting into it (*see* Fig 2.22). This practice of 'prising' chips of wood away and not

Fig 2.23 Riemenschneider's mastery of cutting technique is quite breathtaking in this detail from the limewood 'Elevation of the Magdelane', Bayerisches Nationalmuseum, Munich.

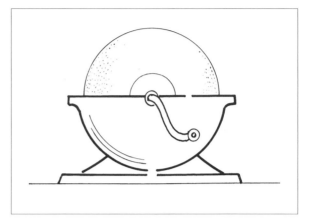

Fig 2.24 A 1920s hand-cranked, water-cooled grinding wheel would never heat the blade.

allowing the edge to enter and leave the cut cleanly is very common. As a way of blunting a carving tool on wood, you could hardly do better.

◆ Whether a grinding wheel has drawn any of the temper at any time.

Heating the blade repeatedly to below the well-known 'blue' colour (which indicates overheating and loss of hardness), but still heating it to far more than 'hand hot', may also lead to loss of edge-holding ability. Great care must be taken not to allow the blade to heat up significantly during grinding.

◆ The subtle effect of some modern grinding wheels on the crystal structure of the edge.

Minute cracks and striations may appear in some sorts of steel from the high-speed impact of the abrasive grit, so making the edge more liable to decay. This is more likely to happen with a coarser stone. Always finish off grinding on the finest wheel and leave enough metal for hand-working beyond any effect of the grinding.

In my experience there is little difference in the steel and edge-keeping qualities of most old and new tools – and I have in use a range of over 230 tools, old and new, but all from the best quality manufacturers. Individual tools of all ages and makes seem to vary in their edge-holding properties because so much depends on variations in steel, tempering and the treatment of a tool in the processes of carving and grinding. When it comes to the forging or shaping of tools, however, there does seem to be more of a difference between old and new.

So, to help you buy the best tools, here is some summary advice.

■ Never buy tools just because they are cheap, and definitely not from dubious sources.

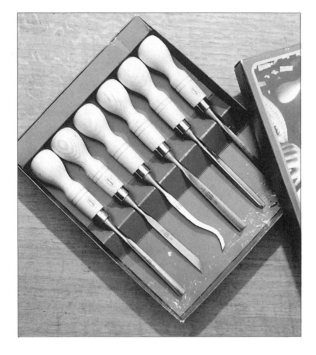

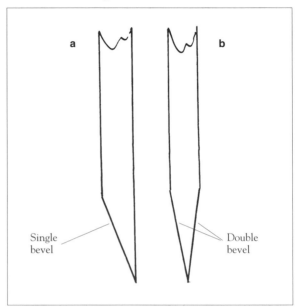

Fig 2.25 A 'starter' set of carving tools. I regard the small front bent chisel (third from the left) is a highly dubious choice for beginners, but must be bought with the set whether it will be used or not.

Fig 2.26 (a) Carpenter's and (b) carver's chisels require different bevel arrangements.

■ Always buy from firms with a long-standing good reputation to protect; who label their tools; are justifiably proud of what they make; and who can supply catalogues and other information.

■ When you are beginning buy your good quality tools from a few different sources and compare them yourself. Do not commit yourself to buying too many tools of the same make at this stage – you might eventually be unhappy with them.

■ If in doubt contact a few carvers and find out which tools they use frequently and what they think of them. Bear in mind we are all biased to some extent.

■ Buy the best tools that you can afford and do not stint on quality. It is better to buy a few, good tools, than more of lower quality. Tools are meant to last a life time and you do not want to regret what you have bought. Avoid box sets (*see also* page 90).

In this way you can be fairly sure of getting tools that are the best currently available – made from the best quality steel, using the best possible techniques.

Now let us look at how the blade can be shaped in its cross-section, longitudinal section and width for different applications.

CROSS-SECTION

Woodcarving blades have only a dozen or so different cross-sectional profiles, although there may appear more to a beginner. And even these dozen or so shapes reduce to three:

■ Straight
■ Curved
■ Angled.

It is when these profiles are multiplied by the changes possible along the length and the width, that we arrive at the huge numbers of different types that are actually available.

The cross-section of the blade is seen by looking end-on at the edge of the tool.

Straight blades

Tools with blades which are straight across the width are called **chisels**.

In normal woodworking, the chisel is a very common tool, having a bevel on one side of the cutting edge and a flat face on the other. Woodcarving chisels differ from those used in carpentry by having a bevel on *both* sides (*see* Fig 2.26). The reason for this is explained in the section on shapes and function (*see* page 79); the carpentry chisel is used mostly with a

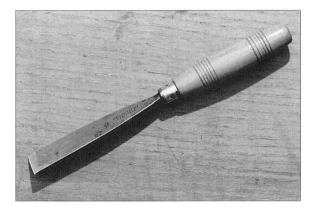

Fig 2.27 Basic firmer chisel.

Fig 2.28 An old socketed firmer chisel, tapering straight to the edge.

Fig 2.29 The splayed allongee shape naturally arises as a bar of metal is thinned to a working edge. Earliest chisels may well have kept the original bar, bound in thong, as the handle; sockets and tangs were later refinements.

– presumably connected with the workers of roofs. The word chisel also comes from the French *ciseau*, – which is a blade with parallel edges and a definite bevel. Of the two shapes, the long splay – termed 'allongee' by carvers – is by far the older (*see* Fig 2.29).

The ordinary straight woodcarver's chisel is designated no. 1 in the Sheffield listing.

When the cutting edge of the chisel is at an angle to the long axis, the tool is called a **skew chisel (skewed chisel)**, **skew** or **corner chisel** (*see* Fig 2.30). A straight version of this tool, as opposed to anything bent, is a no. 2 in the Sheffield List. Like the firmer chisel it has a bevel on both sides and can be

different purpose, although it is usual for carvers to have a few.

Another name for the woodcarver's chisel is a **firmer** or **firmer chisel** (*see* Figs 2.27, 2.28). This term was first recorded a couple of hundred years ago and seems to come from the French *fermé*, meaning a roof truss. It was applied to a chisel with a blade splaying from the handle, and with no apparent bevel, called a *fermoir*

Fig 2.30 Basic skew chisel.

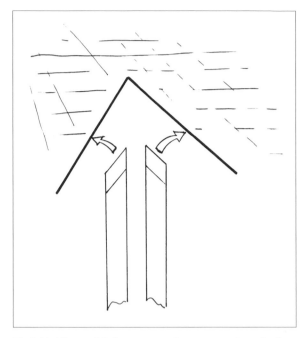

Fig 2.31 The useful skew can get into corners from both directions by turning it over.

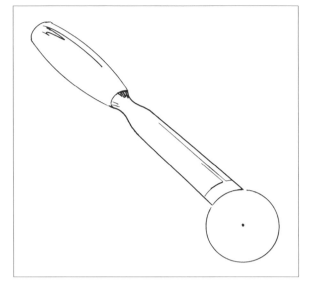

Fig 2.32 A sweep is, by definition an arc, a proportion of the circumference of a circle.

Fig 2.33 The flattest gouge, seen from above, is almost indistinguishable from the truly flat chisel.

Fig 2.34 The flattest gouge (left) and a chisel (right) seen end on.

used either side up, with the cutting edge facing left or right (*see* Fig 2.31).

Curved blades

When the actual cutting edge of the blade is curved to a greater or lesser degree, it is referred to as a **gouge**.

The curvature is known as the **sweep** of the blade when this curvature is an amount of an arc from a given circle (*see* Fig 2.32). The different radii of the circle determine what the curvature looks like. Sweeps range from very flat (no. 3), which is almost, but definitely not, a chisel (*see* Figs 2.33, 2.34), to a true semi-circle (usually no. 9) (*see* Fig 2.35).

The no. 9 is the last sweep in the series that can be 'rocked' through its cut (*see* Fig 2.36). The smaller representatives – approximately ⅛in (3mm) or less – are known as **eye tools**; they are used to form the 'eyes' where some types of acanthus leaves meet (*see* Fig 2.37).

After this the side walls elongate and the mouth deepens. The gouge takes on more of a **U** shape (nos 10 and 11), with no. 11 having the deepest walls (*see* Figs 2.38, 2.39).

To go over this numbering system for straight-bladed gouges: the flattest gouges are no. 3; the semi-circular ones are no. 9; and there is a deepening range of sweeps in between. There are two **U**-shaped gouges

Fig 2.35 Sweeps range from the flat to the semicircular.

Fig 2.36 Only gouges with a sweep can rock or rotate through their cut. This slicing action, in either direction, is a primary carving technique.

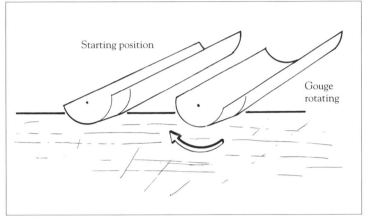

Fig 2.37 A small semicircular carving tool is rotated into part of the hollow between acanthus leaves, forming the distinctive 'eye'.

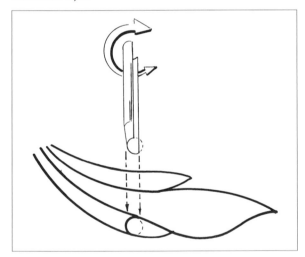

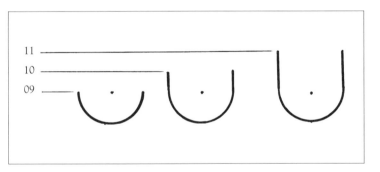

Fig 2.38 From a semicircle, the walls of the gouges extend to form U-shaped profiles.

Fig 2.39 From semicircle on the left to the deeper U-shape on the right.

(nos 10 and 11) with curves based on semicircles and elongated walls.

This nomenclature is not always as neatly defined as stated here and some differences occur between makers. For example, a firm may make *fewer* divisions in the range – making the no. 10 the true semicircle and only having the no. 11 as the **U** shape. Remember also that these tools include a degree of hand-making when comparing them with the manufacturer's charts of 'ideal' shapes.

The principle is that the curves are arranged from flat to very curved, and numbered accordingly. It is a common mistake (and one appearing in many publications) to assume that when each sweep of

gouge is given a number, this number applies to gouges that take their curvature from a particular diameter of circle, no matter what the width. In other words, that smaller or narrower gouges are segments of the larger

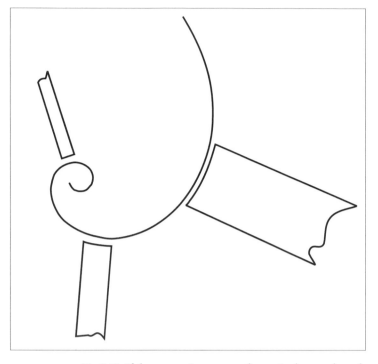

Fig 2.40 If the sweeps in a range of a particular number of carving tool are joined, the result is a spiral *not* a circle, although the sweep of any particular tool will describe a circle.

Fig 2.41 Any gouge with a 'sweep' – a portion of a circle – will cut a circle according to the size of radius.

ones. So no. 6 gouges whether ¼in (6mm), ½in (13mm), ¾in (19mm) or 1in (25mm) wide might be assumed to have an increasing amount of the same radius circle. This is not true.

If you were to join the ends of cuts made by the range of say no. 6 straight gouges by pushing them into a flat wooden surface, the result would be a spiral, *not* a circle (*see* Fig 2.40). This shows that the gouges of any designation *keep a proportionate depth as they decrease in width*. This is true of both British and continental systems. How the geometry was first decided appears to be lost, along with the original patterns, in the mists of time. The sweeps perpetuate because when the swage blocks that are used to form the profiles wear out, a new one can be taken using a tool as a pattern; the original information is never needed. Perhaps the curves were progressive Archimedian spirals, and not circles at all. However, remember that *every gouge – other than the U-shaped – will cut a true circle if allowed to follow its own cut* (*see* Figs 2.41, 2.42).

By stamping the edges of your gouges into a piece of card or tracing paper, it is possible to find which widths and numbers of gouges will join up in the same circle. A second numbering system of your own, using perhaps Roman numerals or letters, can then be added

Fig 2.42 U- shaped gouges are obviously not able to do this.

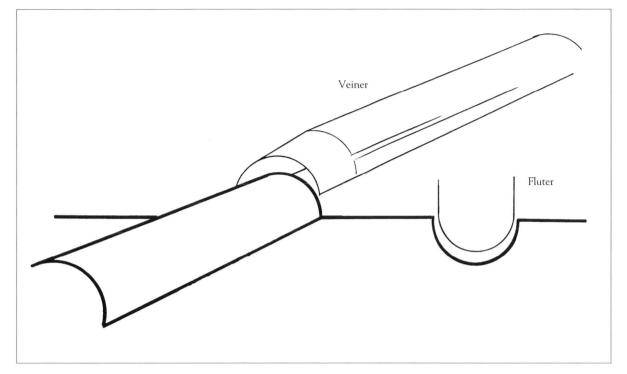

Fig 2.43 A veining tool is one used upside down to shape the veins in, for example, foliage; fluters were used to cut channels.

Fig 2.44 'Flutes' and 'reeds'.

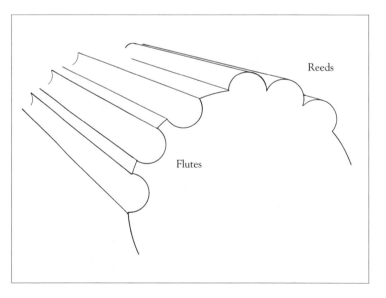

to the handles. This may be important for carved work such as mouldings. For most work, however, carvers come to know which chisel cuts which curve, and will manipulate a gouge to fit a particular cut if exactly the right one is not to hand.

A flat gouge is termed exactly that – a **flat gouge**. A gouge with a pronounced sweep is termed a **quick gouge.** Carvers talk about **flatter** or **quicker** gouges as the curvature varies one way or the other. As the curvature increases, the gouge is said to become quicker. There may an interesting relationship with the phrase the 'quick and the dead'. A quicker gouge is, in a sense, more 'alive'; in the first rough stages of carving, a quick gouge can remove wood much faster and more vigorously than a flat gouge.

The nos 9, 10 and 11 gouges, because they are based on semicircles, do not become quicker or flatter, only wider or narrower. The width of the tool is the diameter of one particular semi-circle. These gouges are called either **veiners**, or **veining tools** if they are small (approximately ⅛in (3mm) or less; or **fluters**, or

fluting tools, if anything much larger (*see* Fig 2.43). These terms describe the principal use to which these tools were put: the no. 9, for example, can be used upside down to shape the reeds or veins in foliage (*see* Fig 2.44). A **flute** is a decorative channel cut into a surface and can be easily cut with these deeper U-shaped gouges.

Fig 2.45 A basic V- or parting tool.

Fig 2.46 Apart from the standard 60° parting tool, narrower and wider versions are available for different purposes.

Angled blades

By far the most common angle to be used is a V shape.

It is helpful to see this tool as two chisels joined together by one edge to make a V shape; for obvious reasons it is called a **V-tool** (*see* Fig 2.45).

Another common name for this shape is a **parting tool**, so-called because among other things it is used to separate or divide one area of carving from another. This is most easily seen in shallow, relief carving where the subject is 'relieved' from its background.

The angle formed between the two sides can be more, or less, acute: the three normal angles are 45°, 60° and 90° (*see* Figs 2.46, 2.47). The angle is chosen according to the work for which the parting tool is

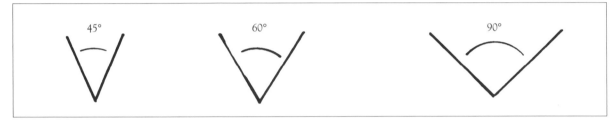

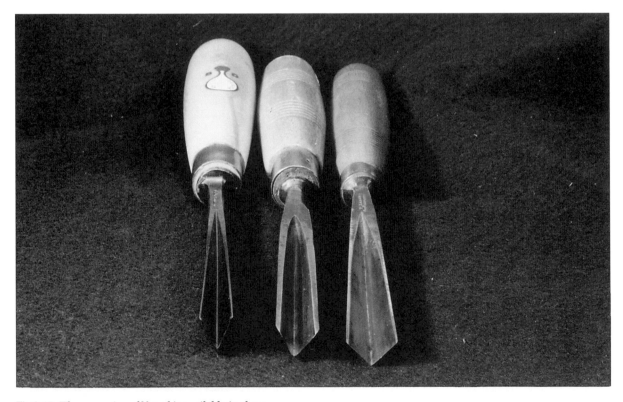

Fig 2.47 The same size of V-tool is available in three different angles: 45°, 60° and 90° (left to right).

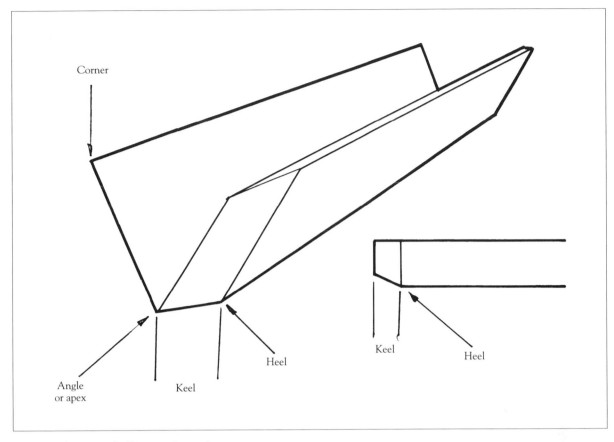

Corner

Angle
or apex

Keel

Heel

Keel

Heel

Fig 2.48 The parts of a V- or parting tool.

needed. If you have to choose only one type, the 60° angle is probably the most useful, being the medium shape. The junction in the bevel between the two faces of the parting tool is called the **keel** and, like a keel in a boat, it has a guiding function (*see* Fig 2.48).

You may come across other, more unusual, tools which have an angled cross-section of some sort (*see* Fig 2.49). These were originally developed in the furniture trade for particular work, such as cleaning between the elements of a design. They are little used in general carving; most of their work, if not all, can be done with other tools and they are nearly redundant these days. If you are starting carving, in particular, these tools should not really be considered. However, they are worth knowing about. Their names are rather fanciful and it is not hard to imagine some Italian carvers, many of whom found their way to the East End of London in the heyday of furniture carving, having a private joke over their pasta one day which somehow caught on. Some may have been designed by the founder of the tool suppliers Alec Tiranti Ltd.

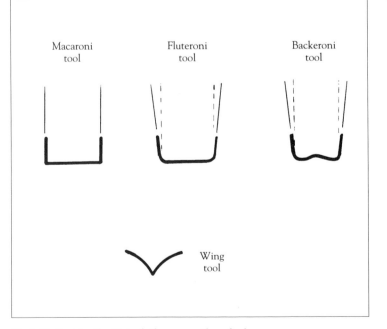

Macaroni
tool

Fluteroni
tool

Backeroni
tool

Wing
tool

Fig 2.49 Besides the V- tool, there are other, far less common tools which are angled in cross-section.

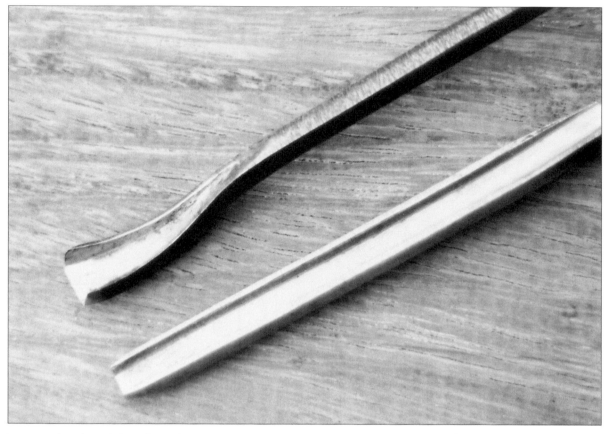

Fig 2.50 Short bent (left) and straight macaroni tools.

Fig 2.51 The straight chisel normally has flat faces. The oval shape of the lower tool is an attempted innovation, but I find its smooth corners make it less easy to grip.

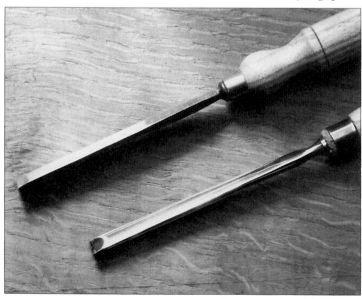

These angled tools include the following tools.

The macaroni

This is equivalent to three chisels joined together with two right angles in between (*see* Fig 2.50). It is sometimes called a **trench** or **trenching tool**, and is a bit like half of a rectangle. It will cut to both the left and the right sides.

The fluteroni

This is a sort of softened-off macaroni with rounded corners. The sides are still straight, but leaning out a little.

The backeroni

This is a fluteroni with the central in cannel curving slightly in.

The wing tool

This is aptly named, and is the equivalent of two gouges edge to edge, rather than the two chisels that make up

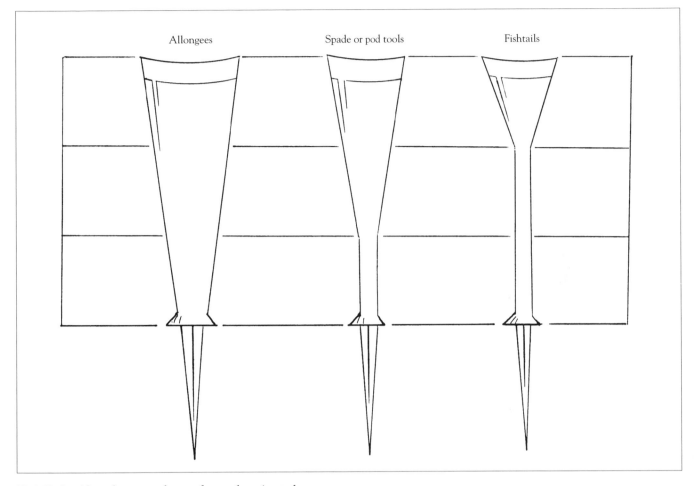

Allongees   Spade or pod tools   Fishtails

Fig 2.52 A guide to the nomenclature of tapered carving tools.

the V-tool. This tool was used to clear wood between two beads, shaping the beads themselves at the same time. A **bead** or **reed** is the opposite of a **flute** or **channel**, sticking out as a semicircular moulding.

Having considered the various shapes of woodcarving tools by looking *across* the blades, let us now turn to the shapes along their length.

LONGITUDINAL SECTION

A blade can be straight or bent between the handle and the cutting edge. These two broad themes contain several variations.

Straight tools

The sides of these tools may be parallel along their length or may splay outwards from the handle. Straight woodcarving tools with *parallel* sides are the ones usually called **straight**.

The splaying or tapering starts either directly from the shoulder of the blade, or begins after some length of shank. The shank can in fact be quite long with the blade a mere appendage, fanning out at the end. The tapered tools have their own names depending on the variable ratio of taper to shank.

Straight, parallel-sided gouges or chisels

These are by far the most common and useful woodcarving tools, although a few, specialist carvers may have more of other types. In terms of the Sheffield List, these tools are the ones numbered 1 to 11 and also include the straight parting tools.

Straight, tapered chisels and gouges

These are lightweight versions of the straight, square-ended tools, while still retaining the same sweeps or curvatures. The consequences of the splaying shape are twofold:

■ The corners are made more prominent. This is most important for getting into corners, as when lettering.
■ They are of lighter weight and give greater visibility. This facilitates more precise cutting and makes them excellent for precise cutting and finishing off.

One disadvantage of splayed blades is that their cutting edge becomes narrower as it is sharpened. This means that they have a shorter effective life than parallel blades.

The names given to these tools vary a bit between manufacturers and some have, predictably, been obscured with time. A fairly uncontroversial classification would be as follows (*see* Fig 2.52):

■ The **allongee** tapers, or splays, from the shoulder straight out to the edge (*see* Figs 2.53, 2.54). This is probably one of the oldest shapes of chisel as the act of beating out a lump of metal tends to produce a splayed shape more easily. The name comes from the French *allongement*, to elongate. As straight gouges and chisels get wider, they also become bulkier; for a tool wider than approximately 1½in (38mm) it may be worth

Fig 2.53 The allongee shape.

Fig 2.54 The allongee is a lighter tool for the size of the cutting edge. The side view (above) shows the taper often merges into the bevel, which may be indistinguishable.

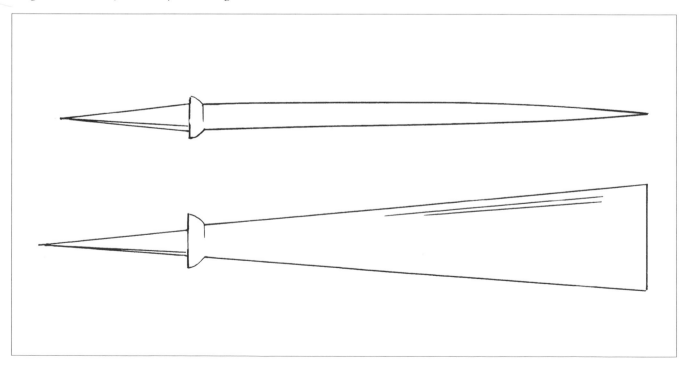

having the less cumbersome allongee shape – trading the slow loss of width over time for the lighter use.

■ The **fishtail**, at the other extreme, has a long, square shank with a suddenly expanding blade at the end – which does indeed look like the tail of a fish (*see* Fig 2.55).

■ Between the allongee and the fishtail can be variable lengths of shank or taper somewhere in the middle (*see* Fig 2.56). Old books often refer to these middle tapers as **long-**, **medium-** or **short-pod** tools or, collectively, as **spade tools** or **spade gouges**. Here the word 'pod' may come from *podium*, referring to a foot or leg – the prominent shank. Bear in mind that shank also means a leg, or at least part of it.

When considering buying any of these splayed tools, it is important to bear in mind that a fishtail to one manufacturer may be a spade tool to another. You need

Fig 2.55 The basic fishtail shape.

Fig 2.56 Tapered gouges: nomenclature varies between manufacturers. You need to decide what you want to achieve, and ask if the shape of tool will do it for you.

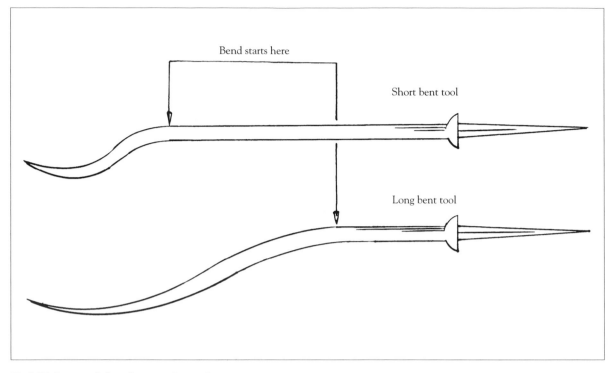

Fig 2.57 Long and short bent carving tools.

Fig 2.58 The crank of a front bent gouge curves in the opposite direction to a back bent gouge.

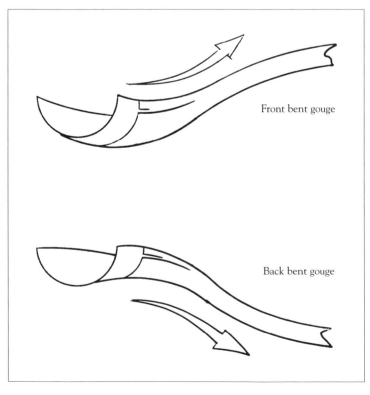

to check this detail with illustrations and not assume manufacturers use the same name for the same shapes.

The actual blade sweeps normally correspond to those of the other straight gouges and the tool numbering reflects this fact. The last digit (or two digits) of the listing are the same for all blades with the same sweep, regardless of the different longitudinal shapes. In this way if you like the sweep and size of a particular parallel gouge, but would like it as a fishtail, you should be able to get this version of the tool using the numbering system.

Chisels may also be allongee, spade or fishtail with a long shank.

Bent tools

The bend is seen by looking at the side of the blade: it will curve one way and then the other. The bend itself can start from one of two places (*see* Fig 2.57).

■ It can start from the shoulder of the tool, as a long, continuous, snake-like bend: the long bent tool.
■ It can start much further away, towards the working edge after a straight shank. This creates a short crank-like bend: the short bent tool.

The short bend, in turn, can bend in opposite

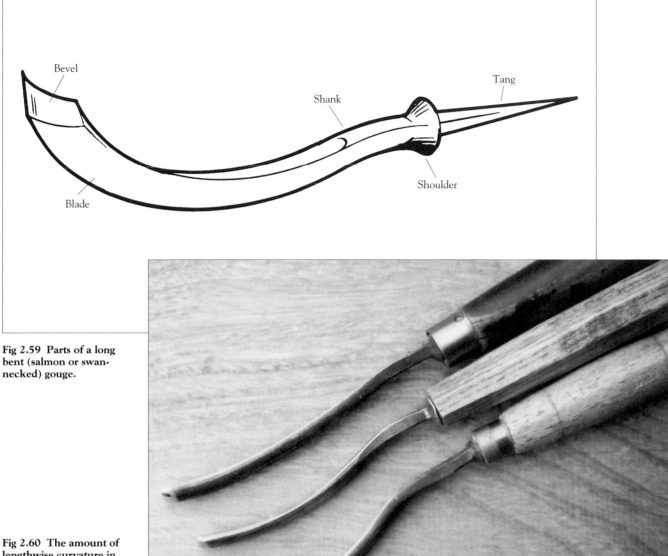

Fig 2.59 Parts of a long bent (salmon or swan-necked) gouge.

Fig 2.60 The amount of lengthwise curvature in long bent gouges varies between manufacturers. Some have so little curve as to be little improvement on the straight gouge.

directions (*see* Fig 2.58):

■ Towards the front first: a front bent
■ Towards the back first: a back bent.

Let us look at these bent woodcarving tools in more detail.

Long bent tools

These tools, which are invariably gouges not chisels, have various names: **long bent**, **curved**, **salmon** or **swan-necked** gouges (*see* Figs 2.59, 2.60). The curvature is long and elegant and enables the carver to get into a shallow recess without the handle fouling the wood.

V-tools also come in a long bent version, but not chisels.

Short bent tools

Again there are various names: **short bent**, **shallow**

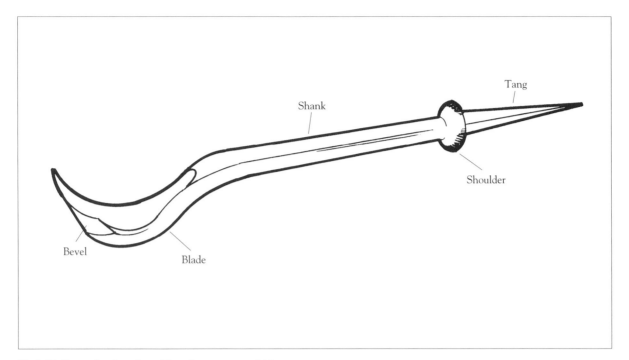

Fig 2.61 Parts of a short bent (front bent or spoonbit) gouge.

Fig 2.62 Basic front or short bent gouge.

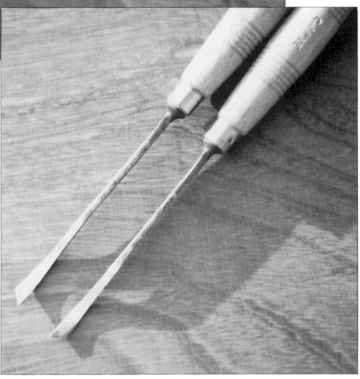

Fig 2.63 Short bent chisel.

Fig 2.64 Short bent skew chisels come in pairs.

bent, **front bent** and **spoon** or **spoonbit gouges** (*see* Figs 2.61, 2.62). Sometimes the simple term **bent gouge** is used; this implies the type with the short bend to the front but this is not necessarily the case. The term is best avoided and replaced with something a little more precise.

Short bent tools may not be gouges, but fishtail chisels or skew chisels, in which case they have a long shank.

The short bent chisels and flattest gouges are called **grounding tools** or **grounders** (*see* Fig 2.63), because they are used to work the backgrounds of relief carving.

A **short bent skew chisel** can have the cutting edge skewed to face the left or right. These are usefully

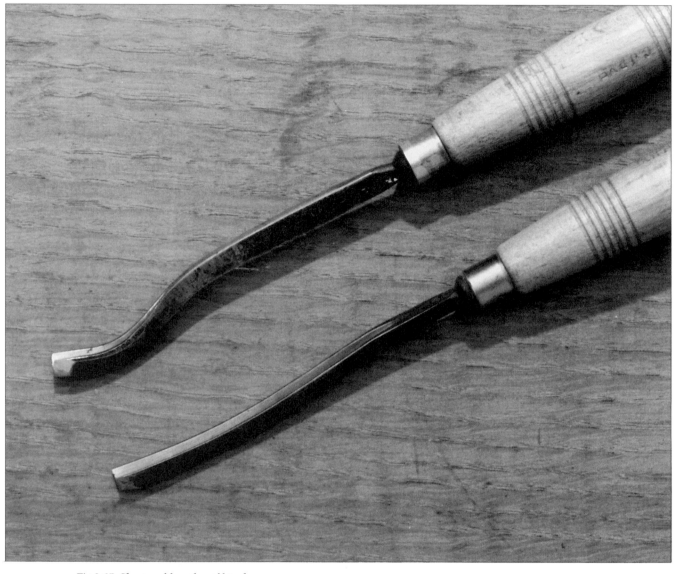

Fig 2.65 Short and long bent V-tools.

bought in pairs (*see* Fig 2.64). **V**-tools and macaroni tools can also be in a short bent form (*see* Fig 2.65).

The tightness of the bend allows the carver to get into recesses which are deeper than those accessed by the long bent tools – the crank-like shape keeps the handle even further out of the way.

The amount of bend that any manufacturer gives to both short and long bent tools varies considerably – not only between manufacturers but even between batches of tools coming from one manufacturer. Sometimes there seems to be so little curve on the tool that it beggars the description 'bent', and gives

negligible advantage over the straight tools. So you need to be a little wary here, especially if you are ordering unseen tools through the post. Try to examine photographs or drawings of what you hope you are getting, and do not accept a tool with a curve that, in effect, does not do the work it is meant for.

Short bent gouges with the greatest change of curvature in the bend are referred to as **knuckle gouges** (*see* Fig 2.66). These are useful for entering very tight recesses and hollows, such as those found in Gothic carving.

Sometimes, but fortunately not often, a very

awkward job requires such a bend that a special tool has to be made – perhaps with so much of a bend that the edge of the tool is actually facing back towards the handle. This is not too difficult a procedure and Chapter 5 gives you enough working details to tackle this problem (*see* page 229). It is best to start with a tool having the sweep and width you want and simply alter the lengthwise bend to what is needed.

Back bent tools

These tools are similar to short bent gouges, but the curve is made in the opposite way. The odd-looking tool so produced comes into its own when carving a bead or other convex surface which, itself, curves concavely – such as

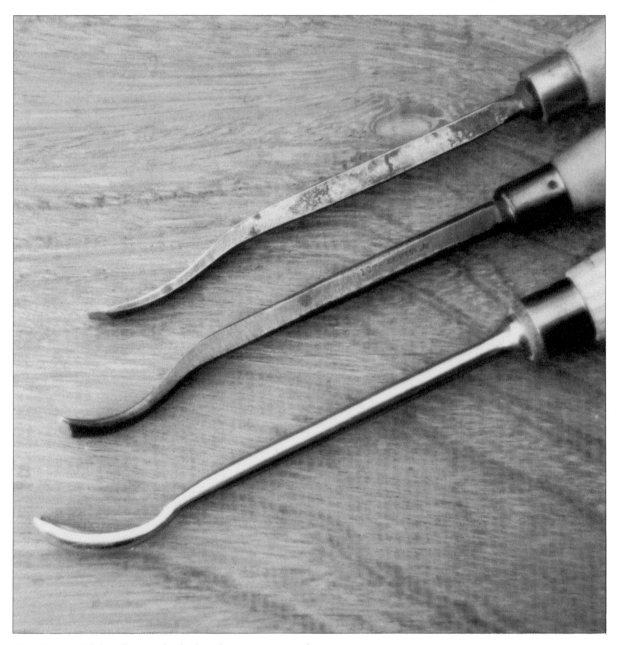

Fig 2.66 As with long bent tools, the lengthwise curvature of short bent tools offered by manufacturers varies considerably, and some versions are hardly bent at all.

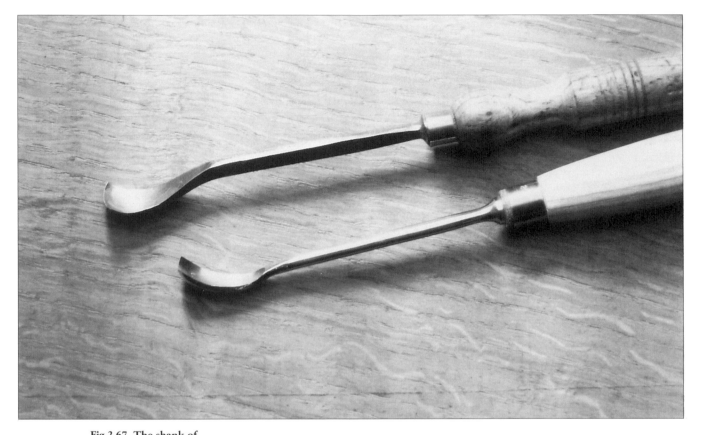

Fig 2.67 The shank of
the front bent gouge is
normally rectangular,
facilitating grip. A new,
polished, circular shape
looks slicker, but I find
that I can grip it less
firmly. This sort of
personal reason is why
it is best to handle tools
first, rather depend on
the catalogue
photographs.

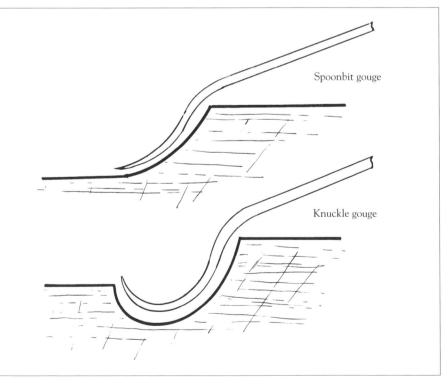

Spoonbit gouge

Knuckle gouge

Fig 2.68 The knuckle
gouge is a tightly cranked
front bent gouge which
gets into deep recesses
more easily.

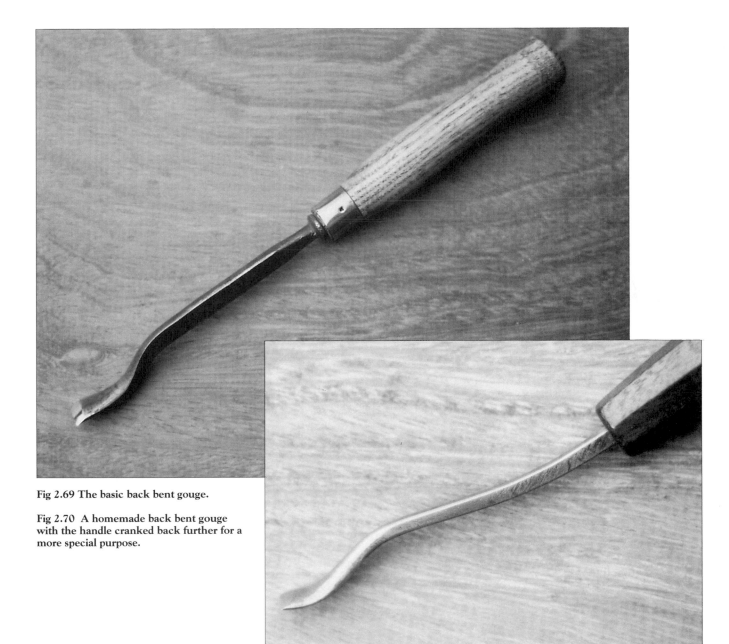

Fig 2.69 The basic back bent gouge.

Fig 2.70 A homemade back bent gouge with the handle cranked back further for a more special purpose.

when a reed travels into a hollow or recess (*see* Fig 2.71).

To put this another way, a convex surface (such as a reed) can be formed by turning an ordinary straight gouge upside down. Sometimes though, when working that shape into a hollow, the handle of this straight gouge can get in the way. Cranking the handle back keeps it clear of the wood: this is the back bent gouge.

All bent gouges can be obtained in the same variety of sweeps as the straight gouges. As with the tapered tools, however, a manufacturer may prefix the sweep number with another to specify a type of bend.

Number 11 gouges (and no. 10 if this has more of a **U** shape than semicircle) are not available in the back bent form as they do not really work upside

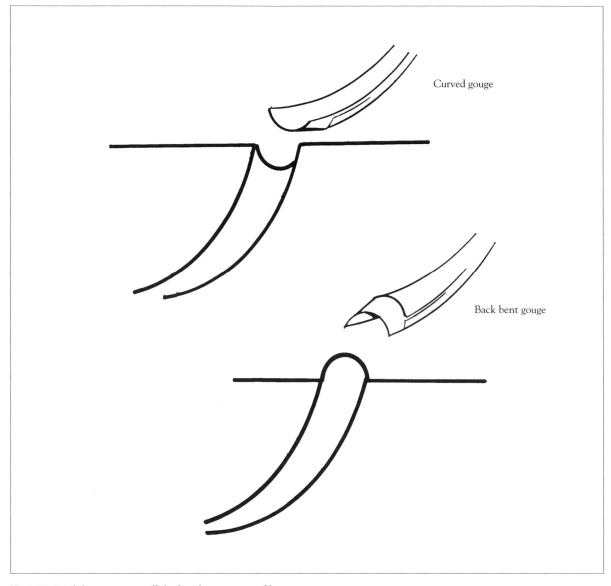

Curved gouge

Back bent gouge

Fig 2.71 Back bent gouges will deal with convex profiles which curve into recesses.

down. For the same reason, the V-tool is also unavailable in a back bent form.

Dog leg tools

The **dog leg chisel** has two nearly 90° bends in its shank, towards the working end (*see* Fig 2.72). It is used, like its counterpart the knuckle gouge, to get into very tight recesses or when undercutting. A **foot chisel** is a more exact version of the dog leg. A **side chisel** has an L-shaped shank; again it can get into odd corners not reached by other shapes.

WIDTH

All woodcarving tools are available in a large range of widths. It is the working edge that is taken into account when measuring the width.

■ Chisels (straight, tapered or bent): the width is measured at right angles across the cutting edge. A skew chisel is measured across the maximum width of the blade, as if it had an edge at right angles.

■ Gouges or parting tools (straight, tapered or bent): The width is measured as a straight line across the widest part of the mouth, at the very edge. This will be

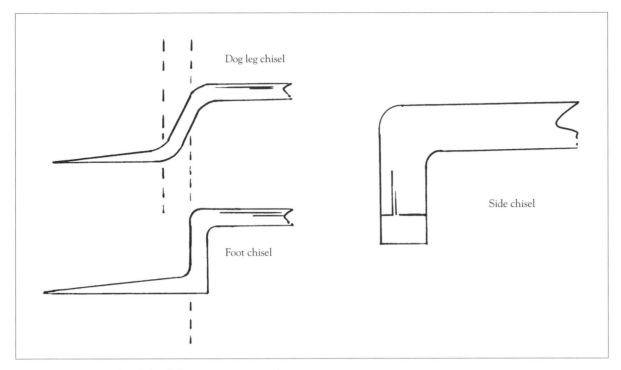

Dog leg chisel

Side chisel

Foot chisel

Fig 2.72 Some specialized chisel shapes.

Fig 2.73 Particular carvers may work with mostly large, or mostly small, tools, depending on the type of work they prefer or specialize in.

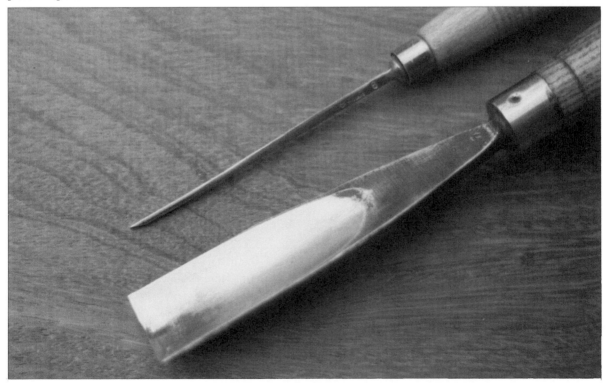

from corner to corner, at right angles to the long axis (*see* Fig 2.75).

The width is usually given both in imperial (inches) and metric (millimetres) measurements but some imported tools use only metric. There is a conversion table in the Reference Section at the end of the book (*see* page 348).

Widths start from very small, delicate tools of ⅟₁₆in (2mm) and range to large 2in (50mm) brutes used for sculpture (*see* Fig 2.76). What widths are actually available varies between manufacturers – no one makes all the tools that could possibly be made. Most makers stock a wide variety of the most commonly

Fig 2.74 Skew chisels come in a range of widths. A newcomer should start with something in the middle and only buy different sizes when they are actually needed – which might be never.

Fig 2.75 It is the actual cutting edge which is measured.

Fig 2.76 Width increments, between the smallest and largest for each type of carving tool, account for the enormous numbers that are available.

used tools, having made some selection of sizes to offer the public based on economics. You may need to look around if you need an exact specification. Some manufacturers will consider producing a tool to your special requirements.

LENGTH

The overall length of a woodcarving tool varies between manufacturers (*see* Fig 2.77); you should also consider the length of the handle. Some make a range of tools in both larger and smaller overall sizes.

As a guide, you may expect the blade of a ½in (13mm) gouge to be around 4–5in (100–125mm) from the shoulder to the edge. This is useful when you come across an old tool and are trying to work out how much has been worn away.

The light-weight gouges with mushroom-shaped handles, designed to be held in one hand, are meant for wood engraving or wood cutting prior to printing (*see* Fig 2.78). The principles of sharpening covered in this book also apply to them. Normal carving tools are always held in both hands. If you are *carving* rather

Fig 2.77 Two brand new tools; the difference in length is about 1in (25mm).

than engraving or making woodcuts, then the larger tools, of sufficient size to allow the free use of both hands, are what you need.

There are cheap sets of 'carving' tools around which are very small and look like the nibs of old

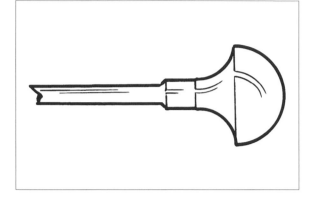

Fig 2.78 Such mushroom handles are for wood engraver's burins.

dipping pens. They are made of soft metal and are meant for cutting soft linoleum and the like. They are not suitable for carving wood and should be avoided.

SUMMARY

I have described in this section, in some detail, the sorts of tools that are available, and the various terms you may come across.

▪ Gouges come in a series of curves or sweeps, from very flat to very quick or deep.

▪ This range of gouges can either be straight, or bent in various ways along the length of the blade.

▪ The straight gouges can have parallel sides, or sides which taper out from the shank or handle, splaying to varying degrees.

▪ The bent gouges can bend along the whole length of the blade (long bent), or just at the far end away from the handle (short bent).

▪ Short bent gouges can be bent in either of two directions: so that the mouth or hollow of the gouge is at the front (front bent), or at the back (back bent).

▪ This array of tools can be generally smaller or

Fig 2.79 Different manufacturers shape the tool shoulders in different ways; some taking more care than others.

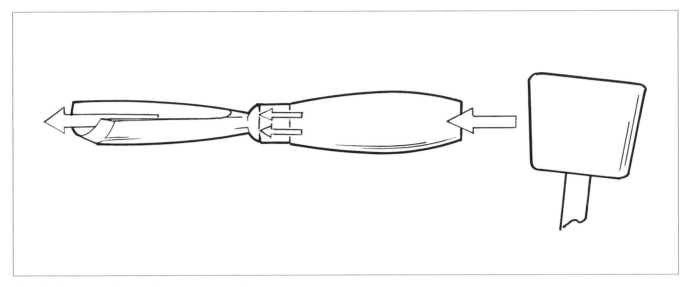

Fig 2.80 The force of a mallet blow is taken and transmitted by the flat shoulder.

larger, and can be obtained in a large variety of widths.

When you buy a tool you will need to know:

- What sort of **sweep** or curve you want
- Whether, and in what way, you want the tool **bent** or **tapered**
- How **wide** you want the tool to be.

The section on selecting and buying tools explains further how the shapes of these tools relate to their function, and includes a discussion of other considerations which need to be taken into account before buying any tools (*see* page 90).

Shoulders

FUNCTION

The shoulder of a woodcarving tool, sometimes referred to as the **bolster** or **stop**, is the protuberance in the shank of the blade where the tang penetrates the handle. The word 'bolster' seems to be used here in the same way we use the word elsewhere, meaning a cushion or pad.

The flatness of the shoulder, as it meets the wood, prevents the tang being driven further into the handle and splitting it. The shoulder is, in effect, a sort of joint. It is particularly important when a carving tool, such as a large gouge, is struck with a mallet; the impact of a blow on the handle arrives at, and is taken almost entirely by, the shoulder (*see* Fig 2.80). The

Fig 2.81 A beautifully forged shoulder with a good size and shape, seated well on the handle.

force pushes on into the blade itself. The tang is not unlike a nail and mallet blows can be repeatedly – even unwittingly – heavy, especially on larger sculpture tools. The shoulder works with the ferrule to stop the sharp tang forcing its way into the wood of the handle. Historically the shoulder pre-dates the ferrule, presumably because making metal tubes was not easy.

Some carvers and firms insert a hard **leather** or **rubber washer** between the shoulder and the handle

Fig 2.82 The same shoulder from beneath; it is obvious that trouble has been taken in the shaping.

Fig 2.83 Leather washers like this are more for consistency of appearance than for function.

to smooth this transmission of energy, but this is not actually necessary with a properly fitting shoulder (*see* Fig 2.83).

SHOULDERLESS TOOLS

Not all carving tools have a shoulder. A shoulder is really only necessary, as is the ferrule, when there is a danger of splitting the handle. Light tools, which are only worked fairly delicately by hand, do not need the added protection of the shoulder and ferrule as the pressures on them are small. However, one very important feature of these shoulderless tools is that the end of the tang is squared off – this helps resist any further penetration of the tang into the handle.

At the most, these shoulderless tools can be lightly struck with the heel of the hand as carvers sometimes do. However, avoid the dangers of overusing this technique (*see* the section on using a mallet in Chapter 4, page 192).

A bad practice is to exert sideways leverage on such tools as this can also lead to splitting the handle, if not bending the tool or breaking its edge.

CORRECT SHAPE

The shoulder is formed quite early on when the tool is made, and it seems that the forming is often hurried in the rush to get on with making the blade itself. A look at a broad range of carving tools will verify this – the shoulders come in all shapes and sizes. They may be too large and overhang the ferrule; sometimes they are ridiculously small and only the ferrule prevents them pushing, cone-like, into the wood; sometimes they are badly offset to one side. But, to be fair, some manufacturers take a lot more care over the forming of the shoulders, and the tool as a whole, than do others.

The main features of a correctly shaped shoulder are as follows:

■ The part of the metal in contact with the handle should be *flat* (*see* Fig 2.86). It is not uncommon to

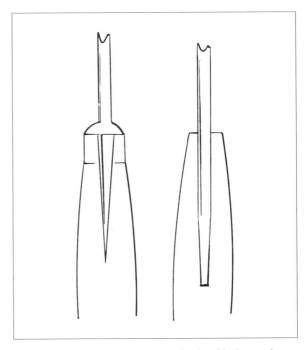

Fig 2.84 The flat end to the tang of a shoulderless tool acts in a similar way to a shoulder, inhibiting the splitting of the handle.

Fig 2.85 Typically, shoulderless tools are light weight and are used for finishing and delicate work.

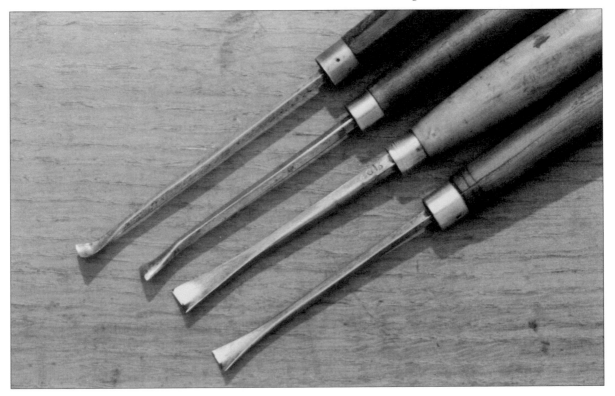

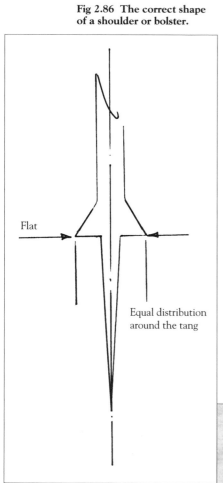

Fig 2.86 The correct shape of a shoulder or bolster.

Flat

Equal distribution around the tang

Fig 2.87 It seems hardly worth making a shoulder like this one.

Fig 2.88 This blob-like shoulder may stop the tang penetrating the handle but will seat badly and lies to one side of the blade. Laying a straightedge on the photo will show you how far the tang is off line as well.

Fig 2.89 Perhaps half a shoulder is better than none.

have handles without ferrules relying entirely on the flatness of the shoulder to prevent the wood splitting.

■ The metal of the shoulder should be distributed equally, and evenly, around the shank.

■ The shoulder size should relate to the size of the tool – larger tools needing appropriately larger shoulders. The shoulder should not overhang the ferrule, although this latter point can have as much to do with the handle being too small as the shoulder being too large.

Tangs

FUNCTION

The tang is the means whereby the blade itself can be fitted with something more comfortable and amenable to the hand than steel (*see* Fig 2.90). The word 'tang' comes, through Danish, from an Old Norse word *tangi*, meaning a point or spike. In dialect, tang has also referred to a serpent's tongue and an insect's sting; and interestingly connotes a penetrating taste.

The use of a tang is only one option, however. Another method, better in some ways but involving more labour and materials, is to form a conical socket

Fig 2.90 A strong, straight and well-made purposeful tang.

Fig 2.91 A socketed shipwright's chisel with an iron end ferrule; such a strong socket will take far more punishment than one with a tang.

into which the handle is fitted. This seems to have been quite a common method in the Bronze Age, when casting the socket was part of casting the tool itself. You can see examples of these tools, along with tanged chisels and gouges, in the National Museum of Wales, Cardiff. As early as the Iron Age, when the forging of tools had just started, socketed gouges were being made – one of these can be seen at the Lake Village Museum in Glastonbury, with a handle turned in oak. The Egyptians and Romans, whose tools can be seen in many museums, also commonly used sockets as well as tangs on their chisels.

The socket probably fell out of favour because a tang is less labour-intensive to make. The socketed blade can still be seen in heavy chisels used to cut mortise-type woodworking joints and in wheelwrights' and shipwrights' chisels (*see* Fig 2.91), sometimes found in second-hand tool shops.

The socket, merging into the blade, gives a much stronger tool that can be repeatedly and forcefully struck – consider that a 1½in (38mm) gouge may only have a ½in (13mm) shoulder and a ¼in (6mm) tang

behind it. The strength accorded by the socket was originally important when the metal of the blade had poor edge-keeping qualities and the woodwork was monumental – heavy work by today's standards.

Before damp-proofing, tools were more prone to rust, especially in the tang: which is hidden away in the handle. If oak was used for the handle, as it frequently seems to have been, it would react with the iron of the tang when moisture was around. This corrosion of the tang, even without the wood being oak, is still seen quite often in old tools that have not been kept in dry conditions. A socket, being a bigger mass of metal, resists this corrosion for much longer.

The socket is, therefore, tougher both mechanically and in its ability to resist the effects of time and damp. Early toolmakers would have appreciated that, bearing in mind the effort involved in making larger, heavier tools, socketed handles were a better investment of effort.

Sockets are still common in many cultures today, but they do make tools heavier. When it comes to smaller sizes, the socket tends to be so much bigger than the blade itself that the tool becomes cumbersome and even tiring to use. However, should you come across any of these old socketed tools remember that they can be re-shaped into large, very tough, gouges for sculpture.

Another option, instead of using a tang or a socket, is not to have a wooden handle at all. The whole carving tool can be made from a bar of steel – like a stonecarving chisel – and is struck with a metal hammer. The metal part forming the 'handle' is made more comfortable by binding it with leather thong or some type of cane. This way of making carving tools is quite useful if you are making your own, as there is significantly less work involved in working a blade into one end of a simple bar of metal. This can be of particular importance in countries where energy is considered more precious than it is in Britain, and it is in these cultures that this sort of tool is most common.

TYPES

There are three types of tang, requiring slightly different approaches when it comes to fitting them into the handle (*see* page 65):

- Tapered
- Untapered
- Square ended.

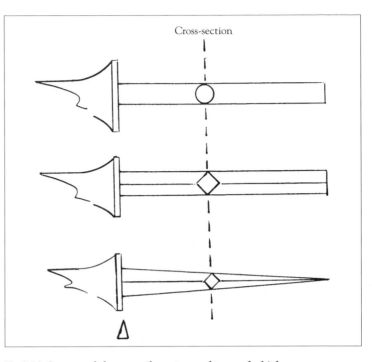

Fig 2.92 In general there are three types of tang, of which the square tapering sort is the most common.

Fig 2.93 The parallel round tang is unusual and does not 'bite' the wood like square-sectioned tangs. In this case the tang, and shoulder, are strong and well made. There should be no problem providing the tang grips the hole in the handle tightly enough.

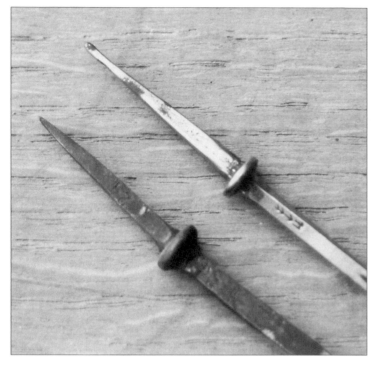

Fig 2.94 A straightedge applied to the photograph will demonstrate how far the two tangs are from true.

Fig 2.95 Where a tool has a tang bent at an angle to its axis, some of the mallet blow or driving force will go into flexing the tool – possibly bending it further.

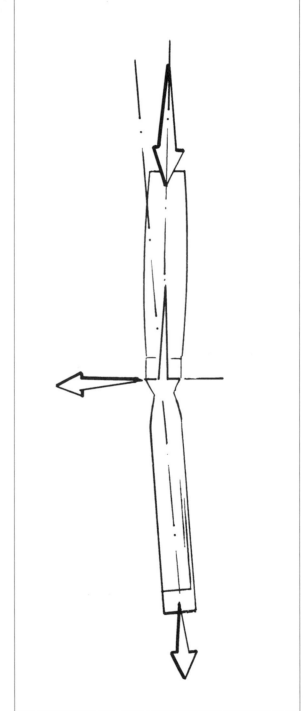

A small point about all these tangs is that they have a square section; the corners bind into the wood and stop the handle turning on the blade. A parallel, round tang is occasionally used, but this cannot bite the wood in the same way as a square-sectioned tang and is therefore not as good.

CORRECT SHAPE

A tang can be made well or badly, with some manufacturers performing better than others. The tang has several important functions – often disregarded – and, like the shoulder, the shape of the tang may function efficiently or inefficiently.

◆ **The tang must be made without too many lumps and bumps, and should be straight.**
The tang allows the handle to be fitted. Some carvers try to protect the tang from rust by soaking it in oil and pouring a little more into the hole before actually fitting the handle.

◆ **The tang must be in a straight line with the blade.**
This, if nothing else, affects the very feel of the tool in your hand. From the arm, the hand grips the handle of the gouge in a straight line of intention. This intention wants to be carried straight through to the cutting edge without veering away. Some carvers do

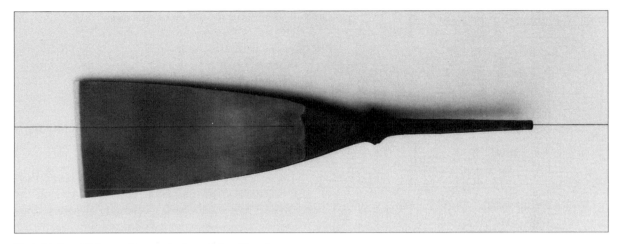

Fig 2.96 In addition to the poorly shaped shoulder, the tang of this tool is well off the axis.

put up with tools the handles of which are bent at an angle to the blades and only realize how much more satisfying the tool feels when the handle and blade have been lined up correctly.

◆ **The tang must not be bent at an angle.**

I have seen this angle as much as 20° out from true. If such a gouge is struck heavily with a mallet, even with a good shoulder and ferrule, the bend can become gradually worse and the tool threaten to break (*see* Fig 2.95). The tang, shoulder and shank are made of a

softer-tempered, less brittle metal compared with the blade itself. This is quite deliberate, allowing the impact of a blow to be absorbed and transmitted through the metal without it breaking under the stress. Should there be some angling away from the central axis of the tool already, there will be a tendency for the softer metal to bend further. Bending can also happen when the tool is used inappropriately – like a small crowbar – to lever pieces of wood away (*see* Fig 2.97).

Fig 2.97 A good way to bend the tang or break the blade is to use the tool to lever away pieces of wood.

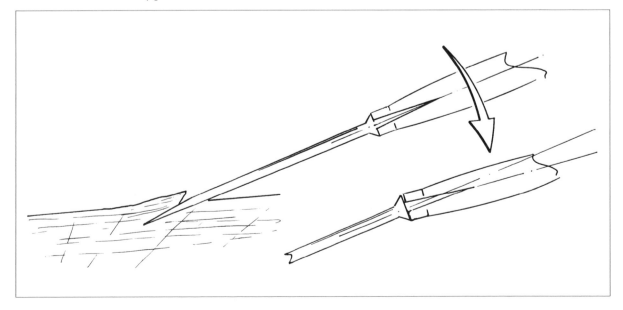

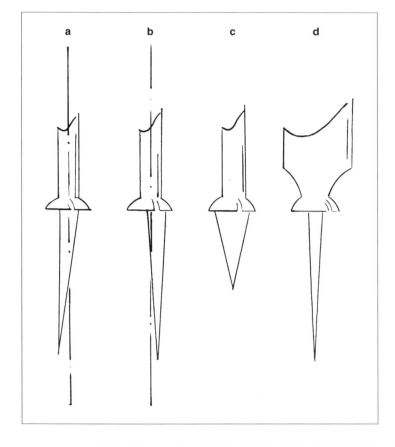

◆ **The tang should not be offset.**

The tang is correctly aligned when it runs down the central axis of the shank and blade. If it is parallel to this axis but offset to one side, fitting a handle without the shoulder overhanging the ferrule becomes more difficult. This fault also affects the feel of the tool as discussed in the first point above.

◆ **The tang should be of a size and shape appropriate to the work that the tool can reasonably be expected to do.**

The tang should not be too short and fat as this provides little purchase on the handle and interferes with the shoulder; nor should it be too long or thin in a larger tool as this provides a point of weakness (*see* Fig 2.99).

There can be a problem with tangs in older tools which are partly, or completely, rusted away. All might not be lost: see the section on correcting carving tool faults later in this chapter (*see* page 73).

Fig 2.98 Some faults with the tangs: (**a**) angled to the axis line; (**b**) parallel to the axis line but to one side; (**c**) too short with not enough shoulder; and (**d**) too long and thin for the size of the blade.

Fig 2.99 When we get to carving tools of this size, 2½in (65mm), a tang only ¼in (6mm) wide is beginning to look a little inadequate.

If you buy tools without handles, carefully inspect the tang along with the rest of the tool, bearing the above points in mind. Some faults can be corrected but where they cannot – or perhaps you do not feel you *should* have to correct them – return the tool with the appropriate explanation and ask for a better one. Putting up with manufacturing faults does nobody any favours.

Handles

OVERVIEW

This chapter started by looking at carving tools from the end furthest away from us: the blade and shank. Then we turned to the shoulder and tang. Now we come to the nearest part of the whole tool, the handle, which is often undervalued.

Supplying tools with fitted handles is a phenomenon of mass production over the last 100 years or so. There is at least one advantage: if the tool is supplied already 'handled' and – as the tendency is today – already 'sharpened', then in theory at least you can consider yourself up and running for the nearest piece of wood.

Carvers used to buy their tools unhandled, with just the steel blade and its naked tang. Unhandled tools can still be bought from some suppliers. The carver would then make and fit a handle personally. This was usually from a square piece of wood, subsequently shaped octagonally and without a ferrule. This meant that – depending on the wood to hand and the mood of the carver – the handles would all be distinct. Without the ferrules the handles may not have lasted as long, but replacing them would not have been considered a problem. Old handles of a factory-made type often show marks, glyphics or notches as the carver tried to make some tool handles stand out from others.

Today, manufacturers rarely provide more than three sizes of handles – all exactly the same shape – for the whole range, size and variety of their carving tools.

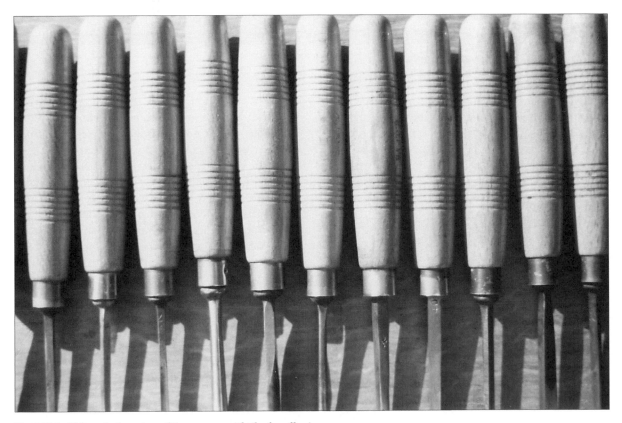

Fig 2.100 Although there is nothing wrong with the handles in themselves, when such similar mass-produced handles are aligned on the bench, their similar appearance can be confusing.

Fig 2.101 Different handles, also in different types and colours of wood make tools more immediately recognizable on the bench.

In fairness, this is probably as much as they may reasonably be expected to provide as they are primarily makers of carving tools, not handles.

Factory-made handles are therefore convenient, but all the handles are more or less the same;

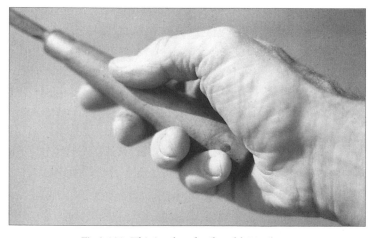

Fig 2.102 This is what the 'hand·le' is about.

handmade handles involve additional effort but result in handles of a more individual and personal kind. This needs to be considered a little further because there are definite advantages to handmade handles, making the additional effort worthwhile. The handle makes the carving tool more comfortable in the hand, but there is more to it than that.

The handle lies between the blade, which works the wood, and yourself, who directs the carving. Its very name describes its function: it is the bit you 'handle' and actually hold in your hand (*see* Fig 2.102). Lying as it does between the blade and you, it must have a relationship not only to the size and shape of the blade, but also to the hand or hands holding it. The handle plays a vital role in establishing the comfort, strength, efficiency, balance and 'feel' of the whole tool. A tool – which may be perfectly sharpened – may not 'feel right'; it sits awkwardly in the hand; perhaps it is not one to which you feel attracted. This in turn will affect how you carve, in anything from a subtle to a significant way.

It is not the tools themselves which decide

whether a carving is successful or not – a whole array of mental factors and attitudes surrounding the act of carving itself come in to play as well.

A tool appears to respond to the amount of effort, even love, that is put into its care. Such an attitude of care and attention to the carving tools feeds into the process of carving. It is hard to abuse a beautiful tool, one into which a lot of care and effort has been put. It is as if the tool draws your best effort towards itself. Carving tools are the vehicles through which creativity and pleasure flow. A carver absorbed in carving will forgot the tools – at this point the carver is working directly with the wood, without any tool in the way.

This is the first reason for making your own handles, or at least some of them. You are making the tool personal in a way which is not possible with the blade itself. After all it is *your* hand on the handle, not a mass-produced average hand. Besides this, there are several other reasons for not buying factory-made handles.

◆ **A mass-produced handle looks like every other mass-produced handle.**

It is quite possible to have 40, 50 or more carving tools arrayed on the bench and at work. Every carving tool that a carver possesses may be on the bench among wood chips, sawdust, pencils and other tools. In such cases similarity between gouges and chisels can cause confusion and irritation. It is important for efficiency and continuity of purpose that individual tools are readily recognized and picked up (*see* Figs 2.100, 2.101). This is accomplished far more easily if the shape, size, type of wood or colour of the handles is varied. It helps to distinguish at least some of the handles on your carving tools, even if you do not do it for all of them.

◆ **The overall length of the carving tool can be controlled by varying the length of the handle.**

For example a particularly short carving tool can be given a better overall working length – and a longer useful life – by increasing the length of the handle (*see*

Fig 2.103 Effortless carving by the great master Riemenschneider: St Barbara, Bayerisches Nationalmuseum, Munich. Carved in about 1515 in limewood.

Fig 2.104 It is possible to lengthen a short tool with a custom-made handle to the normal overall length.

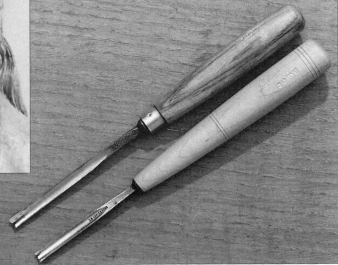

Fig 2.104). Another example would be fitting an extra long handle to a large, flat gouge; this gives the tool greater slicing leverage and speed for cleaning and finishing backgrounds (*see* Fig 2.105).

By flattening one side of the handle of a straight gouge, the handle can be lowered that little bit extra which gains vital access for the cutting edge in a hollow for which a bent tool, of the same shape, is not available.

◆ **The handle can be suited to both the hand and the blade.**

Because of the limited variety of mass-produced handles compared with the large variety of carving-tool shapes and sizes, such handles can often be entirely the wrong size or shape for the tool. As *hands* vary as well, the handle may also be uncomfortable.

The handle of a sculpture gouge needs to be gripped comfortably and held easily for long periods (*see* Figs 2.106, 2.107). There are shapes which are more suited to mallet work, tending to bind into the hand better and not sliding through.

Bought handles very often have a thick layer of varnish which can cause your hand to become unpleasantly warm and sweaty, even slippery (*see* Fig 2.108). There may also be ridges and sharp corners to make the hands sore – these are often found at the very end of an octagonal handle. Octagonal handles are good shapes for setting down on an inclined plane, for instance, when lettering a panel, as they do not roll

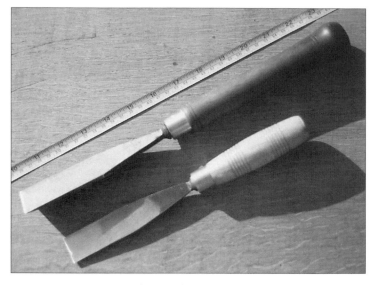

Fig 2.105 The extra long handle facilitates the flattening of backgrounds.

Fig 2.106 This design of handle I have developed for sculpture gouges . . .

Fig 2.107 . . . held by the hand well. In use it tends to grip more firmly.

Fig 2.108 A thick layer of varnish over the whole handle has congealed into a glob on the ferrule.

so easily; but end corners, if they are not softened, can work into the palm of the pushing hand.

Varnish can be removed with sandpaper, followed by oiling the wood; sharp edges and corners can be filed or sanded away. This allows you to take some control over some of the qualities of your carving-tool handles – the next step would be to make the handle from the beginning.

If you have a lot of tools with mass-produced handles, consider remaking the handles a few at a time – starting with favourite tools. You may be able to see some ways of re-shaping or altering the existing handles to make them more personal, distinctive or better functioning.

It is not difficult to make handles for your woodcarving tools, and the time invested is not much compared to the years over which you may be using them. Once the importance of handle quality is realized, no further encouragement will be necessary.

Of course there is nothing to stop you going straight ahead with mass-produced handles and producing wonderful carvings. At the end of the day handles are not carvings, only part of the means towards that end. What is being promoted here is an attitude of positive regard for carving tools in the hope that this attitude will make the carving itself more satisfying and successful. This attitude or approach works with creative potential, rather than against it.

SHAPES AND IDENTIFICATION

From the illustrations it can be seen that handles can have many possible shapes – some very traditional, e.g. London Pattern, or South Kensington, that relate to carving schools, some a little more unusual.

When you come to choose the shape and size of handle, you will need to bear in mind the shape and size of the blade to which the handle will fit, the 'roughness' of use to which the tool will be put, the size of your hands and so on. There is a large degree of

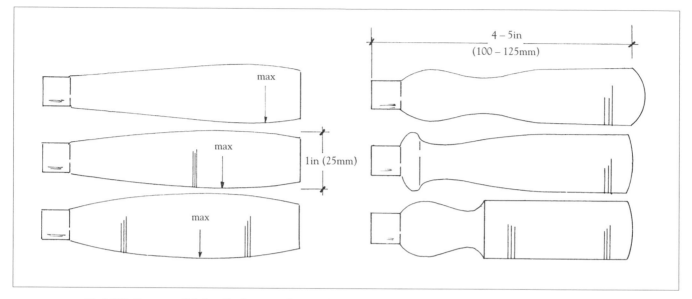

Fig 2.109 Some possible handle shapes and approximate sizes. The maximum thickness of the row on the left can, of course, be varied.

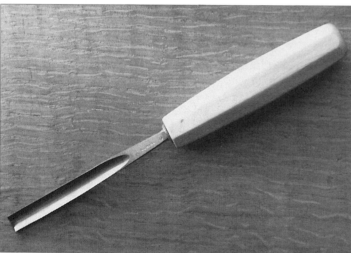

Fig 2.110 Although much care may be taken in making a carving tool, the limited range of handles that a firm can provide may mean the tool ends up with one that is too large.

Fig 2.111 Roughly the same size tool, fitted with different sizes and shapes of handle by different manufacturers.

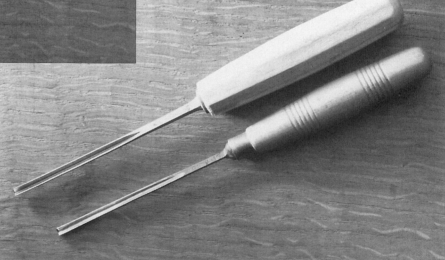

free choice, with no hard and fast rules, but here are some useful guidelines.

Size

■ A good, overall length for a woodcarving tool is somewhere between 9 and 10in (225 and 250mm), so you need to adjust the length of handle to suit. Around 4–5in (100–125mm) for the handle is common (*see* Fig 2.112).

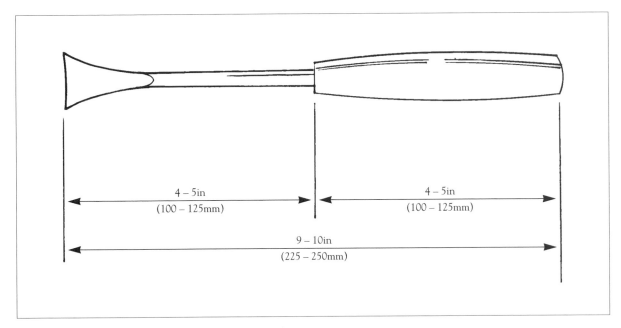

Fig 2.112 The overall length of a carving tool will involve a balance between the length of the blade and the handle.

■ The width of handle is usually ⅞–1in (22–25mm) at its maximum point, but should be larger for bigger hands.

Shape

■ Large gouges need larger, heavier handles.

■ Thin, delicate gouges suit longer, thinner handles.

■ Short, small gouges can have the length of the blade made up in the length of handle.

■ A carving tool that is struck a lot with a mallet might be held better with a more wedge-shaped handle – a shape which grips into the hand. The wedge does not want to be too conical; this in itself can feel uncomfortable. Fatter, barrel shapes tend to pop out of the hand. The concavity of a wedge-and-ball, 'pattern-makers' handle gains a good purchase for the first finger and thumb.

■ Make sure there are no hard corners to dig into the palm of the hand that is pushing the handle.

■ With barrel-shaped (London Pattern) handles, the point of maximum bulge can be varied in its position along the length. So can the amount of this bulge in relation to the length. This will be a matter of what feels right.

■ Octagonal handles are gripped much better than round ones and do not roll on the bench. They are made by shaping a square-sectioned piece of wood,

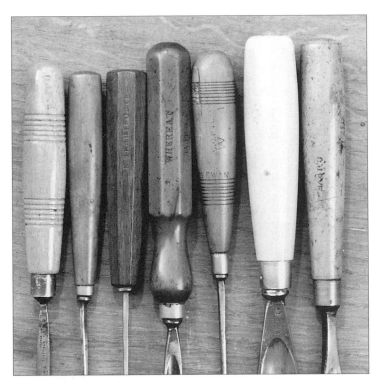

Fig 2.113 Some classic handle shapes.

rather than by using a lathe. Turned handles go back to Roman times and no doubt the octagonal ones are equally old. To put a ferrule on an octagonal handle shaped by hand involves some accurate whittling – so

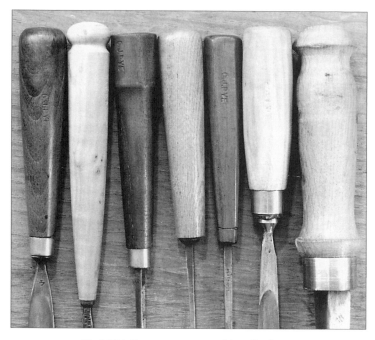

Fig 2.114 Some more unusual handle shapes.

invariably these handles did not (and still do not) have ferrules. If they split then it is not too much effort to make another.

Ferrules

■ A tool used for light work will probably not need a ferrule, or even a shoulder. However make sure the handle is made from tight, straight-grained wood.

■ A larger tool, doing more work, will benefit from a ferrule at the tang end – making sure the wood does not split here.

■ Where a tool takes a lot of pounding from the mallet, an additional ferrule on the end of the handle will cause it to last longer – preventing the wood splitting and mushrooming out.

WOODS

Handles need a resilient hardwood with close, straight grain, that has been properly seasoned (definitely not green). Certain factors are important in determining the suitability of a piece of wood to be used for making handles.

Resilience

Wood can either be taken from near the centre of the tree (heartwood) or towards the outside (sapwood). The wood taken from towards the outside, even though the tree is still called a 'hardwood', can be soft and open-grained. Wood for handles should be taken from the tougher heartwood – although not from the actual

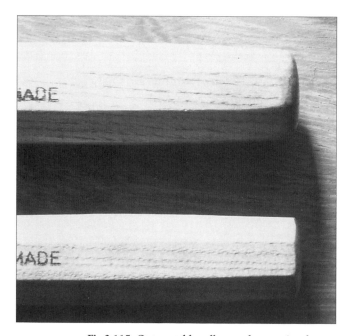

Fig 2.115 Octagonal handles can have quite sharp corners (bottom); round them over to make them more comfortable.

Fig 2.116 The wider end of the top handle is a better target for the mallet than the other, which reduces towards a point.

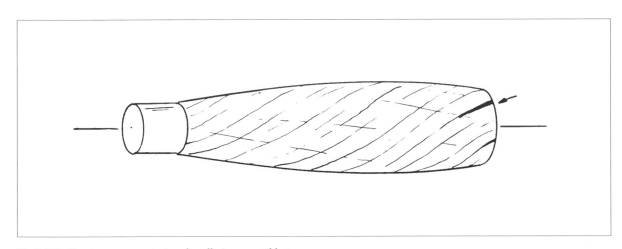

Fig 2.117 Short or cross-grain in a handle is susceptible to splitting, especially when a mallet is used.

centre of the tree. This would be the toughest, hardest option. Some woods, like ash or hickory, have a natural springiness which greatly adds to their resilience.

Straight grain

The grain of the handle should run along its axis, not diagonally across it, even in part. This is especially important if a mallet is to be used: cross-grain in the handle can split from a blow on the end (*see* Fig 2.117). Uneven, difficult grain can also create problems when fitting the tang into the handle. Knots may be a problem depending where they are, their size, and whether they are 'alive' or 'dead'. They can be an attractive feature, as can burled (burred) wood, but you need to be careful when using the mallet.

Close grain

Trees which have grown very quickly produce broad annual rings and relatively light, soft wood – the heartwood can be as soft as sapwood. Use a tight, close grain, where the tree has grown slowly. Usually it is just a matter of selecting and putting aside odd bits of wood for use as handles when you need them.

Species of wood

The following list, which is by no means complete, may be useful in selecting wood for a handle:

■ For tools struck heavily with a mallet: box, ash, hickory, pau marfin
■ For tools occasionally struck with a mallet: any of the above, plus beech, oak, fruit wood such as cherry, apple or plum, maple, hornbeam

Fig 2.118 close-up of a brass tang ferrule showing the inside bevel.

■ For tools rarely or never struck with a mallet: any of the above, plus rosewood, teak, mahogany.

FERRULES

A **ferrule** is a metal collar binding around the end of a handle to strengthen the wood against splitting. The word itself relates both to the Latin *ferrum*, meaning iron, and to the Old French word *virelle*, meaning a bracelet. Many terms show the great importance of the Norman and French influence both on stonecarving and woodcarving in Britain.

The ferrule can be fitted at either the tang end (a **tang ferrule**), or the free end of the handle (an **end ferrule**).

Fig 2.119 Such 'internal' ferrules are more popular for the mass-produced handles of continental Europe. Note the offset hole.

Tang ferrules

Such ferrules reinforce the wood against the tang being driven, spike-like, into the end-grain. When force is exerted sideways on the blade, the ferrule prevents the handle splitting. More delicate carving tools, and those with good, flat shoulders, do not actually need a ferrule – although one is often fitted to the handle as a matter of course.

Manufactured ferrules are normally made of brass, which resists stretching and does not corrode. If you cannot buy purpose-made, loose ferrules, then a strong piping or tube with walls about $\frac{1}{16}$–$\frac{1}{8}$in (2–3mm) wide will substitute. A short trip to a scrap yard or metal suppliers will produce enough ferrule metal to last a lifetime.

The size of the tang ferrule should relate to the size of the blade or, more exactly and ideally, its shoulder and tang (see Fig 2.120). The shoulder itself can rest on the edge of the ferrule, but an overhanging shoulder is uncomfortable. The amount of wood

Fig 2.120 The relation of the shoulder or bolster to the ferrule.

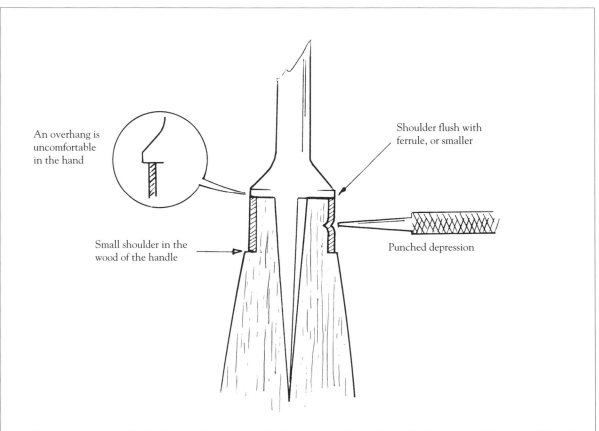

An overhang is uncomfortable in the hand

Shoulder flush with ferrule, or smaller

Small shoulder in the wood of the handle

Punched depression

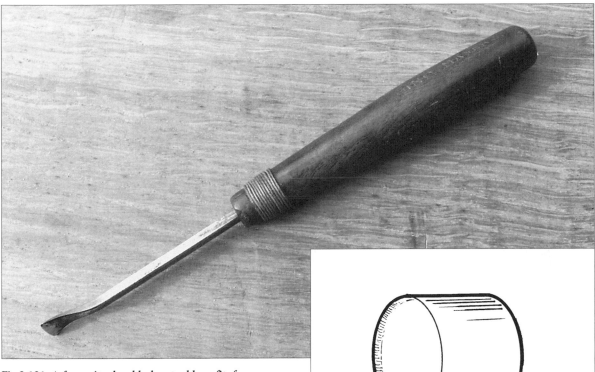

Fig 2.121 A favourite shoulderless tool benefits from a lovely bit of ferrule improvisation.

between the tang and its ferrule should be neither too great, in which case the wood gives, nor too little (for instance if the ferrule is inordinately thick), in which case this part of the handle is actually weakened.

One important feature of a ferrule is that it has a bevel on the *inside* of one end. This end is offered to the wood of the handle, which is made a touch oversize. Tapped home, the inside bevel pinches the wood tightly and the ferrule compresses the wood, allowing for the handle to shrink a little (*see* Fig 2.122).

End ferrules

If a tool is going to be struck heavily with a mallet, the life of the handle will be considerably extended by banding the free end with a thick ferrule. The metal needs to be thicker walled than that for a tang ferrule, and preferably made of iron. Many types of piping will be suitable.

With a steel or iron ferrule on the end of a large sculpture gouge, a soft-metal 'dummy' mallet, such as is used by stonecarvers, can be used instead of the normal wooden mallet. This sort of mallet is made of soft, annealed iron and has the advantage that a good weight is possible without bulking up the size.

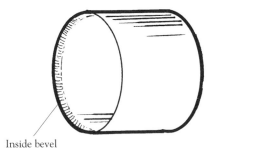

Inside bevel

Fig 2.122 The inside bevel is offered to the handle first and jams the ferrule in place by compressing the wood.

Fig 2.123 If a hard mallet strikes the unsupported end-grain often and hard enough, the wood will start to burr over.

Making and fitting ferrules

Mark the selected tube and cut it squarely with a hacksaw or pipe cutter. Clean up and remove any burrs on a bench stone or grinding wheel. (Be careful here: grip the tube in self-locking 'Mole' grips, and apply it, *lightly*, to the side of the wheel.)

An inside bevel can be formed with a round file or a small, conical grinding wheel – such as those designed to fit into an electric drill. It is also possible

Fig 2.124 (Top) When the grain of the handle runs out of the axial line there is a danger of it being split by the mallet.

Fig 2.125 (Above) A sculpture gouge fitted with an end ferrule.

Fig 2.126 (Right) Even such an iron ferrule can itself burr over after weeks of hard mallet work.

to use a piece of broken, round file mounted in a drill for the same purpose.

■ For a tang ferrule: the end wood of the handle, onto which the shoulder of the blade sits, should finish flush and square with the free edge of the ferrule. Flatten the end wood after the ferrule is fitted with a sanding block.

■ For an end ferrule: allow the wood to extend a little way out of the metal tube. With use the wood will eventually mushroom over, taking the metal of the ferrule with it, giving rise to less wear and tear on the mallet. You may like to start this process by planishing over the corners with a hammer first.

When any type of ferrule is fitted, it should butt onto a little shoulder formed in the wood (which must be made with the handle) just enough to merge the wood comfortably with the metal.

Sometimes, as an added precaution, a centre punch is used to make one or two depressions in the side of the ferrule – this locks it on in case the wood shrinks or it works loose.

MAKING HANDLES

The hole into which the tang will fit must be aligned along the central axis of the handle. To achieve this bore the hole first, whatever shape handle is being made. If the hole is true, and the shape worked around the hole, then the tang – and the blade – will align correctly along the handle.

It is also helpful, but not necessary, to start with a square-sectioned piece of wood which is a little oversize and overlength. The wood does not need be planed, but can be accurately bandsawn; a little trouble taken over the initial accuracy of the blank makes the following stages easier. Mark the centres at each end of the wood, drawing diagonally across the corners, and use a point to punch a small starting depression at the point of intersection. This will prevent the drill bit wandering as it starts to bite.

Once you have a squared-up, centred block you can bore the hole.

Boring the hole

Whether the tang is tapering or parallel in section, it helps to drill an accurate pilot hole first (e.g. ⅛in (3mm)). An appropriate diameter drill bit can then be used.

■ If you have a *parallel round tang*, make the final hole an exact tight fit along its whole length.

■ For a *parallel square tang*, bore the hole a size which is halfway between the diagonal of the square and one of its sides (*see* Fig 2.129). Test the fit of the hole first on a piece of scrap wood. The corners of the tang bite and lock into the wood of the hole.

■ For a *tapered tang*, bore a guiding pilot hole about ⅛in (3mm) diameter and use the twist method of fitting the handle which is described later (*see* page

Fig 2.127 This result of an offset hole demonstrates the need for accurate boring.

Fig 2.128 On a lathe, a hole can be drilled easily and accurately 'between centres'.

Fig 2.129 Hole size for a parallel square tang.

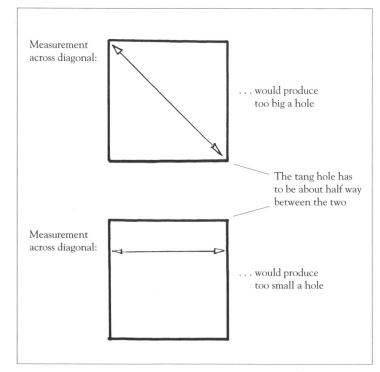

Measurement across diagonal:

. . . would produce too big a hole

The tang hole has to be about half way between the two

Measurement across diagonal:

. . . would produce too small a hole

69). If the wood is something like box, with a propensity for splitting, then bore in a second hole about a third of the depth of the first hole. Take a measurement of the diagonal of the tapering tang a third of the way down from the shoulder and make this the diameter of the second hole.

There are various ways to bore the hole accurately. The easiest method (whether you are intending to turn the handle or not) is to bore the hole on a lathe. The wood automatically lines up axially between the centres.

The next best method is to use a pillar drill, which is the lathe turned, in effect, vertically. The handle needs to be aligned correctly using a simple jig. Pass a screw perpendicularly through a plate of plywood, MDF (medium-density fibreboard), etc. Clamp the plate to the pillar drill table so that the drill bit descends dead on the point of the screw.

To use the jig, place the centre of one end of the wooden blank onto the screw point and lock the pillar drill to start a little above the other end. For the pilot hole of ⅛in (3mm), you can hold the wood in position with one hand and lower the drill with the other. Clear the hole of sawdust regularly and there will be little problem with the wood twisting in your grip. If some clamping method is available with the drill then do use it.

If you have neither lathe nor pillar drill, bore the hole using an ordinary wheel brace or electric hand drill. The problem still remains of how to bore the hole true; the tried methods of a helper's eye, or a set-square placed as a guide on the bench next to the drilling, can work well here.

Once the pilot hole has been drilled, the size of the hole can be incrementally enlarged as necessary. Hold the wood in a vice and allow the bits to follow the hole of the preceding one.

Shaping the handles

Octagonal handles

Try and get these as accurate as possible, although what really matters is the *feel* of the handle – test this often. There should be enough width of wood remaining at the tang end for any shoulder to seat correctly. Bore the holes first using the information given earlier about the shape of the tang (*see* page 65).

1 Start with an accurately planed, square piece of wood with the centres marked at each end.
2 Draw the profile of the handle on one face of the wood and cut the waste off cleanly using a bandsaw or coping saw.
3 Use Sellotape or masking tape to replace the bits sawn off and, turning the wood over 90°, draw the profile again.
4 Saw off the waste a second time and you should end up with a four-sided profile of the final handle.
5 Smooth the faces squarely with a spokeshave, rasp, file, etc.
6 Chamfer the corners by eye in the same way to give the eight sides.
7 Octagonal handles, as mentioned before, invariably do not have ferrules. To fit one, it is either a job for the lathe, or a matter of paring or rasping the wood into shape.

Fig 2.130 Sizing down to a close fit for the ferrule.

Fig 2.131 Cleaning the end of the finished handle with the skew.

8 Sand the handle smooth; round over the end that will push into the palm of your hand and seal the wood as for the turned handle below.

Turned handles

If several handles are being made, first bore them all as one procedure – referring to the information given earlier in the section on boring the hole (*see* page 65).

1 Bore the hole first with the drill bit in a Jacob's chuck, at the drive end of the lathe. Use a slow speed and feed the wood from the tailstock to the necessary depth. Mark the depth of the various drill bits with masking tape.

2 Remove the wood and the Jacob's chuck from the lathe and fit the normal drive centre. Reverse the wood on to the lathe so the point of the revolving centre is in the hole and tighten up.

3 Rough the handle to a cylinder and move in the tool rest as close as possible.

4 Fit the ferrule next; mark its length and a little extra onto the end of the wood. Using a square chisel and calipers, carefully reduce the wood to the *outside* diameter of the ferrule, keeping the shoulder square.

Stop the lathe and try pushing on the ferrule; remember to offer the end of the ferrule with the inside bevel to the wood.

5 By trial and error, creep up on a final diameter where the ferrule pushes on tightly (*see* Fig 2.130). You may need to take the handle off the lathe and, with the ferrule on the edges of a vice or piece of tube, tap the ferrule home.

6 An end ferrule is fitted in a similar manner.

7 Now, with the ferrule in place, shape the handle: Round the handle end to fit comfortably in your hand. Do not run the wood completely down to the ferrule, but leave it a shade proud where they meet – a definite, but *small*, shoulder remains.

8 Sand and then burnish the handle with shavings. The wood can be left like this, acquiring the natural patina of use, or sealed with a coat of cellulose lacquer, varnish or shellac. Cut the sealer back finely – do not give the surface a shiny or glossy finish. This makes the grip uncomfortable, slippery and possibly dangerous.

9 Use the point of a turning skew chisel to trim back the excess wood at the ferrule end but take care not to cut into the revolving centre (*see* Fig 2.131).

10 Remove the handle from the lathe, hold it in a

Fig 2.132 An old carving tool in which the blade has been fitted to the handle with gutta-percha.

Fig 2.133 To fit a handle, hold the tool so that the shoulder rests on, and is gripped by, the jaws of a vice, with the tang vertical.

vice and finish off both ends with a chisel and sandpaper. Flatten the hole end so that the blade shoulder fits flush to the wood. Seal the ends as before.
11 Finally, punch a ferrule-locking depression on each side – a nail will do for this. A thick end ferrule may need a small hole with a nail tapped in.

FITTING HANDLES

Faults with the blades, and especially the shoulders and tangs, need to be corrected as far as possible to give the best chance of fitting a handle well. These are dealt with later in the section on correcting carving-tool faults (*see* page 73).

Old carving tools can be found with quite large – and not particularly accurate – holes for the tangs, filled with gutta-percha (a resinous gum from a Malayan tree). The tang has been pushed accurately into the gum which has then set like hard, black horn, fixing the blade neatly and securely in position (*see* Fig 2.132). This is a trick worth remembering. Modern equivalents (for example two-part plastic filler, such as for car bodies or wood) will repair a handle – perhaps correcting too large a hole, or one that is offset. The only snag is that there is more of a problem if you ever need to remove the tang from the hole again.

To knock on a handle, the blade must be held properly (*see* Figs 2.133, 2.134). If the blade is set upright so its cutting edge is against a resistant surface and the handle is thumped on, there is a problem. The tool has nowhere to travel and as the energy from the mallet

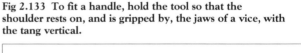

blow cannot be released, the blade may crack. This is particularly true of U-shaped blades where the bevels on either side act as wedges, squeezing the sides together.

The other point to mention is not to thump too freely, but take the fitting of the handle in a relaxed and easy way.

A metalworking vice with soft metal linings is the best sort to use; but a woodworking vice is an alternative, first packing out and protecting any wooden linings with scrap hardwood.

Grip the chisel by the blade or shank so that *the shoulder is supported on the jaws of the vice* and the tang points straight up in the air.

The method varies for parallel and tapered tangs.

Parallel tangs

If the holes are the right size, the parallel tangs, both round and square, should knock straight on with a mallet.

Tapered tangs

◼ Tap the handle, with its pilot hole, on to the tang a little way then twist it around both ways – the tang is being used to ream out the hole (*see* Fig 2.135).

◼ Tap the handle a little more and twist again. Remove the handle and tap out the dust.

◼ Keep repeating this process with the handle in one hand and the mallet in the other, taking the handle off now and then and tapping out the dust. You will fairly quickly get a rhythm and before long will have set the handle down on the tang to within ⅛in (3mm) of the shoulder.

Fig 2.134 The best way to grip a tool for fitting the handle is beneath its shoulder.

Fig 2.135 The 'tap and twist' method of fitting a handle.

Fig 2.136 Using a wedge of hardwood to knock off the handle.

■ At this point clear the dust out one last time and select which part of the handle – perhaps a pleasing bit of grain – you want to appear and where. Also if the tang and hole are offset, now is the time to look for 'compensating errors'.

■ Now tap the handle home and there should be no problem of splitting. If your tang and holes are true the blade will be aligned along the axis of the handle.

One final point: the method by which the tang is heated and burnt into the handle is only appropriate if a hole cannot be bored and you are really desperate. While no doubt it is fun, it also charcoals the wood inside, allowing the handle to work loose; it can be messy and not without its dangers – both to the lungs and a wood workshop; and it can, if care is not taken, damage the tool tempering. It is also much slower than anything described here – all in all it is not a method to be recommended.

REMOVING HANDLES

Although problems of sticking do arise with old tools and rusty tangs, the handle of a woodcarving gouge or chisel normally comes off without much difficulty. This is especially true of tools that have tapered,

square tangs – these lock securely in place during use, but release from the wood fairly easily when required.

For the following methods of removing handles, grip the blade in a vice by a substantially strong part such as the shank, just beyond the shoulder. If an engineer's vice with metal jaws is being used, protect the blade from being marked with hardwood pieces.

Never grip quick gouges – and especially U-shaped ones – across the blade. The pressure of the vice can crack the metal which, having been hardened and tempered, is more brittle than flexible.

Method 1

With the blade held firmly in the vice try the handle a little while gently twisting it. Sometimes this is all that is necessary. Be careful as the handle can come off very suddenly, so make sure that nothing is in the way of your elbow as it travels backwards.

Method 2

A wedge of hardwood, looking like a large screwdriver head and long enough to grip, is applied to the ferrule if it is visible around the shoulder (*see* Fig 2.136). Strike the wedge firmly with a mallet. If

Fig 2.137 Problems in removing the handle may arise when the shoulder is very tight to the ferrule.

nothing happens, apply the wedge to the other side of the ferrule and repeat. The handle should knock off fairly easily. Beware, again, that if you are too enthusiastic the handle can disengage from the tang suddenly and take flight across the workshop. Using an actual screwdriver for this purpose can damage the

Fig 2.138 Name punches.

ferrule, which is normally only made of soft brass.

Method 3

When the shoulder sits tight up to the edge of the ferrule, the wooden wedge cannot get a purchase on the handle to knock it off. You need to approach the joint between the shoulder and the wood from the side with an old chisel, trying to loosen the handle and gain enough space to apply the wooden wedge. Be careful not to damage the ferrule with the chisel or screwdriver. If you do, the ferrule may need filing or touching up on a grinding wheel.

Method 4

Sometimes warming and drying the handle a little with a hair dryer causes it to release the tang.

Method 5

If all else fails – say with an old tool where it is certain the tang has corroded and practically bonded with the wood – the handle has to be sacrificed. First use a hacksaw and pliers to remove the ferrule, sawing diagonally along its length. Grip the blade in the vice by the shank, with the shoulders resting on the jaws and the handle straight up. Split the handle from the top end using an old chisel. The wood can be pared away to reveal the tang.

FINISH

Smooth the handle with fine sandpaper so it feels well in the hand. Sandpapering and burnishing with another piece of the same wood, or wood shavings, is an adequate finish in itself.

A coat of varnish, cellulose lacquer, sanding sealer or shellac – rubbed back with fine wirewool – can be used to seal the wood; this can be done on the lathe.

Thick, heavy varnish should be avoided as it becomes uncomfortable and slippery when the hands are warm. It is not necessary to wax the handles as, if frequently used, the wood naturally becomes burnished and acquires its own patina. Bought handles which are already glossily varnished can be rubbed back to the wood with sandpaper and re-finished.

If woodcarving tools are unused for some time, a light wipe with linseed oil (raw) on the handles will take care of the wood.

Soaking the end of the handle in varnish or thinned PVA (polyvinyl acetate) glue overnight – which penetrates the end fibres – increases the resistance of the wood to damage and splitting when it is hit with a mallet. On the other hand, there may be a danger of skin sensitivity with handling.

NAME PUNCHES

It is not a bad idea to stamp your name on your tool handles, or in some way mark them personally. If you have acquired old gouges and chisels and intend to continue using the handles, then you can add your name to any already stamped on. There is a great sense of continuity, seeing tools passed through several hands and being aware of contact with a carver who may be long dead.

Support the handle in a **V**-like trough of wood to stop it rolling. Line up the punch and try to mark both sides of the handle with a single sharp strike using a hammer.

The Reference Section contains sources of name stamps (*see* page 345).

Carving-tool faults and their correction

A 'fault' in a carving tool may be seen as anything that interferes with its working efficiency. This would include, among other things, the carbon steel being of inferior quality, perhaps having unsatisfactory edge-keeping quality from the original tempering; incorrect forging of the shape; or a poorly fitting handle. Faults also include poor sharpening – but more of that in Chapter 3.

Some variation in quality may not be seen as a fault. And faults may, or may not, be something you wish to correct. Some matter more that others. I am suggesting here that a critical look should be taken at your carving tools to see if there is any way of improving their performance or feel; or even how they may be made more attractive to use.

More, or even most, often faults lie in the actual shaping of the tool itself when it was forged: in the blade, shank, shoulder and tang. Some manufacturers produce superbly shaped carving tools; others, sadly, do not.

At the risk of producing anecdotal evidence, I started carving with a dozen tools, but in a few months I had built up a list of tools that I could usefully carve with. I duly sent off an order for about 40 tools to a reputable firm (but one which can remain anonymous). When I examined the tools, I found that I needed to send back nearly half of them; distributed

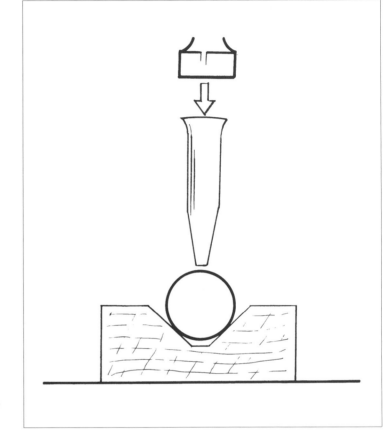

Fig 2.139 A former of wood is used to hold a round handle safely while it is name stamped.

among these tools were all the faults which will be dealt with below. The steel and edge-holding properties themselves were excellent but the shaping was unacceptable. The tools had been carelessly made and should not have passed the factory inspection. Out of the tools I was sent as replacements, I returned another six . . . .

The faults which follow have occurred both in my own tools and those of other carvers, and the reasons why they may be considered faults – the effect of the fault – will be given. The question is whether the 'fault' or condition makes a difference to you as the user. Some carvers do very good work with tools I would have considered faulted to a degree that would make me want to do something about them.

So, to some extent, it is a question of attitude. The approach I would like to promote in this book is one where manufacturers make tools to the best of their ability and carvers love the tools with which they work, their quality and efficiency.

So, check over your tools, both old and new, as they are acquired. Work through those that you have, and gradually bring all your carving tools up to a level where you can justifiably be proud of them. But do not be obsessional about them, they are a means to an end only.

If you need to return a carving tool to the retailer or manufacturer, point out the problem quietly but assertively and there should be no problem with getting a replacement; it is to be hoped that you are also helping the manufacturers improve their products.

Old and second-hand tools have their own problems and these will be dealt with later (*see* page 92). Starting with the blade, and working through to the tang, here is a check list of some faults, including those of the handle, together with some notes on what might be done about them.

BLADES

Steel

One of the advantages of a beginner not buying too many tools of the same make, is that a comparison of steels, through direct experience, is possible. There is not much you can do yourself if the blade is discovered to have poor edge-holding qualities, other than attempt

to re-harden and temper it. This is explained in Chapter 5 (*see* page 233) and can be quite successful.

It is also possible for a tool to have a 'soft spot' where it seems to lose an edge very quickly. 'Blueing' of the metal by over-grinding will produce the same result – see the section on bench grinders in Chapter 3 (*see* page 135).

A winding blade

This is mainly a problem of tapered chisels and gouges – such as fishtails – and short bent tools. The blade has been forged so that, if the edge is looked at directly end-on, there is a degree of rotation or winding around the true axis (*see* Fig 2.140).

The resulting tool feels less certain, more 'self-conscious' in the hands than when the blade and edge are aligned properly to the square shank. The winding must always be compensated for and the tool will line up inappropriately for setting in and finishing cuts.

There is not much to be done without re-heating and shaping, although a bold approach would be to attempt a cold re-shaping, using a vice and heavy grips. This may be possible, provided the bending is to be done in the soft, annealed part of the blade, such as the shank. Otherwise, if the shape is not acceptable, the tool will have to be returned.

Asymmetry of the blade

Here the blade, with or without winding, bends away to one side. Again this is more often, but by no means

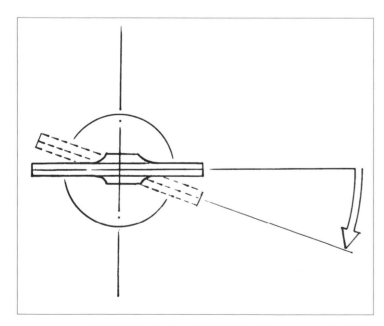

Fig 2.140 A winding fishtail blade. The same rotation fault can be seen in poorly forged short bent tools.

Fig 2.141 A front bent chisel with the blade offset to one side.

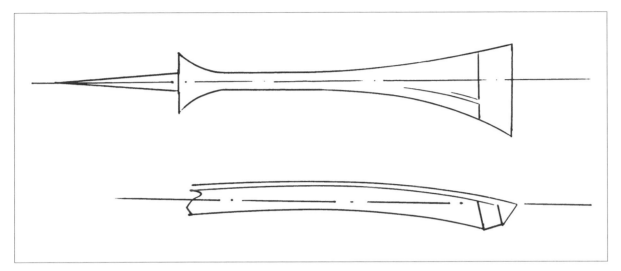

Fig 2.143 Different thicknesses between the walls of a V-tool make their equal sharpening more difficult.

always, to be found in tapered tools. If it is a small problem, a tapered gouge or chisel may be ground back to symmetry – with some loss of useful life – or a cold bend attempted. But, for the most part, any significantly asymmetrical tool should be returned.

Unevenness of metal thickness

When the blade is forged from the hot metal blank, the red-hot metal is placed in one (concave) half of a former and hammered with a matching (convex) shape – the result is a particular shape and sweep of blade.

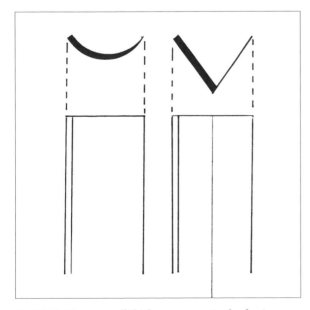

Fig 2.144 Uneven wall thickness occurs in the forging process when the in cannel forming block is misaligned.

If the two parts of the former have been accurately lined up, the sweep will have an even wall thickness across the width. The cannel (the inside curve or V-groove) will also line up symmetrically along the axis and not wander, or be offset, to one side. Sometimes, however, less than the desired accuracy of matching is achieved at this stage, and the tool may pass from the factory to point of sale without being removed by quality controls.

If the metal of the wall is of uneven thickness, it becomes very difficult to set the bevel correctly or sharpen the edge evenly. The edge towards one side, being thicker than the other, will need a longer bevel to get the same cutting angle (*see* Fig 2.145).

This problem is especially frustrating with the V-tool – difficult enough to sharpen evenly at the best of times – where walls of different thicknesses can make the tool impossible to sharpen correctly. Another

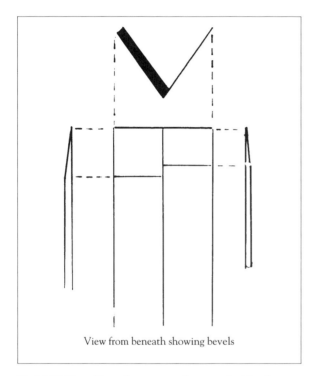

View from beneath showing bevels

Fig 2.145 To achieve the same angle on each side of a parting tool with uneven wall thicknesses, the bevels always end up different lengths.

Fig 2.146 Poor alignment of the in cannel with the axis of the blade again produces uneven wall thickness.

problem with the V-tool is when particularly thick metal is left along the junction of the two sides by the maker as a precaution against the tool cracking at this point when it is bent in the forging.

It may be possible to reduce the wall thickness to a level of evenness by grinding. Otherwise replacement is the only option.

Bad alignment of the cannel can have the same effect on a V-tool (*see* Fig 2.146), making the sharpening an unhappy experience, but is less of a problem than uneven wall thickness.

Bent tools

Bent tools are bent for one purpose only: to enable the carver to get into recesses where the straight tools have difficulties. The principle is bend the blade further and get in deeper. You will find a range of bends being offered by manufacturers, and a range of definitions of what a 'bend' is.

With so many tools ordered by post today, tools are often only seen as drawings or photographs in catalogues and are not actually handled. They can arrive looking quite different from what was expected. Two tools of the same width and sweep, from the same manufacturer, may have dissimilar bends.

For example, some manufacturers make spoonbit gouges with such a shallow bend that the tools are of little advantage over the straight versions.

What matters is how useful the shape of a carving tool is to you – as the carver actually using it. Shallow bends have their place, as in working shallow backgrounds ('grounding'), but deeper bends are also needed – and when you order one, a deep bend is what

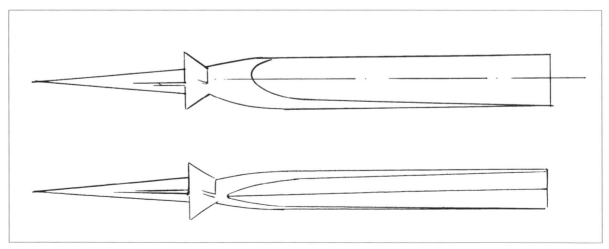

you should get. If what you have received is unacceptable, return the tool with a note of the problem; if there is no improvement, try another maker.

Do not attempt to change the shape by cold bending as this is too near the area of tempered metal (*see* Fig 2.147).

Blade surface

Some makers take a lot of trouble to polish up the surfaces of their tools to make them attractive. Others leave the outer faces with the rough, black oily surface resulting from quenching the hot metal on the outside, and only polish the inside to show the straw tempering colour. New, polished tools are often protected from damp by being given an oily, or greasy, coating.

Oily surfaces on carving tools are more of an irritation than a problem as there is a tendency for the grease or black oil to get on to the work via the hands. Rub the blade with a de-greaser like paraffin until no more oil comes off. Fine emery paper can be used on the more dense black finishes, as well as to smooth off sharp corners and edges along the length of the blade.

For pitting and roughness of the surface see the section on second-hand tools in this chapter (*see* page 93).

SHOULDERS

Inappropriate size of shoulder

Shoulders, or bolsters, can be filed or ground down if they are too large.

Too small a shoulder – more of a protuberance than a shoulder – can be forced into the wood by a mallet. If the tool is for light work only, for all practical purposes this will probably not be a problem. For heavier work, this state of the shoulder is unacceptable.

Rounded underface

The 'face' is the underside of the shoulder. It should be flat and sit tight against the end of the wooden handle (*see* Fig 2.148). If the face is badly rounded, not only will there be a gap between the shoulder and the wood – which is uncomfortable to hold – but there is a danger of the metal being forced further into the wood and splitting it, especially if there is no ferrule on the handle. If the face of the shoulder is not truly flat, it is easier to make the handle look as if it is fitting properly.

To create a flat face on the underside of the shoulder, grip the blade in a vice (preferably a

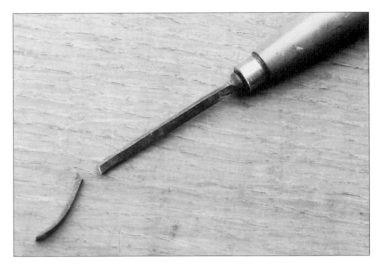

Fig 2.147 You cannot cold bend the hardened part of a blade, however misaligned, without this happening.

metalworking vice) with the tang pointing upwards and the shoulder resting on the jaws. Drop a washer which has a hole slightly larger than the diameter of the shoulder, over the tang so that it rests on the vice. More than one washer may be needed, adjusting the shoulder of the tool so that its face stands out a little proud of the hole. Set the tang perpendicular to the washer. With the washer acting as a jig, a file can now

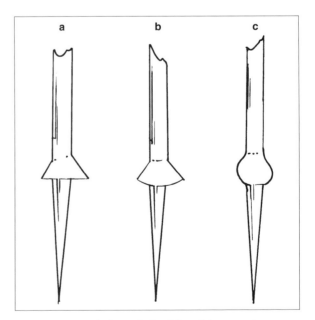

Fig 2.148 Some faults with shoulders: (a) unevenly distributed around the blade; (b) rounded undersurface; and (c) misshaped altogether.

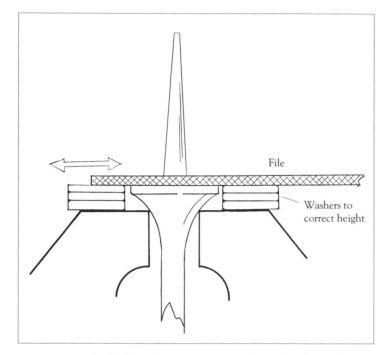

Fig 2.149 A file and washers can be used to flatten the under face of a shoulder so that it seats well on the handle.

be used to flatten the undersurface of the shoulder (*see* Fig 2.149), creating a good face to sit on the wood of the handle. Take care not to bite into the tang.

TANGS

Tang off the axis line

To get a blade dead in line with the handle, the tang must be on the central axis of the blade. The consequences of a bent tang have been discussed earlier in this chapter, in the section on tangs (*see* page 50).

The tang may have been bent in the original making, or bent by rough use. It is possible to still align

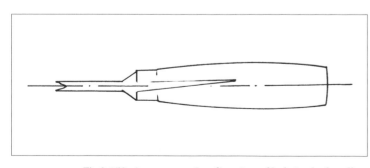

Fig 2.150 A compensating direction of hole in the handle enables the blade to be lined up along the axis of the tool.

the handle by boring the hole at a compensating angle (*see* Fig 2.150) – in effect, compensating errors – but this is not easy to get right. It is far better for the tang to be straight in the first place.

An angled tang can often be straightened by cold bending. The blade should be gripped in the vice as described for flattening the bottom of the shoulder, and tapped gently with a hammer – working from the shoulder end. Remember that a tang – or any metal – will not take much bending backwards and forwards before it weakens.

If cold bending feels risky, use a gas torch to heat the tang up to dull red and then bend it. While you are doing this, protect the blade itself from the effects of the heat by wrapping it in a wet rag.

If the tang is of adequate bulk and length, grinding and filing is also an option.

Tang parallel to, but off, centre line

This is a problem created in the initial forging and is at its worst when the shoulder overhangs the ferrule. Proper fitting of the blade along the true axis becomes impossible.

Options for dealing with this problem lie in grinding and filing the tang into the central axis – if there is enough metal in it. If not, consider offsetting or packing the hole in the handle. Otherwise, if you do not want to live with it, send the tool back.

Inappropriate size of tang

It may seem obvious that a large gouge needs a large tang to fit strongly into the handle, and that other sizes of blade need an appropriate amount of tang. But the first you may know about a tang being too small is the handle bending about the shoulder. It is more often a problem with larger tools.

If you are making your own handles, you will buy the carving tool 'unhandled' and can immediately inspect the tang. Otherwise you will have to knock off the handle to have a look. Send the tool back if it is a new tool.

If the tang is corroded – as in an old tool – a few more options are described in the section on tangs later in this chapter (*see* page 94).

HANDLES

Hole offset or too large

For either of these conditions it is best to make a new hole. Plug the old one with a dowel of the same size –

and wood if possible – gluing and tapping it in. Find the position for the new hole by lining up both ends of the handle between centre points, and rotating it.

An oversize or offset hole can also be packed to the side with slivers of wood.

Inappropriate size or shape

Look at whether the size of the handle is too small or too large; whether the shape is what you want; the suitability of the wood for the use of the tool; and whether a ferrule is needed at the tang end, or another needed to protect the handle end against the mallet.

To some extent, if there is wood to spare, handles can be re-made. If not, it may be a case of making an entirely new handle, keeping the old one for a different tool.

Varnish

As mentioned previously, some manufacturers cover their handles with thick varnish. This is not a pleasant surface compared with thinner, less glossy finishes.

Varnish like this can be removed with fine sandpaper or stripper (followed by washing); and the handle burnished with another piece of wood. Wipe the wood occasionally with a little linseed oil, or seal the wood with a thin coat of shellac or varnish, rubbed back with fine wirewool.

The best finish and patina comes from the effect of being regularly used in the hand.

SELECTING AND BUYING WOODCARVING TOOLS
Shapes and function

The subject of woodcarving itself (i.e. how to carve) is not the principal theme of this book – although information about carving will inevitably infuse it. It is intended that carving, as such, will be covered in more detail in a future book.

For the newcomer to woodcarving, it is not just

Fig 2.151 A variety of tool cuts, depths, open and filled spaces and rhythms are used in this detail from Riemenschneider's 'Crucifixion Altar' in Detwang, outside Rothenburg. Many of the tools that were used are clearly apparent.

the choice of woodcarving tools that is bewildering, but the fact that being able to choose the right tools means knowing, at least to some extent, what to do with them. What carving chisels and gouges are in an academic sense is fairly straightforward, but what does one actually *do* with them? The following information is included as a brief guide to newcomers to the craft. In this section are some pointers to the functions of the various woodcarving tool 'families' and what they can be expected to do. This is by no means an exhaustive guide, but should help you decide what tools you need for the work you have in mind. In the following section is an approach to buying tools needed to start carving.

One point to remember is that when a carver is working, carving as such is only taking place when the tool is actually cutting the wood. So the more 'down time' (that is time sorting out another tool to use), the slower and more irregular the pace of working. With trade carving on a number of repeat items, or in

lettering, a rhythm is built up after a while; the order in which each tool is used is established and refined so that maximum efficiency is achieved. The cuts proceed in a set order and the down time is reduced to a minimum – and the resulting work appears as swiftly as possible with a uniform appearance.

When a one-off piece is being carved, the down time is kept as low as possible in a different way. The carver uses the tool in his or her hand for as long as possible and makes the tool do the work of several others – not putting the tool down until another is really necessary. Against this, though, it should be said that there is a danger of making work look uninteresting by using the same cut too often.

So the functions of tools are not completely fixed and static. One gouge can be made to perform functions more naturally ascribed to another and the normal 'brief' of the tools is to some extent flexible. But there are also times when you must have one particular tool for the work at hand, and none other will substitute.

Some guidelines for newcomers follow, describing what they may expect a particular family of woodcarving tools to do.

Straight chisels (firmers)

To begin with the obvious: firmer chisels are used when straight lines are needed – as in cutting letters or setting in straight edges (*see* Fig 2.152). Lettering can need a wide range of chisel sizes to cut the varying lengths of uprights, diagonals and horizontals. Use chisels for working over lightly convex areas to produce a finished surface and, if they are presented in

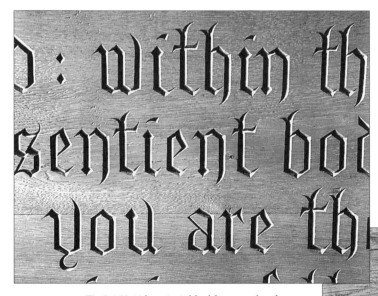

Fig 2.152 (Above) A blackletter style of script such as this has minimal curved elements and so few gouges are used. (Right) Straight chisels play a very important part in most lettering.

Fig 2.153 The skew chisel cleans up an otherwise inaccessible corner.

a slicing or skewed fashion, they will trim the outside edges of curves.

Straight corner chisels (skew)

The essential working part of this tool is its long, pointed corner, enabling it to enter and clean corners and angles where normal square-ended tools – chisel or gouge – cannot reach. Different angles of skew will give the skew a longer or shorter corner, for dealing with different recesses.

The skew chisel – held something like a pencil – can be used in a scribing way for running and shaping curved edges. It will shape the corners and edges of grooves left by a V-tool (*see* Fig 2.153). This produces a very flat relief; used in this way, the skew is quite a delicate tool. It can also smooth lightly convex surfaces, giving more of a slicing cut than the square firmer.

Remember that the longer the point of the skew chisel, the more fragile it is. If the point is rocked from side to side when it is sunk in wood, it is very liable to snap off and remain embedded (*see* Fig 2.154).

Short bent chisels (grounders)

A **grounding tool** or **grounder** is primarily concerned with finishing the backgrounds in relief

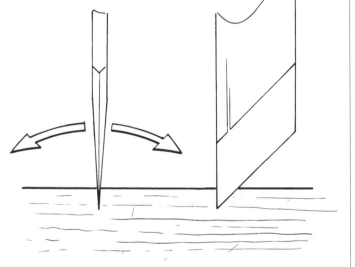

Fig 2.154 A good way to snap the point off a skew chisel is to rock it from side to side while it is embedded in the wood.

carving (*see* Fig 2.155). 'Grounding' describes the deeper, flat-bottomed cutting that is needed to sink a background.

A grounder may be a short bent chisel or a short bent gouge of the flattest sweep. In some ways the flattish gouge profile is the preferable cutting edge – the corners are free of the wood throughout the cut and there is less tendency for them to tear the fibres

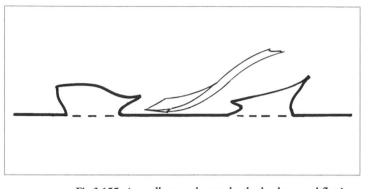

Fig 2.155 A small grounder works the background flat in a relief carving.

compared with a flat chisel. The amount of bend in the grounding tool (or any bent tool) dictates how much it can be used, in what circumstances, and how well the cutting edge can get into an appropriate position to cut.

Short bent chisels can also undercut in other contexts and can clean grain where straight tools cannot reach. Use them to chamfer or clean the inside of curves, as, for example, in Gothic tracery.

Short bent corner chisels

These tools, sometimes called **corner grounders**, can get into recesses and corners where square-ended tools

Fig 2.156 Simple grooves with the V-tool will add a lot of flair to a simple foliate carving.

cannot reach. They come into their own where undercutting has been created and deep corners need to be got at.

The skewing of the edge in relation to the rest of the tool can be to the right or the left; one reaching where the other cannot, or where the grain needs a particular direction of cut. As both directions inevitably need to be cut at some time or another, buy them as a matching pair. Short bent corner chisels are the sort of tool that may not be used very often, but when they *are* needed it is because nothing else will do.

Splayed chisels (fishtail or spade tools)

The spade or fishtail version of any parallel-sided tool gives two extra benefits.

▪ The corners become more prominent, allowing cuts to continue into angles normally inaccessible to the parallel sort of tool. For example, use fishtail chisels to cut the flat ends of serifs in lettering.
▪ These splayed tools are much lighter than the straight tools – they feel more dextrous and so are used mainly for finishing work, for example, in smoothing rounded surfaces.

There is a cost to these benefits, however: the cutting edge loses its width with sharpening and these blades have a shorter working life than parallel-sided ones. For this reason, and because of their lightness, they are unsuitable for rough work. Keep these splayed tools for the lighter, final stages of carving, allowing other tools to take the brunt of the preliminary work.

Parting tools (V-tools)

These very useful tools are made with different angles – producing a different openness of groove or straight-sided channel (*see* Figs 2.156, 2.157). Use the **V**-tool on its own to run a shallow, decorative and finished groove in the surface of a carving, for instance on a bread board, or delineating hair, feathers or leaves.

Chamfering the edges of **V**-grooves creates a type of low relief carving. The tool is also used with special knives to produce 'chip carving' – a geometrical, surface decoration.

In relief carving, much preliminary work involves outlining and defining an area to be blocked out (*see* Fig 2.158). The **V**-tool is indispensable here and its alternative name of 'parting' tool suggests this use. And, if the tool is tilted to one side, a degree of simple undercutting is possible, for example under carved leaves.

Fig 2.157 A front bent skew cleaning the curved groove between reeds.

Fig 2.158 A V-tool can be used to outline a relief carving in successive levels to the required depth. A gouge is used to remove the waste and other tools to 'set in' to a predetermined line.

Straight gouges

The parallel-sided gouges, of all sweeps and sizes, are the general carver's most called-upon tools. They are at work right from the start of a carving, with the preliminary roughing out, through to establishing the main forms and masses ('bosting in') and on to the final surface finishing. It may be helpful to elaborate a little on how gouges are used.

The 'quicker' carving tools do indeed remove wood in more bulk – and therefore more quickly – than the flatter gouges. Flat gouges in turn produce shallow, polished facets which can be worked over the surface of the wood – modelling, smoothing and completing it.

In making a gouge cut, one principle is not to let the corners dig in. The middle part of the sweep cuts, but the corners remain in the fresh air, slightly above the surface (*see* Fig 2.161). This is a different technique from deliberately using one of the corners to make a cut in the manner of the skew chisel. If the

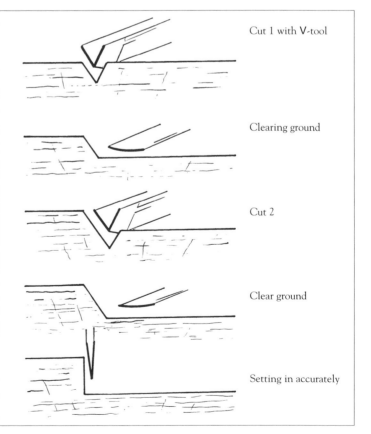

Cut 1 with V-tool

Clearing ground

Cut 2

Clear ground

Setting in accurately

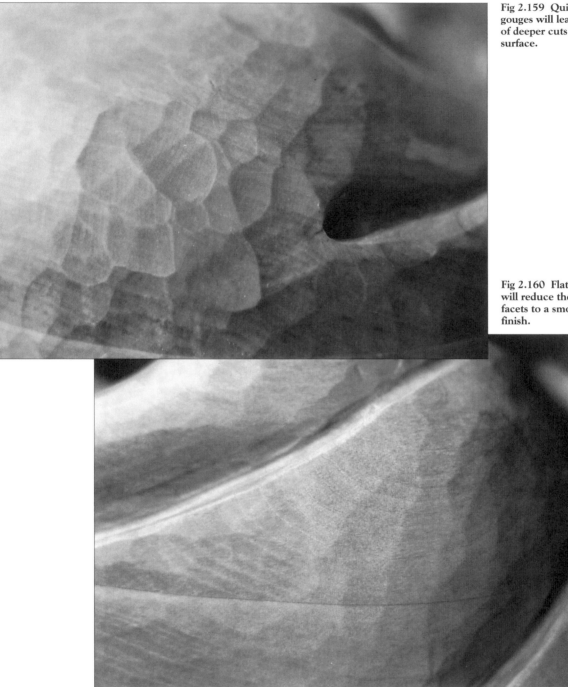

Fig 2.159 Quicker gouges will leave patterns of deeper cuts on a surface.

Fig 2.160 Flatter gouges will reduce these deeper facets to a smoother finish.

corners of a gouge are buried in the wood during its cut then not only is some control lost, but the wood fibres are torn, which produces a ragged surface. There is also the danger of breaking an embedded tool. If deeper cuts are needed, select a deeper gouge.

Another important use of a gouge involves matching the particular sweep, or curve, of the cutting edge to a precise, matching curve to be cut in the wood (*see* Fig 2.162). Clean, precise shapes can be outlined in this way and repeated; one application of

Fig 2.161 Digging in the corners of the gouge will tear wood fibres, not cut them.

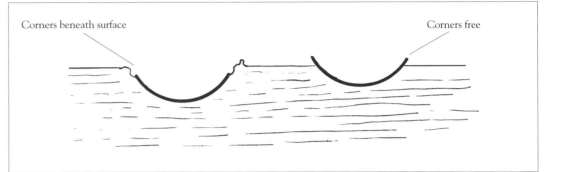

Corners beneath surface

Corners free

Fig 2.162 Matching the curve to an exact requirement to set in a clean, sweeping edge.

this technique would be to carve mouldings.

'Setting in' involves outlining a main subject from its surroundings, perhaps cutting away the background. Setting in uses the sweeps of carving tools in a similar way to that mentioned above, and is one of the reasons why carvers build up large numbers of carving tools in different sweeps and sizes.

This principle – of tool profiles matching the curves of edges being cut – also brings clarity and a precise beauty to the carving of letters in wood.

The term 'bosting in' comes from the French

ebauché, meaning to sketch. It describes that stage in the carving process which is a little further into the work than the preliminary roughing out. It is used when the main forms and masses are being defined or 'sketched in'. What is being sought are the primary planes, forms and movement of the work – the masses and forms that underlie and support the final details. A variety of straight gouges, often fairly flat, or even chisels are used extensively in this vigorous stage. Getting these early masses and moving forms correctly established is an extremely important – if not the *most*

Fig 2.163 The beads in this old carved moulding were cut with a gouge in the reversed position.

Fig 2.164 Gouges can be used in either a 'normal' or an 'upside down' position.

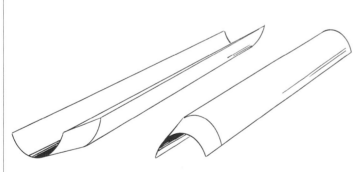

important – stage in a carving. There is a tendency for beginners to start working the final details before the main body of form has been expressed. Not only will those details which have been carved too early be cut away as the work progresses, but these details may well be in the wrong place altogether. When the underlying form is established first, the details fall naturally into place.

With the exception of the very deep gouges, all gouges give *two* cuts: one with the tool entering the

Fig 2.165 Veiners will produce a 'softer' cut than the V-tool.

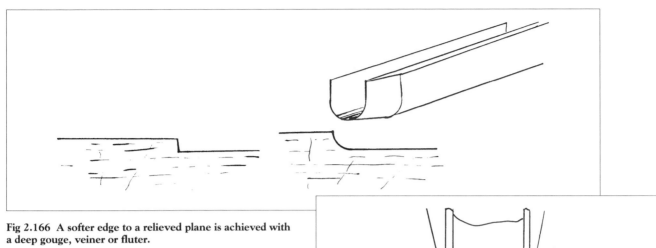

Fig 2.166 A softer edge to a relieved plane is achieved with a deep gouge, veiner or fluter.

Fig 2.167 Sideways pressure is exerted on the wedge-like bevels of a U-shaped gouge, and if the tool is buried deeply in the wood the walls may be squeezed together sufficiently to crack the metal.

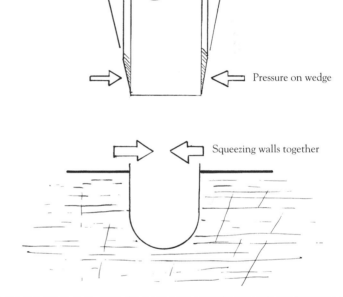

Pressure on wedge

Squeezing walls together

wood in the normal fashion, the other with the tool reversed (upside down), which produces a convex cut (*see* Figs 2.163, 2.164). So, in buying one of these tools, you are getting more value than you thought for your money.

Fluters and veiners, by producing deep cuts, grooves or channels, can be used to produce decorative work in their own right. They will also create a softer outline to a relief form (*see* Figs 2.165, 2.166). An object, or area, can be faded or blended more into the background if it does not have a hard junction where the two planes meet – such as might be made by the parting tool.

As a final note there is a distinct risk of U-shaped gouges cracking if they are powerfully embedded into wood; the outer bevels act as wedges to squeeze the walls of the gouge together (*see* Fig 2.167).

Splayed gouges (fishtail, spade or pod tools)

What was said about spade and fishtail chisels applies to these tools as well. Being thinner, the splayed gouges are quicker and easier to sharpen than parallel-sided gouges and hold a finer edge. But for the same reasons they are less economic, becoming slightly narrower with each sharpening.

Splayed gouges are not suitable for heavy work, but are excellent tools for finishing (*see* Fig 2.168). Their lightness and shape makes them easier to manipulate as they obscure less wood; and their prominent corners will run surfaces into sharper angles

Fig 2.168 A flat fishtail gouge would have helped clean the central leaf into the corner in this old oak moulding.

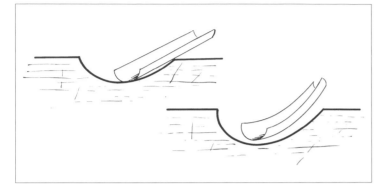

Fig 2.169 The straight tool will start to foul the edge of a recess. The same sweep and size of tool in a curved form will make the cut.

and recesses. Fishtail fluters negotiate curves more easily than the straight, parallel fluters. The blade following through after the cutting edge has less tendency to jam in the wood.

Fishtail gouges have great value in lettering, for example curving end serifs.

Long bent gouges

The bend in these tools enables the gouge to enter deeper recesses and hollows (*see* Fig 2.169). Because

the sweeps match, when the blade or handle of a straight gouge fouls the wood around a recess a simple change can be made to a similar curved gouge. Bent tools can only rarely be used upside down.

Short bent gouges

These gouges will enter yet deeper hollows than those entered by long bent gouges. The deepest hollows are entered by the most cranked tools, 'knuckle gouges' – a name expressing their shape.

In practice, the handle of a short bent gouge often swings through a large arc to produce what is quite a small cut. Make sure the cutting edge is travelling through the wood, and not just being levered at the bend.

Short bent gouges are used in high relief carving where the ground is sunk well back; in undercutting; in pierced work, such as Gothic tracery, working the inner curves especially; and in modelling internal curves at any stage in a carving where the hollow is more than a straight tool can cope with.

Back bent gouges

Earlier, in reference to straight gouges, it was mentioned that two types of cut can be made by presenting the blade in different ways to the wood. A concave groove or facet can be cut with the inside of the gouge upwards (the right way up). This type of cut is the one normally associated with gouges; and long and short bent gouges will take the carving into deeper and deeper hollows.

Fig 2.170 A deep hollow worked by a small front bent gouge.

Fig 2.171 A back bent gouge will negotiate a profile where a straight gouge would fail.

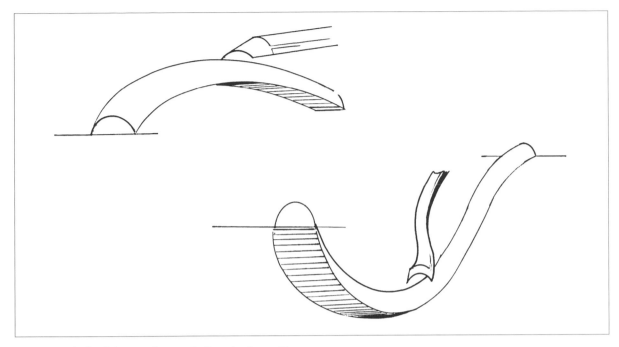

Fig 2.172 The back bent tool enters hollows in the upside down position.

The second way of cutting involves reversing the tool so that the inside of the gouge points downwards (upside down) – against the wood. This presentation produces a rounded or convex cut (*see* Fig 2.172). Now, if the long and short bent profile enable the gouge in the first position to enter hollows, then the back bent profile allows a similar access for the gouge in the second, more difficult, reversed position.

Selecting and ordering

MAKING THE CHOICE

The contents of this chapter so far will have helped you gain an understanding of the 'anatomy' of woodcarving tools, how they work and what might be done with them. But if you are starting off without carving tools at all, there comes a point when you need to take the plunge and buy some. Which ones and how many? Or what if you want to expand your range?

Here are some notes that might help make the choice.

◆ **Buy only a few carving tools to start with.**

Time is needed to understand each tool as you carve so that you become familiar with it and discover what it can do for you. Time will also be needed to sharpen the tools, which can be slow and at times frustrating to

begin with. On the other hand, too few tools can be frustrating as well, and your work may be limited by not having the right tools.

As a guideline, around a dozen or so carefully selected tools is a good starting number. A suggested list, and how it is arrived at, is given in Table 2.1 (*see* page 91).

◆ **Base your choice on need.**

At the start you may have no idea of what it is you want to carve – how big it will be, or how complex. You will almost certainly need more tools than you initially buy. The best approach – whether you have no carving tools or many – is to increase their number as and when the need arises.

Make the most use of what tools you have available and make a few notes as you go along. If you feel that a particular gouge would be right for the job, if only it were wider, narrower, bent or shaped in some way, you can use what has been said earlier in the chapter to describe the difference you need accurately.

◆ **Use your gut feeling.**

Having said that the choice of carving tool is best decided rationally – basing your need on previous experience – there is also a place for a more intuitive approach, especially if you do not know what you actually want to carve. So if you see a carving tool that 'grabs you', or fills your head with ideas of what might be done, or that you can feel and see yourself using, then the chances are that your heart is speaking to you, and you should listen.

SELECTING THE TOOLS

At the start, some decision as to *what* tools to buy needs to be made. At the risk of duplicating an earlier section in this chapter, here are some guidelines.

◆ **Avoid cheap tools.**

Cheap tools are almost always made of poor steel, badly tempered and incapable of holding an edge for long – even if they have been polished up to look smart. They are often shorter than usual with cheap-looking ferrules.

Expense is relative. Although top quality carving tools may appear expensive, they are meant for a lifetime's use. Through them you may have years of pleasure, creativity and perhaps even earn your living. If there is still any doubt as to the value of carving tools, it is worth reflecting on the relative cost of a few hours at the cinema, eating out or setting up in other crafts.

◆ **Buy from reputable manufacturers.**

Buy from well-established firms with a reputation to protect in the marketplace. They will have useful lists of their tools and additional information available.

It is particularly useful if they are using a standard numbering system such as the Sheffield List so that you can refer between makes. If not, and you are able to inspect the tools, take along an impression of the cuts your present carving tools make by stabbing their edges into a flat piece of wood or cardboard. With this in hand, you can make a comparison between the sweeps you have at home, the variation of sweep or shape you want, and what is on offer.

◆ **Try various makes to start with.**

Different makers seem to have different strengths, for example in the bends of their tools, the thickness of metal or the finish. Some makes of tool are more attractive to some individuals. But before settling into the well-known rut of 'brand loyalty', do try out different makes. It is worth experimenting this way even if you have quite a few tools already.

◆ **Avoid boxed sets.**

This is the way many people start: a boxed set of woodcarving tools as a Christmas or birthday present. This *can* work out well, but equally as often, does not. The giver will usually be unaware of what quality the tools are or may have bought some of the cheaper tools to be found on market stalls. Even when the quality is excellent, the choice of tools has been made by other people: firstly by the manufacturer and secondly by the giver of the set.

Poor quality, or poor selection, can cause a lot of frustration and, sadly, has been known to put people off carving right from the start.

The choice of tools is a very personal issue, as has been stressed before. In effect, the tool kit grows with the carver. However, if you already have a boxed set, do not despair! They may be exactly what you need. If they are not what you need at the moment, but they are good quality tools, sooner or later you will use them.

◆ **Inspect the tools.**

Use the information given in this chapter – and summarized in the next section on new and second-hand tools (*see* page 92) – to check over your tools for faults when you buy them. There is no reason to accept substandard tools when by returning them you should get the quality you are paying for. On the contrary, by keeping manufacturers on their toes with your discrimination, carving as a whole is being done a long-term service.

SUGGESTED STARTING KIT

Having just spent the last few paragraphs suggesting that other people should not be allowed to make decisions about the carving tools you need, this section may seem a little out of place!

My experience has shown me that although someone can understand all that has been said about woodcarving tools – about quality, the different shapes, what they do and so on – there can still be an initial lack of confidence when it comes to buying some to start with. This is not such a surprise as confidence will only really begin when you actually lay your hands on the tools, and start using them.

The following tool selection is based on several things: my teaching experience, both private and in adult education; discussions with other carvers; what I started with; and what tools are on my bench more often than any others. My initial selection of carving tools perform basic, useful functions. From here onwards, acquire tools by working out your needs.

Bear in mind that any carving book will give you a different set of carving tools with which to begin. There are at least three reasons for this:

■ The apparent vastness of choice among carving tools and makes

■ The wide-open field that is carving design, with different projects requiring different tools or approaches

The unique preferences, not to say prejudices, that individuals (including myself) have about what we like and what we think is right – about *anything*, never mind carving tools!

Eventually, you will know *yourself* the work to which you are inclined – the scale, size and detail. Perhaps it will be lettering or wildlife, huge bowls or duck decoys, abstract sculpture or netsuke.

What you must do is *start* – with something, anything, but start. Problems then become something to get your teeth into. And this is also a good way to see your first carving as well. It is easy to worry about different aspects of what you want to do before you have started carving. Once you get going, you have experience to learn from, and what previously seemed difficult becomes tangible and approachable.

The tools I suggest you buy are listed in Table 2.1, where the numbers refer to the Sheffield List.

No.	Width (ins)	(mm)	Description
01	¼	6	Straight (firmer) chisel
01	½	13	Straight chisel
02	⅜	10	Skew (corner) chisel
03	¼	6	Flat gouge (straight)
03	½	13	Flat gouge (straight)
06	½	13	Medium gouge (straight)
06	1	25	Medium gouge (straight)
08	⅜	10	Quick gouge (straight)
10	¼	6	Quick gouge (straight)
11	3⁄16	5	Fluter (straight)
39	¼	6	Parting (V-) tool
*	⅜	10	Short bent flat gouge
*	⅜	10	Short bent medium gouge

Table 2.1 An initial selection of woodcarving tools.

Consider also buying the following tools:

- Right and left short bent skew chisels, ⅛in (3mm)
- Larger fluter and smaller veiner
- Bent and fishtail tools in any of these sweeps and sizes.

There are also some variations, according to the interests of the woodcarver.

Sculpture

You may find the smallest tool that you need is 1in (25mm) going up to approximately 1½in (38mm). It is possible to buy 2in (50mm) tools, but in practice they require a lot of effort with the mallet. In the long term these smaller tools, while apparently slower, are less tiring to use and eventually more work is achieved with the same effort.

Miniature carving

The shapes above are still more than likely to be needed but in this case the range is reduced in size, perhaps to ¼in (6mm) and below.

Lettering

Lettering requires more straight chisels – if not a full range in small increments, as straight lines are a prominent feature in many styles of lettering. The curves of the letters will need to be matched and fishtail gouges and chisels used for the serifs.

Miscellaneous

Other interests such as violin-making or carving duck decoys suggest their own requirements: more curves to match scrolls and finer veiners and V-tools for featherwork.

ORDERING THE TOOLS

Today, ever larger numbers of carving tools are bought through the post; often it is not possible to see and handle woodcarving tools locally. You will, therefore, need a good idea of what tools you want.

◆ **Get hold of catalogue information.**

Good manufacturers and suppliers readily distribute their catalogues. Study them and check that the particular numbering system coincides with what you want and what you expect to receive.

◆ **Keep an accurate record of your order.**

Mark the sweeps of the tools you have sent for, and the date you sent the order. It is quite useful to record the exact shapes of your blades by pressing them into a board of thin wood. It is then easy to compare the impressions with what the manufacturers are offering.

◆ **Check over the carving tools when they arrive.**

First, see that the sizes and shapes are exactly what you expected. Second, inspect for faults and problems using the information on pages 73–9. Decide whether any fault is something you can deal with simply or not; return any unacceptable tools, with a polite explanation, asking for a replacement.

Perhaps the impression is being given that faults in woodcarving tools are common; they are more common than might be expected. Fortunately, toolmakers have been improving their quality as the market grows and the competition increases. The main purpose of the following section on faults or problems is to prevent someone being at a loss when they occur, and to inform them of what sorts of remedies are possible.

New and second-hand tools

Because of the increasing interest both in carving itself and old tools in general, second-hand carving tools are not as common as they used to be – nor are they necessarily cheaper than their new equivalents. However, they still crop up in markets, second-hand tool shops, car boot sales and so on, and are worth looking out for. Once people know of your interest in carving, you may well find that you are given tools and wood. There is a welcome feeling today that it is reprehensible to waste such assets. So you may well acquire some old tools and with luck they will bear such illustrious names as Addis and Sons, Herring or Ward and Payne.

With a new tool you can be reasonably sure of its shape, size, quality and so on. But these old tools can have certain problems that actually make them less than attractive propositions. It is these problems that will be dealt with in this section, thus helping you to make an informed decision as to their worth to you as a carver. Unless you like collecting these old tools, do not buy a

tool *merely* because it is old. Reviving older woodcarving tools and putting them back into successful service, however, can be a very satisfying undertaking.

Bear in mind all that has been said previously about assessing new carving tools – these observations can be applied to old carving tools as well. In addition, the following points should be looked at.

Length of blade

It is a fact in carving that the most useful tools are those that wear down quickest because of continuous sharpening. Therefore, it is often the case that the blades of the most useful-looking, old woodcarving tools are considerably reduced in length (*see* Fig 2.173(a)). Not all of a blade is tempered for cutting wood – an amount towards the handle is left softer and more resilient. Whether a carving gouge has worn beyond the tempered steel, or not, can only really be assessed by using it.

Some tools, such as parallel-sided gouges, can take a lot of sharpening, and thus shortening, in their stride. With other carving tools – fishtail and short bent carving tools for example – the effect of sharpening can be seen more quickly (*see* Fig 2.173(b)). The effective life of such tools is less as it takes a far shorter time to reduce the blade beyond its useful shape or workable hardness. When a carving tool is no longer useful for carving, it will be reborn as something for opening paint tins or making holes.

Old tools can therefore present two problems:

■ They may no longer have any useful temper or

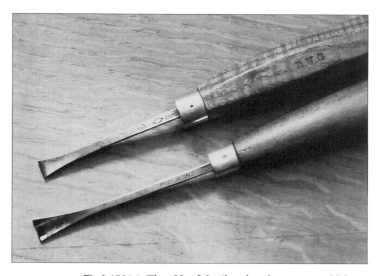

Fig 2.173(a) The older fishtail tool at the top started life about the size of the lower one.

Fig 2.173(b) The two front bent gouges on the left have worn back considerably compared with the newer tool on the right.

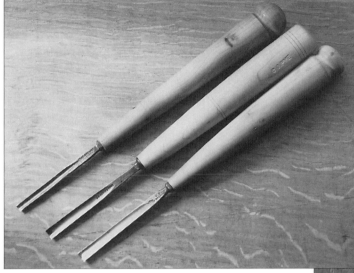

Fig 2.174 Short, old tools can be brought back into circulation with handles of extra length.

Fig 2.175 A badly rusted surface, but not pitted enough to affect the cutting edge which lies more towards the centre of the steel.

hardness, making it impossible for them to hold an edge.
■ The shape may be so shortened that it is no longer of any use.

The answer to both these problems is heat treatment: either re-tempering or re-shaping (the means is described in Chapter 5). Assuming the steel is good quality, and you are willing to take the time and trouble, there is no reason why such tools cannot be usefully reborn within the realms of carving.

Rust

The effect of storage in a damp place – unfortunately the lot of many old tools – is corrosion of the metal parts. The iron, taken originally out of the earth as iron ore, is naturally returning to its stable compound, ferrous oxide. Corrosion appears as smaller or larger areas of pitting or flaking in the surface. In second-hand shops tools are often given a wipe of oil to inhibit the corrosion so the rust will not necessarily look reddish brown but will appear dirty black.

The extent and, more importantly, the *depth* of pitting has to be assessed (*see* Figs 2.175, 2.176). Because carving tools have bevels – both on the inside and the outside – the actual cutting part of the steel is *within* the blade. Take, for example, a firmer chisel with equal bevels on both sides where the cutting edge is set in the very middle of the blade. Only very severe corrosion would reach this far in. Although a blade may look corroded, the point is that if, after sharpening, the *actual cutting edge* is free from corroded pits, there will be no marks or scratches in the wood following its cut. Effectively the tool is as good as new.

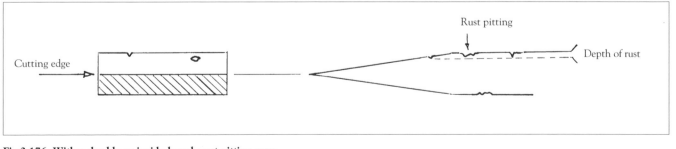

Fig 2.176 With a double or inside bevel, rust pitting may not be deep enough to affect the actual cutting edge.

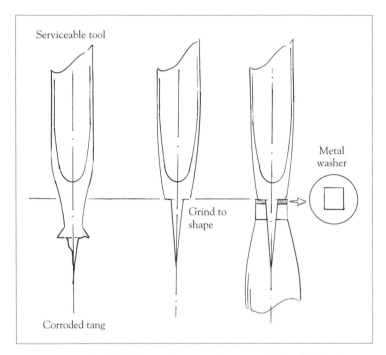

Fig 2.177 A new tang may be ground into a blade where the original tang is corroded. A washer with a square hole will act as a shoulder.

With gouges, the amount of bevel set on the inner surface varies depending on the tool and how it is used. It does no harm to go beyond any pitting on the inside by forming a longer than normal inner bevel – so again pitting of a gouge blade may be easily overcome (*see* Chapter 3, page 110).

If the pitting is so deep that it appears in the

Fig 2.178 A gouge which had lost its tang through rust back in use.

cutting edge when the blade is sharpened, the effect is to leave a scratch in the wood. This is not acceptable for work left straight from the tool and not sanded. A tool may be worth grinding back, beyond particularly bad pitting. The metal itself can be cleaned up with small grinding wheels (such as those fitted to power drills), slip and bench stones, and grades of emery paper. Certainly the tool can be soaked in oil or an anti-rusting agent to prevent further damage.

Rusted tangs

Corrosion affects the tangs of old tools as well as the blades. If the blade of a carving tool with a handle is affected by damp in this way, assume at least a similar effect on the tang. The handle may protect the tang from moisture, but equally the wood can hold moisture in, and against, the metal. Badly rusted tangs may appear as looseness of the handle – which may give a surreptitious opportunity to inspect the tang. The tang can be so badly corroded as to be thinned almost to nothing – stopping short at the shoulder and making the tool weak and liable to bend or break.

What is most important is the blade, as this is what does the cutting and finishes the surface. The tang is only a means to holding the blade, with the help of the handle.

If the blade is usable, form a new tang by grinding one into the metal in its normal position but of necessity more towards the cutting edge (*see* Fig 2.177). Substitute for the shoulder (bolster) proper by grinding two shoulders into the metal, and sitting these onto a washer. Make the diameter of the washer that of the ferrule, and file its hole square to take the new tang. Take care to grind the new tang in line with the axis of the tool and big enough; at the same time make the new shoulders square and in line. While grinding, dip the blade in water or wrap it in a wet rag to keep it cool. It does not matter if the tang itself heats up as this needs to be softer anyway.

This way of reinstating the tang works well. Because the blade is effectively shortened, the loss of overall tool length can be made up by fitting a longer handle.

Broken blades

This is usually to be seen where some sad, old carving tool has already been used to open paint tins or as a screwdriver. Judicious grinding can sometimes salvage these blades, but be careful not to overheat the steel and draw the temper. Remember that the steel is

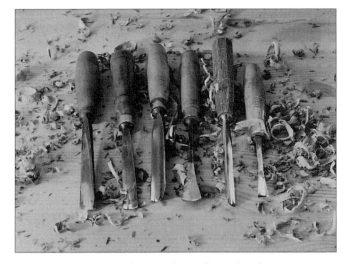

Fig 2.179 Lining up tools in use keeps their edges from knocking against each other.

Fig 2.180 Careless placing of tools on the bench will cost time in damaged edges.

thicker nearer the shank of the tool, and a longer bevel is needed to get the cutting angle that is wanted. Re-tempering the blade may also be necessary (*see* Chapter 5, page 235).

Broken tangs may be approached as if they were badly rusted (*see* previous page).

CARE OF WOODCARVING TOOLS

Carving tools need looking after:

Fig 2.181 Delicate edge versus the cast iron foot of a clamp – an unequal contest. Clamps are commonly used by carvers. Be aware that they are an easy source of damage to cutting edges which have taken time and effort to achieve.

- When you get them
- As they are being used
- During the times they are idle.

This is most simply achieved by cultivating good habits. Before dealing with specific ways of storing and looking after carving tools, a few more general thoughts might be useful.

◆ **Deal with mechanical faults and problems with your carving tools straight away.**

Rather than let a lot of small concerns build up, deal with the problem as and when it is noticed if at all possible. The object is to get your tools feeling so comfortable and working so well that you need hardly give them a thought. This includes sharpening carving tools as they are obtained.

◆ **Maintain a good level of sharpness.**

The emphasis here is on *maintenance*. Aim for the best level of sharpness you can achieve, then maintain or

improve this level – rather that oscillating between good and bad conditions.

◆ **Put the tools away in the state in which you would like to get them out.**

It is frustrating to get out a carving tool only to find it needs sharpening – or dealing with in some way – before it can be used. Far better to have tools sharp, working well and ready for immediate use. So have a rule: tools are not to be put away unless they are as sharp as you would like them to be when you next pick them up – it will save more effort than it creates.

◆ **Protect the carving tools properly at all times.**

Essentially this means respect: respect for the carving tools and what they can do. Protection applies to mechanical damage, especially to the cutting edges, and to the effects of damp. Carving tools which are used continuously do not rust. So the longer the tools are unused, the more precaution they need from damp. This matters most to carvers working in garages and sheds at the bottom of the garden. If possible, bring the tools into the house between carving sessions.

◆ Never lend out tools.

Make this a rule – even to friends. Woodcarvers have a degree of specialized knowledge and personal concern about their tools that is rarely shared sympathetically by others. It is not unknown for the 'friend' to be looking for a screwdriver while ostensibly asking for a chisel. The exception may be another carver whom you can trust to return the tools in the condition in which you lent them.

Storage possibilities

GENERAL POINTS

◆ Put carving tools away, and out of the way.

Large numbers of tools on the bench at any one time are in danger of being damaged if their edges knock against one another as you are working. By all means leave out the tools you are immediately using, but make a habit of clearing away redundant tools – and make sure they are put away sharpened.

◆ Periodically wipe the tools with an oily rag.

If tools are not being used for some time – or perhaps towards winter if the workshop is not heated, or is a little damp – this will 'keep them sweet'. Wipe the blades clean with a fresh cotton rag before handling them again.

◆ Store them safely when not in use.

There are several methods of storing woodcarving tools – all attempt to store them out of harm's way, but ready when they are needed. The methods described below all have advantages and disadvantages. You may find a mixture the best way of storing your particular range of carving tools.

TOOL ROLLS

This is an old and well-tried method of storing and transporting carving tools. The handles of the tools are held in opposite rows of pockets but are staggered so that the blades of one side lie between the handles of the tools on the opposite side (see Fig 2.182). The handles support the blades and edges and, when rolled up, the tools nestle together preventing them knocking against each other. The material itself can help protect the tools from damp.

Some measurements for an average roll are given in Fig 2.184, but consideration could be given to having larger or smaller rolls with dimensions appropriate to your tool sizes. You might try lining up a few sample tools and

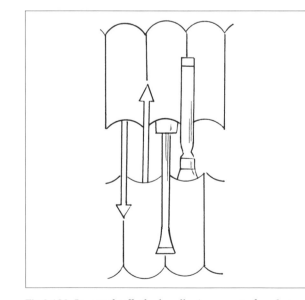

Fig 2.182 In a tool roll, the handles in one set of pockets support and protect the blades of the tools on the opposite side.

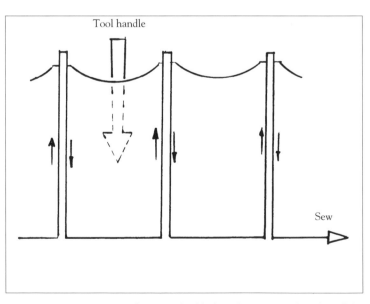

Fig 2.183 For more strength, sew a double line that crosses the edge of the pockets.

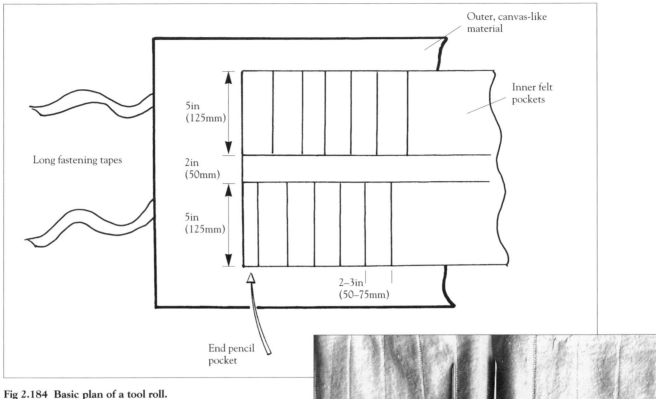

Fig 2.184 Basic plan of a tool roll.

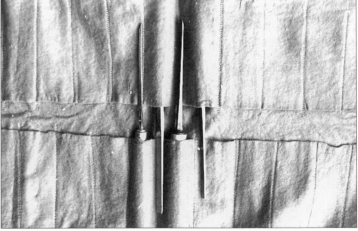

Fig 2.185 Cosy, safe and portable – the simple tool roll. This one will take a particular size range, but you could organize the roll according to sweep or shape.

gauge the pocket sizes with a flexible tape measure.

Tool rolls are easily made with a sewing machine, Use baize for the inner pockets and an outer piece of tough material such as canvas. This should fold over the ends of the blades for additional protection, as well as strengthening the outside of the tool roll. Sewn-on tapes are used to tie the rolls up between use.

A good, manageable size might take between 24 and 30 tools. With larger numbers of tools, the rolls start becoming a bit cumbersome. Several smaller rolls are a better option. These tool rolls need replacing every so often as – with the best will in the world – the sharp tools will cut them.

Without good organization, tool rolls are continually being opened and closed to put tools away or get them out. One idea is to have rolls filled according the frequency with which the tools are used. A roll can be left open on the bench, but a lot of space is being used by tools that are not in use. It is better to leave the tool roll open somewhere away from the bench, but close by.

The greatest advantage in storing woodcarving tools inside fabric rolls is enjoyed by those who do not have a permanent workplace The tool roll can then be stored somewhere convenient, perhaps in a wooden box such as a carpenter's toolbox, with other equipment.

A type of tool roll which contains a row of elastic loops along the centre can be bought commercially, but is not recommended. Passing the sharp edges through the loops without cutting them, or your fingers, can be quite a palaver. Also the blades themselves are looser than in the pocketed tool roll, with a resulting increased risk of the delicate edges

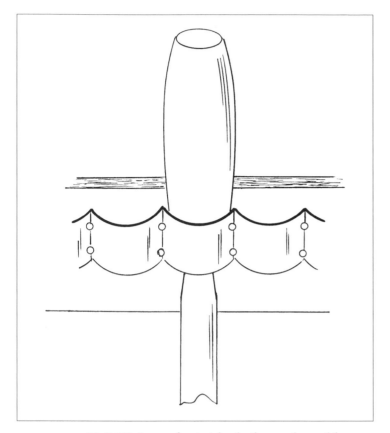

Fig 2.186 Loops of material or leather can be used for storing tools.

being damaged. This sort of roll may have its place for other bits and pieces, however.

RACKS

This method of holding carving tools can be very convenient. The carving tools are within easy reach, and can be easily returned after use. The bench can be less cluttered and the tools at your disposal can be easily seen.

Two types of rack are frequently used.

Loops of material

Leather strips or old car seat-belts are tacked at intervals along a board at the back of the bench. Blades are inserted edge down, and the tool is supported by its handle (*see* Fig 2.186).

There are some problems. For this type of rack to work, the tool handle must be wider than the blade – or the tool will fall through the loop. This limits the size of tools to about 1in (25mm) or narrower, depending on the size of the handles.

The blades also need to be heavier than the handles, and as some blades are much smaller and lighter relative to the handle, their handles tend to fall over and across others. The edges beneath can touch or knock one another, with possible damage. You should consider protecting the edges of some tools with vulnerable corners – such as fishtail and skew chisels – by means of a cork pushed onto the end.

Wooden shelf

An alternative method to loops is a rack, made by boring and cutting various sized holes and notches into a shelf of wood (*see* Fig 2.187). The holes take tools where the blade is smaller than the handle; the notches where the opposite is the case – normally gripping the blade by the shank.

This is a firmer, safer arrangement than the loop method of holding tools but not so easy to adjust. To begin with, guesses have to be made as to what tools you may eventually have – and the holes, notches and necessary clearance between blades, estimated.

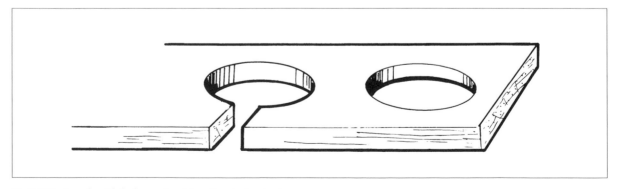

Fig 2.187 A rack with holes and notches for storing tools.

Fig 2.188 Reversing every other tool in a full drawer will safely fit more in.

Drawers

Lay out the carving tools in the drawer with the blades in one direction. Use different drawers, or parts of drawers, for different sweeps or shapes of tools. This can work very well as a storage method, especially if the drawers are part of the carving bench or close at hand. 'Drawers' can be shallow boxes made with simple butt joints and plywood bases; they do not need to be elaborate.

Metal multi-drawer cabinets which are sold for office filing are exactly the right size for storing woodcarving tools. These units are available with 5, 6, 9, 10, or 15 drawers and can be bought second hand. The drawers can be easily labelled and – being metal – they will last indefinitely. Such drawers will need lining to protect the edges of the tools. Self-adhesive, cork floor tiles are useful for this, but use the unvarnished tiles as these protect the contents of the drawer from the damp better.

If all the tools are laid out neatly pointing in one direction, there is little danger of the tools clashing against each other when the drawer is slid open or closed. The smallest tools, especially those with round handles, may roll a little but a few wooden dividing strips, acting as racks, will prevent this.

LONG-TERM STORAGE

There may be an occasion when carving tools have to be stored for a length of time – perhaps several months. Above all protect them from damp: wipe the blades with the same sort of oil used for sharpening, or better still wrap them in oily rags. Protect them from damage either by rolling them up in rags or in their own tool rolls. Finally, keep them in a polythene bag in a dry place.

Bench discipline

This chapter deals with carefully selecting your carving tools; the following chapter discusses working your tools up to their most efficient and sharp condition. Caring for your tools before and after use has been dealt with above. However, the discipline of looking after them also involves the time when they are actually used. Again, some basic practices will help.

During carving

◼ Avoid levering or prising wood chips away with the chisel or gouge as this can break an edge – cut the wood cleanly.

◼ Avoid scraping the edge across the cut wood as the tool leaves it – this action will dull the edge.

◼ When a tool such as a skew has entered the wood, do not rock it from side to side. There is a real danger of breaking the corner and leaving it buried in the wood.

◼ Use a mallet only when the tool can take it, and be particularly careful with shoulderless tools.

When the tools are on the bench

The danger is not so much one of rust or mechanical damage to the tool, as the carefully sharpened edges chipping and knocking up against each other or metal objects. So to help guard against this:

◆ **Line up the tools parallel with the blades in the same direction.**

The tools should be lined up at the back of the bench, or out of the immediate working area. They will look a little like a series of piano keys, which is not a bad way to regard them. It is better if the edges point forwards as the tools can be recognized more easily from this direction. This is a really excellent habit to get into right from the start of a carving career. The discipline of always putting down your tools in a row not only protects them from each other, but by making the

tools easier to find, speeds up the carving process and adds enormously to the overall awareness and flow of what you are doing.

◆ **Try not to have too many tools on the bench.**

If a lot of woodcarving tools are needed on a particular job, organize them so that the tools that are least frequently used are out of the way and lined up towards the back of the bench. Bring forward the ones needed for the immediate tasks.

◆ **Periodically clear the bench.**

Repeating a point made above: make a habit of tidying up the work area of surplus tools and putting them away after first making sure they are sharp. Also clear the bench of wood chips and other bits and pieces occasionally – this can coincide well with natural breaks for brewing up.

◆ **Keep tool edges away from anything metal.**

Quite a few metal objects can be on the bench: clamps, holdfast heads, compasses, metal rulers and so on. The sharpened edges of woodcarving tools only have to touch these things, or each other, to damage the edge sufficiently to leave scratch lines.

◆ **Beware of the dangers to carving tools when moving around and adjusting work.**

This is the time when – because the attention is elsewhere – tools can be rolled about against each other, or knocked to the floor.

◆ **Touch up any damage to edges straight away.**

If an edge does get chipped or damaged accidentally, make a point of dealing with it as soon as possible. If you wait until you need the tool again, it will be when you want to carve, not sharpen.

SUMMARY

Looking after your woodcarving tools from the moment you first get them, through their sharpening, while they are being used, to when they are stored, involves a degree of discipline. Discipline can be seen as developing good working habits – efficient methods of going about things that not only save time and energy, but also facilitate carving itself.

By understanding and caring for woodcarving tools, in themselves and for what they can do, there is less to get in the way of carving itself. Tools are not ends in themselves – when it comes to actually carving, the heart and mind always play the principal part. Discipline and care can nevertheless be seen as making a very important contribution to the same end.

Fig 2.189 A cork will protect delicate corners, either on the bench or when the tool is stored.

SHARPENING WOODCARVING TOOLS

Aims

To emphasize the importance and benefit of having sharp woodcarving tools

To make clear what 'sharpness' is, and what factors contribute to a sharp cutting edge

To describe the sharpening process in general terms and, in detail, how specific types of woodcarving tools are sharpened

To describe the equipment needed to sharpen woodcarving tools, and using and caring for it

To advise on how to maintain sharpness with the least effort

To look at the problems and benefits of electrical sharpening methods

To promote, through being at ease with the sharpening process, more confidence with woodcarving itself

Each of the aims will be considered in a little more detail in turn.

Emphasizing the importance and benefit of having sharp woodcarving tools

Beyond carving itself, sharpening and looking after woodcarving tools is the main task undertaken by carvers. A master woodcarver once told me that when costing a piece of work, he would allow up to one-third of the allotted time for sharpening and maintaining his tools. This is a stunning bit of information for newcomers to take in, as it was to me at the time. After all, the carving beckons – who wants to spend hours sharpening?

The view of many newcomers – still maintained by others who have been carving a while – is that sharpening is a chore which has to be tolerated in order to get on with the carving itself. The marketing of pre-sharpened tools caters to these feelings – but unfortunately the 'spontaneously self-sharpening'

woodcarving tool has yet to be invented, and the task of sharpening tools will remain, as it always has, something the carver must undertake.

Even though there is hardly a book on carving that does not start with *some* information on the subject of sharpening, and information is given out by tool manufacturers themselves, students at carving classes still turn up with badly sharpened tools or even tools so useless that no sharpening could reclaim them. The reason is twofold: firstly the student does not feel, or comprehend why, sharpness is important; and secondly, the information on sharpening is still inadequate, insufficient or unclear.

What is needed is a change of attitude to some extent. Carving tools should not be seen as separate from the woodcarving itself. Sharpening is not the bane and penance of the carver but part of the process – a process that involves yourself, working with your design, the wood, your carving tools and the high quality of their cutting edges. All these factors support each other as the whole process moves towards a satisfying end.

Sharpening woodcarving tools is not a particularly difficult skill to learn and exercise and, in itself, *can* be enjoyable. Its real importance only becomes obvious with experience, so a beginner has to be convinced of

Fig 3.1 Brightly polished, pre-sharpened tools.

the advantages to be had from really sharp carving tools, in order to put in the effort needed to learn the skills of sharpening. This chapter will try to help with learning such skills and getting a feel for their importance.

Making clear what 'sharpness' is, and what factors contribute to a sharp cutting edge

---

As with carving itself, knowing what you are looking for is halfway to finding it. What, then, is this magical sharpness: is it always the same, for all carving tools, at all times, for all woods?

This chapter has a theme which follows the old axiom: 'To give someone a fish is to feed them for a day. To teach someone to fish is to feed them for the rest of their life.' Those who have been given a set of unprepared carving tools as a present must face the problem of sharpening them first. Without proper instruction, this can lead to a frustrating experience – ending, not uncommonly, in the whole notion of carving being abandoned before it has even started.

With a gift of pre-sharpened carving tools, at least one gets to carve wood for the day. But without the

necessary sharpening skills the tools dull, begin to cut less well, and dissatisfaction and frustration arise.

Describing the sharpening process in general terms and, in detail, how specific types of woodcarving tools are sharpened

---

There is method, basic to the sharpening of all woodcarving tools, that can be taught and learned. The key approach given in this chapter will be adapted for different shapes, sweeps and sizes of blade to achieve what you want in a particular case, and in the quickest and most straightforward way.

Some of the techniques of sharpening may seem awkward at first – and certainly there are some tools that need more care than others – but they are well within the capabilities of anyone dextrous enough to carve.

Describing the equipment needed to sharpen woodcarving tools, and how to use and take care of it

---

If sharpness and carving tools are inseparable, acquiring carving tools means acquiring the means to

Fig 3.2 Sharp tools are a real pleasure to use.

Fig 3.3 A habit of regular stropping will maintain the keenness of the cutting edge.

Fig 3.4 Signs of an electrical sharpening system: slightly hollow bevel and coarse, lengthwise scratch marks on the bevel, all polished over.

sharpen them. Once you invest money in carving tools, you need to invest a little more on the sharpening equipment, and learn to use it. There are various options in sharpening, including electrical help. But at the basic level, you do not need much in the way of kit so the cost can be less than that of a few carving tools. And, in the same way that good quality carving tools last a lifetime, so will good quality sharpening stones.

The following chapter explains what equipment you need, why you need it and how to use it; as well as how to look after the various bits and pieces so that they last a long time.

Advising on how to maintain sharpness with the least effort

Sharpening and maintaining sharpness of tools is essential to the woodcarver. It needs to be accepted and not seen as a chore or an interruption to the work. The meditative quality of sharpening can be enjoyed; as can the self-respect and joy in achieving and using a beautifully sharpened blade. There is also the opportunity to take stock of how the carving is progressing.

While fostering this attitude, ways can be found to minimize the effort of sharpening and maintaining the cutting edges; creating routines, rather than big events that stand out for their tediousness. It is also likely that if you have a resistance to the discipline of sharpening, then the chances are you will have problems with the discipline of carving itself.

Looking at the problems and benefits of electrical sharpening methods

If there were a means of sharpening carving tools electrically so as to produce exactly the correct qualities of shape and sharpness, safely and easily, then certainly this would become an option. However, the electrical devices available today have benefits *and* drawbacks. They are helpful in some areas but can cause problems in others. It is not simple, or even sometimes possible, to achieve the shape and quality you aim for using electrical methods. The place and use of electrical sharpening or honing machines will be gone into in more detail later (*see* page 189).

Promoting, through being at ease with the sharpening process, more confidence with woodcarving itself

---

Both this chapter and Chapter 2 take the attitude that the carving tools should not get in the way of the carver's intention. Tools can get in the way both physically, by being, for example, poorly shaped, and mentally, as when frustration arises from not being able adequately to sharpen a particular tool or achieve the effect or surface finish that is wanted.

The answer to these sorts of problems lies largely in the idea of discipline: self-imposed habit patterns and approaches to tools, sharpening and carving itself. Such disciplines ease the way towards what the carver wants to achieve, and command over woodcarving tools and their sharpness removes one of the major barriers between the carver and the carving.

THE NEED FOR SHARPNESS

When woodcarving tools are compared with the tools used in woodturning, one difference quickly becomes obvious: turning tools can be used straight from the grinding wheel. This is far from the case with carving tools.

There is nothing to stop you attempting to carve straight from the grinding wheel, if that gives you the effect you are after. But carving tools normally undergo a far more involved process of sharpening before they are ready for use on the wood and the would-be carver can get down to work. Without doubt, this need to sharpen carving tools has caused many a potential carver to become a woodturner.

The reason why turning tools can be used in such a comparatively rough state is because of the high surface speed of the wood revolving beneath the cutting edge, which requires short, tough bevels (see

Fig 3.7), and the peculiar application of the cutting edge to the wood. Woodturners regularly supplement cutting with sandpaper, finishing turned shapes to exploit the natural beauty of the wood.

In carving, especially carving realistic forms, the cuts of the tools can be left as a surface finish in their own right, but this means producing cuts worth leaving (see Fig 3.8). Carving involves many more (and more complicated and delicate) shapes of tools compared to those used in turning and requires a much more involved approach to sharpening than could be achieved from a grinding wheel.

Until quite recently, there were no 'ready-sharpened' woodcarving tools. Tools came with a bevel roughly ground, or *set*, by the factory. It was accepted without question that a carver would sharpen them exactly as he or she wanted. Although pre-sharpening has its advantages, carvers need to sharpen different tools in different ways and for different purposes. This is what the factory would have expected when they sent out tools 'set but not sharpened'.

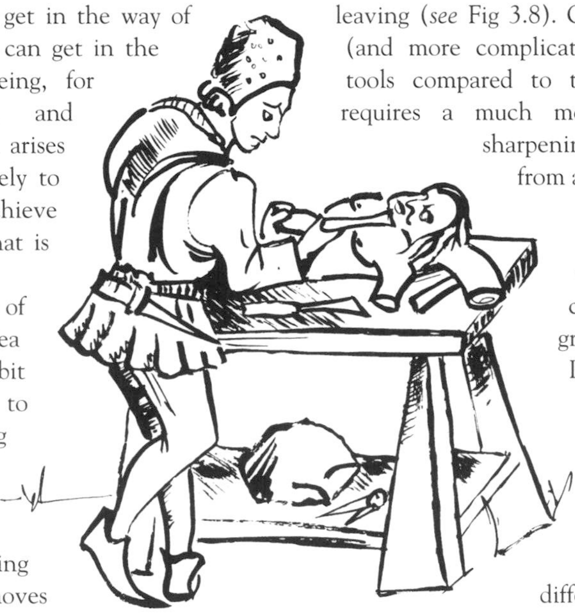

Fig 3.5 (Above) Based on a 1470 German woodcut.

Fig 3.6 The nose of a woodturner's spindle gouge.

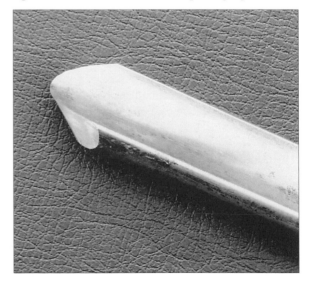

In this chapter, the emphasis is on the set carving tool which requires sharpening, and where even the bevel might need re-setting. Unless stated otherwise, these are the sort of tools that are being referred to. This seems to be the most useful approach as pre-sharpened tools can easily be included when it becomes necessary or appropriate to re-sharpen them. There is a section dealing especially with the advantages, disadvantages and peculiarities of pre-sharpened tools later in this chapter (*see* page 188).

The skill of sharpening the cutting edge 'just so' – and keeping it sharp – is a skill which, for the woodcarver, comes before everything else. Without it, all other skills of design, artistry and execution of a work will suffer. And, as a skill, it must be learnt. Its value cannot be overestimated.

To put in the effort to learn and practise this skill, motivation is needed – the effort must be seen to be worthwhile in terms of results. So what exactly are the advantages that tool sharpness gives to the carver?

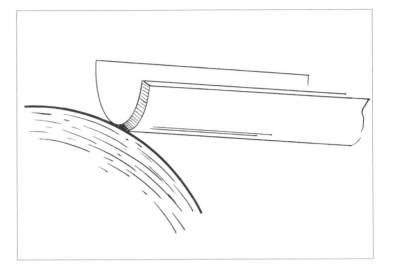

Fig 3.7 The very short bevel of this roughing gouge makes it suitable for turners but entirely inappropriate for carving.

Fig 3.8 Vigorous cutting in this sketch model of a head by Gino Masero gives the face a completely different character from how it would be if it were sanded smooth.

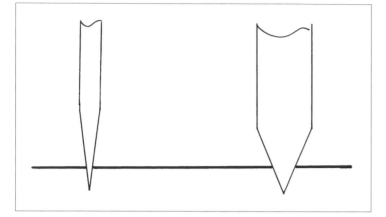

Fig 3.9 It is an obvious principle that the thickness of a wedge relates to the amount of effort required to push it into the same material.

Fig 3.10 Sharpening refines the crystal lattice of a cutting edge to a level which cannot be seen by the naked eye.

Why is such a high degree of sharpness needed? The following are some answers, but not in order of importance.

Effort

The cutting edge of a woodcarving blade is nothing more than a wedge of steel, a fine wedge, cutting and prising the wood fibres apart. The angle of the wedge is the angle at which the bevel of the carving tool is set, and this can vary under different conditions. The bevel also needs to be the correct shape – which will be dealt with in more detail in a section on the bevel later in this chapter (*see* page 110).

A common reason for finding that cutting through wood is harder work than it need be, is the incorrect setting of the bevel angle as a preliminary stage to sharpening (*see* Fig 3.9). When this is

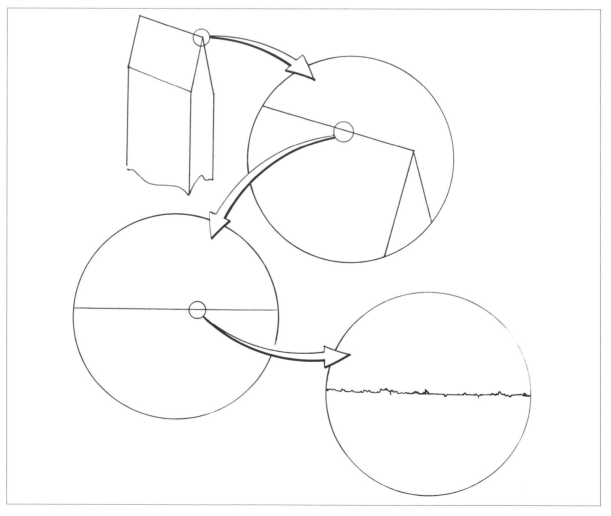

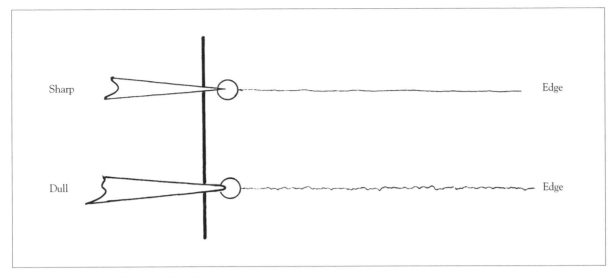

Fig 3.11 As the crystal lattice of the edge wears down, so more effort is needed to push it through the wood fibres.

changed, the amount of effort needed to cut the wood will decrease.

A microscope, applied to the very edge of a carving tool, shows a crystalline structure. The cutting edge is a wall of molecules making up a crystal lattice. When the blade cuts, this wonderful crystal edge is pushed into a similar microscopic world of wood fibres, prising it apart. When a tool is sharpened, the thickness of this crystal edge is refined down to the most slender state possible – the minimum thickness, given the angle of bevel, that will separate the wood molecules and fibres. Eventually this resistance will start to erode the microscopic structure of the steel, and from a thin peak of crystal, a thicker, rounded and broken edge will form (*see* Fig 3.11). Forcing a passage against the resistance of the wood becomes more difficult as the tool becomes blunt.

The amount of effort needed to carve is affected by:

- The angle of the bevel
- The refining of the bevel edge by further sharpening.

When less effort is needed to cut, speed of carving increases, in turn enhancing efficiency. Speed and efficiency also depend on the carver's approach to the work: the method and how the tools are used. Nevertheless, sharpness is indispensably linked to the swiftness and effectiveness with which a work is executed. So, less effort, quicker work, and greater efficiency.

Control

With most woods, and correctly sharpened tools, cutting *across* the grain need not be much different from cutting *with* the grain. It is even possible, with some woods and the right technique, to cut cleanly *against* the grain if necessary – providing your tools are sharp enough.

Because sharpness makes all directions of cut available, sharp carving tools will help the carver achieve and control whatever form he or she is seeking.

As a corollary, blunt tools will be inhibiting. They do this mechanically (because of the difficulty in cutting with them), mentally (because blunt tools continually intrude into the overall intention of the carver) and emotionally (because of the frustration that arises).

Appearance

Along with control over the form, a really sharp carving tool will leave a beautiful, polished facet as it cuts away a wood chip. The bevel follows behind the cutting edge and burnishes the wood. This effect is best seen when the wood is cut with the grain, but also occurs with sliced cross-cutting.

Such clean cutting may be all the surface finish that a carving needs in order to arrive at its finished state. Blunt tools, however, tend to tear wood fibres rather than cut them and leave scratchy lines, although this can also be the result of bad carving technique. This is when rasps, files and sandpaper will

Fig 3.12 A detail of 'The Banquet at Simon's' by Riemenschneider (1490–92). Light toolwork on the peak of the hat suggests fur, and therefore status; plain surfaces balance with strong areas of tool cuts; and a V-tool was used to draw in details in the background.

Fig 3.13 A smooth surface makes available to the carver a different kind of beauty.

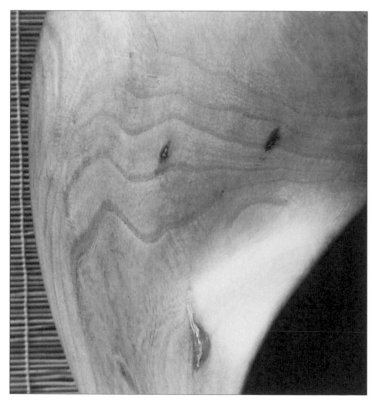

be used as expedients.

Tool cuts in the wood have been called the 'fingerprints of the carver'; they are unique in a way that a sanded surface is not. A sanded carving looks, and feels, very different from one left straight from the chisel. The freshness of cutting, with crisp lines and edges, will all too easily be removed by sanding. The definite changes of plane that makes carving look different from modelling will be smoothed and rounded over. The effect of injudicious sanding can be to make a piece of carved work look as if it has been sucked a while, like a boiled sweet.

Using tools with sharp cutting edges, and accompanied by good technique, at least *gives you the option* of a surface finish left straight from the chisel. Many carvers have never experienced this option because their tools are not really sharp. Sandpaper may be resorted to for the finish, whatever the cost in loss of detail or deviation from the original intention. Once really sharp tools have been used, an entirely new range of options is often seen.

If a sanded finish is wanted from the start, say to show off the natural colour and beauty of the grain, it is still worth working towards the final surface with sharp cutting edges. Sanding is never an enjoyable task and the less time and effort spent on sanding, the better. Odd scratches in otherwise cleanly cut facets of wood can be ignored as these will be taken out with the sanding. Bear in mind that using tools on a sanded surface will blunt them. Choosing a smooth sanded finish is *not* the same as finishing with a sanded surface only because someone is incapable of sharpening their tools properly, or has a poor carving technique.

Safety

This may seem contrary to what is expected, but blunt carving tools are actually more dangerous than sharp ones. Encouraging youngsters in schools to work with blunter tools, in the hope that this will lead to fewer mishaps, is actually a mistake.

Putting aside hazardous techniques and habits of carving, such as putting parts of your body in the way of the blade, a blunt tool needs more effort behind it to force it through its cut. When the blade eventually reaches fresh air again, it is still being propelled by this excessive force. So it tends to leap out of the cut in an uncontrolled manner. It is far better to take easier cuts, with less effort, and in a controlled way, than to be continually jerking a blunt tool out of the wood.

Enjoyment

One of the most tangible pleasures of teaching woodcarving is to see the joy and recognition on the face of someone who uses correctly and truly sharpened tools for the first time. They may have been working away – sometimes for years – with effectively blunt tools even though they have tried their best to sharpen them.

This is the real case for sharpness: working with blunt tools is a real chore and rarely appreciated for the burden it is until sharp tools are used. Sharpening carving tools is less tedious than working with blunt, badly, even wrongly, sharpened tools.

On the other hand, sharpening itself can be a worthwhile use of time. A break from carving to touch up an edge can give you time to stop and think, assess what you are doing and consider the next step. Without wanting to create too romantic a vision, I find that sharpening on a stone can be soothing – a quiet, healing sort of activity that contrasts with the energy often found in the actual cutting.

Finally there is the sheer joy to be felt when a fine edge of steel slices through a good piece of wood. In a silent workshop it makes a noise, a sort of sliding, whispering, as the shaving comes away. The simplicity of the action and the feel of control and command, even when striking the tool with a mallet, is why many people carve. All this is facilitated by really sharp carving tools.

PRINCIPLES OF SHARPENING

Fundamentals

What is sharpness and how do we measure it? Is there a difference between 'sharp', 'sharp enough' and '*really sharp*'? The answer to these questions lies largely in what we wish to achieve, but also in our attitude.

The meaning of the word 'sharp' includes such connotations as keen, fine and clear, as well as biting, piercing and acute. The word refers to wit and temper, as much as to the cutting edge of a carving tool. Woodcarvers certainly need their tools and wit to have these qualities – if not their temper. There is also the carver's adage to be borne in mind: 'Dull tools make dull work.'

The essential characteristics of a sharp carving tool are these.

■ The edge will cut through wood more easily than a blunt one with the same angle of bevel.
■ It will leaving a shiny, polished facet, without scratch marks.
■ The surface left from clean tool work may be seen as finished – giving a particular clean and sparkling quality to the work.
■ The carving tool cuts more or less as nicely *across* the grain as with it; the sharpness makes negotiating curves easier, where one side of the curve will be against the grain.
■ The proper shape of a sharp edge, for example with its corners retained, works as efficiently as possible.
■ Grooves and cuts can be lain down next to each

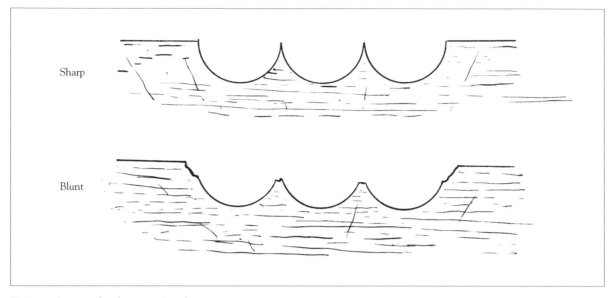

Fig 3.14 One test for sharpness is to lay grooves next to each other.

other without tearing up or crumbling the ridges of wood in between (*see* Fig 3.14).

■ Using a sharp carving tool is less of a physical effort than using a blunt one.

■ Without doubt such tools are more of an aesthetic pleasure to use than dull ones.

As was said above, some wood sculptors, working on large sculpture with the intention of using files and

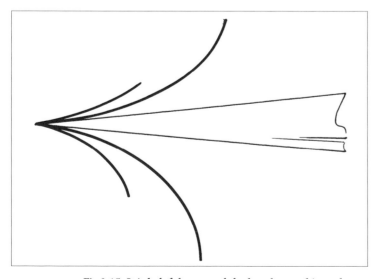

Fig 3.15 It is helpful to regard the bevel as nothing other than a very refined wedge, cleaving the material.

rasps afterwards, can afford scratches on the surface of the wood or torn grain from tools which are a bit dull as these marks will be removed. As a conscious decision this may be justified on the grounds of expediency – a case of 'sharp enough' with less 'down time'. More often than not, however, it is a case of the sculptor not knowing, having not been taught, or not bothering to maintain the cutting edges.

It is the cutting of the tool in the wood and whether it achieves what you want it to that matters. With experience you will become acutely sensitive to the feel of the tool as it is working. You will also see what is happening from the path of the gouge or chisel, and will know how to make equally sensitive adjustments to the edge.

Bevels

FUNCTION

The **bevel** is that shape taken by the thick, supporting metal of the blade as it thins down to the fine cutting edge which actually penetrates the wood. It can be flat, rounded or hollowed along its length, and there may be a bevel on one or both sides of the cutting edge.

The bevel on a woodcarving tool is in effect a wedge which cuts and prises fibres apart against resistance (*see* Fig 3.15). As wood fibres from different species of tree bind together in different densities and strengths, differences in the wedge-like quality of the

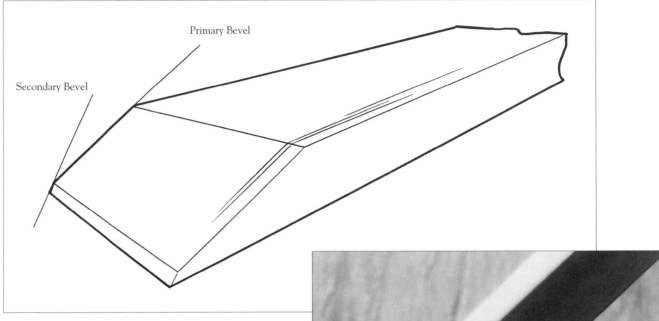

Fig 3.16 Sharpening on a secondary bevel is not the best option for carving tools.

bevel are required to deal with this resistance efficiently.

In the same way that carving proceeds from the main masses and form through to the final details, sharpening a carving tool is a refining of the underlying bevel. The importance of the bevel is often neglected by beginners who tend to sharpen the very edge only (*see* Fig 3.16), producing a secondary bevel that gradually thickens in size. Getting the bevel the correct shape is a major part of sharpening correctly.

'SET' OR GRINDING ANGLE

The **set** of a carving tool is the angle at which the bevel has been ground on a blade – how long or short it appears. Carvers usually talk about longer or shorter bevels, rather than an actual angle, because this is how they appear.

Invariably, a bevel will be set on a carving tool when it leaves the maker, whether it has been sharpened further or not. The grinding may be part of an automated process in some factories, or involve a skilled person using an industrial grinding wheel. But this bevel angle, pre-set by the manufacturer, is *not* necessarily the one that is wanted by the carver (*see* Figs 3.17, 3.18). There are various circumstances in which a different angle – a longer or shorter bevel – may be needed.

Fig 3.17 The bevel offered by the maker of this tool is about 45°. It may never occur to a newcomer to carving that this can, and needs to be, changed.

One problem with pre-sharpened tools is that while the bevel may indeed be set at a useful angle, it may not be *the* most useful working angle for the needs of that particular carver. Someone buying a woodcarving tool for the first time may assume that the shape of the bevel found on the blade is the correct angle for the tool and can not be altered. It *may* be the correct set of bevel, but then again, it may not.

If the angle of bevel you need is different from the one which has been ground onto the tool, then the bevel will need re-setting first. This usually involves re-grinding.

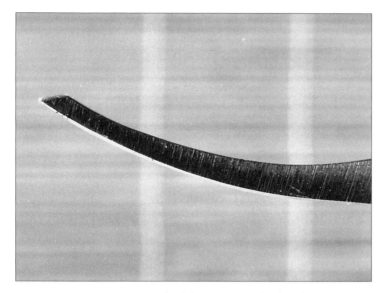

Fig 3.18 A new back bent gouge with a bevel of 45° – again, the carver needs to decide the appropriateness of this angle.

Fig 3.19 The relationship between sharpness and strength.

SHARPNESS VERSUS STRENGTH

There are two factors working against each other in the set of the bevel. As the bevel becomes longer and the wedge effect sharper, the tool, in theory at least, is able to work its way through the fibres of the wood with less effort. But the cost is in loss of strength – there is less metal to buttress the cutting edge (*see* Fig 3.19). As the bevel becomes longer, the cutting edge becomes weaker, until the fibres of the wood may be hard enough to damage the cutting edge before being cut themselves.

BEVEL ANGLE

Correctly assessing the bevel angle (or length) comes as a matter of experience. The overall angle usually varies between 20° and 30°. Remember, however, that blades are of different thicknesses; and this will affect how long the bevel appears.

The question arises as to what bevel angles are needed and under what circumstances? The determining factor is the hardness of the wood fibres.

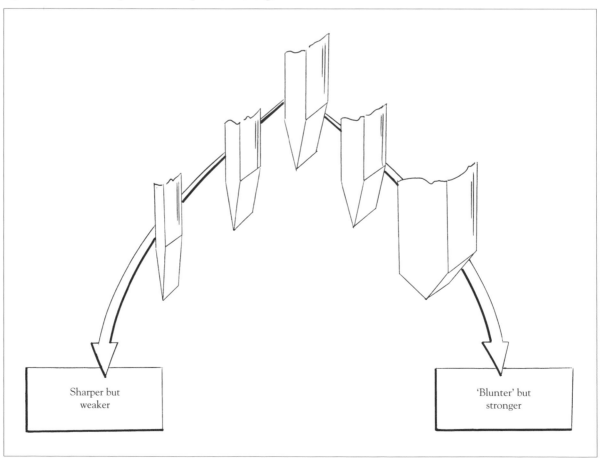

Sharper but weaker

'Blunter' but stronger

Wood varies between soft at one end of a range (e.g. pine) and very hard at the other (e.g. boxwood), with medium degrees of hardness in between (e.g. limewood). The terms 'soft' and 'hard' are functional ones and should not to be confused with the biological terms 'softwood' and 'hardwood' (*see* Chapter 8, page 299).

The most common woods used for carving fall into a middle range of hardness and the bevel on manufactured tools, usually set around 25°, is appropriate for these. The woods in this middle range of hardness include lime, walnut, oak, and mahogany, but even these woods vary in density and hardness depending on the circumstances in which they were grown, whether there are any hard knots and so on. A bevel set at 20–25° will be suitable for most situations and medium hardness material. It looks about twice as long as the thickness of the blade when there is a bevel on one side only.

Soft wood include pines: northern pine, yellow pine, etc. These timbers were extensively used in the past, especially during the Regency period, for carvings on fire surrounds and panels. To reproduce these pieces

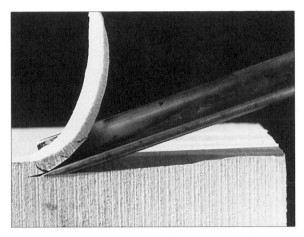

Fig 3.20 The wedge-like action of the bevel is evident here.

Fig 3.21 What some different bevel angles look like.

Fig 3.22 Different bevel angles are needed to deal with different resistances of wood fibres.

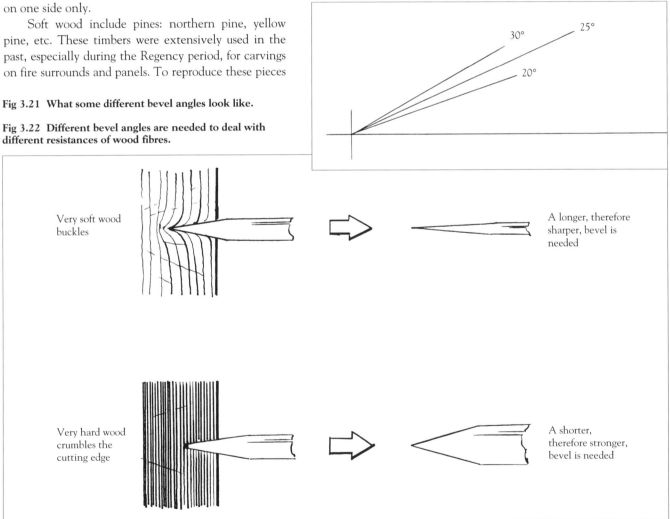

Very soft wood buckles

A longer, therefore sharper, bevel is needed

Very hard wood crumbles the cutting edge

A shorter, therefore stronger, bevel is needed

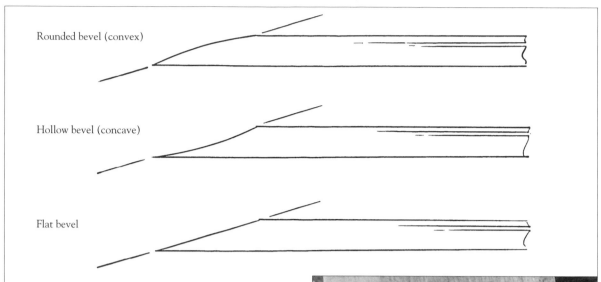

Rounded bevel (convex)

Hollow bevel (concave)

Flat bevel

Fig 3.23 Three types of bevel profile.

and effects today, top quality pine may still be used.

It is often thought that the softer a wood is, the more easily it can be cut. But what actually happens is that the softer fibres buckle before the wedge of the cutting metal (*see* Fig 3.22). The fibres may not resist – stay still long enough – to be cut cleanly and they tend to tear. So what is needed for carving these soft, pine types of wood is a *longer* bevel, a sharper edge, than might be expected. The keenness divides the fibres *before* they crumble, giving proper clean cuts.

However, with a longer bevel, the strength of the cutting edge is reduced. If a carving tool with a longer bevel suitable for pine is used on a harder wood such as oak, the cutting edge will disintegrate and produce a scratched and torn surface. It was not unusual in the past for a carver to have more than one set of carving tools. A special set of tools with extra long bevels was kept solely for work on these very soft woods.

Some exotic woods available today, such as lignum vitae, are extremely hard. Conversely, the bevels for these woods need to be shorter for cutting edges to survive.

If a carving tool is not cutting easily or satisfactorily – even though the edge appears to be as sharp as possible – it may be that the bevel length needs adjusting to be a little longer or shorter.

What is being sought at the end of the day is the longest, and therefore sharpest, bevel compatible with strength.

Fig 3.24 A hollow ground bevel with a secondary bevel from heel to edge.

FLATNESS

The bevel can have three different contours from the heel to the edge (*see* Fig 3.23):

■ Hollow (concave)
■ Rounded (convex)
■ Flat.

In the previous discussion about the bevel angle, the assumption was made that the bevel was simply *flat* between heel and edge – without any secondary bevels. This is the correct shape, and there are several reasons why this is the best option.

Hollow bevels

A hollowed contour (*see* Fig 3.24) comes from applying the bevel to a circular grinding wheel which

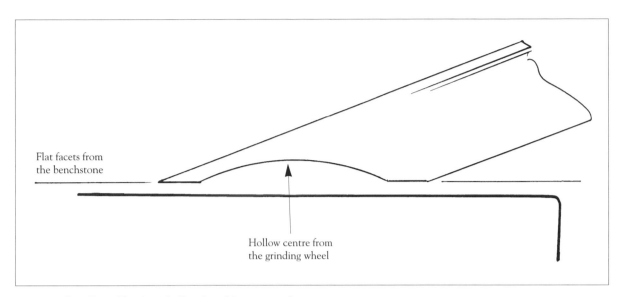

Flat facets from the benchstone

Hollow centre from the grinding wheel

Fig 3.25 The effect of honing a hollow bevel (exaggerated).

grinds its own shape into the metal. From the grinding wheel the tool may be sharpened on flat oilstones, but not enough to remove the hollowness completely. A hollow in the bevel continues to exist between the two flat surfaces produced on the oilstones (*see* Fig 3.25).

It might be thought that a slightly hollow-ground bevel is a better option than a truly flat one, as the blade is more free to follow the cutting edge. With this benefit, however, come two disadvantages. The first is the inherent weakness in a hollow bevel. As the hollowness encroaches on the cutting edge, the angle of the bevel becomes more acute. The edge becomes sharper and sharper, but – being less supported – weaker and weaker.

Fig 3.26 A carving tool bought with the bevel set but not sharpened is usually flat because of the large diameter of industrial grinding wheels. They may also be quite even and a good size, like this one.

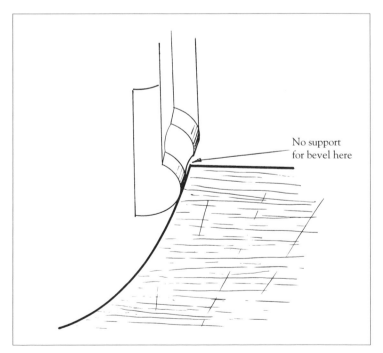

No support for bevel here

Fig 3.27 It is difficult for a hollow-ground bevel to self-jig.

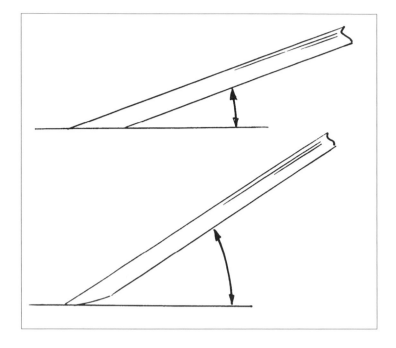

Fig 3.28 Although the edge may look sharp, the cutting edge of a rounded bevel is a thicker point of contact with the wood than a flat one.

Fig 3.29 The greater cutting angle produced by a rounded bevel.

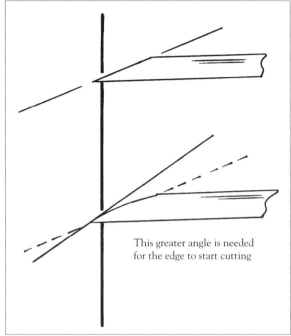

This greater angle is needed for the edge to start cutting

Secondly, a hollowed bevel rides up on the edge of a cut, say when setting in, and working feels awkward and inaccurate compared with a truly flat bevel. This relates to a 'self-jigging' action that will be discussed later (*see* page 118).

Leaving a hollow bevel is not necessarily a quicker way of sharpening a carving tool either. With correct grinding, it takes the same time to flatten across the whole bevel – so making the edge stronger and lining up more accurate – than sharpening from heel to edge.

Rounded bevels

Some hollowness, or concavity, towards the centre of the bevel is preferable to a rounded or convex bevel. A rounded bevel is produced by altering the angle at which the blade is presented to the grinding wheel or oilstones – lifting and lowering the handle.

At the cutting edge, the rounded bevel has the opposite, obtuse, profile to that of a hollow-ground tool, with two effects. In the first place, a thicker wedge of steel has to be pushed into the wood, involving more effort (*see* Fig 3.28). Secondly, the carving tool will start to cut the surface of the wood *with its handle positioned higher than would the same tool with a flat bevel*. In other words, a rounded bevel gives a greater cutting angle (*see* Fig 3.29). The lower this angle, the more control a carver has when cutting –

the carver's hands rest on the wood and work more surely. The higher the cutting angle, the more awkward and uncontrolled the cutting becomes.

Rounding the bevels of woodcarving tools is a frequent and major cause of their handling, and cutting, badly with unnecessary effort. The problem is more common than one where the bevel is flat but with an incorrect angle. A seemingly small change from round to flat bevels makes an enormous difference to the quality and control of cutting.

The exception to the rule comes in the long and short bent chisels and gouges. A slight rounding of the bevel is acceptable as an extension of the bent or 'rounded' shape of these tools – helping to jig the edge through their hollow cut.

Flat bevels

Flat bevels cut most efficiently and contribute the greatest amount of strength to the edge for its sharpness, compared with hollowed or rounded bevels. The cutting angle can be accurate and low; and the bevel will self-jig along the face the edge is cutting.

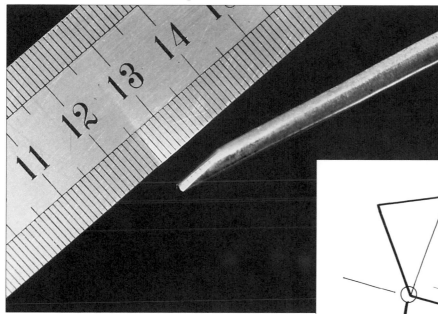

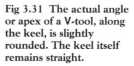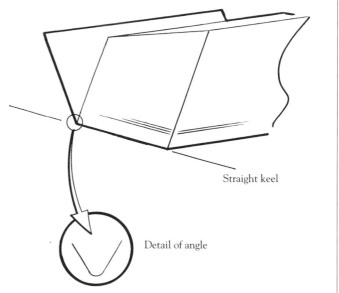

Fig 3.31 **The actual angle or apex of a V-tool, along the keel, is slightly rounded. The keel itself remains straight.**

Straight keel

Detail of angle

Fig 3.30 **A flat bevel; note the slightly rounded heel.**

It is no more trouble to sharpen a flat bevel than any of the other shapes so far discussed. The practicalities of producing accurate, flat bevels is dealt with later in this chapter.

One final point about **V**-tools: the keel, the line of metal at the angle of the two sides, is the main part of the bevel that is rubbing the wood during its cut. As such it should be like the bevels of other straight tools – flat from the cutting point to the heel. However, the keel is slightly softened by rounding it from side to side and is not kept as a knife-like angle (*see* Fig 3.31). This helps the blade slide along its groove and cut curving lines more easily.

Secondary bevels

Some carvers sharpen only the very edge of their carving tools, producing a small secondary bevel. This in effect thickens the wedge of metal as the angle of the secondary bevel must be greater than the primary one (*see* Fig 3.32). The secondary bevel gets longer with each sharpening, increasing the cutting angle of the tool. Eventually the tool will need re-grinding.

Sharpening a secondary bevel is more often than not an ill-directed habit. It takes the same amount of time and effort to present the bevel flat to the oilstone and produce a continuous, flat bevel from heel to edge at the outset, as it does to produce a secondary bevel. A blade with a flat bevel will only need re-grinding if, say,

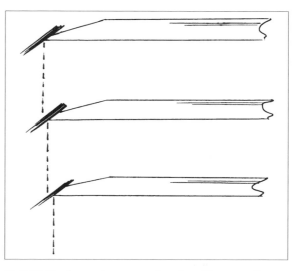

Fig 3.32 **Re-sharpening a secondary bevel increases the bevel angle at the actual cutting edge and therefore the effort needed to cut wood; the tool will need re-grinding at some point.**

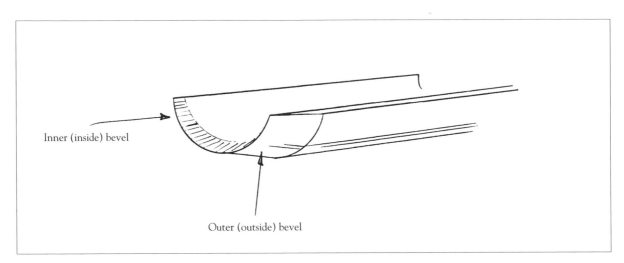

Fig 3.33 Inner and outer bevels on a carving gouge.

a corner is broken, not because the bevel angle has changed. So secondary bevels cannot be recommended.

INNER AND OUTER BEVELS

If you compare a carpenter's chisel with the flat firmer chisel used by a woodcarver, one difference is immediately apparent: the carpentry chisel has a bevel on one side only, the firmer chisel has a bevel on *both* sides. An echo occurs in carving gouges, where another bevel is also found on the inside (*see* Fig 3.33).

A lot of books on woodcarving neglect the inner bevel altogether. The practice in the woodcarving trade has always been to sharpen an inside bevel onto straight gouges for the several advantages it gives. It may be helpful to summarize the advantages.

An inner bevel on a straight carving gouge

■ eases away the wood chip or shaving from the blade as it cuts, allowing the cutting edge to proceed through the wood with less effort,

■ facilitates using the gouge in a reversed, upside down position,

■ shares the overall bevel angle with the outer bevel – which can then be longer – lowering the cutting angle and giving greater tool control,

■ strengthens the cutting edge by placing it more towards the centre of the steel where it is buttressed on both sides.

It is only fair to say that these points are debatable. It is worth looking into the reasoning behind the use of inner bevels a little further. The difference between the single-bevelled carpentry chisel and the double-bevelled

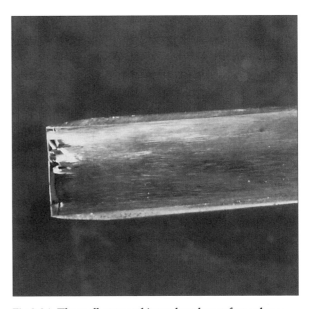

Fig 3.34 The well-stropped inner bevel seen from above.

firmer chisel can be used to illustrate some important aspects of how woodcarving tools and bevels work.

Carpentry chisels are used mainly to make woodworking joints – such as mortise and tenons – and paring accurate, flat surfaces prior to glueing up. The flat face causes the tool to be 'self-jigging': as the edge enters the wood, the flat underside of the chisel rests on the cut surface, which then acts as a guide, or jig, for the rest of the blade (*see* Fig 3.35). The chisel will cut accurately in a straight line, provided it is pushed sympathetically.

There is no equivalent flat face to a carving chisel – the flat bevel may have *some* self-jigging quality but,

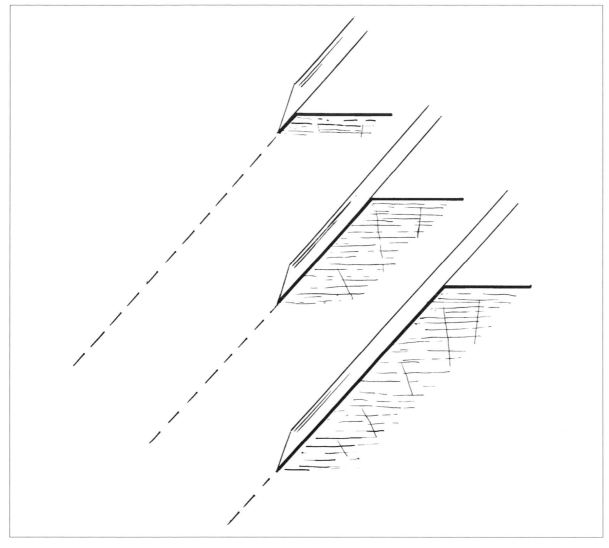

Fig 3.35 How the flat face of a carpenter's chisel is self-jigging and runs along the line of its own cut.

being so short a surface, it is negligible. Although carved surfaces can look very flat, on close inspection they have usually only been worked smooth to *appear* flat to the eye. Often a finger can detect shallow facets where the surface has been finished with a flat (no. 3) gouge.

In normal use, woodcarving chisels and gouges enter and leave the wood continuously in a fluid procedure which is not aimed at creating surfaces for exact, functional purposes. This self-jigging quality is not, therefore, appropriate. However, carvers often have a few carpentry chisels in their kit for those occasions when true flatness *is* required.

As a practical exercise take a carpentry chisel and with the *unbevelled* side of the blade down, cut a flat face across the edge of a piece of softwood. The jigging action can be observed assisting the blade line up. Now try to leave the wood through the same cut by lowering the handle. You will find this is difficult – if not impossible – to do cleanly. The edge snatches and breaks out the wood in front of the blade.

Turn the chisel upside down so the bevel is towards the wood and repeat the exercise. You will see how much more difficult it is to cut a truly flat face, while at the same time how much easier it is to cut out of the wood by lowering the handle (*see* Fig 3.36).

When the bevel is down, the heel end of the

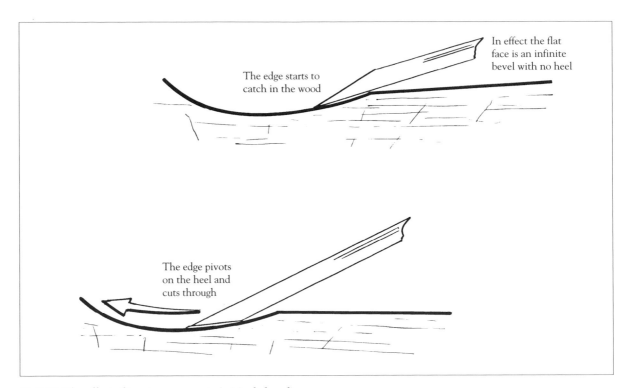

The edge starts to catch in the wood

In effect the flat face is an infinite bevel with no heel

The edge pivots on the heel and cuts through

Fig 3.36 The effect of turning a carpenter's (single bevel) chisel upside down is to allow the cut to pivot on the bevel heel. Try this.

bevel acts as a fulcrum, lifting the edge to bring it out of the wood. This ability of carving chisels and gouges to pivot around the heel and remove wood chips and shavings is essential to the act of carving.

Many beginners fail to understand that shavings of wood can only be removed cleanly if the cutting edge is moving *through* the wood. It is not enough to cut into the wood with a gouge and lever down on the handle to prise a wood chip away – this only bluntens the edge, and might actually break it. The edge can only work with the heel in the way described, and the chip or shaving be cut cleanly, if the edge is actually

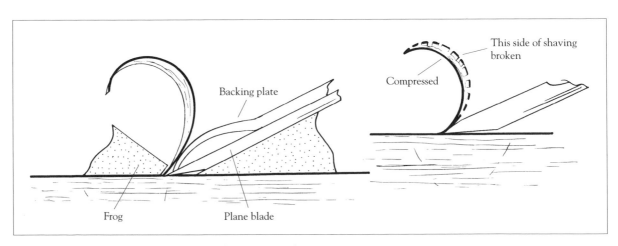

Backing plate

This side of shaving broken

Compressed

Frog

Plane blade

Fig 3.37 The inside bevel helps to curl the shavings up and away from the cut, in the same way as a joiner's plane.

pushed forwards through the wood.

If you take a long shaving with a double-bevelled firmer chisel you will find that the shaving curls up and away from the blade and that it does not remain straight (*see* Fig 3.37). A similar curling effect is seen in a carpentry plane. This curling is the result of the shaving being forced upwards by the top bevel (against the backing plate in a plane). The underside of the shaving is broken but the top remains intact and compressed. The different tensions curl and clear the shaving away from the blade as it is cut.

Putting an inner bevel (in cannel) on to carving gouges imitates the effect of a double-bevelled firmer chisel and – as the inside bevel curls the shaving away – the edge cuts through the wood more easily (*see* Fig 3.38).

Another occasion where an inner bevel is an advantage occurs when a gouge is used upside down, with the mouth (in cannel) to the surface of the wood. In this position, a gouge will shape rounded forms, beads, reeds and so on; the inner bevel enables the edge to negotiate and leave the cut more easily. Being such a shallow angle, the inside bevel normally lacks a true heel, and merges more with the cannel, but it helps nevertheless.

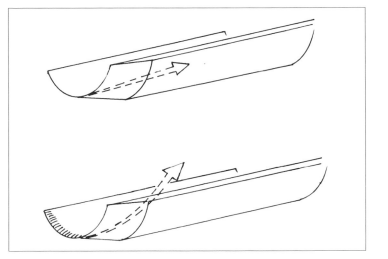

Fig 3.38 The shaving is directed by the inner bevel out of the mouth of the gouge, easing the passage of the tool.

The actual amount of bevel on the inside varies. It tends to be longer on a flattish gouge and can be as much as one-third of the length of the outer bevel. The quicker the gouge, the shorter the inner bevel. The deepest, **U**-shaped gouges (nos 10 and 11) are not

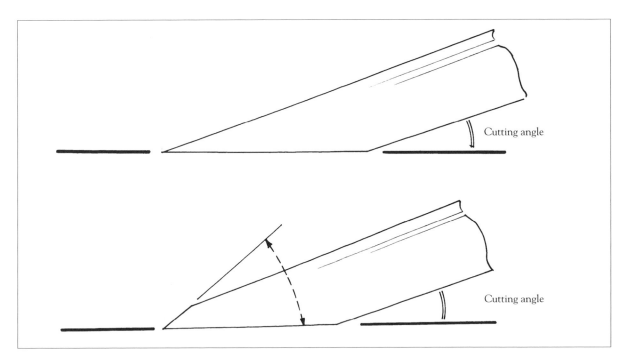

Fig 3.39 Although a short inner bevel makes for a greater overall angle (below), this is not at all the same as a solid wedge of this angle, which would need considerable effort to push.

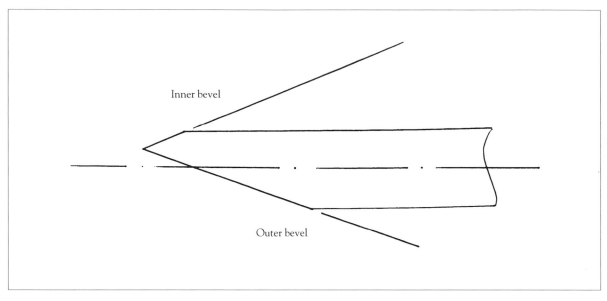

Inner bevel

Outer bevel

Fig 3.40 The ideal cutting profile for most gouges throws the cutting edge towards the centre.

used upside down and will have very short, tight bevels, serving only to direct the shaving up and out of the narrow cannel better.

A low cutting angle – the angle at which the carver offers the tool to the wood in order for it to start cutting – gives greater tool control. A low cutting angle is caused by a smaller outer bevel angle as it rests on the wood. But as we have seen, this means a weaker edge. An inner bevel keeps the cutting angle lower while making the edge stronger (*see* Fig 3.39), throwing the cutting edge towards the centre of the metal and effectively buttressing it from both sides. Being short, the inner bevel does not have the same effect as making a whole, single bevel with a combined angle of both inner and outer bevels.

When considering the strength of the edge it is important to remember that when the edge rocks out of the cut on the heel, quite a lot of pressure is exerted on it by the wood chip. The cutting edge of a blade with a single bevel is only supported by the steel on one side. With an inner bevel as well, the cutting edge is moved towards the *centre* of the blade, and is now buttressed by the steel on both sides – bracing and strengthening it. Carvers tackling very hard woods may consider placing the cutting edge quite far towards the centre of the blade by sharing the total angle of bevel more equally between the inside and outside.

CUTTING PROFILE

The configuration of the **cutting profile** – a section through the cutting edge – varies between tools. Not all tools have the same thickness of metal, or the angle or disposition of inner and outer bevels for example.

U-shaped gouges (fluters and veiners) and V-tools, which are not used in the reverse or upside down position, tend to have a significantly shorter inner bevel.

The flatter the gouge, the longer the inner bevel is. This points to the use of these gouges in the reverse position as a principal function.

Inner bevels are not normally put on the curved and bent gouges. The curve of the blade itself directs the edge through the cut; and these tools are never used upside down.

Not all carvers take the trouble to add an inner bevel to their gouges, but there are enough good reasons and advantages to make this practice worthwhile.

The cutting edge

If you examine the metal of a blade's cutting edge under a microscope, a crystalline structure can be seen. The carbon and iron, together with any other additions making up the steel, form themselves into tense crystal lattices. These lattices are the 'grain' in the metal, formed by the forging and heat treatment,

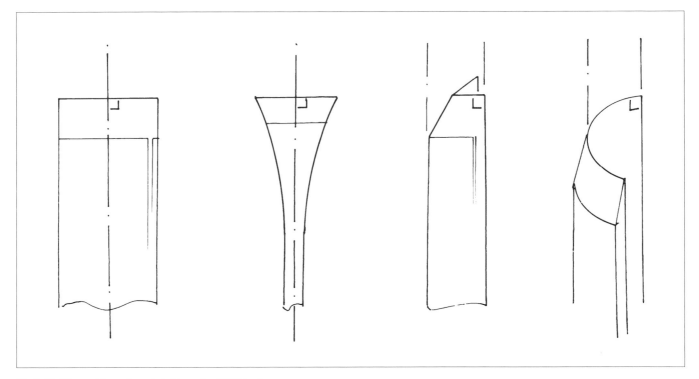

Fig 3.41 The cutting edge at right angles (90°) to the longitudinal axis.

which give it strength and resilience.

This wonderful edge is a refinement of the bevel. But, in addition to the flatness of the bevel, the best cut, feel and efficiency is only gained from the carving tool when a certain form is given to the cutting edge and bevel as a whole. This form includes:

- Edges at right angles to the blade
- Straight edges
- Proper corners
- Evenness.

These particular features need to be borne in mind while sharpening. They can be regarded as standards at which to aim.

SQUARENESS

Carving tools, with the exception of skew chisels, are sharpened with the cutting edge at right angles (90°) to their longitudinal axis (*see* Fig 3.41). Other than the skew chisel, it is not necessary to give carving gouges skewed edges, although there are some that have recently appeared on the market. This needs exploring further as it relates to useful ideas about the actual technique of carving.

Fig 3.42 Over-grinding at the factory has produced a wavy edge, feathering to the left – this must be straightened early on in the sharpening process.

Skewed fishtail *chisels* go back a long way. Etchings depicting carvers at work from the Gothic Renaissance period (around 1480–1530), which includes the work of such pre-eminent names as Tilman Riemenschneider, depict such tools in use –

but not skewed gouges. The Science Museum in South Kensington, London has an example of a Chinese skewed fishtail chisel with a socket instead of a tang, dating from around 1850, in their collection (inventory no. 1875–53) *see* Fig 5.31.

Skewed gouges have never been the standard kit of the carver anywhere. That skewed fishtail chisels have a long history reflects the general usefulness of the skew *chisel* to the carver. The corollary can also be made: the reason that skewed gouges have never appeared as standard reflects their lack of usefulness, even though carvers might need a skewed edge under some circumstances. The modern attempt to market skew gouges is an attempt to answer a need which is not really present; at the same time sacrificing other useful qualities that right-angled edges have.

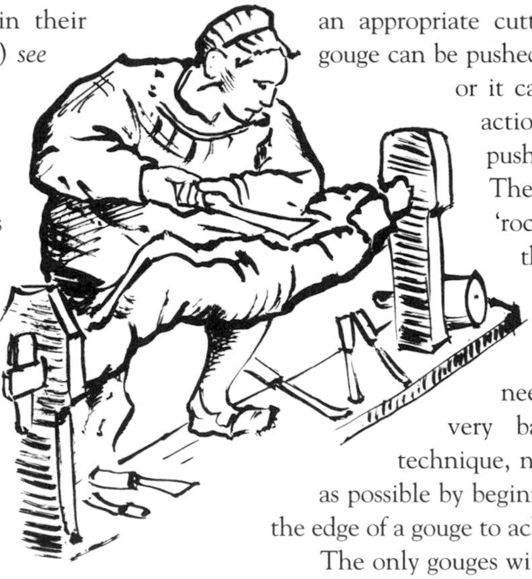

One point given in favour of such gouges with skewed edges is that their skewness causes the tools to slice the wood in a similar fashion to a guillotine. However, this effect can be achieved more simply by an appropriate cutting action with the tool. A gouge can be pushed dead straight along the wood or it can be given a winding, slicing action by rotating the wrist of the pushing hand as the tool advances. The gouge is thus rotated or 'rocked' through its cut, slicing the wood (*see* Fig 3.44). This 'slicing cut' can be made to the left or the right and to a greater or lesser degree as is needed. Such a slicing cut is a very basic and important carving technique, needing to be mastered as early as possible by beginners. There is no need to skew the edge of a gouge to achieve this particular effect.

The only gouges with which this slicing cut is not possible are those based on a **U** shape (nos 10 and 11). As the sweeps of all other gouges are based on arcs of circles, the edges can be applied with a winding stroke. Firmers can also be used with a slicing action.

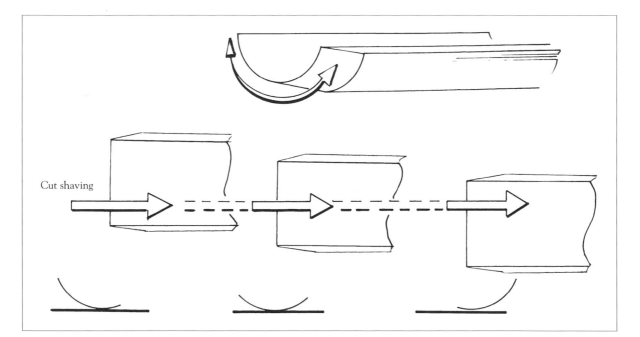

Cut shaving

Fig 3.43 (Above) From an engraving by Hans Burgkmair, around 1400.

Fig 3.44 The slicing cut: a basic and very important carving technique.

The 'square-on' orientation of a cutting edge is also essential for clean setting in – the tool being lined up accurately and easily in the wood. A skewed edge makes setting in more difficult. Again, for all practical purposes, almost any corner can be cleaned easily with a small range of straight and short bent skew chisels. It is necessary to skew a gouge to produce a long corner for this sort of purpose.

STRAIGHTNESS

The cutting edges of carving gouges and chisels can have one of three profiles (*see* Fig 3.45).

■ The central part of the edge may protrude beyond the corners to some extent – it is said to be *nosed*.
■ The central part of the edge may recede behind the corners – the corners protrude and can be described as *winged*.
■ The central part of the edge may be a straight line with the corners – in addition to being at right angles as discussed above.

Each option gives rise to different effects as the tool is used.

Nosed edges

A woodcarving tool bought set but not sharpened (that is with the bevel ground to a rough shape) quite often has a 'nose' or 'lady's finger' appearance: the centre of the edge protrudes beyond the corners to a rounded point (*see* Fig 3.46). The effect may also be

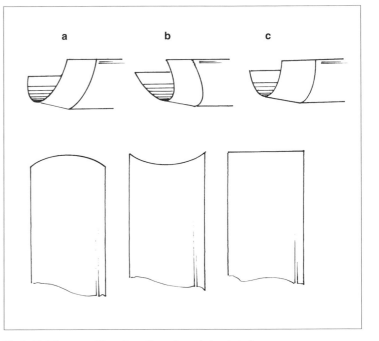

Fig 3.45 **Three profiles of cutting edges: (a) pointed or nosed; (b) winged; and (c) straight.**

called 'pointed'. V-tools may also appear this way with the angle pushed forward, sometimes quite far beyond the corners. These shapes are a product of the forging, with the shape perpetuated in the grinding. Beginners often assume, wrongly, that this must be the correct shape for the tool, whereas the manufacturers assume

Fig 3.46 **Nosed cutting edge in gouges straight from the factory.**

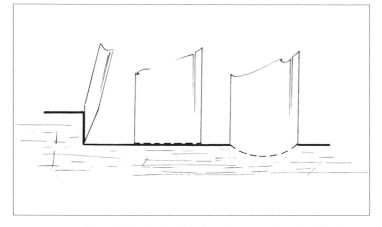

Fig 3.47 Setting in cleanly to the next plane is difficult with a nosed edge which tends to leave cut marks.

Fig 3.49 Setting in cleanly to the next plane is difficult with a winged tool as the corners tend to cut further than intended.

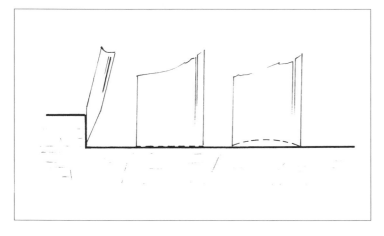

Fig 3.48 A bullnosed gouge tends to tear the wood towards the sides of its cut.

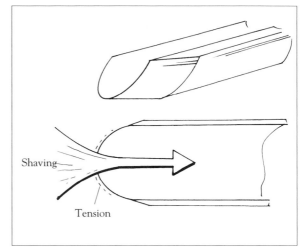

the opposite page.

The final, and least important, reason for not having a nose on gouges or V-tools involves the way in which these carving tools like to cut wood (*see* Fig 3.48). With a nosed centre to the cutting edge leading and cutting the wood before the sides enter, the central part of the shaving advances prematurely up the cannel, creating tension with the sides. Even if the wood towards the sides of the cut is not actually torn, there is still a tendency to produce less of a clean surface. This effect is increased with the extent of nosing. To some extent, a build up of tension like this must happen with a straight-edged gouge, but tension is always quickly and adequately relieved as the surface is cut before the wood underneath.

Winged edges

Going to the other extreme, a cutting edge with the corners advanced gives rise to similar problems of setting in as a nosed gouge. However, the contour of the blade is generally more useful than that of the nosed tool as the corners are still available. The wood at the surface is cut before the wood in the centre and not prised away uncleanly.

Straight edges

Straight edges give the best of all worlds: clean setting in, useful corners and clean cuts. Sharpen all gouges, chisels and V-tools, straight or bent, with the cutting edge in a straight line from corner to corner, as well as being at 90° to the longitudinal axis. In this way

that the carver will be altering it.

This pointed state of the cutting edge is the least useful of all the three options for several reasons. In the first place, 'setting in' – the purpose of which is to relieve one plane of the design from another – looks best when the planes purposely and cleanly meet. It is difficult, if not impossible, to get an exact straight bottom to the cut when a bullnosed gouge enters the wood as a stab mark will always tend to occur (*see* Fig 3.47). The round end is the wrong shape to set in crisply and cleanly, except for very particular conditions where some feature of a carving, such as a moulding, calls for it.

The second reason why a nosed gouge or chisel is a poor option is that, with this profile, the useful *corners* are lost. This is dealt with in more detail on

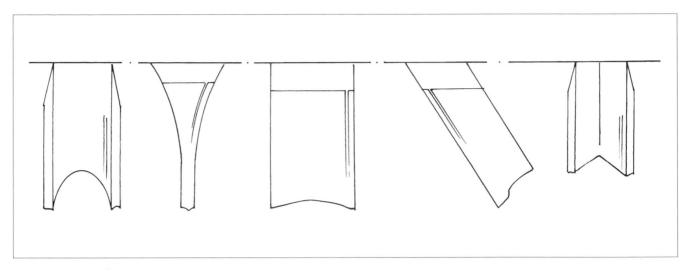

Fig 3.50 Straight edges.

Fig 3.51 The corners must be considered an extremely important part of the cutting edge.

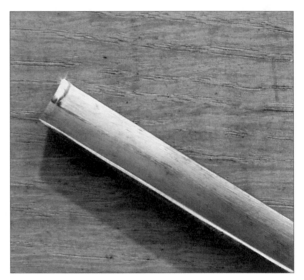

accurate setting in and full use of the edge is possible.

A wavy or notched edge is usually not acceptable – depending on the degree of irregularity and whether it has any effect on the work. If care is taken, sharpening the edge to such a shape can be avoided.

CORNERS

The importance of maintaining the full width and shape of a woodcarving tool, right into the corners, needs stressing. Beginners in particular do not appreciate, or make full use of, the corners of gouges or chisels. It is all too easy to over-sharpen the corners and reduce a tool's usefulness.

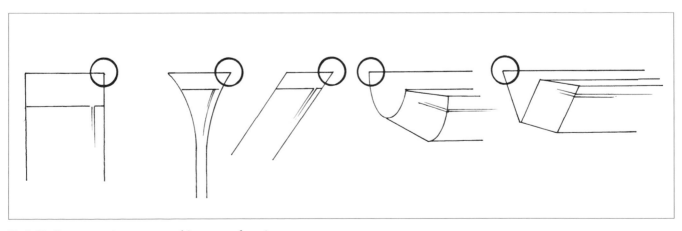

Fig 3.52 Corners are important working parts of carving tools and should be kept.

Corners are singled out for use continuously in the routine of carving: joining surfaces or planes neatly and accurately; setting in; cleaning into angles and corners and so on. Corners are often used more in the fashion of knives. A tool such as the skew chisel is really only a glorified corner; and a skew with its long pointed corner missing is effectively crippled. Fishtail tools also have emphasized corners for getting into awkward recesses.

Paying attention to the corners of all carving tools is an important aspect of sharpening.

Fig 3.53 Uneven wall thickness in a V-tool may cause later difficulty in sharpening.

Fig 3.54 Edges and heels parallel.

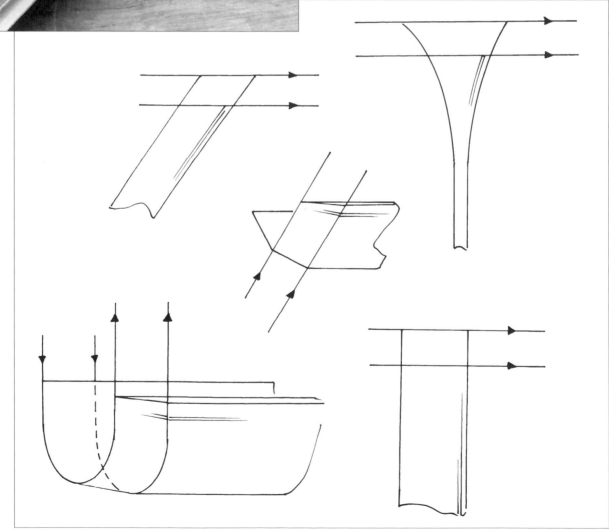

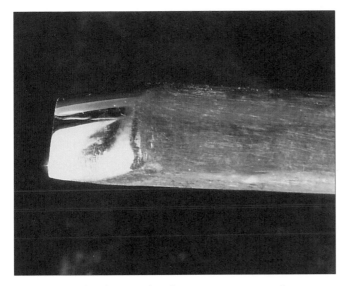

Fig 3.55 A tool with a straight edge, corners present and flat, and a polished bevel.

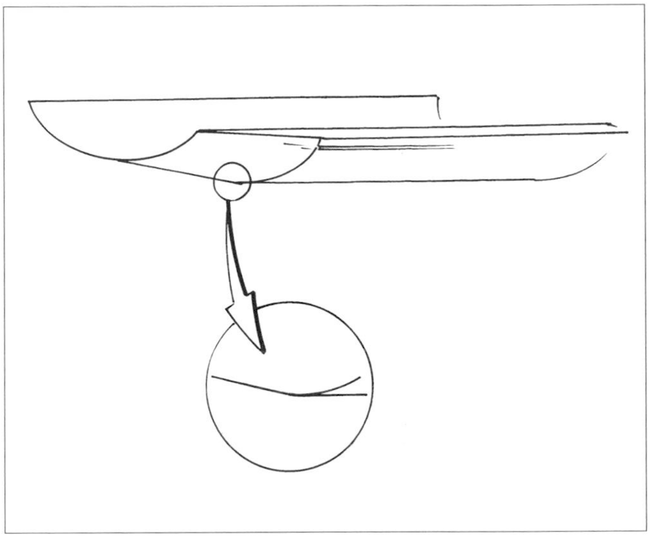

Fig 3.56 *Slightly softening the heel smooths it through its passage.*

EVENNESS

The steel of which a carving blade consists ought to be of even thickness across its width and along its length. An uneven thickness can mean some parts are weaker than others.

Uneven wall thickness can become a real problem in the **V**-tool. If the two sides are not of equal shape and thickness – with the cannel lined up truly down the centre – the tool can be impossible to sharpen correctly (*see* Fig 3.35). The condition needs to be corrected first before time is wasted on sharpening.

With an even wall, when any flat bevel is shaped evenly from side to side the heel will lie parallel to the edge (*see* Fig 3.54).

The heel

The **heel** is the angle formed as the bevel meets the blade proper – one can imagine the cutting edge to be the 'toe'. The importance of the heel in the carving stroke has already been mentioned, but a couple of further points need to be added.

Firstly, a flat bevel will make the angle of the heel quite sharp and well-defined. When the bevel and heel follow after the cutting edge, they rub the surface of the wood and burnish it – which adds tremendously to the appearance of the work. However, if the heel is too keen a ridge, it will roughen or score the surface of the cut as it passes, rather than smooth it. To avoid this

effect, the heel needs to be *slightly* rounded over, smoothed and polished – but *only* the heel, keeping the rest of the bevel flat.

The best way of smoothing the heel is on a fine benchstone, not the grinding wheel. Leave the heel until after the blade, with its flat bevel, is completely sharp, and then soften the definition of the heel as a final act.

This softening also applies to the heels of the **V**-tool, that is the two proper heels and the point at the base of the keel, where the keel meets the main body of metal. Rounding the keel over slightly prevents a sharp angle scoring the bottom of the groove. It also helps the tool slide round and navigate corners more easily. The keel itself should be kept flat straight.

One further refinement involves removing facets towards the sides of the heel; thinning the metal here gets the corners into tighter recesses (*see* Fig 3.57). The facet can be produced on the fine grinding wheel, after the tool has been sharpened; take care not to remove metal from the actual corners of the cutting edge. Although this feature can be useful on any carving tool (for example a skew chisel) it can weaken the edge. Do it to a particular tool when circumstances require.

In brief

Sharpening a carving tool for the first time is a matter of aiming to do the best you can, but it must be attempted

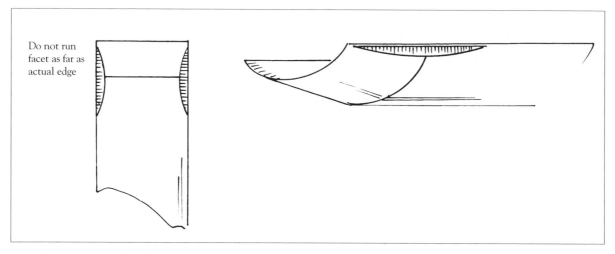

Do not run facet as far as actual edge

Fig 3.57 Facets in the side of the bevel allow the corners to get into tight recesses more easily.

in the right way. There is no point in spending an equal amount of time sharpening the tool wrongly.

All the points so far discussed – the bevel with its appropriate angle and shape; the cutting edge and its profile; the heel and so on – may seem a little much for a beginner to take in all at once. Some tools are not so easy to sharpen and it may be that you concede a little on the shape. But do the best you can. Then each time

Fig 3.58 The white line or line of light – the visible edge – is seen by orientating the edge to a light source. A little practice will soon make this an easy procedure.

the edge needs touching up, improve it a little further until the tool arrives at as perfect a shape and sharpness as you can make it.

I have tried to make the information arise naturally and logically out of how carving tools work for the carver, and what can be expected from them. The following summary gathers these points together for reference and gives an overview of what you are looking for.

◼ Keep the bevel flat, from edge to heel, with an even thickness from side to side and no secondary bevel.
◼ The angle (length) of bevel needs to be adjusted according to the hardness of the material. Overall angles vary from 15° to 30°, with 20–25° being suitable for most purposes.
◼ There are many advantages to working an inside bevel onto straight gouges and throwing the cutting edge towards the centre, especially in those tools that will be used in the reverse, upside down, position.
◼ The cutting edge, with the exception of skew chisels, should be square-on to the longitudinal axis of the tool.
◼ Keep the corners.
◼ Make the cutting edge straight from corner to corner and parallel to the heel.
◼ Slightly round over and polish the heels after sharpening.

The secret of success

There is a particularly straightforward approach to sharpening carving tools which, if followed rigorously,

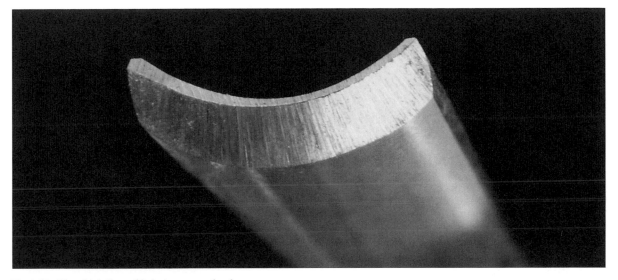

Fig 3.59 The thick line of light in a completely unsharpened tool. Note the thickening to the left.

is more or less guaranteed to lead to the cutting profile and edge that is wanted.

Look at the end of any unsharpened gouge, which has only been set by a manufacturer. The very blunt edge can easily be seen reflecting light and appears as a thick, shiny line (*see* Fig 3.58). This is called the **white line** or **line of light**. These terms will be used synonymously to refer to the visible edge.

This line of light is the primary guide to the state of the cutting edge. By constantly checking the thickness and distribution of this visible line while sharpening, the quality of the potential cutting edge is monitored (*see* Fig 3.60). The thicker the line of light, the thicker the edge of steel, and vice versa. As a carving tool is sharpened, the line gets thinner and thinner. When the edge reaches 'sharp', the line of light will have disappeared. The crystalline structure of the edge has been made so thin as to be no longer visible to the naked eye.

To reflect the light, the edge of the carving tool must be orientated to the light source in a way that displays the white line. It is possible to think the white line is gone, only to have it reappear when the blade is turned around a little.

When the edge is approaching sharpness, the line of light attenuates and can be a little difficult to see. Sometimes a magnifying glass is useful for having a really close look at the line, helping to decide what state the edge is in. Pushing the edge into a piece of medium-hard waste wood will also toughen and

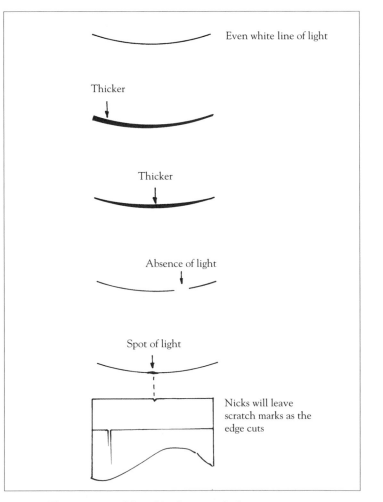

Fig 3.60 The evenness of the white line reveals the thickness of metal along the cutting edge.

Fig 3.61 (Right) The white line of light is getting thinner, but now it is thicker towards the top.

Fig 3.62 Scratch marks on the bevel can result from the action of specific abrasive stones.

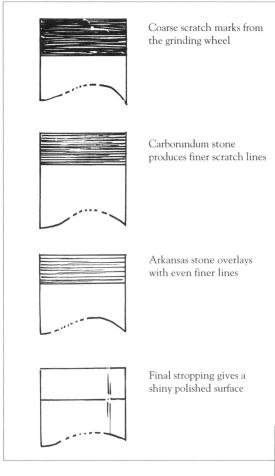

Coarse scratch marks from the grinding wheel

Carborundum stone produces finer scratch lines

Arkansas stone overlays with even finer lines

Final stropping gives a shiny polished surface

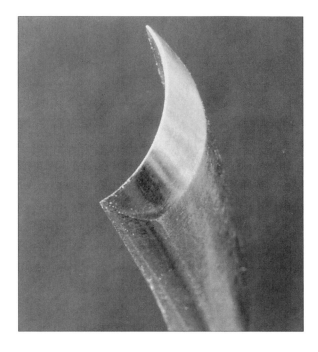

emphasize the edge to reveal any white line or speck.

Sharpening that produces an uneven line of light means that some parts of the edge are thicker than others. Continuing to sharpen in the same way will produce an uneven, wavy, cutting edge – perhaps with missing corners. Small spots or areas of light along the edge will be echoed in scratches to the surface of the

Fig 3.63 The scratches towards the heel as well as the polished metal towards the edge would suggest that the bevel is rounded and not flat.

Fig 3.64 Coarse bevel scratches – as with the line of light you will need to orientate the blade to examine them most clearly.

wood as it is cut.

This line of light is the first indicator of the state of sharpness of the cutting edge. Returning to the unsharpened carving tool, look at the *bevel* where scratch marks – probably quite coarse – will be seen. These marks result from the grinding wheel abrasives which were used to set the bevel. The scratches will change in appearance as the bevel is sharpened on various grades of stone (*see* Fig 3.62). From these marks information about the state of the bevel can be gained: its flatness, evenness, how it is being applied to the oilstones and so on.

So there are two indicators we can use to assess how the sharpening is coming along:

- The white line of light
- The bevel surface.

Both the line of light and the bevel scratches show where metal is to be removed and – equally as important – where metal is *not* to be removed.

The key word in using these two indicators is *evenness*. Sharpening involves a balance between removing and leaving metal from the bevel; and proceeding in an even, regular way (*see* Fig 3.65). The secret of successful sharpening is, constantly, to allow the line of light and the surface of the bevel to guide the next step, maintaining an even appearance from start to finish.

Where part of the white line is *thicker* than another part along the edge, this part must be worked on specifically – at whatever stage in sharpening you are at – to bring the line back to a uniform thickness. It is important to put this same point the other way round: where the line is found to be *thinner*, this part of the edge needs to be left alone and consciously avoided until the rest of the metal has been brought to the same state of thinness.

As the abrasives used to sharpen the blade get finer and finer, so do the scratch marks in the metal of the bevel. The scratches of finer abrasives overlay and hide those of the previous ones until a final polished surface is achieved. These marks can be observed on the bevel at any stage in the sharpening process and the position at which the blade is offered to the sharpening stones should be adjusted (*see* Fig 3.66).

For example, say a firmer chisel is put from the grinding wheel to a flat benchstone. If the handle is inadvertently raised, more of the bevel towards the cutting edge will be worked on. The edge will thin according to the line of light – it may even disappear

and the tool thought to be sharp. Indeed this is often an expedient with beginners, who try to move the sharpening process on more quickly by raising the handle and working more on the edge. But the bevel will actually be rounded or secondary.

What has happened will immediately be obvious if the scratch marks are looked at occasionally – they will not be evenly distributed across the face of the bevel. By checking the bevel, the handle can be lowered appropriately and flatness of the bevel re-established.

SUMMARY

Starting with the grinding, through to the final sharpening, retain an even white line of light, right up to its final disappearance. Continually check this and

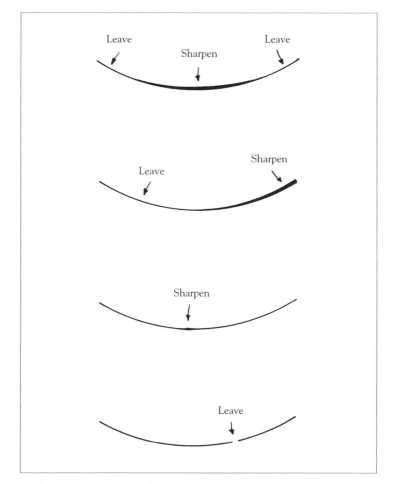

Fig 3.65 How the state of the white line of light indicates the next step in sharpening. Always strive for evenness. In the bottom example, it might be best to return the whole edge to a visible line first – missing points such as this are tricky to deal with.

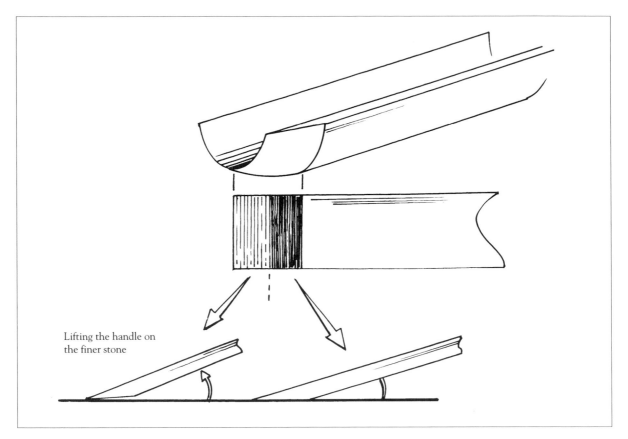

Lifting the handle on
the finer stone

Fig 3.66 Finer and coarser marks on the bevel can indicate lifting the handle – which makes the line of light disappear quicker and rolls the bevel.

the bevel surface, maintaining a uniform appearance to both. The main points, therefore, are:

- The line of light
- The surface of the bevel
- Evenness from start to finish.

If this advice is followed, there is no reason not to achieve straight, acutely sharp cutting edges, complete with corners and flat bevels.

EQUIPMENT

The equipment needed to sharpen woodcarving tools is relatively straightforward. It consists entirely of an assortment of abrasives which remove unwanted metal from the blade. There is no trickery in it. These abrasives can be thought of as a scale, or range. At one end there are very coarse abrasives – represented by the grinding wheel – for removing metal quickly. At the other end are finely dressed strops, the cut of

which polishes the metal. Between these two extremes lies a spectrum of artificial and natural stones with graded, abrasive qualities

A blade moves along this scale from coarse to ever finer abrasives in the sequence of shaping and sharpening its cutting edge. Not all the elements in the scale are necessary or appropriate on any particular occasion. With practice, the carver can skip stages and feel free to move around the scale, up or down, according to what is needed at that moment.

A few terms need clarifying. Technically, the **grinding wheel** or **grindstone** refer to the abrasive wheel itself and not the machine. In practice, the wheel is inseparable from the machine which is termed either a **grinder** or **bench grinder.**

Oilstone, benchstone, whetstone and **honing stone** all mean the same thing. The word **hone** comes from an Old English word for a stone, so 'honing' means 'stoning'. And the word **whet** derives from the Old English *hwaet*, meaning quick or active; so a

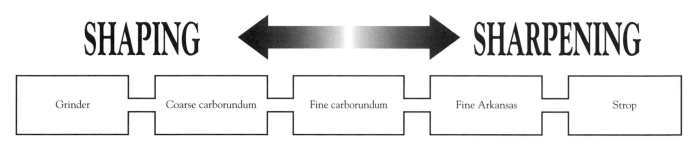

Fig 3.67 Sharpening is a process which starts with initially shaping the cutting part of the blade, and moves through a spectrum of abrasives to the final, sharp cutting edge. At a later time, different stages will be taken up and moved through, depending upon what the edge needs to return it to a correct state of sharpness.

whetstone was a sharp active stone, to be differentiated from ordinary ones. **Whetting, honing,** and **stoning** synonymously describe the act of sharpening a tool on a benchstone. All these words are in common usage and have become a little confused.

A point that was made about woodcarving tools themselves also needs to be made about the equipment needed to sharpen them. It is false economy to buy inferior quality of either. Like the carving tools, the expense is really an investment in personal satisfaction as well as time and money. Good quality sharpening stones will last at least the lifetime of the carving tools themselves. As long as they are looked after properly, they only need to be bought once.

The sequence of sharpening a carving tool involves working along the range of abrasives in the following order:

■ The grinding wheel
■ Coarse benchstones (and slipstones)
■ Fine benchstones (and slipstones)
■ Strops.

The bench grinder sets the bevel and squares the edge. Then the benchstones and slips refine and sharpen this shape, with the strops polishing to the final working edge.

First we will look at the equipment in a little detail, then general information will be given on how to use and care for it. Finally, points related to working the individual shapes of tools will be dealt with.

Bench grinders

Whether a bench grinder is really needed or not depends largely on the sizes, and numbers, of carving tools to be managed. A carver with only a few, small tools may find that a coarse benchstone will adequately do the job of a grinder. A sculptor, on the other hand, with only a few but nevertheless large gouges would find it laborious only to use benchstones; a bench grinder would save a lot of time, especially as some sculptors tend to use their carving tools ruthlessly. A grinding wheel at the coarsest end of the abrasive spectrum removes the most metal, most quickly.

A newcomer, who does not know whether they are going to be hooked on the craft of carving or not, should probably leave the grinder to start with. Working with flat bevels, tools only need re-grinding when they become damaged. It may be a matter of having access to a grinder, rather than actually owning one. So a grinder, while not essential to begin with, can save a lot of time, especially where there is serious blunting or breaking to the edge of a tool. Most carvers end up with one.

TYPES

Modern grinders are electrically driven. There must be some treadle- or hand-operated wheels out there – not without their advantages – but they are very unusual today. Some of the following discussion is applicable to them, but note that working arrangements that allow *both* hands to be kept free for controlling the tool on the wheel are the best.

Electrically driven grinding wheels can be 'dry' (fast running) or 'wet' (slow running). On some dry grinders an abrasive belt may replace one of the wheels.

Dry bench grinders

Dry bench grinders with two abrasive wheels are the cheapest option. These wheels are mounted directly on to either end of the motor shaft and so turn at the same speed as the motor – somewhere around 2900 rpm.

Fig 3.68 **This sort of low-tech grinder has been largely superseded by electrical grinders; although slower and more 'friendly', less control over the tool is possible because one hand is always occupied turning the wheel.**

There are protective guards around the wheel as well as in front as the high speed and cutting ability throws off particles and sparks quite violently. However, properly used, a good quality machine is quite safe, and being

Fig 3.69 **A typical dry bench grinder, modified with a longer tool rest.**

Fig 3.70 **Removing the grinding wheel: one end will have a thread going the opposite direction to normal to prevent the wheel unscrewing in use.**

about the simplest machine in the workshop, will last a long time.

The motor size of dry bench grinders varies between ¼ and ½ hp, the smaller size being quite adequate for the needs of the carver. The two wheels will be of different grit but the same size and positioned either end of the motor shaft. Diameters vary between about 5 and 8in (125 and 200mm). A wheel of at least 6in (150mm) diameter is required.

The wheels themselves are made of artificial stone, usually based on vitrified aluminium oxide or silicon carbide. 'White' wheels designed for use on high speed steel (as used for woodturning tools) can also be used on carbon steel, though a fine grit is usually unavailable. Because there is an option of two wheels, a machine is normally supplied with a 'coarse' and a 'fine' grit of stone. It is useful if these terms are known to match those for your (artificial) benchstones. There are many excellent and reliable makes on the market, as well as cheap imports. The wheels and bearings of the latter tend to be inferior and wear quickly.

Wheels can be easily replaced from engineering suppliers, changing them to other available grits. The size of wheel should remain the same on either end of the motor spindle to keep the machine balanced and prevent undue strain on the bearings. Always follow the manufacturer's instructions when changing wheels.

When one or both wheels are replaced or removed from the grinder, for whatever reason, they will need *balancing* on the machine – rather like motor-car tyres need balancing. There is often some spot on the wheel denser than another and, revolving at high speed, the

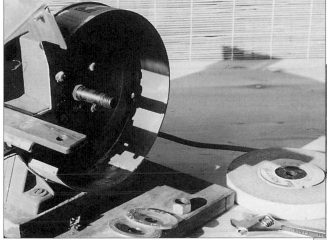

Fig 3.71 The free spindle after the wheel is removed.

Fig 3.72 The lowest point on the wheel is marked with a pencil.

centrifugal force of this imbalance can create unpleasant vibration as well as stressing the bearings.

To balance the wheels of a high-speed dry grinder follow these steps.

1 Unplug the machine and remove the wheel guards from both sides.
2 Remove one wheel completely (*see* Figs 3.70, 3.71).
3 Spin the remaining wheel freely, and when it comes to rest, mark the lowest point on the rim of the wheel with a pencil (*see* Fig 3.72). Repeat this a couple of times and you should be able to locate any 'heavy' spots as gravity will pull these consistently to the low point of the free swinging wheel.
4 Remove this wheel and fit the other one to the opposite side.
5 Mark the second wheel similarly to the first.
6 Now replace both wheels, *lining up the pencil marks to opposite sides*, so that heaviest point of each wheel counterbalances the other when the machine runs.
7 Tighten the wheels according to the manufacturer's instructions and replace the guards.

Wet bench grinders

The motor of a wet grinder usually has the same standard rating as a dry grinder, but the speed of the wheel itself is decreased by some reducing drive. This makes them a little more complicated and larger, although both wet and dry machines need space to work around. The wheel speed will be around 50–100 rpm which is slow enough not to fling water out of the trough in which it revolves. The water constantly flushes over the wheel, washing away particles and

cooling the blade, but obscuring what is going on.

There is usually only one, larger-sized grinding wheel on wet grinding machines; the wheel is approximately 8in diameter by 2in thick (250 x 50mm). A separate buffing wheel may also be included in the arrangement. These wet grinders can be significantly more expensive than the commoner, dry running bench grinders. Their advantages consist of eliminating the danger of tool over-heating; not flinging out sparks; and generally operating in a gentler way. The Swedish Tormek range can be recommended as good quality and reliable machines.

Alternatives

Cheaper options for grinding involve using an electrical drill attachment or flexible shaft (*see* Fig 3.74). These are inexpensive alternatives but suitable only when a small amount of light grinding is wanted, or as a temporary expedient. A bench grinder is a better alternative for the busy carver.

Quite small grinding wheels are available for drills and flexible shafts. These can be useful for some preliminary shaping – for example putting an inner bevel on a large gouge, while the blade is gripped in a vice. However, they do not have the same safety

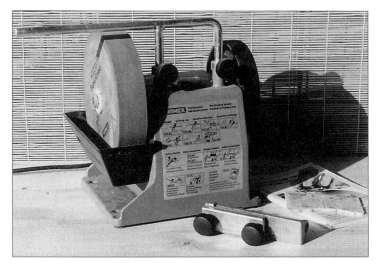

Fig 3.73 A wet grinder with the larger slow wheel in its trough on the left and a buffing wheel on the right.

arrangements as bench-mounted grinders and extra care needs to be taken in their use – choosing the slowest drill speed and wearing proper eye protection.

SPEED AND FRICTION

Dry grinders are designed to move metal quickly: the wheels are coarse and the speed is high – sparks of white hot metal shoot off dramatically into the air. While this may seem fun, it can create two problems.

First, it is very easy to grind off more metal than you intended (over-grinding). Sometimes it is better to use a coarse benchstone and take a little longer to set the shape precisely, rather than risk over-grinding and destroying the shape.

The second problem lies in the heat generated by friction between the fast-moving surface of the wheel and the tool. Over-heating the cutting edge – turning the surface blue ('blueing') – seriously damages the steel. A short foray into the world of physics is relevant here. By understanding how the heat is actually generated, steps can be taken to minimize it.

The difference between heat and temperature, while not often appreciated, is of real, practical importance to the carver. Simply put, 'temperature' is measured by thermometers whereas 'heat' is the combination of this temperature with the *mass* of an object. To take a common example: a dinner plate can have a *lower temperature*, but *more heat*, than a spark. So a spark landing on the skin may hardly be felt – its mass is very small and the heat disperses rapidly into the skin. But a dinner plate at a lower temperature has far more heat available to raise the temperature of the skin.

Referring back to carving tools, two principles arise.

▪ The larger a chisel or gouge, the slower its increase in temperature on a grinding wheel.
▪ The temperature of the thinnest parts of a blade – the parts with the least mass – will increase in temperature faster than in other thicker parts.

In other words, the tools which are most susceptible to over-heating are the smaller ones. And the parts of the tools most vulnerable are the corners and edges, for example, the point of a skew chisel and the corners of fishtail gouges.

The hardness and toughness of carving-tool steel is brought about by specific heat treatment, a process which can be undone by re-heating the blade. Above a certain temperature (around 235°C) the metal starts to **anneal**, softening towards its original unhardened state. When a blade turns blue on a grinding wheel, the temperature will have reached somewhere around 300°C. It now loses its ability to hold a cutting edge and dulls rapidly. Blueing usually occurs in one spot on the edge or corner first. Easily done, blueing happens very quickly.

Unfortunately the loss of hardness in the blued cutting edge cannot be rescinded and further heat treatment is needed to restore the temper. This is dealt with in Chapter 5 (*see page 235*), but normally it is simpler to regrind the blade back to an unaffected part without further blueing. This is obviously a great waste of time and steel. It needs to be avoided from the start by understanding what conditions lead to excess heat production.

The amount of heat is related to the amount of *friction*, which is a product of two things:

▪ The speed of the wheel surface
▪ The pressure with which the tool is applied.

So the following three things should be borne in mind while grinding a carving tool.

The mass of metal

The effect of the amount of metal being offered to the wheel on how quickly the temperature rises has already been mentioned. Grinding with a fast, dry grinder should not be taken beyond a certain thinness of metal – not only because of possible over-heating but also because metal needs to be left for the finer abrasives to work on.

Pressure

A light pressure, enough to steady and direct the tool,

is all that should be applied, allowing the wheel to do the work. The faster the wheel, the lighter the pressure. Even though these dry grinders work quickly, many users still get impatient and apply the bevel too arduously and for too long. At fast speeds, events happen quickly.

A small point is that the coarse wheels, with more open grain structure, cut away more material but actually create less friction than the finer stones. Blueing tends to happen more often on the finer stone – due also in part to the metal being thinner at this stage.

Surface speed of the wheel

The speed of a commercial grinder motor is fixed, but what actually matters is the *surface speed* of the rotating wheel itself. The surface speed of larger wheels is proportionately faster than smaller ones – motor speeds between grinders being similar. An 8in (200mm) wheel generates a quarter more heat than a 6in (150mm) one at the same rpm and working in all other ways equally.

A serviceable slow-speed bench grinder is not difficult to make. Slow surface speeds reduce the heat generated by friction enormously. Some notes and guidance for making a slow-speed grinder follow on page 140.

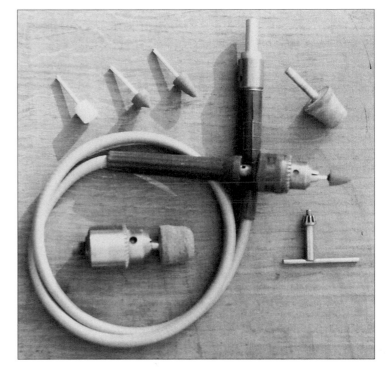

Fig 3.74 This sort of inexpensive flexible shaft is not designed for speeds higher than that of a power drill or grinding wheel take off. Besides small abrasive wheels they can be fitted with burrs and cutters for working directly on wood.

SUMMARY

Over-heating a carving tool on a dry grinder – blueing the steel – is more likely with:

- Faster speeds of motor
- Larger diameter wheels
- Finer grit wheels
- Thinner metal
- Smaller tools
- Increased pressure
- Longer periods of contact

So, to prevent over-heating the metal:

- Bear the above principles and points in mind while working with the grinder.
- Constantly monitor the temperature of the blade with your fingers on its back; never let the metal get warmer than can be comfortably handled.
- Always keep a container with cold water next to the grinder; dip the blades in as often as necessary to keep them cool.

If these points are remembered and the advice is followed, using a dry grinder need never be a problem.

Wet grinders eliminate the problem of heat generation by revolving at a slow speed and steadily flushing the blade with water. Even with a lot of pressure you could never blue the edge and, in this respect, they are excellent and safe machines.

Disadvantages with wet grinders include the following.

- Water washing over the edge of the tool makes the edge less easy to scrutinize so more of a sense of 'feel' is needed.
- The wheels tend to be softer and wear more quickly than their dry counterparts.
- The wheel should not be left standing in the water of the trough unused for a long time as water soaks into the wheel and unbalances it.
- Wet grinders are usually larger machines than dry ones and the cost must certainly be a consideration.

The abrasive surface of a **belt grinder** moves at a much greater speed than that of a wheel. Although a thin belt dissipates heat faster than a solid wheel, the effect is offset by the speed. One advantage of these

Fig 3.75 A simple homemade slow-speed grinder: the motor is slung in the box beneath and its hinged weight tensions the belt; the tool rest has been moved out of the way for the photograph.

machines is that the grinding takes place on a flat surface, so producing a flat bevel more easily. They are less common than double-ended, wheel grinders but are worth considering. Remember to check the adequacy of the tool rests.

MAKING A SLOW-SPEED GRINDER

For many years I have been using a slow-speed dry grinder which I made. It has several advantages.

■ The low speed was otherwise unavailable.
■ The size and grit of the wheels are of my own choosing.
■ The cost proved to be much less than the cost of buying a high-speed new machine.

About 400 rpm produces a surface speed using a 6in

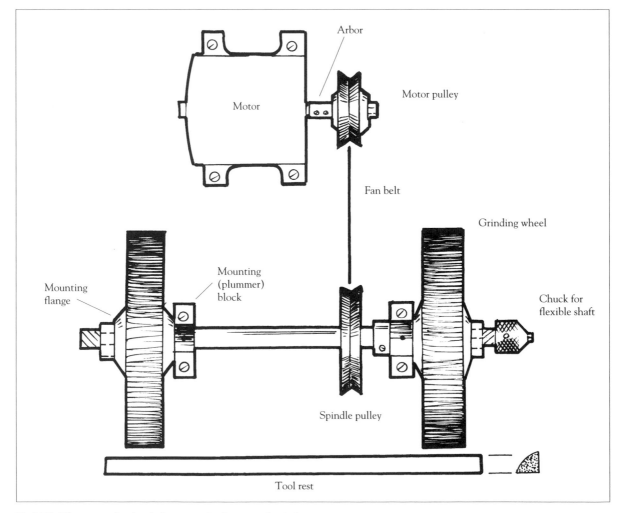

Fig 3.76 The parts of a simple homemade slow-speed grinder.

Fig 3.77 View from beneath of the motor: hinged by one edge the weight of the motor tensions the belt.

(150mm) wheel of about 3 feet (1m) per second. This speed, about one-seventh that of a similar-sized commercial grinder, reduces the generation of heat drastically – in fact by the same ratio. The possibility of over-shaping and over-heating becomes much less, although the wheel still revolves at an efficiently useful speed.

Making a slow-speed grinder is a straightforward project for anyone who has the practical skills to be woodcarving already. It mostly involves the assembly of parts – with a little improvisation – rather than clever metalwork.

The motor from a washing machine, pump, etc. can be picked up cheaply from second-hand tool shops or scrap yards. Look for the information plate giving the power rating and speed: a motor size of ¼–½ hp (185–370W), single-phase and in good condition with mounting lugs is needed. Make sure all the electrics are safe and appropriately earthed.

The bearings, spindles and matching grinding wheels can be bought new (*see* the Reference Section, page 345). Fitting a useful chuck at one end of the spindle is also possible. Always get the best quality stone, at least 1in (25mm) wide. A car fan-belt (not your own!) links the pulleys and is tensioned by the weight of the motor (*see* Fig 3.77). It is then a matter of fashioning and assembling the tool rests, belt guard, etc. to suit. The grinding wheels should rotate *towards* the user.

The speed of the motor, which is known, is reduced by the pulleys so that the wheel rotates at a slow surface speed. The basic formula for relating the speeds and the pulley diameters is:

$$G \times S = M \times D$$

where

G = the speed of the grinding wheel (rpm)
S = the diameter of the spindle pulley
M = the speed of the motor (rpm)
D = the diameter of the drive pulley (on the motor).

The slow speed of a homemade wheel is much safer than a high-speed wheel but nevertheless it is still fast enough for accidents to happen. When improvising,

Fig 3.78 Dressing stone (left) and dressing wheel.

Fig 3.79 The wheel has hammer-like projections that spin on the surface of the grinding wheel and break it down, producing a fine level surface.

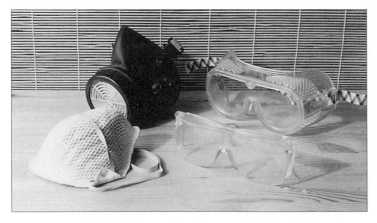

Fig 3.80 Safety and equipment, which should always be a part of any workshop, is particularly important when dressing the grinding wheel because of the dust.

the onus of responsibility for safety rests on the improviser and an attitude of thoughtful caution is needed. The moving parts of the assembly that are not actually used – the fan-belt and pulleys especially – should be enclosed. The fastenings, such as bolts, and the motor, spindle and grinding wheels should be secure and inspected at intervals. With these precautions and observing normal safety rules – such as are described next – there is no reason why such a slow-speed grinder should not prove to be a great asset to shaping and sharpening woodcarving tools.

SAFETY AND CARE

When you buy a grinder, whether wet or dry, read and observe the manufacturer's advice. This is usually well thought-out and is as much for the user's benefit as the manufacturer's own protection.

Manufacturers often advise the 'running in' of new stones. This means running them on the machine for several minutes before applying a tool; the idea is that any flaw or crack in the stone – enough to cause it to fly apart – is given a chance to reveal itself. Always tap a wheel before mounting it: a dull sound may indicate a hairline crack; although well-tested in the factory these stones are brittle and may get knocked in transit. Keep the wheel running true and use all the surface uniformly.

The following points need to be emphasized.

■ Keep wiring from any machine neatly out of the way, not trailing over the floor or work surfaces. Do not drip water from the cooling jar over the motor, electrical connections or plug.

■ Guards, rests, etc. should be properly adjusted and *used*. Face or eye protection is necessary as grit and sparks are quite capable of penetrating the eyeball. Face masks are also advisable as the dust produced by silicon-carbide or aluminium oxide wheels or ground metal cannot be 'user friendly'.

■ Tie back long hair and do not wear loose clothing such as cuffs and ties; serious injury can be caused if these are caught in a wheel.

■ Never stab at the wheel, which can lead to 'digging in'. Approach the surface positively but gently, working as much as possible from the fixed tool rests. The side of the wheel can be used, but *very* lightly, and should never be worn away.

■ The surface of the wheel will need dressing occasionally to keep it flat and true. A **dressing stone** (sometimes called a **devil's stone**) or **dressing wheel**, is drawn carefully across the spinning stone to level it (*see* Figs 3.78, 3.79). This is a simple but particularly dusty operation for which the use of face masks and eye protection is imperative (*see* Fig 3.80). Consider the strategic placing of a vacuum nozzle.

Benchstones

There are two sources of benchstone: artificial and natural. Alternative, synonymous names for benchstones are: **oilstone**, **whetstone**, **honing stone** and **sharpening stone**. Both artificial and natural stones will be needed.

Generally the artificial stones are coarser than the natural ones and follow the grinding wheel in the sharpening process: refining the shape and starting the sharpening proper. The natural stones can cut extremely finely, removing hardly any metal at all, and it is these stones which put the keen, final edge to carving tools.

ARTIFICIAL STONES

Types

Artificial stones are often referred to as **Carborundum stones**. This is actually a trade name for vitrified silicon-carbide that has entered general

circulation. There are three available grades (coarse, medium and fine), having different sizes of cutting crystals or grit. The speed at which they remove metal from the blade varies – the coarser the grit, the greater the quantity of metal removed and the faster the cut.

The middle grade is often unused, with sharpening passing straight from the coarse stone to the fine one. This is reflected in the fact that a **combination stone** is available, with one side coarse and the other side fine (*see* Fig 3.81). Such a combination stone is the most economic option for the carver. Buy the largest surface size available, 8 x 2in (200 x 50mm), which is easier to use and can sharpen a wider range of tools.

Oils

All these sharpening stones must be used with oil. The oil is not being used as a lubricant, instead its purpose is to float away the abraded particles of stone grit and metal. Without this, the gaps and pores between the cutting crystals fill and the stone glazes over (*see* Fig 3.82) so the metal of the blade slides without being cut. It follows that it is possible to use too little oil, but not too much. Although experience will tell you when a balance has been struck, do not be mean with the oil.

After a while the oil becomes a fine, black pulp. Regularly wipe off this oil, metal and grit slurry with a cotton rag, and replace it with fresh oil.

The best oil is the readily available, light lubricating oil used for bicycles, sewing machines, etc. (e.g. '3-in-1'). Some oils, such as linseed oil, dry in contact with the air and would

Fig 3.81 Combination stones are a laminate of coarse and fine Carborundum grits.

Fig 3.82 Reflections from a glazed oilstone indicate that the pores are clogged with stone and metal particles.

Fig 3.83 Only light oil should be used on oilstones.

rapidly clog the stone. Such oils, and thick motor oil (designed for a different purpose), should not be used.

At a pinch, water will do the job of washing away the ground-off grit and steel pulp from the pores of the stone. It will soak in more quickly than oil and will disappear more easily; it also evaporates. However, it is an expedient that will do no harm when the can of oil suddenly runs out.

If the oil is diluted with paraffin, it produces a keener cut on the stone – as does the water. Proprietary honing oils are premium quality light oils, but in practice are of no apparent advantage over the commercial light oil already mentioned.

It is easy to get oily fingers from sharpening carving tools, and equally easy to transfer the oil to a carving. Hang a kitchen roll and a cotton rag near the benchstones. You may need to wash your hands with soap and warm water, especially if you are undertaking finishing cuts.

Care

Sharpening stones are brittle and will crack or damage easily if you drop them onto a hard surface. Keep them in boxes, bought or made, and covered when not using them (*see* Fig 3.85). Grit or dirt in the oil, which interferes with the way the blade travels on the stone surface, should always be removed. Wipe off the black slurry after using the benchstone and never let it dry on the surface as this clogs it.

Wash the stone periodically in paraffin

Fig 3.84 The oil on the stone will slowly soak through a wooden box and start leaving oil stains like this on the carving bench. This is another point in favour of having a separate sharpening area.

Fig 3.85 Keep your oilstones in a box and covered when not in use.

(kerosene), petrol or warm dilute sodium bicarbonate solution. Scrubbing with these liquids will loosen and clean a clogged stone.

A new stone soaks up oil like a sponge unless it has been previously impregnated with oil by the manufacturer. If it has not, you need to 'prime' the stone by soaking it in light oil, diluted with a little paraffin, for a few hours (or overnight) before use.

If a box to fit the benchstone is not available,

mount the stone between wooden endblocks (*see* Fig 3.86). With the endpieces of wood level with the abrasive surface, the possibility of damaging the edge of a tool by running it off the stone is eliminated. Screwed from beneath, the glued-on end pieces can be trimmed down as the stone wears and gets re-dressed.

To stop the stone, in its box or mounting board, from moving around when sharpening is underway, tap panel pins into the corners underneath and nip them

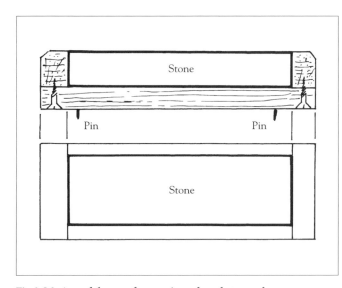

Fig 3.86 A useful way of mounting a benchstone; the nipped-off pins are shown overlength, in reality they need only protrude a small amount.

Fig 3.87 Close up of the pinched-off pin that prevents the box from moving during use.

Fig 3.88 Typically, the end of a stone will be avoided and remain flat . . .

Fig 3.89 . . . but the centre will wear down. After a while this affects sharpening and the surface then needs levelling.

off (*see* Fig 3.87). The pin stubs will project enough to anchor the board or box to the bench, however it is placed.

Dressing worn stones

It is not just metal that is removed during honing – crystals of stone are abraded as well. After a while the stone will no longer be flat and a concave shape starts interfering with sharpening. At this point the surface of the stone needs **dressing**, or flattening, once more.

You can delay the wear on the stone by sharpening evenly over the whole surface as much as possible. Even so, the stone normally erodes towards the centre as the parts nearer the edges are naturally treated with caution (*see* Figs 3.88, 3.89). Rather than using a combination stone, separate coarse and fine stones can be turned over to work on a second flat face before having a 'levelling session' for both sides. It is a

Fig 3.90 An extremely hard cast alloy block meant for dressing stones.

Fig 3.91 An old saw blade, with the handle removed and the teeth rendered flat and safe, is mounted on a wipeable manufactured board. This, together with light oil and an abrasive grit, is the simple means of flattening a benchstone.

Fig 3.92 Mix some oil and grit on the flat surface . . .

Fig 3.93 . . . rub the stone firmly backwards and forwards for a while . . .

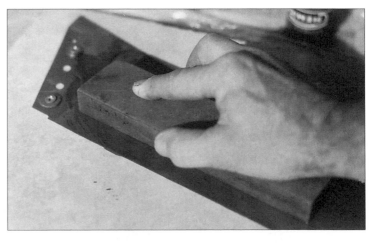

good idea to dress all sharpening stones at the same time as the procedure is a bit messy – although less time-consuming and more straightforward than is generally thought.

To level a benchstone you need:

■ Another hard, *flat* surface such as thick (plate) glass, a stone or slate slab, or a metal sheet (an old saw blade mounted on a piece of wood is suitable)(*see* Figs 3.90, 3.91).

■ An abrasive to cut the stone back such as Carborundum grit (say 400), valve-grinding paste or even fine sharp sand (using a fine grit gives a smooth finished surface to the stone).

■ An oil (one part) and paraffin (four parts) mix which will wash the particles around and maintain the cutting action of the abrasive.

■ A straight edge such as a metal ruler.

■ Newspaper and polythene to keep the table or bench clean.

Method

1 Make a slurry of the abrasive and liquid on whatever flat surface you are using (*see* Fig 3.92).

2 Set the face of the stone onto it and rub it backwards and forwards and in a circular motion (*see* Fig 3.93). Be methodical and lean your weight onto the stone a little.

3 After a while, wipe the straight edge (the metal ruler) across the surface, scraping off the sludge. You will see the extent of the worn depression in the stone

Fig 3.94 . . . and wipe with a straight metal edge. The new flat surface is seen encroaching on the hollow, sludge-filled, centre.

Fig 3.95 It does not take long before the surface of the stone is truly flat.

clearly (*see* Fig 3.94).

4 Continue rubbing the stone, reversing the grip and, if necessary, topping up the abrasive or oil. Keep checking the surface of the stone with the straight edge – eventually no depression in the middle will appear, showing the surface to be truly flat (*see* Fig 3.95).

5 Rinse the stone in fresh oil and paraffin, and it is ready for use again.

NATURAL STONES

Types

Before the days of industrially made whetstones, 'natural' stones were all that was available. These stones have some evocative names: Charnwood Forest, Shammy, Dalmore and Turkey stone. Originally they were quarried from specific rock seams, which perhaps no longer exist; today they can sometimes be found in second-hand tool shops.

The hardness and cutting quality varies between the types of stone and even within one type – depending from where in the seam of rock it was taken.

Fig 3.96 Washita stone has a characteristic mottled or granular appearance.

Two natural stones, still readily obtainable, are the Arkansas and Washita. They are available as benchstones and slipstones, are fairly consistent in quality and are much more expensive than manufactured stones. However, they are essential for honing the keen edges needed by the carver.

Arkansas and Washita stones are types of what is geologically known as 'novaculite'. Today, most of this material is quarried from limited seams in Arkansas, USA by the Smith's family business. They have quarried and prepared the stone for commercial use since 1885 – although before then it was used by the native Americans to make spear and arrow heads. Novaculite as a name derives from the Latin *novacula*, a razor, which recognizes the cutting qualities of these fine-grained stones.

Novaculite is graded according to its hardness: the softer the stone, the coarser its cut and vice versa.

The **Washita** is the softest grade, with a cut approximately equivalent to that of a fine Carborundum stone. In fact Washita has little advantage over the cheaper, artificial stone. The Washita is really a medium grade of Arkansas and has a mottled appearance (*see* Fig 3.96). It makes useful slipstones, but the soft nature makes the stone itself less

capable of holding a thin-edged shape or fine angle.

The next grade, harder than the Washita, is the **white Arkansas** which sometimes appears translucent, especially when wet (*see* Figs 3.97, 3.98). White Arkansas is a hard stone which gives a perfect cutting edge to carving tools, following on from the fine

Fig 3.97 The white Arkansas benchstone appears white when new, going grey with oiling. This one, with white mottling on grey, has been newly dressed.

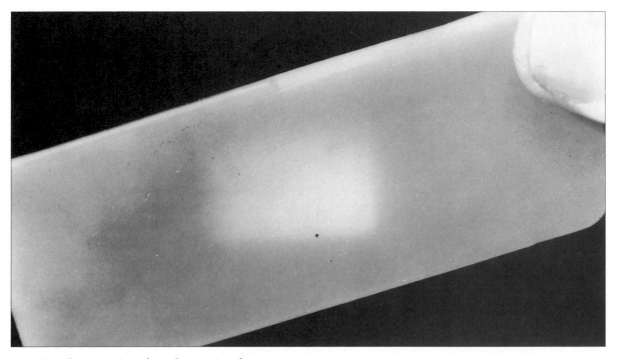

Fig 3.98 A demonstration of translucency in a fine grade of white Arkansas.

Carborundum in the sharpening process.

The hardest grade of novaculite is the **black Arkansas**, the most expensive stone and, luckily, not much use to the average woodcarver (*see* Fig 3.99). These stones cut so finely that it amounts to polishing the blade,

Fig 3.99 The black Arkansas stone, which is very.black in appearance, is too hard for general purposes.

Fig 3.100 The 'standard' boxes that are supplied with 'standard' size stones are often significantly bigger than the stones. Some slips of wood packed around the edge of the stone will keep it stationary in the box.

which carvers more usually undertake by stropping.

The cost of natural benchstones is, again, relative. A good quality one is an investment – they will never get cheaper – and a pleasure to use. Perhaps there is also a little magic in the knowledge that these stones have been wrested directly from the earth, each one unique and irreplaceable.

The stone that is most useful to the carver is the White or Translucent Arkansas. Buy it in the largest surface size possible.

Oils, care and dressing

The same advice applies to natural stones as to the artificial ones. Keep them in a box or mounted and, as they will both clog and break more easily, perhaps a little more care is needed.

OTHER STONES

Water stones

Water stones are marketed as cheaper alternatives to Novaculite-based sharpening stones, but the cost is offset by the quickness with which they wear. The

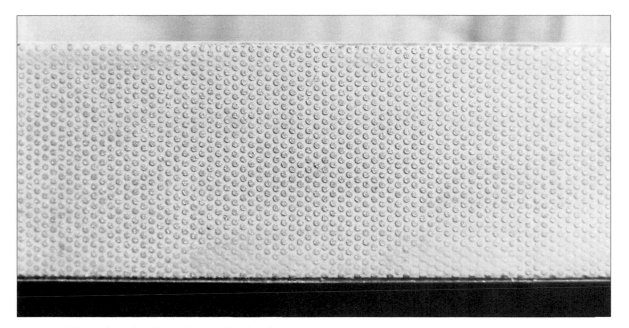

Fig 3.101 The surface of a diamond stone showing the tiny diamond micro-pellets that cut the metal of the blade being sharpened.

range of coarseness and cut is roughly the same as that which has been mentioned above, with 6000 grit being equivalent to the white Arkansas.

Slipstones are not available.

Diamond stones

Modern technology has enabled diamond-bearing micro-pellets, embedded in a polyester-based matrix, to be bonded to blocks of aluminium thus producing whetstones (*see* Fig 3.101). The diamond grit is colour-graded from black (coarse), through red and yellow, to white (the finest). For the woodcarver, the red (200 grit) and white (800 grit) are probably the most useful. At the time of writing these new products are the most expensive benchstones, but being diamond, they wear only very slowly and have an extremely long life. They are used with water, not oil, and do feel different to anyone accustomed to conventional sharpening stones.

Slipstones are not available.

Slipstones

TYPES

Slipstones (or **slips**) are the small, specifically shaped stones that work the insides of gouges and V-tools.

The word slip describes these stones well. Coming from Middle Low German, it retains the original

Fig 3.102 Larger Carborundum slipstones are useful for larger sculpture tools (from left to right): standard; conical; 'kidney'; and square slipstones.

connotations of being small and strip-like ('a slip of paper'); sliding ('slip up'); and letting loose from ('let slip'). These stones do not lie passively on the bench but are actively applied by the fingers.

Slips are available in both artificial and natural stone and in a large number of shapes and sizes (*see* Fig 3.104).

Fig 3.103 Small Carborundum slipstones (from left to right): large and small triangular; square; small and large circular slipstones.

Fig 3.104 (Below) Some slipstone shapes and profiles.

Fig 3.105 (Bottom) Arkansas (about 2½in (65mm) long)(left) and Washita (right) slipstones.

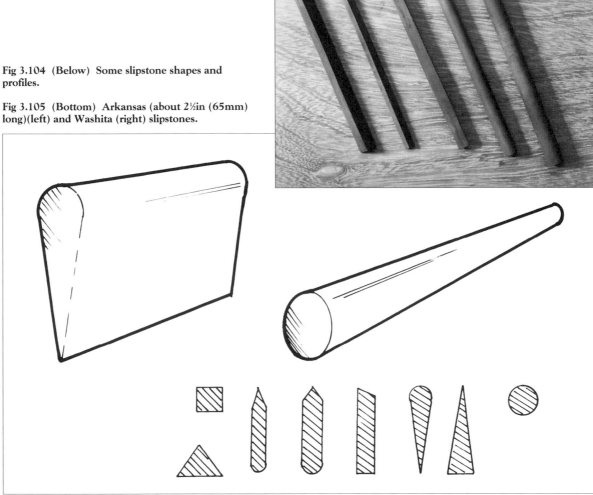

It is the edges of slipstones which are used for shaping: rounded edges (flatter or quicker) shape the inner sweeps of gouges; whereas angled edges suit the V-tool and other angled tools. Conical shapes are also very useful. It is not necessary to have large numbers of slipstones – like carving tools it is best to start with an essential few and build up numbers as they are needed, or as they become available.

A slip is worked up and down the inside of a gouge and if necessary from side to side, creating an inside bevel – a process known as 'opening the mouth'. Or they may simply be used to clean away any burr left from outside bevel sharpening.

A slip that is smaller and of quicker sweep than a particular gouge can still be used, but one that is flatter tends to dig its corners into the metal (*see* Fig 3.106). Where possible match the exact shape to the sweep of the blade, but, with dextrous use, a few slipstones can be made to go a long way. You can alter the shape of a slipstone using the grinding wheel, benchstones or even a file and sandpaper to suit a particular use. With the larger slipstones, one half can be given a rounder profile and the other a flatter one – saving on the cost of two. Leave the surface of the slips, after shaping them, as finely finished as the sides, using, for example, fine sandpaper.

A small set of Arkansas slipstones is available; this, together with a larger round-edge slip, will cover most of what is needed.

CARE

Slipstones, like benchstones, are brittle and easily damaged. They are best kept covered in a box and separate from the rest of the mess on the workbench (*see* Fig 3.109). Slips need preparing before use, keeping clean of grit and, in the same way as benchstones, occasionally reshaping.

Strops

Strop pre-dates the word 'strap' in meaning a strip of leather. It is used, impregnated with a fine abrasive, to give a final, finishing sharpness to the microscopic

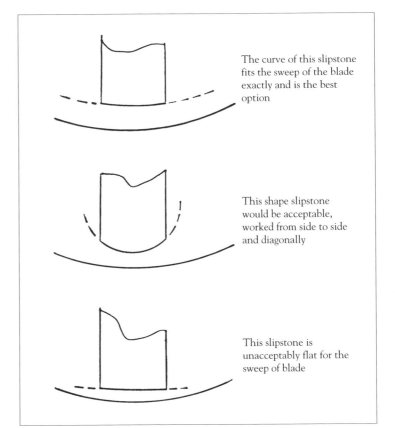

The curve of this slipstone fits the sweep of the blade exactly and is the best option

This shape slipstone would be acceptable, worked from side to side and diagonally

This slipstone is unacceptably flat for the sweep of blade

Fig 3.106 The shape of the slipstone needs to be carefully matched to that of the blade cross-section.

Fig 3.107 Slipstones can be used very delicately for specific and exact sharpening.

Fig 3.108 A very useful set of four small Arkansas slips with different profiles and (above) two triangular slipstones.

cutting edge of a carving tool while simultaneously polishing the bevel. ('Stroppy' people often exhibit an abrasive quality.)

Strops take the form of **benchstrops**, for the outside bevel, as well as **slipstrops**, for working the inside. They are very important part of the carver's kit and are used regularly to brighten up a dulling edge and maintain its sharpness.

Most strops for sale to carvers are too small. It is not difficult to make a good one.

MAKING A STROP

The strop

Strops are best made from the tight-grained, harder type of leather, used for saddles, harnesses, belts and briefcases. This is mostly vegetable-tanned cow-hide. If too *soft* a leather is used, the surface curls up as the tool passes, rounding the cutting edge – more will be said about this effect later (*see* page 186). The firmer the leather, the better. Leather may also stretch or ruck if it is too thin so a minimum thickness of ⅛in (3mm) is needed. A local saddler or hand leatherworker will normally have suitable offcuts (*see* also the Reference Section, page 348).

Fig 3.109 These small slipstones are quite brittle and easily chipped or broken. Keep them safe by some means such as a simple box.

Fig 3.110 A benchstrop with its cover tucked back and ready for use. Also shown are some dressing compounds: proprietary stropping paste (left); a tin of jeweller's rouge powder; and a block of crocus abrasive.

Fig 3.111 The benchstrop.

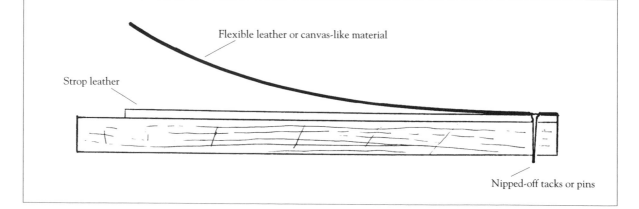

Flexible leather or canvas-like material

Strop leather

Nipped-off tacks or pins

A good size for a strop is 10–12in (250–300mm) long by 3–4in (75–100mm) wide. The leather surface should be untreated so that the pores are still available to take the abrasive. Cut back finishes that have been applied to the leather with a wire brush. Using the leather grain-side down also works.

Mounting the strop

Mount the leather on a block of wood which is a little oversize, fixing it at the top end only. Do not glue it down as a free lower edge can be bent into a slipstrop. A cover of thinner leather or canvas-like material will keep the strop dust- and grit-free when not in use. Nipped-off panel pins in the underside of the mounting board, as with the benchstones, will hold the strop on the bench.

Abrasives

The strop can be dressed with almost any very fine abrasive. Some alternatives which are suitable include:

- Crocus powder
- Carborundum powder (at least 400 grit)
- Finest emery powder
- Finest valve grinding paste
- Jewellers' rouge
- Tripoli wax
- Diamantine (aluminium oxide)
- Brasso and similar proprietary metal-polishing agents
- Proprietary strop paste.

Details of some suppliers are to be found in the Reference Section (*see* page 345)

The abrasive is held to the leather with tallow (preferably), Vaseline, lard or light oil – being very fine, these powders tend to get everywhere. Blocks of some of these abrasives, made up with wax or tallow, are available.

Tools must be wiped after stropping to prevent these greasy compounds from transferring to the wood.

Dressing the strop

1 Sprinkle some of the abrasive powder on to the leather, leaving a ½in(13mm) margin around the edges.
2 Use a finger to rub some tallow into the powder.
3 Repeat a few times by sprinkling on a little more of the powder and working in more tallow to get a uniform colour and consistency. If the abrasive comes as a paste or block, work it straight into the leather.

4 Place the strop in a warm oven or under a grill for just long enough to melt the tallow – which then soaks further into the leather – binding the abrasive to the surface better.
5 When cool, beat the strop with a large chisel or something similar, dragging the strokes *towards* you. This works the dressing in and removes surplus; keep any surplus for re-dressing.

For a while excess dressing may come off the strop and onto the gouges – these will need wiping before use. Although the strop will settle down quickly, blades still need wiping after using it and before carving. Leave a rag by the strop and always wipe *away* from the cutting edge.

CARE

Cover the strop when not in use, keeping it free from grit and dirt.

A strop is *always* used by dragging a cutting edge *towards* you so as not cut the soft leather. The technique is described in greater detail later (*see* page 169). It is easy to nick the strop with a casual, forward stroke. Gashes or nicks can usually be filled with dressing or smoothed by stropping over the area. Over a period of time, the dressing will start to work its way to the near end of the strop; reversing the orientation of the strop now and then, to strop in the opposite direction, will inhibit this effect.

If you are moving to the strop from the benchstones, do not wipe the oil from the blade but allow it to work into the strop – keeping the leather supple and fresh.

SLIPSTROPS

Slipstrops work the inner bevel of a gouge and V-tool and resemble the shapes of slipstones. There are several ways of making them:

- Fold over another smaller piece of the benchstrop leather (*see* Fig 3.112) and dress the fold in the manner described above. A piece 6 x 4in (150 x 100mm), folded on the longer edge, produces a size big enough to keep the fingers clear of the tool's cutting edge. Push the folded part in cannel where it flexes to fit the inside bevel. This type of slipstrop is particularly good for larger gouges.
- Glue *thin* leather to appropriately shaped pieces of softwood and dress the part which fits the carving tool (*see* Figs 3.113, 3.114). Profile the wood with the gouge (or V-tool) that will be stropped; create the shape by

inverting the tool and cutting along, or with, the grain. Be sure to leave enough wood for a safe grip with the fingers well clear of the passing tool edge. Such slipstrops are good for medium-sized gouges and V-tools.

■ Use hardwood in a similar way, but without the leather, and dressing the abrasive straight on to the wood.

Fig 3.112 For larger tools a piece of folded and dressed leather is the simplest. Be sure to make the leather of an adequate size to keep your fingers clear of the blade.

Fig 3.113 Slipstrops.

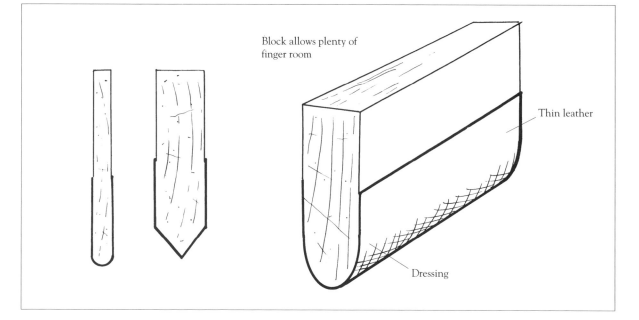

Block allows plenty of finger room

Thin leather

Dressing

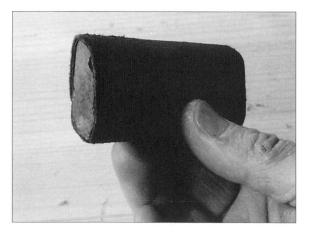

Fig 3.114 A slip of wood shaped specifically and covered with thin leather makes an excellent slipstrop.

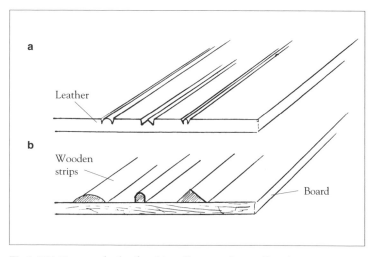

a

Leather

b

Wooden strips

Board

Fig 3.115 Two methods of making slipstrops for small tools.

For the smallest tools, a leather pad constructed like the benchstrop works well. Deeply scored lines of varying widths take the corners of a gouge as its edge is pulled along the leather (*see* Fig 3.115(a)).

Small strips of wood, without leather but dressed with abrasive, can be stuck onto a board or into a shallow box (*see* Fig 3.115(b)). Cut the necessary profiles with particular tools.

The lower edge of the main benchstrop – or a large, folded slipstrop – can be dressed with abrasive for use on the inside of small gouges.

Like slipstones, a few shapes can be made to go a long way.

Care of slipstrops is similar to that of the benchstrops. Keep them with the main strop on the bench, free from dirt or grit. Move the leather *away* from the cutting edge and re-dress notches if they occur. Again, a little oil will keep suppleness in the leather.

Summary

This is a list of the basic equipment needed by the woodcarver to sharpen and look after his or her carving tools.

Bench grinder (optional)
Coarse Carborundum benchstone
Fine Carborundum benchstone
White/translucent Arkansas benchstone
Slipstones: large round-edge slips and conical and smaller slipstones of varying shapes – matching the benchstones in composition
Benchstrop
Slipstrop
Light oil.

METHOD OF SHARPENING

Shaping and sharpening

Here is an overview of what happens when you sharpen a carving tool. It is helpful to conceive of a preliminary stage of *shaping*, before the sharpening of a carving tool proper.

The overall contours and profile of the blade are formed using the grinding wheel and the coarse benchstone and slipstones.

Edges are squared-off and the corners made true.
Inside and outside bevels are set.
The line of light is inspected and adjustments made to get it neat and even; it should be thinned to about the thickness of a Biro line at this stage.

After preparatory shaping comes the actual *sharpening*. Slipstones for the inner bevel, and benchstones for the outer one, gradually thin the visible edge while maintaining a flat bevel, a straight edge and so on. The white line attenuates to a hair's thickness, then disappears altogether. If the honing has been true and even, the whole line disappears at the same time. If not, a little more specific honing will remove any white specks or areas.

If you end up with a poorly shaped edge – through over-enthusiasm or inattention – it must be levelled off square again. Present the tool dead upright to the Arkansas stone and gently draw it over the surface a few times. The amount of white line and the state of the bevel then dictates the next stage: what coarseness of benchstone or slipstone is needed to resume sharpening.

When the white line has disappeared it might be thought that the tool is sharp. However, pushing the cutting edge into a piece of scrap wood may cause the line of light to reappear in whole or part. This is because a **wire edge** (or **burr**) – a feathering of the metal – occurs where the sharpening of the inner and outer bevels meet and hides the white line. Pushing the cutting edge into the scrap wood removes the wire edge at the same time as toughening up the metal and revealing the white line. A few more strokes of careful honing will eliminate the white line. Once more the edge is pushed into the wood, and touched up on the fine stones again if the line returns.

When the white light does not reappear, try cutting *across* the grain of another piece of wood, such as a good quality softwood. The cut surface should be polished and without scratch marks. If scratches occur, a slipstone can be applied to the corresponding tell-tale spot of light with a final touch up on the benchstone. Try the cut again. When a clean, sharp cut has been satisfactorily made, the bevel and edge can be slicked up on the strop.

Cutting profiles

Although there seems a large variety of woodcarving-tool shapes, there are in fact only *two* general profiles across the cutting edge: flat and curved – with a few combinations. Carving tools divide into these profiles in the following ways.

Flat profiles

- Firmer chisels
- Skew chisels
- V-tools (macaroni tools)

Curved profiles

- Straight gouges
- Fishtail and tapered gouges
- Long bent gouges
- Short bent gouges
- Back bent gouges

Combinations

- Deep gouges (nos 10 and 11).

Different approaches, but using the basic procedures outlined above, will master these different profiles.

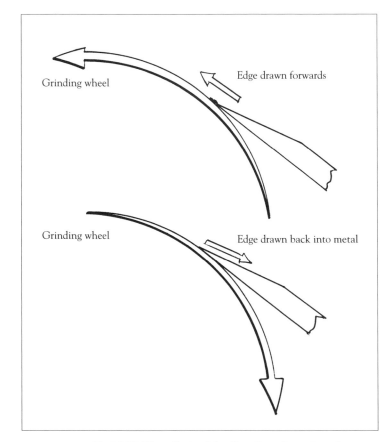

Fig 3.116 The effects of the direction of rotation of a grinding wheel on the feather edge.

The following sections deal with how to use the various pieces of equipment to work these profiles correctly; the specific needs of individual tools then follow.

Basic procedures

Carvers differ in the way they use grinding wheels, benchstones and so on; they differ also in what final shapes and bevel angle they want. Beginners too will eventually develop their own preferences. The methods given here work successfully and are consistent with all that has previously been said regarding cutting profiles and angles.

GRINDING

Grinding wheels shape the carving tools initially: setting the bevel and edge. They may also repair broken or damaged edges.

The grinding wheel should turn *towards* the operator. This is a debatable point as it is sometimes recommended that the wheel should turn *away* from the operator. The reasons for recommending a direction of rotation towards the operator need to be given, as different directions of the wheel have differing effects on the tool (*see* Fig 3.116).

With the wheel turning *towards* the user, metal is peeled back from the edge and towards the handle, leaving a small burr and a strong edge. A wheel turning in the opposite direction tends to draw the metal forward, producing more burr – which tends to crumble off – and an edge which is less strong. The difference can be seen by comparing edges after pushing them into a piece of wood; this removes the metal feathering and allows the stronger metal underneath to be seen.

A second point is that the surface of the wheel rotating towards the user bites into the metal more effectively than one turning away, which tends to bounce the tool more and give a less efficient cut. Wheels rotating away from the user may feel safer because, certainly, the edge cannot 'dig in' – but the correct presentation of the blade to the wheel never causes this result.

Whichever way the wheel rotates, a carving tool can be presented to it in several ways (*see* Fig 3.117).

♦ **Perpendicular to the cutting surface of the wheel.**

Tools are presented in this way (*see* Fig 3.118) as part of the preliminary shaping – straightening or flattening the cutting edge from corner to corner. Be gentle and

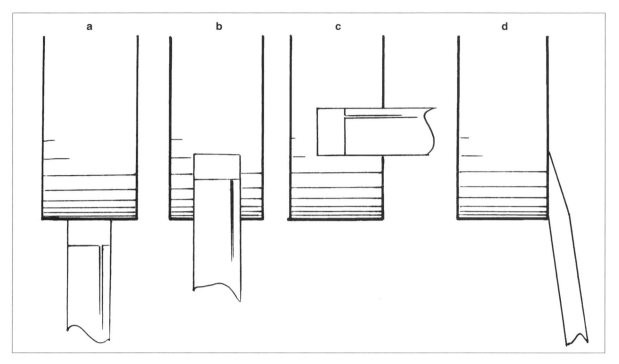

Fig 3.117 Four ways of presenting a carving tool to the grinder: (a) perpendicular to the rotating wheel; (b) in line with the rotation; (c) square on to the rotation; and (d) to the side of the wheel.

Fig 3.118 Perpendicular presentation. (For clarity the grinder's perspex guards are swung up.)

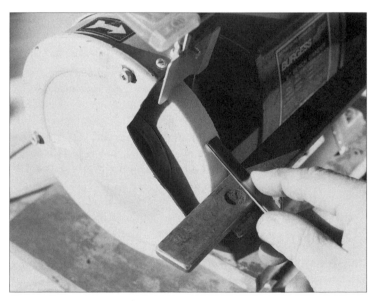

Fig 3.119 In-line presentation.

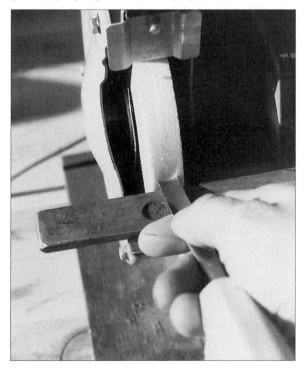

precise. Use the whole surface of the wheel where possible and the tool rests. Always wear eye protection.

◆ **In line with the rotation of the wheel.**

When a tool is offered in line with the grinding wheel (*see* Fig 3.119), the bevel tends to pick up the circular shape of the wheel, producing the 'hollow grind' mentioned earlier. The smaller the wheel, the more

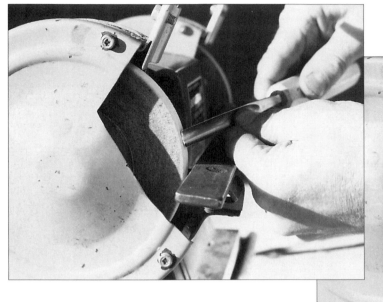

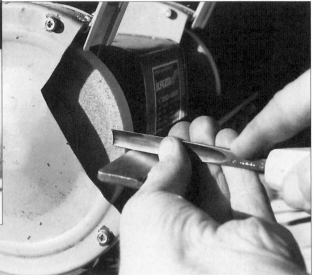

Fig 3.120 Square-on presentation.

Fig 3.121 Touching the carving tool to the side of the grinding wheel.

hollow the bevel. This hollowness can be removed on the benchstone.

◆ **Square-on to the rotation.**

Offering the gouge square-on (at right angles) to the wheel (*see* Fig 3.120) and rotating it from corner to corner – while keeping the same angle of presentation – will produce a flat bevel. This operation involves holding the tool in your hands and steadying your hands in turn on the grinder's tool rest. It is not a difficult technique and if a firm but gentle approach is taken, it is quite safe.

◆ **Touched to the side of the wheel.**

The quickest method of grinding flat bevels onto a gouge or chisel is to start in the normal (in line) presentation to the wheel and remove most of the unwanted metal from the bevel. Then make a final few passes with the tool presented square-on, removing any hollowness. You must rotate a gouge across the *whole* of its bevel surface, whatever the orientation to the wheel. Aim to grind smoothly with any rotating coming from your wrist at the handle; try to produce a clean bevel with no facets.

For a chisel or V-tool, flatten the bevel by touching it carefully and gently to the side of the wheel, using the grinder's tool rest (*see* Fig 3.121). Look at the scratch marks on the bevel and let them guide your positioning of the tool.

Even with a grinder removing metal quickly, impatience may still lead to two unwanted consequences:

■ *Over-heating.* With a fast dry wheel, check the temperature of the blade frequently and *never allow it to rise above hand warm.* This means a pattern of short bursts of light grinding between dipping the blade in cold water.

■ *Over-grinding.* The same regular approach will help prevent over-grinding – a pitfall to be aware of from the beginning. Try not to take too much metal off at a time, but work evenly. Take the white line of light at the edge continuously as your guide. Keep looking at its thickness and the scratch marks on the bevel to be sure of exactly where, and how much, metal you are removing. Bear in mind the shape you are aiming at. If the edge loses its shape, you may need to level it off by presenting the tool perpendicularly and starting the process again.

Method

1 Start by setting the cutting edge, from corner to corner, at right angles to the longitudinal axis. Smooth and clean up this straight edge right at the start on the Arkansas stone.

2 For gouges, set the outside bevel by grinding in line

Fig 3.122 After the edge has been straightened, set the bevel of the gouge on the grinding wheel by smoothly rotating it at the correct angle from corner to corner. Keep checking the result. (For clarity the grinder's perspex guards are swung up.)

with the wheel, rocking the gouge from corner to corner (*see* Fig 3.122) and making a uniform line of light with the heel and edge parallel. Finish at right angles to the wheel – flattening the bevel (*see* Fig 3.123).

3 For large gouges: small grinding wheels in drills or flexible shafts can create an inner bevel quickly, although coarse slipstones are more often used. The white line will thin down – keep it even and uniform.

4 For flat chisels: the grinder's tool rests can be used to help set the bevel equally on both sides. Move the tool from side to side, covering the whole stone evenly. If you do not want to use the side of the grinding wheel (or even

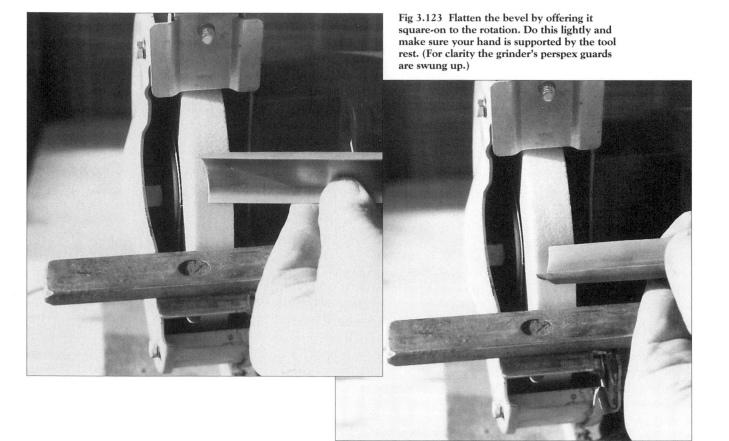

Fig 3.123 Flatten the bevel by offering it square-on to the rotation. Do this lightly and make sure your hand is supported by the tool rest. (For clarity the grinder's perspex guards are swung up.)

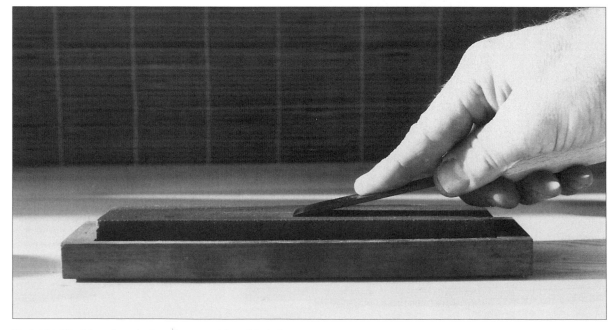

Fig 3.124 Working *along* the benchstone with a chisel; the stone is orientated on the bench end-on to the user.

to grind square-on) to flatten the bevel, use the coarse benchstone.

5 The tool should now be ready for the benchstones.

STONING (HONING)

The two basic carving-tool profiles, curved and flat, are presented differently to the benchstones for sharpening.

■ Flat chisels are presented in line (end-on) with the stone (*see* Fig 3.124).
■ Gouges are presented at right angles (square-on) to the stone (*see* Fig 3.125).

Because of this differing orientation, mount the benchstones so that they can be turned around. Do not fix them permanently in position on the bench with cleats.

   The following procedures to get a straight edge from corner to corner of your tools apply to all types of benchstone, which should be oiled first.

   For both chisels and gouges, hold the blade perpendicular – like a pencil – to the coarse stone and drag it across the surface a few times (*see* Fig 3.126). This is a more exact alternative to the grinding wheel. In both cases, finish off the straight edge on the

Fig 3.125 Working *across* the benchstone; the stone is orientated on the bench square-on to the user.

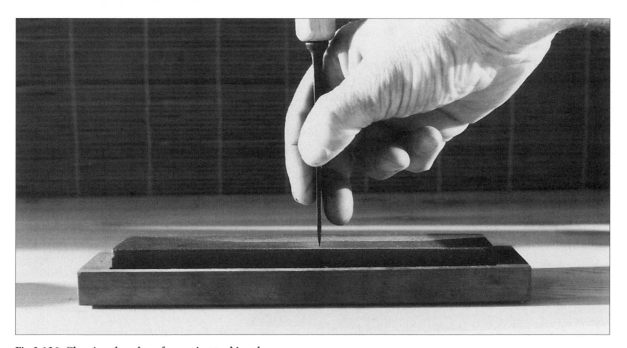

Fig 3.126 Cleaning the edge of a carving tool involves offering it in a perpendicular position and pulling it along a flat benchstone. This is necessary each time you move to a finer stone, refining the edge from the coarser grit of the previous one.

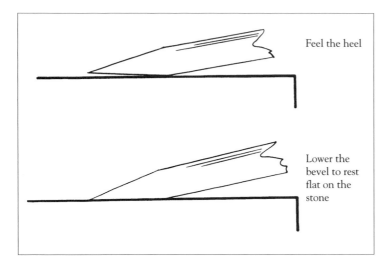

Feel the heel

Lower the bevel to rest flat on the stone

Fig 3.127 How to get a sense of the bevel resting flat on the surface of the benchstone.

Arkansas stone as this produces a strong, smooth, clean edge with which to start.

At any point, when a cutting edge has become unacceptably wavy – or the corners lost – you can reinstate a fresh white line using this procedure. Try not to do this too often as it is wasteful of material. Perhaps only one pass on the Arkansas stone is needed to produce a clean edge from which to re-sharpen.

All other ways of holding the carving tool for sharpening involve the correct use of the *whole* body.

This is important to achieve the right effect. Carving tools are sharpened from the hips not the elbows.

Method – chisels

1 Position the stone on the bench so that its end points away from you (i.e. end-on).

2 If you are right-handed, hold the chisel handle in the right hand with the first two fingers of the left hand on the back of the blade, a little behind the bevel. Vice versa for the left-handed.

3 Place the chisel heel on the near end of the stone. Try to get a sense of the heel resting on the surface (*see* Fig 3.127). Keep your elbows by your sides.

4 Raise the handle until the bevel lies flat on the stone, and then a little more to bring in the actual edge. By raising and lowering the handle a fractionally, learn to feel when the bevel lies truly flat on the surface.

5 Move the chisel forwards and backwards along the benchstone, maintaining the angle at which the tool is presented consistently and keeping the bevel flat. To do this keep your elbows by your sides and rock your whole body backwards and forwards from relaxed knees. You will need one foot in front of the other a little. If you keep your body still and just push the blade backwards and forwards with your arms, there is a strong tendency to raise and lower the handle, rounding the bevel (*see* Fig 3.128). This is called 'rolling the edge'. Keeping the bevel flat requires this whole-body approach.

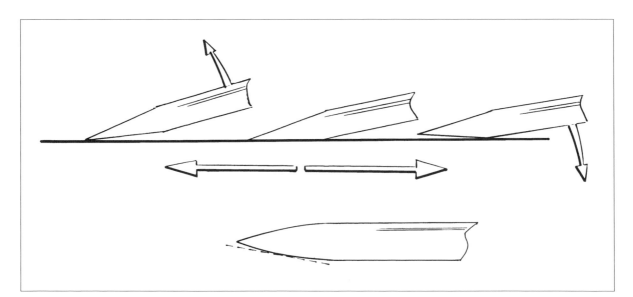

Fig 3.128 Lowering and raising the handle rolls (or rounds) the bevel.

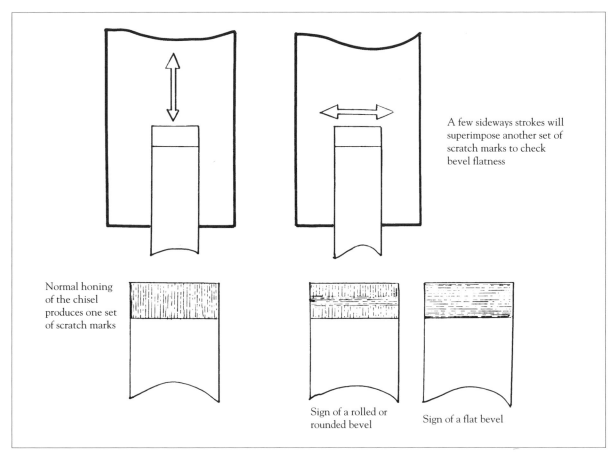

A few sideways strokes will superimpose another set of scratch marks to check bevel flatness

Normal honing of the chisel produces one set of scratch marks

Sign of a rolled or rounded bevel

Sign of a flat bevel

Fig 3.129 Use the appearance of the bevel to monitor the flatness of the bevel.

6 Use the whole of the stone's surface, but keep clear of the very edge. Be careful not to pull the chisel off the stone on the back stroke as this inevitably damages the edge.

7 After a little while turn the chisel onto the opposite side and repeat the action. Counting the number of strokes on each side can help you keep the two bevels equal. Maintain a patient, steady rhythm. Watch the amount of oil on the stone as the edge tends to push it off.

8 Always look at the white line of light, keeping it uniform with sensitive adjustments to the point of contact between stone and metal. Do not raise the handle to make the line of light disappear more quickly. If the line is thicker on one side, try not so much to tilt the tool as to mentally think of more pressure to the other side of the blade.

9 Occasionally, still keeping the bevel flat, make a short, sideways stroke *across* the stone rather than along it. Examine the scratch marks on the surface of

the bevel (*see* Fig 3.129). If the bevel has been rounded, a new mark will appear as a line across the middle. If the bevel is flat, the new mark will extend from edge to heel.

10 Working through the stones in this way and using the white line and bevel scratches, you can maintain an even, flat reduction of the metal to an edge which finally disappears.

Method – gouges

1 Position the benchstone so that its side is facing you (i.e. side-on).

2 Taking a medium sweep (no. 6) gouge as an example: if you are right-handed, hold the handle in the right hand with the first two fingers of the left hand in the cannel or mouth of the blade – about a finger joint back from the edge. Vice versa for the left-handed.

3 Place the heel of the outside bevel in the centre of

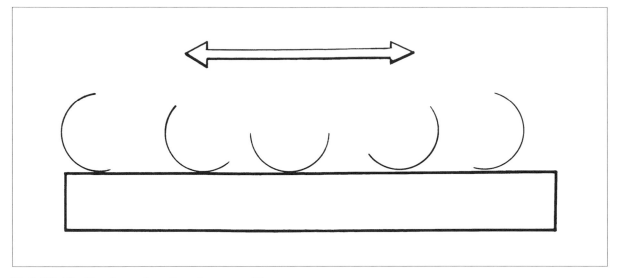

Fig 3.130 The direction and rotation of a gouge while being sharpened on a benchstone.

the stone. Keep your elbows by your sides.

4 Start by getting a feel for how the flat bevel rests on the surface of the stone. Raise the handle until the bevel lies flat on the benchstone, and then a little more onto the actual edge. By raising and lowering the handle a little, learn to feel when the bevel lies truly flat on the surface. With a little practice you can go straight to resting the bevel flat on the stone.

5 Start on the left of the oilstone with the gouge turned onto its right corner. The mouth of the gouge will be pointing towards the centre of the stone.

6 The gouge must now move to the opposite end of the benchstone. In doing so, you must also rotate the blade so that it comes to rest on its *opposite* corner, with the mouth pointing once more towards the centre. This is one sharpening stroke.

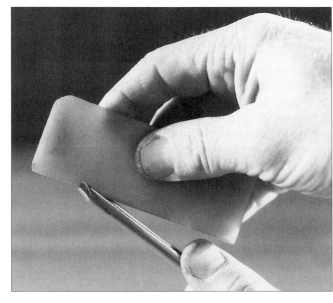

Fig 3.131 Slipstones are used in a partnership with benchstones, rubbing backwards . . .

Fig 3.132 . . . and forwards while maintaining the same angle to the blade.

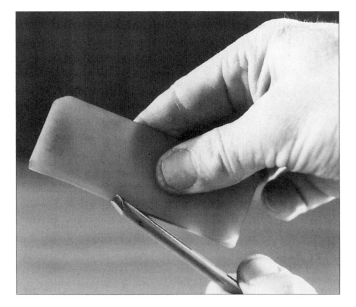

7 Without lifting the gouge from the surface, reverse the movement so the gouge comes to rest on its right corner, over on the left of the stone once more (*see* Fig 3.130). This completes a cycle of two strokes. Notice that the direction of rotation goes *against* the direction of travel, efficiently biting the metal into the stone.

8 The gouge is rocked like this, from one end of the benchstone to the other and back again, in regular even strokes. Use the whole cutting surface, but avoid both a figure-of-eight pattern – which rounds over the bevel – and the very edge of the stone.

9 Present the bevel *flat* all the time. To accomplish this keep the elbows in, rotating the tool handle from the wrist and forearm. Shift the weight of the body from one leg to the other, keeping your back upright and your knees relaxed and slightly bent. This posture has something of the judo stance and balance about it, and should feel comfortable and unforced. If you work from the elbows only, the bevel will invariably become 'rolled' or rounded.

This is the basic technique for gouges, to which some extra points need to be added.

■ Use the slipstones with the benchstones to work the inner bevel or remove the wire edge (*see* page 157). In the sharpening process, the honing of the edge alternates between benchstones and slips (*see* Figs 3.131, 3.132). Slipstones are quite often used first, where an inner bevel is required.

■ Regularly check the state of the white line. If it becomes thicker in one part compared with another, limit the rotation of the blade for a few strokes and work more specifically on the thicker part. Conversely, if some part of the white line becomes unduly thinner, avoid honing that part of the edge. This may mean you have to divide your honing into two separate strokes – lifting the gouge to avoid the thin part in the middle – until the white line is returned to a uniform thickness.

■ To sharpen the whole bevel, the corners must be included, but *it is very easy to over-rotate the handle and sharpen them away* (*see* Fig 3.133). Extra care must be taken with the corners at the end of the stroke so the gouge is rotated neither too much, nor too little. Additionally, all the finger pressure on the gouge tends to lie on the corners at the turn between strokes so pressure needs to be eased a little at this point.

■ The amount of rotation that a gouge needs depends on its sweep – the amount of curve it has. Flat gouges require only a slight turn at the wrist; quicker gouges a lot more. If the wrist action becomes uncomfortable,

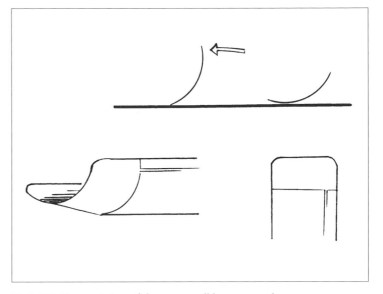

Fig 3.133 Over-rotation of the gouge will hone away the corners.

you may have to hone the edges of the quickest gouges in sectors which you then carefully merge. With flexible wrists this is not normally necessary up to the semi-circular (no. 9) gouges, but the U-shaped gouges can be more of a problem. They are best dealt with as a combination of flat and curved bevels – details will be given in the section on individual tools (*see* page 173).

■ By constantly monitoring the line of light at the edge, and adjusting which parts of the bevel are being honed, a straight, even contour will result. As with the chisels, it is a good idea to make a short stroke with the gouge moving at 90° to the normal direction. The subsequent scratch mark will show you whether the bevel has become rounded or remained flat. As the grade becomes finer, changes in the abrasive marks on the bevel can also be used to monitor how the bevel is presented.

Some carvers sharpen their gouges by rubbing the bevels on a benchstone in the same direction as that described for the chisel above. As the gouge is moved backwards and forwards it is rotated from one side to the other, often in a figure-of-eight pattern. I have always found it difficult with this method either to produce a straight edge with corners, or a flat bevel; it also wears the stone in the centre more quickly.

SLIPSTONING

As a general rule, use the same type of stone on one side of the edge as on the other. So when working the outside bevel on the coarse Carborundum benchstone,

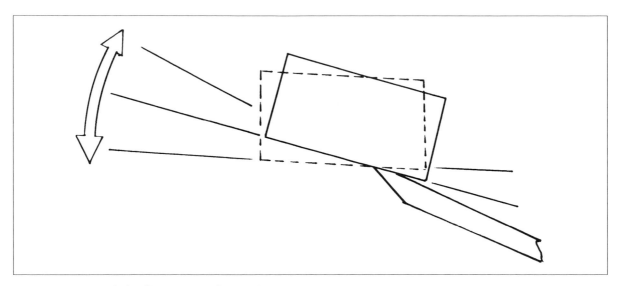

Fig 3.134 Do not rock the slipstone up or down as it is moved backwards and forwards.

use a coarse Carborundum slipstone on the inside – matching grade to grade as the abrasive stones get finer.

Match the curves and angles of the slipstones to the curves and angles of the tools as closely as possible. Bear in mind that you can change slipstone shapes and use some smaller slips on larger tools.

Method

1 Putting an inner bevel to a medium gouge as an example, rest the round back of the blade on the edge of the bench with about 1in (25mm) projecting upwards and at an angle of about 45° away from you.

2 Using some oil – which can be taken up from the benchstone – place the slip into the mouth of the gouge. Hold it between your fingers and thumb at a shallow angle. *Make sure your fingers clear the sharp corners of the blade.* A right-handed person would normally hold the slip in his or her right hand.

3 With firm pressure, rub the stone backwards and forwards; if appropriate, work from side to side and

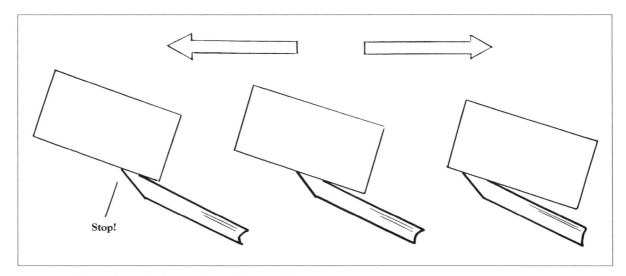

Stop!

Fig 3.135 When pushing the slipstone forward be careful not to come off the edge – leave something like one-third in cannel.

diagonally as well. Keep the angle of the inner bevel flat by not rocking the slip up or down (*see* Fig 3.134). Work evenly across the edge and include the corners but be careful not to over-sharpen them.

4 Do not let more than one-half to two-thirds of the slipstone project from the blade. To put this another way, always keep a substantial amount of the slipstone in cannel (*see* Fig 3.135). This means working in short, rapid strokes. If the slipstone projects more than this, there is a danger of it coming off the blade completely. Almost invariably, the sharpening hand starts a return stoke – only to strike the sharp cutting edge of the tool with the slipstone, or your fingers.

5 Work in conjunction with the benchstone: drawing the inner bevel back with the slipstone; cleaning and working with the benchstone; returning to the slip, and so on. The line of light on the cutting edge is, as always, the guide to where the slip needs to be applied.

An alternative is to rest the gouge in one of your hands and not against the bench. For a right-handed person, the gouge would be held in the left. Allow the hand holding the handle of the gouge to relax so that the round back of the blade nestles in the angle between the thumb and first finger – this hand is supported by holding the elbow into the body. Work the slipstone with the other. This method is more suited to smaller tools and the final, more delicate stages of slipstoning. The work can be held a little closer to the eye.

Another approach that suits some carvers is to fix the movement of the stone and rub the gouge over it – rather than the more usual reverse situation. This method is not recommended as visibility of the edge is not so good.

STROPPING

Method – chisels

1 Line up the benchstrop end-on, supporting the near edge with the fingers (of the left hand for a right-handed person).

2 The strop is *always* used with the blade being drawn *towards* the user – the edge dragging so as not to cut the leather.

3 Hold the chisel around the shank with the right hand. The first two fingers extend along the metal but keep back from the cutting edge roughly the distance of a finger joint.

4 *Place* the bevel flat on the furthest part of the leather and, with firm pressure, draw the tool along the strop towards you (*see* Fig 3.136). Try to maintain the angle and work on the *bevel*, not the edge as that will will take care of itself.

5 At the end of this stroke *lift the chisel clear* and place the bevel flat on the strop at the far end again. Draw the blade towards you for a second stroke.

6 This action is repeated a few times on one side of the chisel, then the chisel is turned over for an equal number of strokes on the other side. You can strop the

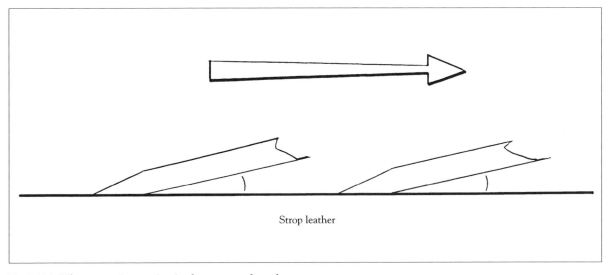

Fig 3.136 When stropping, maintain the same angle and always *drag* the edge to avoid cutting the leather.

Fig 3.137 Using the benchstrop involves rotating the gouge as it passes along the leather while keeping the bevel consistently flat on its surface.

tool quite vigorously, in which case it makes a slapping sound on the strop as it is placed for each stroke.

Method – gouges

1 With the strop end-on, hold the gouge like the chisel, with the extended fingers in cannel.

2 Start at the far end of the strop with the gouge turned onto one corner. Draw the blade towards you with firm pressure at the same time as rotating the wrist to rock the gouge onto its other corner (*see* Figs 3.137, 3.138). The gouge arrives at the near end of the strop facing the opposite way. Keep the bevel flat by maintaining the angle of presentation.

3 *Lift the gouge clear of the leather*, and return it to the far end for a second stroke. This time place the gouge on the *opposite* corner and repeat the rotating stroke –

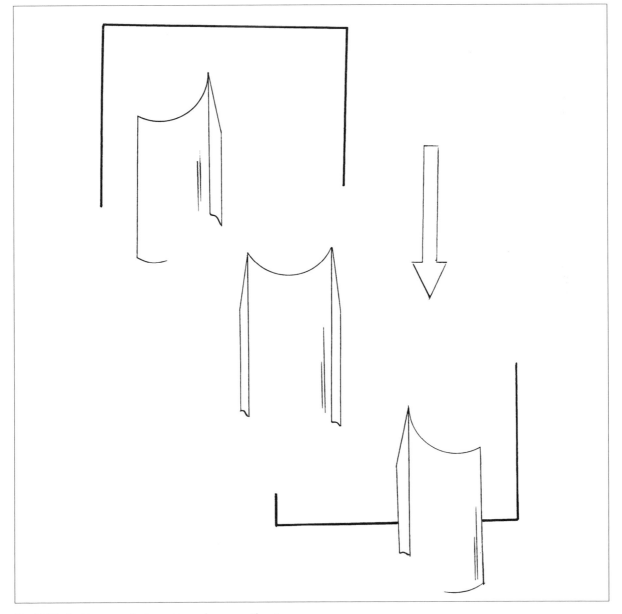

Fig 3.138 As the gouge is drawn towards you on the strop, it must be rotated to cover the full surface of the bevel. Change direction of rotation with alternate strokes.

Fig 3.139 The hand that steadies the strop must be kept out of the way of the returning cutting edge.

this completes a cycle.

4 Repeat the cycle several times. Do not land heavily on the corners.

5 After a few cycles of stropping use the slipstrop on the inside.

6 Only a few passes are needed to maintain the edge; stropping can be quite a brief business.

Safety

There are two dangers in using the benchstrop.

Cutting the leather

Running the tool into the strop is avoided by making

sure the blade is lifted clear of the leather surface on the return strokes. Develop a habitual action that automatically ensures this.

Cutting your hand

The danger is cutting the hand that is steadying the strop – the thumb, especially, can be caught by a negligent, forward stroke of the carving tool returning through the air (*see* Fig 3.139). The edge is now extremely sharp and this danger must be taken seriously.

The strop needs *some* steadying as it tends to be pulled towards you as you use it. Pins beneath the mounting board (described in the section on making a strop, *see* page 155) will largely anchor it, and only a light touch of the hand will be needed to steady it. This steadying hand *must be positioned to the side of the working area out of the path of the blade entirely*. The position can be to one side, at either end of the strop.

By experimenting with the safest yet most relaxed hand position – and by being mindful of the movement of the tool – the danger of cutting yourself can be eliminated.

SLIPSTROPPING

1 Position the gouge or **V**-tool as when using slipstones.

2 Again, the slipstrop must move *away* from the cutting edge. Place it on the inside bevel and push it forward with firm pressure into the air and beyond the edge (*see* Figs 3.140, 3.141).

3 Return the slipstrop *clear of the cutting edge* and position it for a second, forward stroke.

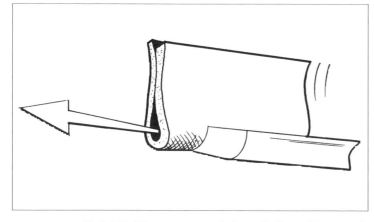

Fig 3.140 Slipstrops must only be pushed *out* of the cannel in order to avoid cutting the leather.

Fig 3.141 The leather slipstrop will deform to fit the sweep of the gouge as it is pushed forwards.

As with slipstones, be aware of the fingers and the very sharp cutting edge.

Individual tools in detail

These notes should be read in the context of what has been said previously about:

■ The shapes and profiles that carving tools need
■ The use of the shaping and sharpening equipment.

Study and refer to this information first. I have tried to avoid repetition as much as possible but, for the sake of clarity, some is unavoidable.

With accurate grinding it is possible to go straight up the scale to the finer stones and save time. The skill of knowing which stones to use, and when, comes with practice.

Decide first on your bevel angle. As a guide, an overall angle (including an inside bevel) of 20–25° is a useful, average one. In practical terms, a length of bevel between two and a half and three times the thickness of the blade would be approximately right.

■ Without an inside bevel: all the angle is taken on the outside.
■ With an inside bevel: make the inner bevel between one-quarter, to one-third, the length of the outer bevel.
■ With a chisel: the angle of bevel is divided equally between both sides.

It may be helpful in the beginning to make a wooden template of what the sharpening angle looks like in order to get some feel for it. In practice, no experienced carver estimates these angles to accurate degrees; it is done more by the feel and whether the tool cuts as they want.

FLAT CHISELS

1 Grind the edge square and establish the corners. The coarse benchstone may be preferred, especially for finer tools. The white line of light should be unbroken along the whole length of the edge.

2 Make one or two perpendicular passes on the oiled Arkansas stone to clean and refine the white line.

3 Grind the bevel flat to the required angle on both sides of the chisel, with the heel parallel to the cutting edge. The edge should be in the centre of the blade. Make the white line an even ½in (1mm) thick at this stage. Use the side of the grinding wheel to remove any hollowness in the bevel, or leave until the next step.

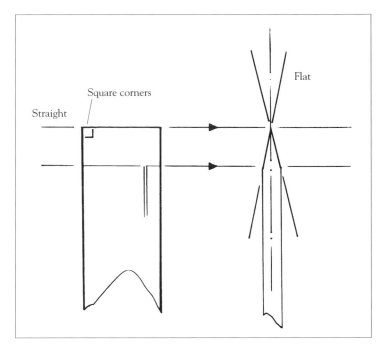

Fig 3.142 Features of a correctly sharpened flat chisel.

4 Set the oilstone end-on, present the bevel flat and hone both sides. Repeat equally on both sides, regularly checking the white line and bevel scratches.

5 When the line of light becomes hair thickness, push the edge into a piece of clean scrap wood to remove any burr. A little more work may then be necessary on the coarse stone to return the line to uniformly hair thin.

6 Set the Arkansas stone end-on and proceed in the same way. After every 10 strokes on each side push the blade into scrap wood to emphasize the line of light and strengthen the edge. As the line thins, push the edge into the wood every five, then every couple of strokes. Do not raise the handle to make the line disappear quicker, but proceed patiently.

7 When the line is no longer visible, and not reappearing when the edge is pushed into the wood, try carving across the grain of a piece of softwood. Look to see if the line returns or if there are scratch marks on the cut surface and touch up the edge appropriately on the Arkansas stone.

8 Once a polished clean cut has been produced, strop both sides equally and wipe the blade carefully.

SKEW CHISELS

1 Grind the skew angle first: 40–45° for general use, around 30° for more delicate use. Present the blade to

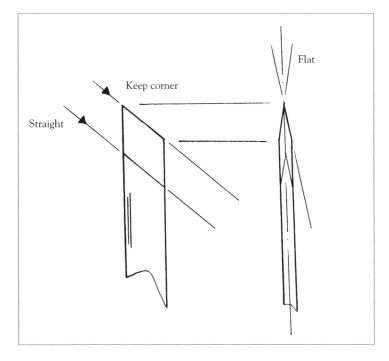

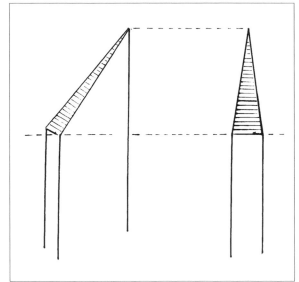

Fig 3.143 Features of a correctly sharpened skew chisel.

Fig 3.144 The initial setting of the skew chisel angle makes it looked wedge-shaped.

the wheel so as to keep a straight line along the edge. This grinding will make the edge look wedge-shaped, narrowing to the long point (*see* Fig 3.144).

2 Make one or two perpendicular passes of the edge on the Arkansas stone to clean and refine the white line.

3 Grind the bevel flat, with the heel parallel to the cutting edge. To do this, position the handle at a

Fig 3.145 When the cutting edge of the skew is moved across the stone, the handle must be angled over the side. (For clarity the oil is not shown.)

corresponding angle to the side of the wheel. Work more on the thicker end of the wedge and remember that *the point can be over-heated very easily.* Keep the cutting edge in the centre of the metal.

4 The skew is offered to the benchstones so that the edge orientates in the same way as the edge of a firmer chisel – across the width of the benchstone. The handle angles out over the side of the stone: to one side for one bevel; the opposite for the other.

5 Hone the skew in the same way as a firmer chisel: two fingers exerting gentle pressure on the blade, and working on both sides uniformly. Keep an eye on the white line and avoid over-sharpening the long point – so removing the most important part of the tool. Test the white line in scrap wood.

6 Strop by holding and moving the skew as if it were a firmer chisel, and carefully wipe the blade. Test the edge by slicing across the grain of a piece of softwood.

V-TOOLS

Consider the **V**- or parting tool as two flat chisels, joining to form a cutting angle. As such they should present no more trouble than the chisels themselves. However, the angle needs special treatment as it is a thicker piece of metal. Most problems in sharpening these tools arise from improper shaping at the grinding stage, or inaccurate application of the slipstones.

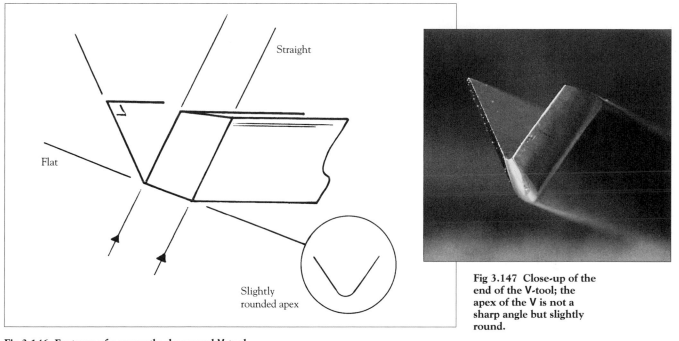

Straight

Flat

Slightly
rounded apex

Fig 3.146 Features of a correctly sharpened V-tool.

Fig 3.147 Close-up of the
end of the V-tool; the
apex of the V is not a
sharp angle but slightly
round.

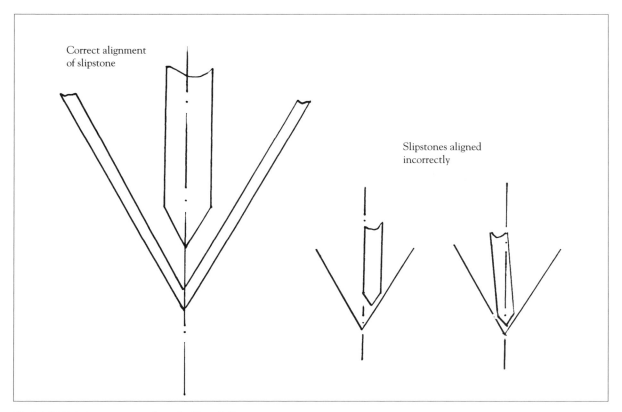

Correct alignment
of slipstone

Slipstones aligned
incorrectly

Fig 3.148 It is important to align the V-tool slipstone
exactly with the apex when working the angle; it is easy to
rub to one side and notch the edge.

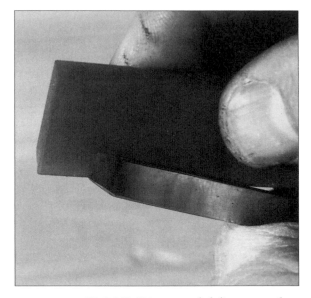

Fig 3.149 Using an angled slipstone on the inside of the V-tool.

Fig 3.150 The three different V-tool angles will need corresponding angles on the slipstones.

As has been mentioned before, the **V** apex between the sides is not actually a sharp angle but *slightly rounded*, both inside and out (*see* Fig 3.147). This is not particularly noticeable, unless the groove cut by the **V**-tool is examined closely, but the rounding over allows the tool to negotiate corners more easily. The keel itself remains straight. It is crucial that the cutting apex and edges of the **V**-tool, the parts which leave the finished cut, are properly sharp otherwise a ragged cut is inevitable. Keep the corners as they are used in deeper cuts sometimes.

Specially shaped, angle-edged slipstones are used

to clean off the wire edge and for working any inner bevel into the angle itself. Only a small inside bevel is needed, working it back every time the tool needs touching up. The slipstone must fit *exactly* into the corner. It is easy to work the slip more to one side of the angle than in the centre which creates a notch (*see* Fig 3.148).

If the sides of the **V**-tool are of uneven thickness, or the cannel is not lined up truly, matching the bevels on either side can be difficult. If it is found that equal matching is impossible, but the bevels are flat and the cutting edges straight, the tool should still be usable.

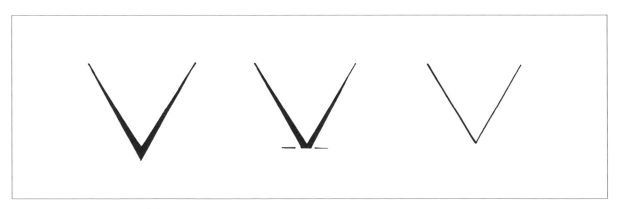

Fig 3.151 When the angle of the keel has been set, the angle of the V-tool will look cut-off. The next step is to remove metal as the bevel is set, reducing the edge to a uniform thinness.

Fig 3.152 Treat one side of the V-tool like a chisel . . .

Fig 3.153 . . . then the other. (For clarity the oil is not shown.)

1 Grind the edges square, with the V-tool perpendicular to the grinding wheel. If the tool was supplied nosed, the edges will now look like two wedges, thickening to the angle.

2 Make one or two perpendicular passes on the Arkansas stone to clean and refine the white line.

3 Set the keel angle by presenting the tool across the wheel; an average angle would be about 20°. Reduce the thickness of the white line at the apex to about ⅟₁₆in (2mm). The outside corner of the angle will look cut off (*see* Fig 3.151).

4 Set the bevel angles on the wheel, treating each side of the tool in turn like a chisel and rendering the white lines to a thickness of the about ⅟₃₂in (1mm). The heel should be parallel with the cutting edges and the V apex aligned dead in the centre. End-on, the angle will still look slightly cut off.

5 Position the benchstones as for the flat chisel and use angled slipstones for the inside. Start reducing the thickness of the edge with the Carborundum, then the Arkansas, stone. There is always a tendency to over-sharpen the corners as they are thinner than the central parts. If the line thins at any point, slightly turn the wrist to exert a little more pressure on the thicker part of the edge and away from the thinner part. Take great care to keep the bevels flat, and check the white line and bevel scratches to make decisions as to exactly how the tool should present to the stone. Push the edge into scrap wood as with the chisel, but do not rock the tool from side to side.

6 As the white line attenuates and disappears, a point of light will be left at the apex, probably projecting a

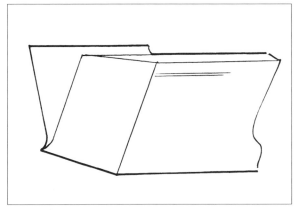

Fig 3.154 A hook may be left towards the end of sharpening; this is caused by the thicker metal at the angle where the two sides join.

little with a hook (*see* Fig 3.154). This is because the metal is thicker at the junction of the two sides. To remove this turn the Arkansas stone side-on and lay the keel flat on the surface. Rock the tool, like a gouge, from side to side and very carefully hone the keel until

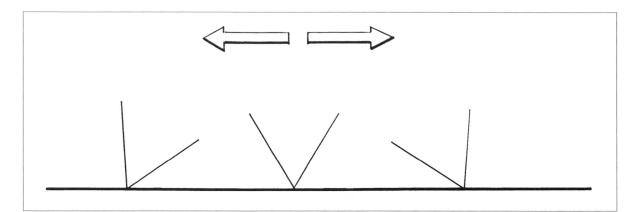

Fig 3.155 Remove the hook by carefully honing the keel. Keep the keel flat on the stone and check the white line.

Fig 3.156 Rounding over the keel of the V-tool by careful rubbing on the benchstone. As always, present the bevel flat and keep checking the edge by its line of light.

Fig 3.157 A specially made V-tool slipstrop. Keep your fingers clear.

the spot of light, or hook, disappears (see Figs 3.155, 3.156). Overworking the keel will dip the apex back. Final spots of light can be removed with the slipstone.

7 If the V-tool ends up with the edge dipping at the apex, wavy, or in other ways unsuccessfully sharpened, one or two perpendicular strokes of the Arkansas benchstone will cut the edge back and reveal the white light from which to start again.

8 Cut across softwood grain as with the chisel; strop inside and out and carefully wipe the blade.

Macaroni tools are treated in similar fashion. Regard them as three chisels joined at two corners which are very slightly rounded. A matching square-edged slip is needed to work the inside.

BENT CHISELS

Sharpen the edges of bent square-end and skew tools in the same way as the straight versions but with a main bevel, in contact with the wood, and a smaller bevel on the upper side. Although the cutting edge is not absolutely in the centre, it is still thrown towards the middle of the metal. The bent V-tool needs little inside bevel.

The main problem comes in holding these tools so that you can present them to the benchstones correctly. Hold the blades like pencils to form the main bevel (see Fig 3.158). Work the reverse, or upper, bevel by turning the tool over and using the end of the stone (see Fig 3.159). Place the stone near the edge of the bench so the tool handle hangs free of the bench surface. A little trial and error may be needed.

GOUGES

1 Grind the cutting edge straight and square and keep the corners. Leave an even white line of at least $\frac{1}{16}$in

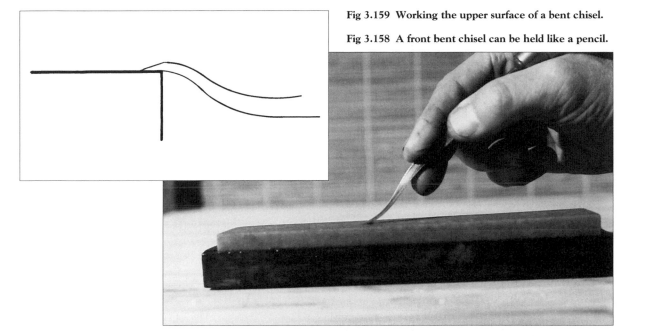

Fig 3.159 Working the upper surface of a bent chisel.

Fig 3.158 A front bent chisel can be held like a pencil.

(2mm), or less if no inside bevel is wanted.

2 Make one or two perpendicular passes on the Arkansas stone to clean any jaggedness and smooth the white line.

3 Start by working the inside bevel with a coarse slipstone held at a shallow angle, and working it evenly from corner to corner. Do not be afraid of working the inside bevel; aim to throw the cutting edge towards the centre of the blade.

4 Shape the outside bevel on the grinding wheel.

5 Position the coarse Carborundum benchstone side-on. Present the bevel flat and sharpen from left to right while rotating the gouge as previously described (*see* page 165)(*see* Fig 3.161). The amount of rotation will depend on the sweep. Keep an eye on the line of light, reducing its thickness to about ½in (1mm).

6 Go now to the Arkansas benchstone and slipstones. Keeping the bevel flat, work the inside and outside bevels in turns – leaving any thinner part of the edge and specifically removing metal from thicker parts. Occasionally push the edge into a piece of scrap wood to remove any wire edge.

7 As the line starts to attenuate, alternate a few sharpening strokes with pushing the edge into the wood. All the line should disappear more or less at the same time, leaving sharp corners and a straight edge.

8 Cut some wood across the grain and see how the resulting cut appears. If there are scratches, look for

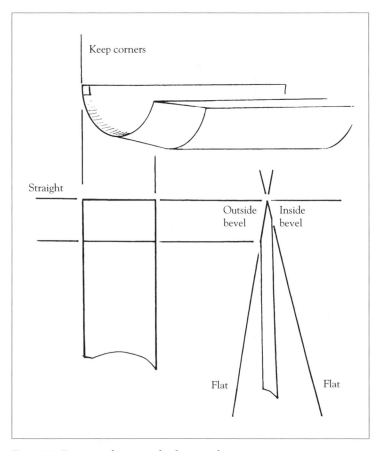

Fig 3.160 Features of a correctly sharpened gouge.

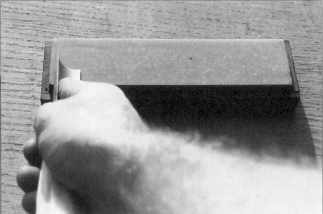

Fig 3.161 Sharpener's view of how a gouge is rotated from one end of the benchstone to the other. The motion is then repeated in the opposite direction. (For clarity the oil is not shown.)

Fig 3.162 This even and thin line of light is produced by the right angle of reflection.

tell-tale spots of light on the cutting edge and remove them with a slip or benchstone.

9 When a clean, polished cut is produced, strop the inside (*see* Fig 3.163) and outside and carefully wipe the blade.

U-SHAPED GOUGES

These are the veiners and fluters: deep flat-sided gouges, (nos 10 and 11). It is helpful to treat them

partly as chisels and partly as gouges – a combination of approaches – while being careful to marry the effects of each (*see* Fig 3.164).

After squaring-off the end and cleaning the white line on the Arkansas stone, grind one flat side, then the other, then the curve in between. Keep the bevels flat and the edge as a straight line. Sharpen on the benchstones in the usual order: turning the benchstone from a chisel (end-on) to gouge (side-on) orientation. The slipstone that is used for the inside curve can be slid up and down the sides.

Keep observing the white line of light, particularly at the juncture of the straight and curved sections, as these points are easily over-sharpened and made to dip back.

It is quite possible to sharpen **U**-shaped tools entirely like gouges, rotating them fully 180° at the

Fig 3.163 Using the slipstrop: start firmly and push the strop out of the mouth of the tool, keeping it at the same angle. Return through the air for a second forward stroke.

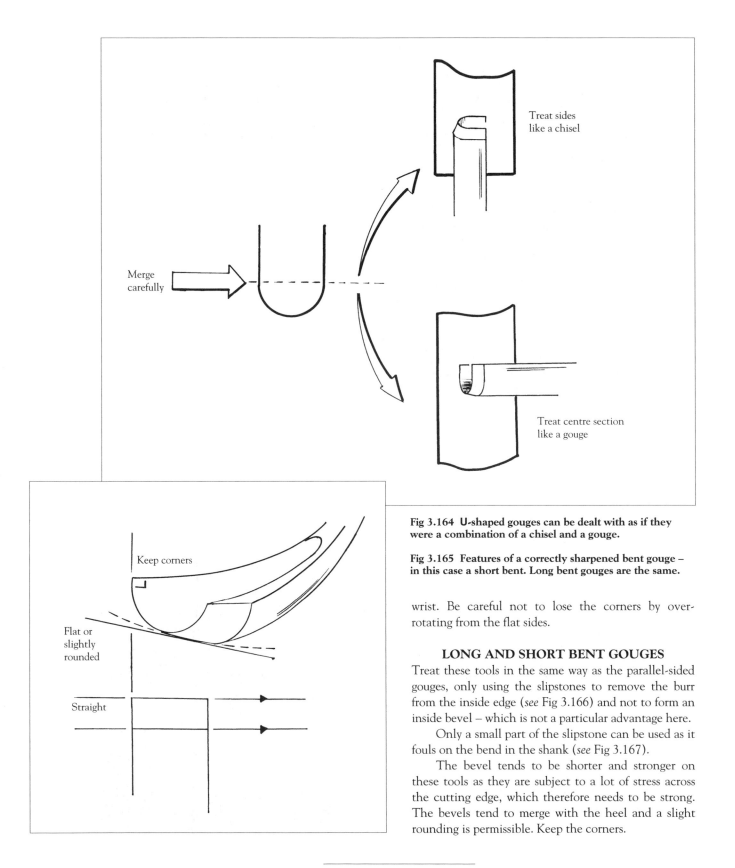

Merge
carefully

Treat sides
like a chisel

Treat centre section
like a gouge

Keep corners

Flat or
slightly
rounded

Straight

Fig 3.164 U-shaped gouges can be dealt with as if they were a combination of a chisel and a gouge.

Fig 3.165 Features of a correctly sharpened bent gouge – in this case a short bent. Long bent gouges are the same.

wrist. Be careful not to lose the corners by over-rotating from the flat sides.

LONG AND SHORT BENT GOUGES

Treat these tools in the same way as the parallel-sided gouges, only using the slipstones to remove the burr from the inside edge (*see* Fig 3.166) and not to form an inside bevel – which is not a particular advantage here.

Only a small part of the slipstone can be used as it fouls on the bend in the shank (*see* Fig 3.167).

The bevel tends to be shorter and stronger on these tools as they are subject to a lot of stress across the cutting edge, which therefore needs to be strong. The bevels tend to merge with the heel and a slight rounding is permissible. Keep the corners.

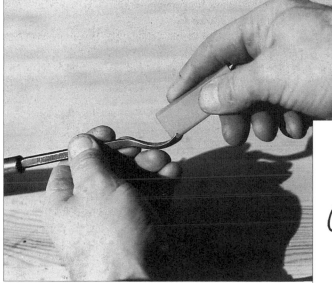

Fig 3.166 Using a slip to remove the burr on the inside edge of a front bent gouge.

Fig 3.167 Only the end of a slipstone can be used with a short bent tool as it fouls on the crank.

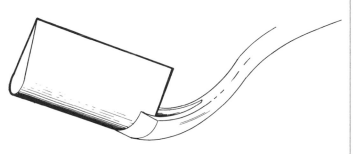

The main problem is in holding these odd-shaped tools satisfactorily so that you can present them correctly to the grinding wheel or benchstones. Some experiment is needed to keep the bevel flat as the handles will swing in quite an arc when the blade is rolling from side to side.

These tools can also be held in a vice and the flat side of a slipstone used on them, like a file.

Fig 3.168 The pattern of sharpening the outside bevel of a front bent gouge is the same as that of the straight one, except that presenting the tool is more awkward. (For clarity the oil is not shown.)

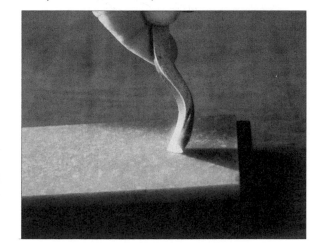

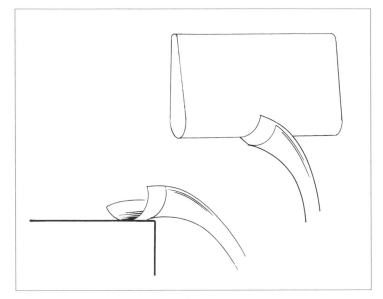

Fig 3.169 Sharpening a back bent gouge involves a lot of slipstoning.

BACK BENT GOUGES

These tools can mostly be sharpened with appropriate slipstones (*see* Fig 3.169). Start as usual by flattening and straightening the cutting edge on the Arkansas benchstone. Place the benchstone side-on near the edge of the bench so that the handle of the back bent gouge can hang free of the bench surface. Present the outer bevel to the stone (*see* Fig 3.170), clean up and

start sharpening like a straight gouge. Keep the corners and a flat outer bevel.

Work as much in cannel with the slipstones (*see* Fig 3.171) as outside with the benchstones – reducing the white line of light until it disappears. The inner surface wants to smoothly merge with the cannel without an actual bevel.

When stropping, only short strokes can be made, with the strop at the edge of the bench, if the outer bevel is to be kept flat. Otherwise you will have to lift the handle to clear the leather and so roll the cutting edge.

TAPERED TOOLS

Long and short pod, spade, allongee or fishtail tools present no problems that are not encountered in the parallel-sided versions. As they tend to have lighter, thinner or more delicate blades, it is easier to over-grind or over-sharpen them, so a little more care is needed especially on the corners. I would suggest you do not use the grinding wheel at all, but start with the coarse bench and slipstones.

The bevels tend to be longer, for finishing cuts, and often merge into the main shank without a noticeable bevel.

Testing for sharpness

There must be something of the cavalier in carvers who evaluate, or demonstrate, the sharpness of a

Fig 3.170 Offering the back bent to the benchstone. (For clarity the oil is not shown.)

Fig 3.171 Slipstones are used with the benchstone to sharpen a back bent gouge.

Fig 3.172 Running grooves together is a good way to check the sharpness of the edge. In the photograph, the scratch line along the groove will no doubt appear as a tell-tale spot of light on the cutting edge. This will need touching up.

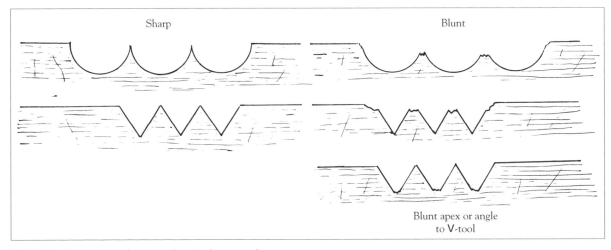

Sharp

Blunt

Blunt apex or angle to V-tool

Fig 3.173 Grooves cut close together in clean wood is a good test of sharpness.

woodcarving tool by shaving hairs from the back of their forearms, or nicking their nails. Presumably they scythe through a lot of body hair when a large number of tools need sharpening.

At the end of the day it is wood that is being carved – and very different types of wood – so it would seem to make more sense to test the cutting quality on spare pieces of the wood kept to one side of the bench,

just for this purpose.

Slicing *across* the grain with a sharp edge will leave a clean, polished cut with no scratch marks; the tool will cut at a low presentation angle and move easily – it may even make a happy 'ssssp' noise. Running a close series of grooves, side by side, is an excellent test (*see* Figs 3.172, 3.173). Assuming the wood is good, the ridges left between the grooves should remain clean and

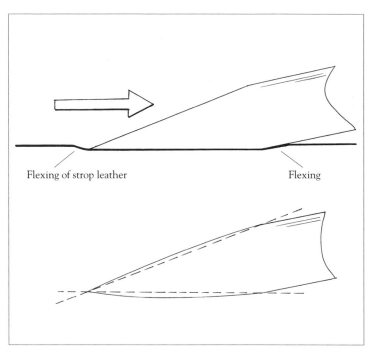

Fig 3.174 A decision has to be made about the notch in this large parting tool: should the whole tool, which is otherwise fine, be sharpened, or just the edge around the notch?

Fig 3.175 After some time of stropping, the bevel starts to become rolled, because even hard leather flexes before and after the edge is passed over it.

intact. If such ridges crumble or the edges of the cuts are torn; if the cuts contain scratch marks or ragged trails; if the cuts are dull or the cutting seems unduly hard work for the wood – some more sharpening is needed.

▨ Look at the line of light for tell-tale spots of white, if necessary with a magnifying glass.
▨ Look at the profile of the bevel itself to see if it is rounded or 'rolled'.

Maintaining sharpness

You could look at this the other way and ask: why do edges lose their sharpness? Given good quality steel and tempering, there are several reasons.

▨ Most beginners wait too long before brightening the cut of their carving tools and thereby make more work for themselves than need be.
▨ Tools can suffer from poor cutting technique.
▨ They may be stored badly.
▨ There is also the effect of the material being carved.

Here are some guidelines to help maintain carving-tool sharpness.

STROPPING
▨ Never let woodcarving tools get into a really dull state – strop them as soon as loss of keenness is felt.

▨ Keep the strops on the benches, in their correct place, along with the working tools.
▨ Get into the habit of stropping the tools *regularly*. The tools become polished and bright and this in itself eases them though the wood.
▨ Strop correctly, keeping the bevel flat and not rolling the edge.

Stropping a blade over a period of time gives rise to another effect which you need to be aware of. The leather of a benchstrop is only firm, not rigid like the oilstones. It 'gives' under the bevel moving along it, curling back to shape when the edge has passed.

This flexing of the strop tends to roll the edge and round over the bevel (*see* Fig 3.175), However, as the cut of the strop is very fine, the effect is only noticeable after a prolonged period of stropping. Even then, this rounding is not so easily seen as the bevel becomes highly polished (*see* Fig 3.176). It may escape a carver's notice that the tool is gradually becoming harder work, or the cutting angle a little steeper – the effects of a rounded bevel.

When a gouge has been used for some time and stropped regularly to keep it keen, try setting the bevel flat on the Arkansas stone – at the original angle – and make a small, sideways movement. The appearance of a dull point of abrasion in the middle of the bevel, contrasting with the highly polished metal, indicates

Fig 3.176 The highly polished bevel, the result of regular stropping, may hide a gradually more rounded bevel.

Fig 3.177 The 'candle' effect: a final rim of polished metal towards the edge – the duller, honed surface creeps towards it as the bevel is flattened. The corners and straightness of the cutting edge will need checking over too.

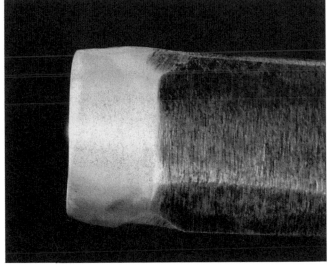

the bevel is rounded. A chisel can be tested in similarly.

Re-sharpen the blade in the normal way and you will see that the initial dull point of abrasion becomes a line; it then quickly spreads over the shiny bevel towards the heel and the edge as the bevel re-flattens. Eventually there is only a rim of shiny metal at the very edge which has not, as yet, touched the benchstone (*see* Fig 3.177). This bright margin has been called the 'candle'. Do not be tempted to lift the handle to get rid of it quickly but carry on with the bevel flat. Stop when the candle is put out, but be careful not to over-sharpen. Begin the cycle of stropping again.

CARVING TECHNIQUE

Tools also become blunt and damaged as much through bad carving practice as failing to strop. Tools should be used to *cut* the wood properly – prising and levering is not cutting and will only damage the edge of the blade.

■ Do not drag the cutting edge across the wood, but enter and leave the cut cleanly.

■ Do not use the blade to lever or prise wood chips away. Cut the tool in, cut it through and cut it out.

■ If a gouge gets buried in the wood try *gently* moving the tool from side to side – *along* the cutting edge, not against it. This is not a good idea with quick gouges. If such gentle persuasion does not work, another tool is needed to carefully remove wood from the sides of the embedded gouge.

■ U-shaped gouges are vulnerable to cracking when they

are forced too deeply into wood. Pressure on the bevels squeezes the two sides together. Never compel these veiners or fluters to cut too much, or too deeply, at once.

STORAGE AND CARE

Care is largely a matter of habit. Start with good quality tools, then:

■ Avoid damaging the edges by the bench discipline suggested in Chapter 6 (*see* page 264).

■ Suggestions for careful storage are made in Chapter 2 (*see* page 96). Check the edges before putting the tools away – in the condition you would ideally wish to find them.

■ Some carvers, when they get to the finishing stages of a carving, have a session of checking every edge for perfect sharpness and touching up any scratch marks they may have let ride in the rough stages of carving. Odd scratch marks may be acceptable where a surface will be sanded or overcut to finish, but not where the naked cuts are left to be seen.

EFFECT OF THE WOOD BEING CARVED

■ Some woods (e.g. teak and some mahogany) contain calcium deposits that dull edges. If this is happening, there is nothing to do but carry on and have a final sharpening session before making finishing cuts.

■ Particles of abrasive remaining in a sanded surface will also take the keenness off an edge, so avoid sanding parts that will be carved later. This applies especially to carving turned work, most of which is sanded on a lathe.

■ Remember that different woods require different strengths of bevel. If a cutting edge is tending to break up it probably means the bevel is too long.

Pre-sharpened tools

Most carving tools are bought by increasing numbers of people wishing to carve as a leisure activity. Understandably they want to get into the wood straight away, without having to sharpen the tools first. Tools catering to this market are available today with bevels set at what seems to be a good average angle and ready sharpened. They may be sharpened by an automatic process or with some degree of hand skill, but they never have inner bevels and are most often shiny and polished.

In my experience, however, there is an intrinsic problem with these ready-sharpened tools. It is not a matter of the steel, tempering or the overall shaping of the tool – all of which may be excellent – but the strength of the edge left by the sharpening process itself.

Certainly a pre-sharpened edge looks sharp – but start carving and it will be noticed that the initial, shiny cut quickly breaks down to leave trails of scratches. When a blade is sharpened on grinding and buffing wheels which drag the metal *forwards* – away from the cutting edge – a microscopic feathering of the crystal edge is produced. This is weaker, or less supported, than when the metal has been drawn *back* from the edge – towards the handle – or sharpened *across* it. After a short while the cut surface is left with lots of little scratches which is entirely unsatisfactory for a finish straight from the edge.

Once these tools have been re-sharpened, using the normal honing methods, the problem vanishes and the quality of the tool can show itself.

So this is something to bear in mind if you are coming new to carving: by all means start with a pre-sharpened edge, but find out how to sharpen and maintain the edges properly, rather than expediently.

The sharpening area

Time spent on sharpening is never wasted, but contributes directly to the quality of the woodcarving

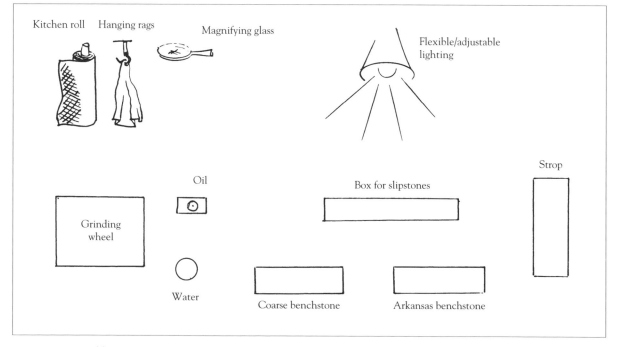

Fig 3.178 A possible arrangement for a sharpening area.

as well as the enjoyment of carving itself. Ways and routines of keeping carving tools keen are worth cultivating. If there is room in the workplace, there are many benefits in setting up a permanent area near the bench specifically for sharpening woodcarving tools. The area set aside need not be very large: enough room to work comfortably and leave important items for sharpening ready to hand. The space warrants good lighting, perhaps its own adjustable light. The grinder, with its cooling water, can be part of the arrangement, or nearby and quickly accessible. The benchstones can be laid out next to the oil; slipstones conveniently placed; and oil, stropping paste, kitchen paper and rags handy. Strops are normally kept on the carving bench next to the working tools.

Another option is a pull-out drawer or ledge – perhaps to the bench – in which the sharpening stones are placed. This is not such a good arrangement as wood chips and dust will always find their way in.

Having the sharpening and carving areas separate helps keep dust and wood chips from one, and oil and dirt from the other. Instead of getting out the benchstones each time they are needed, they are simply waiting to be turned to.

Make the sharpening area pleasant; see it as part of your whole work, and keep it clean. The idea is to make the *means* of sharpening woodcarving tools so easy that sharpening itself becomes no bother whatsoever – and carving itself benefits.

ELECTRICAL METHODS

Electrical means of sharpening woodcarving tools are being pushed more and more in the direction of the carver – marketed with the promise of 'ultra-sharp' edges, in the wink of an eye.

Putting aside marketing claims, the fact is that they may suit some carvers, in some circumstances, but not others. So, looking first at what they are and how they work, some advantages and limitations will be noted. Assessment can then be made as to how useful such machines may be to a particular carver.

Effectively, these machines are like bench grinders, with wheels (or belts) in various combinations. They might actually have a grinding wheel, but always some fast buffing wheel impregnated with a very fine abrasive to hone the edge.

The buffing wheel will be of hard or soft fibrous

Fig 3.179 A typical electric sharpening machine with grinding belt; there are assorted buffing wheels and a take-off chuck (right).

Fig 3.180 The chuck can be used for other abrasive wheels or a flexible shaft.

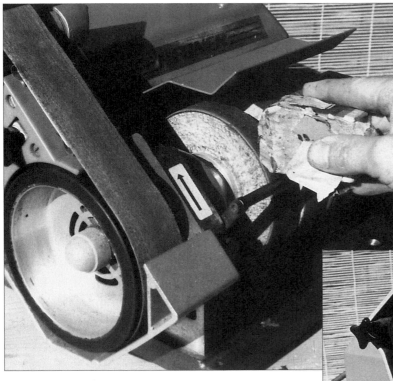

Fig 3.181 The buffing wheels must be dressed regularly with an abrasive compound which is normally supplied by the makers.

Fig 3.182 In this machine there is no means of supporting the tool on the flat section of the belt, which means that the blade has to be held in the air. Besides limiting the control over shaping, hovering the hand like this over the fast moving belt is potentially hazardous.

material, such as felt, and spinning *away* from the user to prevent the cutting edge digging in. This means that the grinding wheel also rotates away from the edge as, invariably, all the wheels are directly connected. Wheels are normally driven directly by the motor and rotate at a high speed, up to 3000 rpm.

In use, a block of proprietary abrasive is pushed against the spinning buffing wheel, melting into it (*see* Fig 3.181). The tool is applied and a sludge of melted abrasive builds up in front of the edge as it polishes the blade and creates the fine cutting edge.

If a carver knows exactly what shape or profile of carving tool he or she wants, and there were quick, accurate and safe electrical methods of achieving it, then this would be a straight option. However, most machines are limited in what they can do. They may be able to achieve enough to satisfy a particular carver, but only a part of what another may want.

For example, there is never a facility to create a proper inside bevel, although the inside of a gouge can normally be 'de-burred' on a softer felt wheel. Nor is there a means of working the inside of a V-tool.

The wheel softness also makes it difficult to produce a flat bevel. At the speed the wheel rotates, it is as if the edge had been stropped many thousand times in a few seconds – and the effect of prolonged stropping is to round or roll the bevel, as was discussed on page 186.

When you sharpen on such a machine, you are involved in a very different process which offers a different product from that which results from hand-sharpening. Without doubt the finished product is achieved much more quickly, but there is more to the comparison than simple speed.

Many carvers enjoy the quiet of carving, as well as that of hand-sharpening their tools. Sharpening can be a moment for reflection before returning to the carving with increased vigour. Sharpening machines can be quite noisy and speedy, and this may be intrusive for carvers with a temperament that prefers quiet.

Following the methods described in this chapter and a regime of maintaining sharpness, little more than regular 'touching up' is necessary. Tools only need to be re-ground or shaped if they become damaged. Tools certainly get hand hot on the buffing wheels, if not in danger of blueing. The speed of the wheels tends to make events happen quickly: over-shaping or plain bad shaping are all too easy. The speed makes them particularly hazardous to beginners who do not yet understand what shape is required of a particular tool. Experienced sharpeners should fare better.

With the wheels turning *away* from the operator, the edge is weaker than one sharpened across or into it. When metal is drawn forwards it produces more of a wire edge, even though it is abraded away by the buffing wheels. The edge tends to crumble and leave fine scratch trails in the cut. Metal drawn back, across or away from the cutting edge to sharpen it leaves a tougher, smoother structure. This has greater resistance and lasts longer. So tools sharpened on abrasive wheels need touching up far more often to keep the same quality of cut. These comments are based entirely on my experience and not any scientific trial.

There is also the matter of cost to be considered – the outlay relative to the amount of use. Such machines would be of more benefit to a wood sculptor with large gouges than an instrument-maker with a few small ones.

Safety factors need to be assessed as well. Some machines have limited wheel guards and no tool rests so the tool is supported by the hand hovering in the air (*see* Fig 3.182). This applies especially to those 'systems' that are sold with an arbor to mount on a free motor.

Rubberized abrasive wheels are very fine, slightly soft, grinding wheels. They can be shaped to suit the hollow forms of internal bevels, and are available on their own to be mounted on a motor shaft or driven spindle. Being soft, these wheels must rotate *away* from the user. Safety considerations in such fast-spinning wheels must be carefully applied.

To be clear about my view on electrical sharpening methods: there is nothing 'holy' about sharpening by hand; nothing intrinsically better in 'hand' over 'electrical' methods; nor anything 'wrong' about buying pre-sharpened tools. Who would go back to a saw pit? The issue really is about what you want and whether you are you able to achieve it.

Sharpening is part of the whole carving package, but it need not be a big deal. Newcomers, buying these machines and quickly producing badly or inappropriately sharpened carving tools, are not doing themselves much of a favour. The fact is, beginners do not know what correct or even satisfactorily sharp woodcarving tools should look like in the first place. This is best learned in a slower, more careful way. Then, when they know exactly how the tools work their best, other approaches can be added to a basic knowledge and skill.

I feel that carvers should learn to sharpen their tools in the traditional way *first*, and not go straight to a position where a machine dictates the shape and cutting of the carving tools. There is then a background of quite subtle knowledge, largely lodged in the hands, and underpinning the carving. An electric machine can then be bought in the light of this basic understanding, to augment it and be incorporated into a well-founded sharpening strategy.

SUMMARY

One aim of this chapter has been that of instilling *self-reliance* – a repertoire of techniques to deal with all shapes and states of carving tools, turning them into exactly what a carver needs to achieve the best work.

The chapter started by looking at some fundamental ideas about 'sharpness'; what features contribute to this end; the necessary equipment and its correct use; how to go about sharpening tools in detail; and finally how to retain sharpness.

It was pointed out that sharpening is a precise skill, but well within the capabilities of someone who has the manual dexterity and wish to carve in the first place. With the correct approach the skills of sharpening woodcarving tools can be gained rapidly to an almost instinctual level.

Like any skill worth acquiring, it *does* take practice. It often involves learning by mistakes and by trying to improve the performance of a tool every time it needs sharpening or touching up. It is not that you cannot carve until you have perfected the skill of sharpening, but by always seeking to improve, doing the best you can and trying for a little better next time, the sharpening will soon become second nature.

The sharpening practices of different carvers differ, with 'grey' areas where opinions differ. What matters is the experience any carver is having of the way a carving tool is cutting and how this fits with the actual carving process. Both the final carving and the process of achieving it matter to the carver.

ACCESSORY TOOLS

Aims

To describe the main tools used by carvers, in addition to woodcarving tools themselves

To give a few notes on their use and place in the woodcarving process

The tools which carvers and sculptors use to achieve the effects they want, to experiment and explore, are many and varied. The tools and equipment discussed in this chapter are commonly

used; in some cases the tools are so common that no more than a few notes, in passing, need be given.

As with woodcarving tools:

- ◾ Buy them as you need them
- ◾ Buy the best quality you can afford
- ◾ Use them safely
- ◾ Care for them and store them correctly.

MALLETS

Mallets are used in woodcarving for the heavier, roughing-out stages and 'setting in', especially in hard woods where handwork is inefficient or too stressful. The word 'mallet' is a diminutive of 'maul', a heavy wooden hammer used for splitting logs. Both come through the French from the Latin *malleus*, meaning a hammer.

Mallets can leave bold work that looks well at a distance besides being a forerunner to finishing by hand – and indeed some carvers do most of their work with a mallet for the boldness, simplicity and flair that mallet

Fig 4.1 A detail from the Tudor facade in Abbey Dore Church, Herefordshire. The mallet work needed to carve the hard oak can clearly be seen.

Fig 4.2 A face from Abbey Dore – note the crisp and simple lines.

Fig 4.3 A detail of Fig 4.2 showing the surface texture straight from the chisel.

Fig 4.4 A collection of mallets. The white one is made of nylon; to its right is a mallet made of mild steel and the remainder are made of lignum vitae.

Fig 4.5 The earliest mallets were made from a waisted log of hardwood (a). Passing a handle through the log (b) made another early type of mallet which had the advantage of striking with the end-grain.

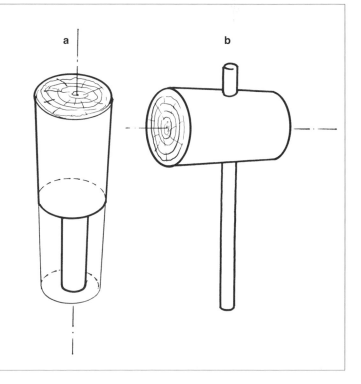

work can give. Carvers tend to collect a variety of mallets of different sizes and weights for different jobs.

Shapes

Woodcarvers' mallets are round, not square. There are definite reasons why this shape is preferred by carvers, and several factors that make a good mallet shape.

The earliest known mallets were Egyptian and were made quite naturally from branches of heavy wood, waisted for a handle (*see* Fig 4.5). Square billets of wood, again with an integral handle, are shown in Roman paintings being used for mortising, as they still are today. Both round- and square-headed mallets have a very long history, continuing up to the present time, and each has its own place. But why the different shapes?

In chopping out a woodworking joint, say a mortise, the flat side of the chisel cuts its own guiding jig. To keep the true face of the joint, the chisel needs to be struck squarely so the force goes straight along the chisel (*see* Fig 4.7). Hence the need for the square, flat face of the mallet.

A carving gouge, on the other hand, is struck from all sorts of directions, as it can be presented to the wood at an infinite number of angles (*see* Fig 4.8). In this case the force is transmitted tangentially. The mallet does not have to be aligned in the exact way a square-faced one must be, therefore a round mallet, which always presents a similar face to the tool handle, can be used and the carver need never look away from the carving and can strike with confidence.

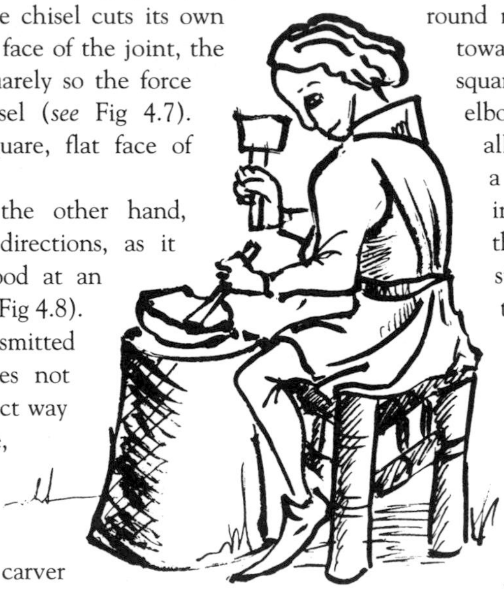

Fig 4.6 Mallets have been used for thousands of years.

As well as being round in cross-section, the round mallet head is also slightly tapered towards the handle (*see* Fig 4.9). Like the square mallet, the blow pivots from the elbow. The tapering head of the mallet allows the face to strike the handle of a cutting tool more squarely – at least in this one direction. A slight belly at the striking point also helps to strengthen this part against wear and tear.

Some other features contribute to a good mallet shape – bear these in mind if ever you make one.

■ The handle should be comfortable, with nothing prominent to cause soreness or even blistering (*see* Fig 4.12). A mallet can be used for long periods of work and you may not notice the effect

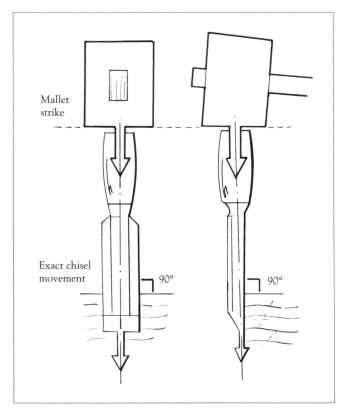

Fig 4.7 The flat face of the woodworker's mallet must line up square to the chisel if it is not to deflect the handle.

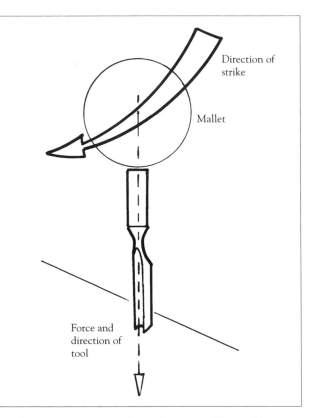

Fig 4.8 The force of the round woodcarving mallet, striking from an infinite number of directions, passes at a tangent down the tool.

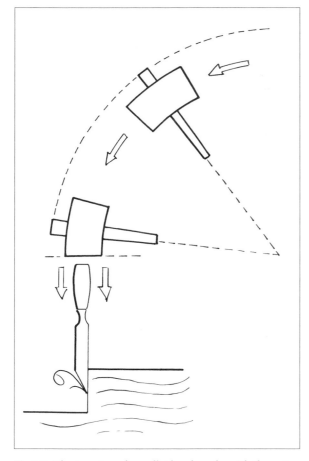

Fig 4.9 The tapering of a mallet head works with the swing from the elbow to give a directed strike.

Fig 4.10 The cylindrical mallet strikes the handle at an angle. This is one of the Lignostone range made of compressed beech veneers.

Fig 4.11 A tapered mallet reflects the swing from the elbow and strikes the handle squarely.

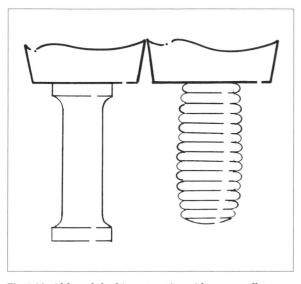

Fig 4.12 Although looking attractive, ridges on mallet handles can make the hand sore with prolonged use.

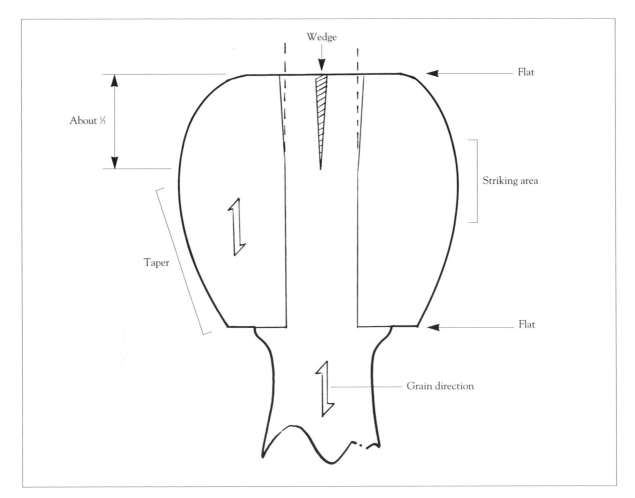

Fig 4.13 Some features of a mallet head.

Fig 4.14 If the new mallet handle were to shrink, the wedge can be driven farther in; at the same time the mallet still sits upright on the bench.

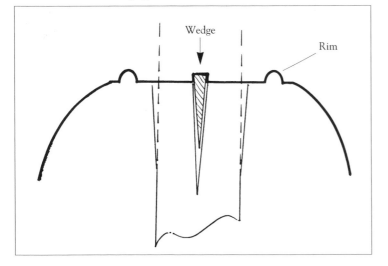

until you put it down. Too fat a shape can make the hands ache; too thin feels a little weak and uncertain.

■ The handle should be firmly wedged into the head of the mallet. A very important point is that the hole for the handle needs to taper out a little at the far end so that the wedged spigot of the handle becomes locked and immovable (*see* Fig 4.13). Indeed, you have to drill the handle out should you ever need to replace it. If this tapered hole is not included, the head can loosen, even with the wedge, although this does not apply so much to smaller mallets, which are used more delicately. A nicety is to form a rim around the top of the mallet – with the wedge being proud to begin with – the wedge is then tapped in further if the handle shrinks (*see* Fig 4.14).

■ A flat top to the mallet head permits it to sit upright on the bench and not roll around.

Wood	Density	
	Approx. lb per cubic foot	**Approx. kg per m³**
Apple	20–40	320–640
Yew	40	640
Beech	45	720
Plum	50	800
Hickory	53	850
Lignum	80	1,280

Table 4.1 Some woods used for mallets. As the weight of the mallet increases, use the densest wood you can to keep the mallet size as low as possible. Remember that other materials such as nylon and brass are occasionally used.

Woods

Mallets with a separate handle are relatively recent, probably stemming from the time when newly discovered and dense woods, such as lignum vitae, could be exploited for their weight and size ratios. Lignum is one of the best woods to use; the diameter of most other woods must be considerably larger to get a similar weight. Almost any hardwood will make a mallet, for example, beech, elm or even fruitwoods (*see* Table 4.1).

Mallets can consist of other materials:

◼ Nylon (originally developed for stonecarving)
◼ Mild steel (these need metal ferrules on the struck end of the carving-tool handle)
◼ Lead-iron alloy (as in 'dummy mallets', again used in stone carving)
◼ Brass.

The use of metal gives a smaller size to the mallet for the weight – and they never wear out. Wooden mallets tend to have one face with end-grain and one with side-grain. The side-grain will bruise and feather away after a while, far more than the end-grain, giving an uneven shape to the mallet. In this context it is worth mentioning Lignostone mallets, made from beech veneers, compressed under enormous pressure with resin glue to result in a virtually indestructible surface of end-grain (*see* the Reference Section, page 346).

The wood in the game balls (or 'woods') used in bowls is lignum. There is a tendency these days to use

Fig 4.15 The difference between a mallet (left) made from lignum heartwood and one made from a branch which is mainly sapwood. Almost all commercial lignum mallets are of the second type.

balls made from artificial materials which are unaffected by the weather – so old bowls often become available. These make excellent mallets, consisting totally of lignum hardwood, not sapwood in the way of most commercially sold mallets (*see* Fig 4.15).

Some pointers to turning up a mallet appear on the opposite page.

Fig 4.16 A bowls ball or 'wood' turned into a mallet.

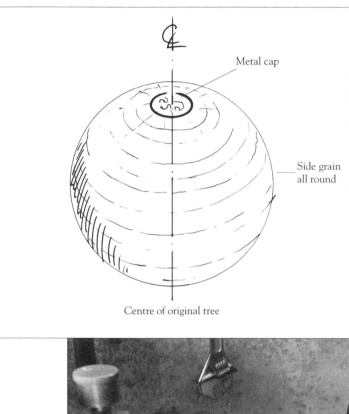

Centre of original tree

The nylon mallets, which are manufactured rather large, can be shaped easily, or reduced in size, on a lathe.

The best wood for the handle is a straight, close-grained bit of ash, hickory or hornbeam, although other woods such as box or yew work well.

Size and weight

Commercially made mallets vary in weight from a light-weight 1lb (0.45kg) to a Herculean 5lb (2.25kg) – the dimensions vary according to the material from which they are made. The individual physical build of the carver, as well as the size of the work and hardness of the wood, will dictate which weight is most comfortable to work with.

It is a mistake for a newcomer to choose a heavier mallet, thinking the work will go quicker. It may well do to begin with, but for most people heavy blows are quickly tiring, as well as stressful on the wrists and elbows. The carving tools and handles must also be fit for heavy mallet work.

It is better to go for light- and medium-weight mallets to begin with – possibly 1lb (0.45kg) and 2lb (0.9kg). If you are not used to the weights, it is a good

Fig 4.17 If two flat faces are bandsawn on either side of the ball, a clamp can be used to stop it rotating when being bored.

Fig 4.18 With the central hole plugged, the preliminary shaping of the mallet can be started.

idea to heft a mallet first, rather than buying it blindly through the mail.

Notes on using the mallets appear later in this section (*see* page 202).

Making a mallet

For those with the ability and a lathe, turning a mallet is fairly straightforward. Read through the following notes first, however, to make sure you have the tools. These guidelines should be considered:

■ The head is bored first with a 1in (25mm) Forstner bit, and the shape turned around the hole using temporary plugs of wood.

■ If you are turning a bowls ball, the centre of the original lignum vitae tree lies underneath the metal caps on either end (*see* Fig 4.16). Bore the hole for the handle here, down the centre. Hairline shakes in the wood can be ignored as they do not affect the performance of the mallet.

■ *Before* raising lignum vitae dust, protect yourself from it adequately.

Method

Turn the mallet head first.

1 Using a slow speed, bore to about ¾in (20mm) from the other end and tap a conical wooden plug into the hole. Reverse the wood and finish boring through to the first hole.

2 Accurately tap in a second plug and mount the wood between centres. Rough the head to a cylinder of maximum diameter (*see* Fig 4.18).

3 Square off the ends of the cylinder and take them down to 1½in (38mm) diameter with a parting tool – leaving only ⅛in (3mm) of thickness to remove around the hole.

4 Using the long point of a skew chisel, reduce the length of the very ends by no more than 1⁄16in (2mm) of wood at a time, scoring into the plug. Each time you have reduced the length of the head, *wind in the tailstock* and take up the slack that is produced. In this way the plug is continuously worked into the hole and there is no danger of the work coming off the lathe: a cut, then a tightening up. When the ends are completely shaved flat, take the work off the lathe and remove the plugs – a Stilson wrench or Mole grips may be useful here.

5 Make a hardwood spigot of a diameter that taps nicely into the hole you have decided is the *handle* end of the mallet. The spigot should enter the hole to a depth of about one-third of the way into the ball. Lignum,

although withstanding compression amazingly, will split more easily – so take care when inserting the spigot not to overforce it. Grip the spigot in a three-jaw scroll chuck. You should now have freedom to splay the hole for the expanding wedge in the handle (*see* Fig 4.20).

6 Using a slow speed and light strokes with a straight-sided scraper, ream out the hole. An increase of diameter of ⅛in (3mm) at the exit – starting from a depth of about one-third of the way in – is enough (*see* Fig 4.21).

7 Replace the plugs. Line up the mallet head on the lathe and shape it with the skew chisel (*see* Fig 4.22). Finish to at least 180 grit and polish with a coat or two

Fig 4.19 Starting to flatten the ends. The problem is how to finish up to the plug.

Fig 4.20 Reaming the hole for the wedge-splayed end of the handle.

Fig 4.21 Carefully skim the hole to about one-third of the way in.

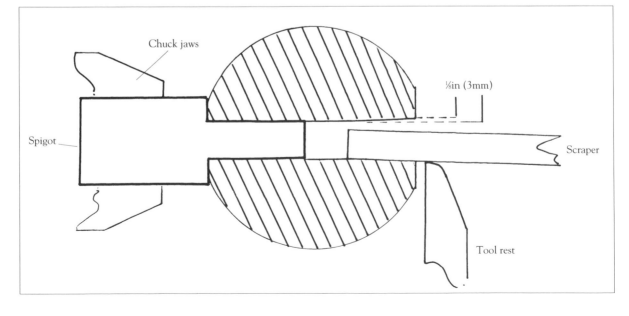

Fig 4.22 The final shape of the mallet head: bellied and slightly tapering.

Fig 4.23 An assortment of handle shapes; comfort is very important.

Fig 4.24 Make sure your handle feels comfortable. Such a ridge may well cause soreness if used for an extensive period.

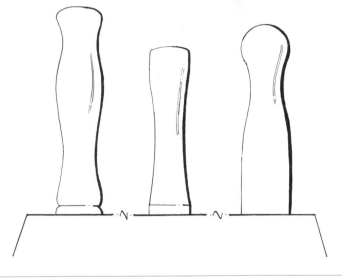

of raw linseed oil. The head is now finished and can be put to one side.

Then turn the handle.

1 The handle is turned as a normal bit of 'between centres' work. Make the spigot that goes through the head about ¼in (6mm) over length and a snug fit. Undercut the shoulder slightly.

2 Feel the handle for comfort; you can take it off the lathe and try it with the head on to get the right shape (*see* Fig 4.23–4.25). Leave the end blips on for the time being and sand well. Burnishing the wood with shavings is the best finish, but it can be sealed with a coat of cellulose lacquer or shellac, finely cut

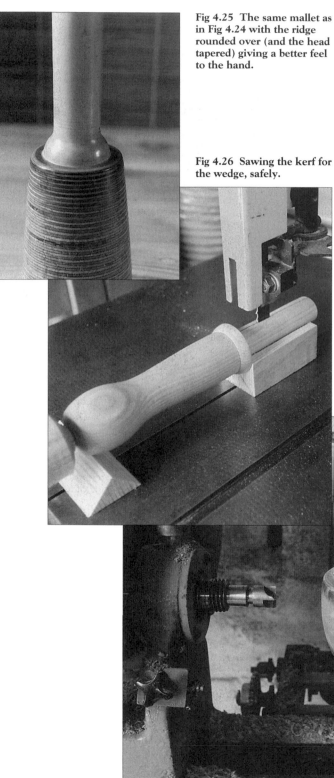

Fig 4.25 The same mallet as in Fig 4.24 with the ridge rounded over (and the head tapered) giving a better feel to the hand.

Fig 4.26 Sawing the kerf for the wedge, safely.

back, if you prefer. Do not create a shiny, slippery surface.

3 Make a support so that the spigot of the handle can be offered to the bandsaw safely and accurately (*see* Fig 4.26). Saw down the centre about two-thirds of the way. A handsaw will also do.

4 Make a long and slender wedge to go into the saw cut. Insert the spigot into the head, making sure the shoulder of the handle is flush against the undersurface. Standing the handle on the bench, drive the wedge home and lock the handle on (*see* Fig 4.27). Trim off the blip, the wedge and the spigot end with a small saw and chisel. Sand and seal as before.

Using mallets

Before using the mallet, it is worth removing as much wood as possible from the carving using the bandsaw or similar tool.

Fig 4.27 Driving the wedge home. It may be an idea to leave the mallet for a while in case the handle shrinks; then tap the wedge finally home, trimming it off so the mallet sits upright on the bench.

Fig 4.28 The usual way to strike with a mallet. The extended thumb helps to guide the carving tool.

Fig 4.29 Precise light striking is possible if the mallet is held by the head.

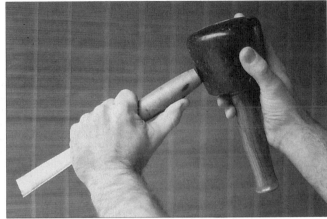

When a lot of work is needed, as in a sculpture, try to work in a rhythmic way. A regular pace will remove more wood and be less tiring in the long run than sporadic bursts of passion.

Keep the elbow of the mallet arm *in* – towards the body – as much as possible and strike so as to include the shoulder. This achieves two things:

■ The stress and fatigue on the elbow and arm is lessened, allowing the work to go on for longer.
■ The weight of the carver can be more readily put *behind* the blow of the mallet; this increases the efficiency of the cutting enormously.

Try to have a sense of your feet in contact with the ground as you are using the mallet so that, braced in this way, the striking force travels forward into the handle of the gouge. The more your body is behind the mallet, the more efficient the cut will be.

Learn to use the mallet with either arm from the start, not just because this shares the work, but because it also avoids having to contort the body at awkward angles to make the necessary cuts to the carving. This is an especially good discipline for lettering.

Do not try to remove too much wood at a time, or cut so deeply as to bury the carving tool.

The tighter the longitudinal curve of a carving tool, the less it should be hit with a mallet. The pressures delivered have to go somewhere, and they may go into breaking the tool.

Work in regular patterns across the surface to be removed. Traditional Japanese carving recognizes this way of working as producing beauty in its own right – carvings may be left in this stage as 'finished'.

Remember that a mallet has two weights, depending whether it is held by the handle or the head

(*see* Figs 4.28, 4.29). Mallet work can be quite delicate, although perhaps not as controlled as handwork.

Besides the mallet, carvers have always propelled their gouges by striking them with the palm of the hand, perhaps building up quite considerable calluses over the years. While this is no doubt a useful

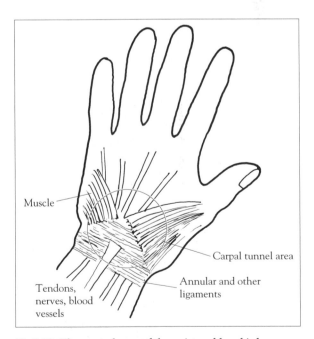

Fig 4.30 The central area of the wrist and hand is less protected by thick muscles or bone. The nerves that pass through this carpal tunnel area are susceptible to trauma.

technique for occasional, light work, there is a real danger of damaging the large numbers of nerves and tendons that pass through the wrist and palm – the 'carpal tunnel' (*see* Fig 4.30). The effect varies

between individuals but thickening here can give rise to a well-recognized, claw-like deformity of the hand – the surgical repair of which is often unsuccessful. If you *must* strike the handle with the palm, use the meaty bit at the base of the thumb or its equivalent on the other side and avoid the centre. Do it lightly and infrequently. Better still, use the mallet.

Care

Mallets should reside – as all wood should – away from direct sources of heat. Very dry atmospheres may cause the wood to shrink. The mallet will recover if kept in a plastic bag with a damp cloth for a while. An occasional wipe with linseed oil will keep the wood sweet – though, unfortunately, this never works with the owner.

ABRADING TOOLS

Such tools are bars of hardened steel with multiple teeth which remove wood as 'spoil', or coarse sawdust, rather than as chips or shavings. Buy the best quality tools when you need them. Poor quality rasps and files quickly lose their cutting ability. There are so many variations, producing varied effects in different woods, that some experimenting may be necessary.

Rasps

Rasps have individually raised teeth giving coarse, medium and fine cuts. The coarser and larger the teeth, the quicker the wood is removed.

Rasp blades are usually straight with a flat, round or convex cross-section, with lengths varying from 8 to 12in (200 to 300mm). Farriers use particularly large rasps on horse's hooves which work well on wood. Look also to suppliers of stonecarving tools.

Files

Files differ from rasps in having fine ridges rather than individual teeth (*see* Fig 4.32), producing a comparatively fine – to extremely fine – cut, depending on the grade. They are very commonly used in metalwork and are useful for producing an intermediary finish between that produced by rasps, and that of sandpaper.

A **single-cut file** has a series of sharp ridges diagonally crossing the blade. The **double-cut file** has a

Fig 4.31 Rasps: the middle one is 2in (50mm) wide.

Fig 4.32 Files (single-cut and double-cut) have ridges while rasps have teeth.

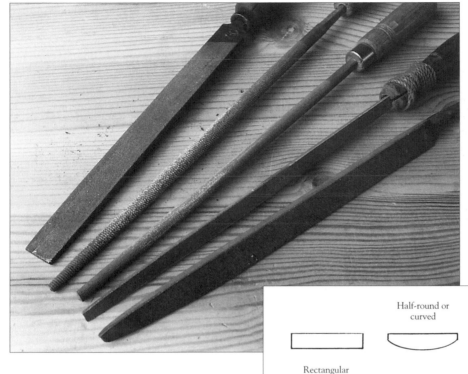

Fig 4.33 Files: flat, round and triangular cross-sections.

Fig 4.34 Files, rasps and rifflers can have any of a variety of basic cross-sections.

second set of ridges crossing the first, producing diamond-shaped teeth; these files remove material quicker than the single-cut file.

The size and spacing of the grooves produces the grade of file: **rough** is the coarsest, through **bastard**, **second-cut** and **smooth**, to **dead smooth**. Sometimes files are numbered according to a Swiss system, in which case 00 is the coarsest and 6 (06) is the finest.

In cross-section, files can be square, round, flat, half-round or triangular, each used for different purposes (*see* Fig 4.34). The variable lengths can be parallel or tapering.

Small, round, tapering files are known as **rat-tail** or – smaller again – **mouse-tail files**. Needle files are slight, very fine versions of these files, often sold in sets for precision metalwork. Needle rasps are also available

Although files are common in tool shops, good selections will also be found in engineer's suppliers. Look also at the files and rasps used for repairing vehicle bodywork and shaping plastic.

Rifflers

Rifflers are small paddle-like rasps, usually double-ended, with a narrow, metal handle in between. The lengths of these tools vary between 6in and 12in (150

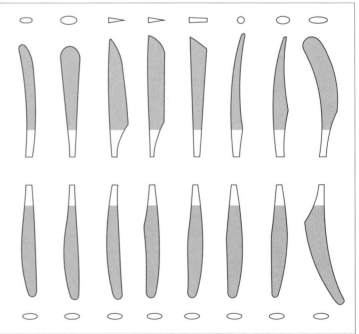

Fig 4.35 A selection of rifflers.

Picture © Alec Tiranti Ltd.

and 300mm), but the cuts all tend to be similar – that is, medium.

The shape of the 'paddle' ends is very variable: straight, curved or angled; round, flat, triangular, convex or knife-like; parallel or tapered. The two ends may be different or the same. Manufacturers will have their own idea of what is most useful, or marketable.

Possibly relating to the Old French *rifler*, meaning to 'scratch, strip or plunder', this bunch of assorted

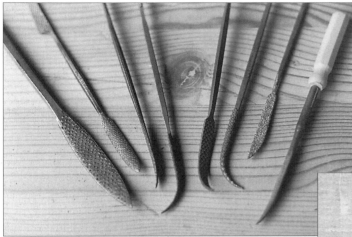

Fig 4.36 Rifflers come in a great variety of shapes and sizes. The second from the right has a coating of tungsten-carbide particles.

Fig 4.37 Surform shapes are only available in basic, simple profiles.

Fig 4.38 Close up of Surform teeth and perforations.

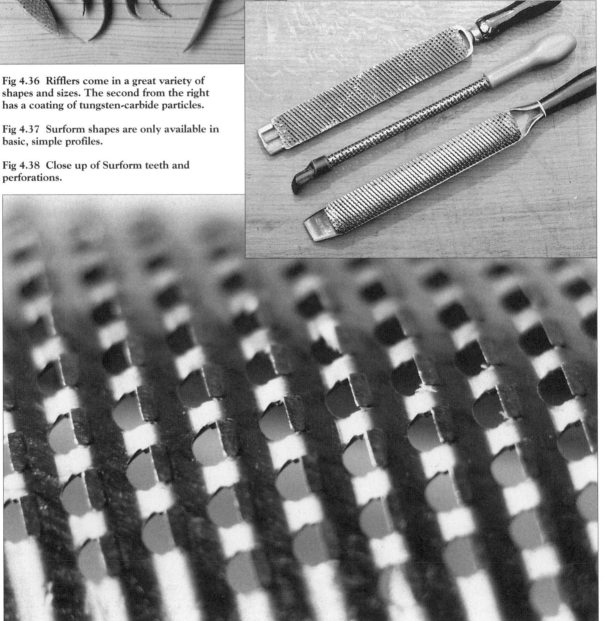

rasps can get into corners and awkward areas which are inaccessible to carving tools and finish them off. They can perform particularly useful functions in undercut and pierced work.

Surforms

The Surform, sometimes known as a **shaper tool**, is a patented rasp of the modern industrial age, made from stamped, sheet steel. Its hardened teeth cut into the wood and the dust passes through holes in the blade to keep the cutting surface clear (*see* Fig 4.38). The blade itself is replaceable and fits onto a separate frame or handle.

The shapes are limited and simple: flat, convex or round; the cuts are either coarse or fine. They remove wood quickly and efficiently to produce a smooth surface with light teeth marks. Children seem to be able to handle these tools well.

Tungsten-carbide

More and more, patented processes for attaching tungsten-carbide grit onto a flexible backing fibre are producing hard-wearing, rasp-like tools. The products themselves may be flexible or, when applied to hard plastic or an aluminium backing, shaped like true rasps or files.

There is usually a colour grading from coarse to fine cut. Although these, along with diamond grit versions, were principally designed for metalworking, the coarsest versions will abrade wood like fine sandpaper.

Using abrading tools

The function of rasps and files is more that of shaping than carving. They are not normally used for producing detail, but for reducing waste wood, rounding, refining, smoothing and exploring. It is always quickest to remove preliminary waste wood with a gouge and mallet.

It is easy to dismiss these tools as simple, or as expedients for those who cannot sharpen or use a carving tool properly – but very beautiful, refined and subtle forms can be made with these tools alone. They come into their own, prior to sanding, in the types of sculpture where very smooth planes are needed to show off the grain of the wood. Rasps start the process, followed by files and then sandpaper.

One end of a file or rasp will have a sharp tang for a handle as the handles are normally supplied separately. The handle itself needs a ferrule to prevent it splitting and can be fitted as described in Chapter 2 for carving-tool handles (*see* pages 61–5). It is better to use a handle to prevent damaging the palm of your hand (*see* Fig 4.39); if it is not possible, remove some of the tang on a grinding wheel.

Both hands are normally applied to a rasp. Binding the far end of a coarse rasp, or wearing a tough glove, will protect your fingers from the metal teeth (*see* Fig 4.40). This is also useful when you want to reverse the rasp and draw it towards you.

Fig 4.39 The tang of a rasp can be uncomfortably sharp to the palm. Fit a simple handle for protection.

Fig 4.40 The far end of this Surform shaper has a useful grip which spares wearing out the fingertips.

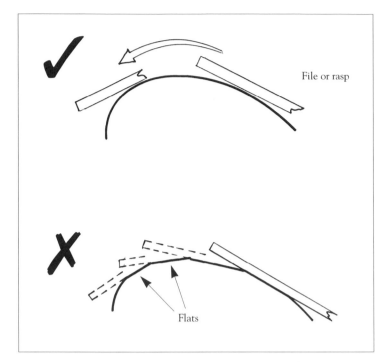

Fig 4.41 **Move the rasp or file smoothly to follow the surface you are seeking.**

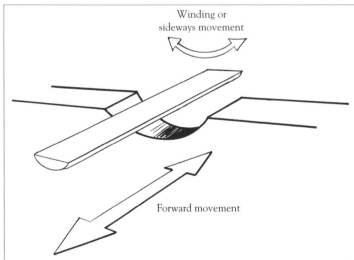

Fig 4.42 **For internal surfaces, a combined action is best with the rasp or file.**

Fig 4.43 **Winding the rasp through its cut is essential to achieve the smooth, unspoilt lines appropriate to this type of work. The rasp is one sold for car bodywork and gives a very clean cut on wood.**

When rasping or filing, strongly visualize the form beneath. As the tools are pushed forwards through their cut, send them around the contours of the shape that you are seeking, rather than producing a series of 'flats' (*see* Fig 4.41). For a good result on the surface make the rasp or file move *sideways* at the same time as moving it forwards. On internal curved surfaces, a half-round rasp or file stroked with this winding type of cut will avoid grooves forming (*see* Figs 4.42, 4.43).

Sometimes, when carving in the conventional way, resorting to a rasp, file or riffler – before returning to the carving tools – can help clarify larger forms and shapes.

The teeth of rasps and files clog with wood, especially those with a finer cut or when working with resinous or moist material. The tools then become inefficient. Try coating them with chalk before using them on these sorts of wood. This does not apply to Surform tools which allow the spoil to pass through the blade.

A wire brush used across the teeth of a rasp will unclog them (*see* Fig 4.44). Dried, resinous wood can be softened with paraffin before brushing, and it is also possible to dig around the teeth with a soft-metal point.

Files and tools with finer teeth need a **file card** – a special, short-bristled wire brush designed for the purpose. This brush is stroked across the teeth.

Care

Files and rasps are often treated badly and thrown into boxes and damp corners. They really deserve better. Never use them as levers as they are brittle and may snap, or even as hammers – when the teeth may fly off. For similar reasons store them carefully, perhaps in a rack to prevent their teeth from clashing together and bluntening. The metal itself is susceptible to rust

which will affect the cutting edges and teeth by dulling them – so store them in a dry place.

Worn abrading tools are worth keeping as they cut less voraciously than new ones.

CARPENTRY TOOLS

Tools which are found quite naturally in the kit of anyone working in wood also have a supporting place among carvers. Cutting away calculated amounts of waste wood with a saw will save a lot of time. As before, buy good quality tools as they are needed.

Handsaws

This group of tools includes saws for cutting straight lines, curves and enlarging holes.

For cutting straight lines

■ **Cross-cut saws** for cutting *across* the grain
■ **Rip saws** for cutting *with* the grain
■ **Backsaws** (such as **tenon saws** or the **'gentleman's saw'**) for cutting in either direction

These saws come in varying degrees of coarseness, with the cut being measured by the number of teeth per

Fig 4.44 Regular use of a wire brush and the smaller file card will unclog the teeth of abrasive tools.

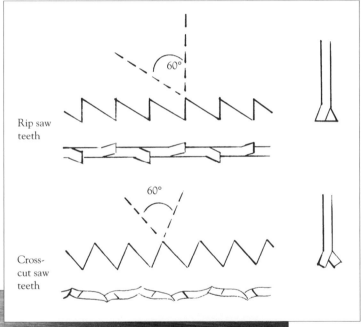

Rip saw teeth

Cross-cut saw teeth

Fig 4.45 You can distinguish a rip saw (for cutting *with* the grain) from a cross-cut saw (for cutting *across* the grain) by examining its teeth. Rip saws have chisel-like points for paring between fibres; cross-cut saws have more knife-like teeth for cutting through them.

Fig 4.46 Disposable saws with such hardened teeth (which cannot be sharpened) are tending to replace the conventional types that need sharpening.

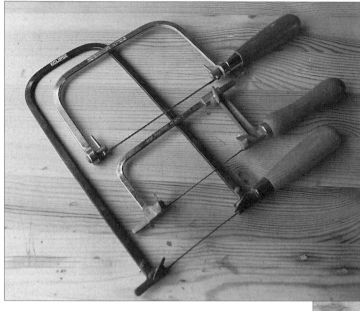

Fig 4.47 Saws for curved work, all with detachable blades that will insert through holes pierced in a carving. The largest is the fretsaw; the smallest takes a thin fretsaw blade; the remaining coping saw is the most useful one to have handy.

Fig 4.48 The bowsaw looks like something out of the ark – and may well be as old. The blade is held in position by removable pins so the saw can be used for pierced work.

inch (tpi) – the lower the number, the coarser the cut is. Such saws are designed to cut in straight lines. First make a positive drawing cut with the saw to guide the subsequent cuts. Hold the handle with the index finger extended and cut rhythmically without jerking the forward pressure.

For cutting curves

■ **Bow saws**
■ **Coping saws**
■ **Fret saws**

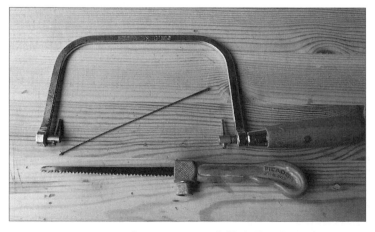

Fig 4.49 The coping saw with blade detached (above). For larger holes, the keyhole saw may be the answer.

These saws have narrow, delicate, replaceable blades for cutting curves. The bowsaw, a really ancient tool, is the largest and coarsest. The fret saw is the finest with a great reach of cut. The blades themselves are usually of one coarseness and can be inserted through holes in the wood to cut internal curves – turning the blades in different directions when the frame gets in the way. Make sure the blade is straight and not twisted along its length, and do not exert too much pressure. Twisting and pressure tend to snap the blade.

For enlarging holes

■ **Keyhole saw**

This is a narrow saw projecting from a handle and used, as its name suggests, for inserting into a preliminary hole and cutting a keyhole shape. From a carver's point of view it can be used to enlarge holes without the reassembling necessary, for example, with a coping saw. Be gentle on the forward pressure to avoid kinking the blade.

Planes

A metal carpenter's plane may be used for: dressing the surface of a panel of wood to reveal the grain; to make drawing on the surface easier; and for joining pieces of

Fig 4.50 Jack (left) and block planes.

Fig 4.51 A view of a plane blade, exaggerated slightly, to show the rounded corners and slight curving of the cutting edge.

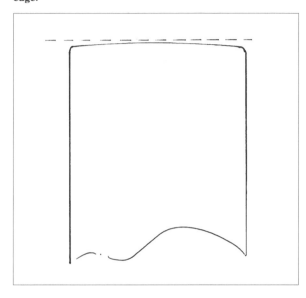

wood. Of the many varieties the **jack plane** and the small, adjustable **block plane** are probably the most useful.

The cutting edge of a plane blade is sharpened so that it is *slightly* rounded, or 'nosed' (*see* Fig 4.51), to prevent the corners digging in and to merge cuts. By moving the plane across the wood, more wood can be removed from a specific place without having to tilt it.

To remove the shavings more easily when working hardwoods move the backing plate forwards to reveal about ⅟₁₆in (2mm) of blade; for soft woods reveal about ³⁄₁₆in (5mm). Sharpen keenly, and lay the plane on its side when not in use; store with the cutting edge retracted.

Spokeshaves

Spokeshaves will smooth large, curved areas – flattening off facets and shaping. **Flat-faced spokeshaves** are used for convex surfaces and **round-faced spokeshaves** for concave ones. Those with the

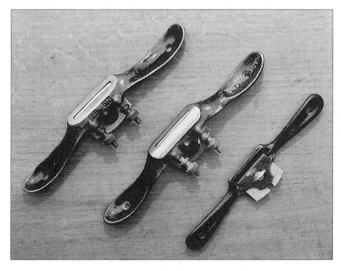

Fig 4.52 Spokeshaves may have a flat or round face.

Fig 4.53 A wooden block which is used to get a better hold on the spokeshave blade for sharpening.

blade adjusted by a screw handle are the most convenient.

Like the plane, the cutting edge of a spokeshave is curved to a slight centre prominence. A cleaner finish and an easier stroke is obtained with the cutting edge presented at a skew to the direction of cut, slicing it in its passage. Try to feel into the curves you are making.

As the blades are quite small, holding them for sharpening can be a little awkward. Grip the blade in a block of wood kept especially for the purpose, jamming it into a deep saw-cut (*see* Fig 4.53). Sharpen as keenly as a carving chisel.

Hand routers

Largely superseded by electrical routers, hand routers may still have their place in levelling a background evenly – for example between letters in relief work. The smallest version is known as an **old woman's tooth**. The name 'router' comes from the Anglo-Saxon *root*, meaning to dig or grub up.

To work most efficiently, remove the bulk of the wood in the normal way and 'set in' with gouge and mallet. A depth gauge made from wooden strips will be useful in this preliminary stage, which should end with about ⅛in (3mm) to spare. Finish to depth with the router – the blade of which should be properly sharp – working with the grain where possible. The surface may still need final grounding with flat (no. 3) gouges or scrapers to remove any tears left by the routing.

Fig 4.54 The hand router is a cheap alternative for those who dislike the noise and speed of the electrical version, but need something for checking the level of backgrounds.

Other tools

The usual array of carpenter's tools includes hammers, brace and bits, wheel brace, screwdrivers and so on – all generally useful to a carver undertaking a variety of work. Although power drills have replaced the wheel brace, for example, it is sometimes simpler to pick up the hand tool from the side of the bench. And, again, the work may need a delicate and precise touch, such as only a slow, hand-controlled tool will give.

SINGULAR CARVING TOOLS

Knives

Very beautiful and complex carvings are created by knife work alone, and some carvers like to mix knives with their conventional carving tools – or at least have one or two knives handy.

Whittling, coming originally from the Anglo-Saxon *Thwitan*, to cut or pare, is the name given to probably the oldest sort of carving, using only knives. Special knives are also used for **chip carving** (*see* Fig 4.55) – where geometrically shaped pieces of wood, mostly triangular, are removed from a panel to produce intricate patterns. Whittling and chip carving, in their sole use of knives, are considered by some to be crafts in their own right.

Many types of knives are suitable, and available, for carving. All are straight-bladed with the names of the shapes varying according to both makers and users. There are, however, probably only five basic shapes to choose from (*see* Fig 4.56). Some knives are angled and drawn towards the user to pare off shavings (*see* Fig 4.57).

Safety considerations point to the danger of knives which fold, closing on the user's fingers. Locking knives, or knives with fixed blades, are much safer – especially for the beginner.

The emphasis on keen sharpening that has been made for carving gouges and chisels also applies to carving knives. New knives still need additional sharpening, on the Arkansas stone at least.

Sharpening

1 Place the oiled benchstone end-on, and lay the blade flat on its surface with the edge pointing away.
2 Lift the back of the blade slightly and stroke the

Fig 4.55 Carving knives, rivetted into their handles. The two different makes on the right show the standardization of shapes.

Fig 4.56 The five basic blade shapes: (a) spear or pen; (b) slant tip; (c) sloyd or clip; (d) spey; and (e) sheepfoot.

Fig 4.57 This orientation of knife blade is designed to be drawn towards the user.

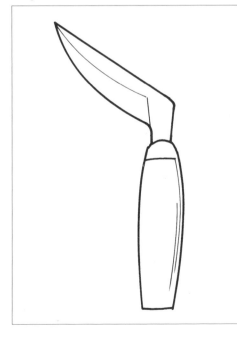

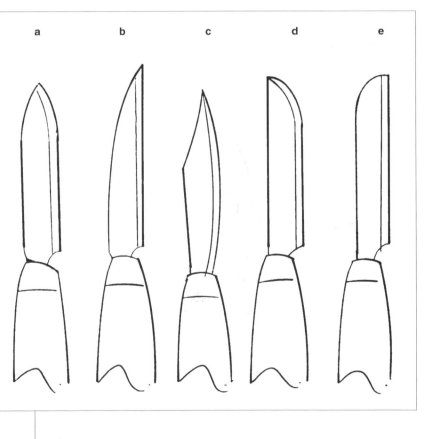

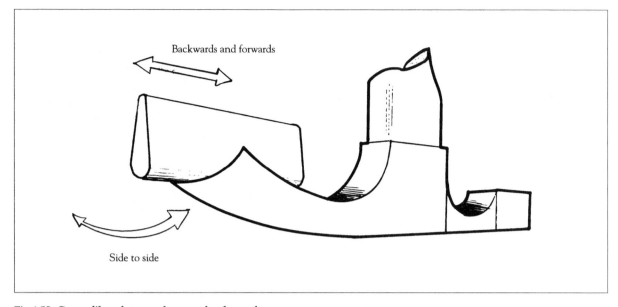

Backwards and forwards

Side to side

Fig 4.58 Gouge-like adzes are sharpened only on the inside, with grades of large slipstone.

Fig 4.59 Is is easy to bury an adze in the timber by trying to remove too much wood at once.

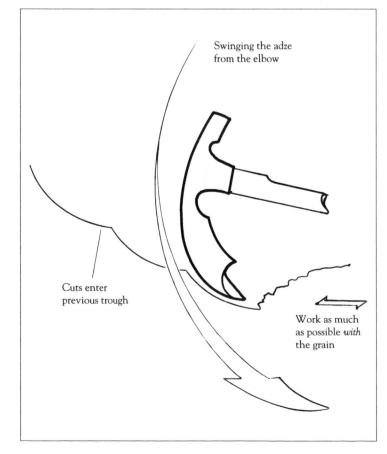

Swinging the adze from the elbow

Cuts enter previous trough

Work as much as possible *with* the grain

edge backwards and forwards, or in a circular motion, on the stone, maintaining the same angle.

3 Repeat equally on both sides. Use the method of looking for the white line along the edge to check the sharpness, as described for carving tools (*see* page 184).

4 Strop by dragging the blade backwards on the strop, at the same angle at which it was sharpened.

Adzes

An **adze** is an ancient tool for crudely shaping wood, and still has its attraction for some carvers of larger sculptures. It is often used with an axe, instead of a mallet and gouge.

Adzes are available in flat or hollow cross-sections, with the blades curved along their length to match the arcing swing from the shoulder or elbow. All adzes have just the internal bevel and are best sharpened with large slipstones only (*see* Fig 4.58).

Adzes have a tendency to bury their edges in the wood and be used like crowbars to lever away a chip (*see* Fig 4.59). A large gouge, propelled through its cut by a mallet, will cut more cleanly and accurately so for most carvers it is a better option.

Scorps

A **scorp** is a strange-looking tool which is drawn towards the user, carving large convex shapes. A similar tool – although not so tough – is the **hook knife**.

Fig 4.60 Miscellaneous, possibly 'specialized', tools: the adze (top); scorp; chip carving knife; and hook knife.

Fig 4.61 Sharpen the scorp with a round slipstone from the inside.

Fig 4.62 A hook knife can be similarly sharpened with slipstones.

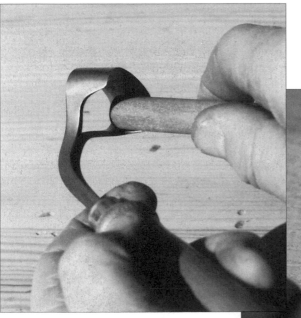

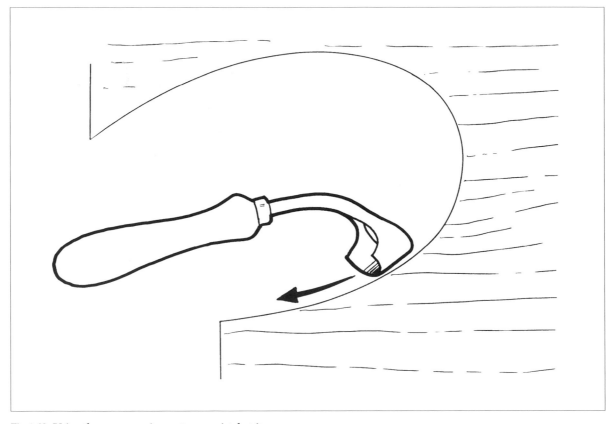

Fig 4.63 Using the scorp requires a strong wrist, but it can be invaluable for working sculptural recesses, with the grain.

The advantage of these tools is that the edge cuts *from the bottom of the hollow outwards* and in some circumstances will give a cleaner finish than a gouge worked in the opposite way. They can also get into deep, sculptural hollows where a carving gouge is impractical (*see* Fig 4.63). They are hard on the wrist, and therefore most of the waste wood needs removing from such a hollow first. This can be done by drilling, with bent gouges or using a burr on a flexible shaft.

These are the sorts of tools that are worth knowing about and having for specific needs or projects – in which case they can be indispensable.

PUNCHES AND FROSTERS

Punches produce specific indentations, such as circles or crosses, when they are tapped onto the wood surface. They were very popular with the Victorians,

Picture © Henry Taylor Tools Ltd

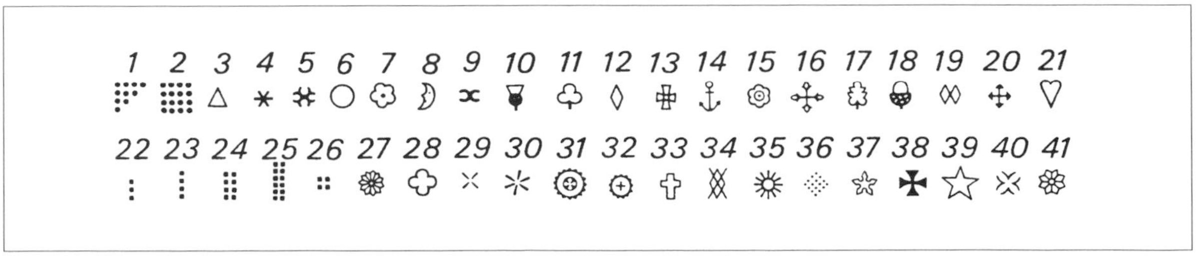

Fig 4.64 A selection of punches.

Fig 4.65 Close up of the working ends of two circular punches (left), two eye punches, and a floret.

who produced a large number of different punch patterns, some of which are still available today (*see* Fig 4.64).

One shape which is particularly useful is the **eye punch**: an oval shape pointed at one end (*see* Fig 4.65). This tool will sink and flatten the bottom of the 'eyes' that form in the junctions between certain sorts of acanthus leaves (*see* Fig 4.66). Eye punches can be easily made by grinding or filing an appropriate size of nail. The eye *must* be carved properly in the wood first – using the punch on its own will only crush the fibres and leaf edges to bad effect.

Frosters or **frosting tools** create a hatched effect of many dotted indentations (*see* Fig 4.67). They are used to finish a background and provide a contrast to some simple relief carving, or even to produce a decorative shadow effect.

Frosters can be bought, or made by filing the flattened ends of large nails or bolts with small triangular files (*see* Fig 4.68).

For the frosting to look its best, clean the surface or background properly with carving tools first. Frosters should not be used to hide rough work or a poor finish. Frosting is only a surface treatment, a contrast, and not particularly meant to be noticed. It is

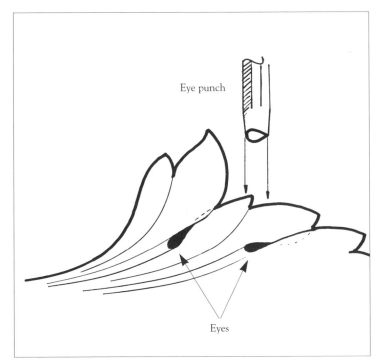

Fig 4.66 Use an appropriate size of eye punch to flatten the bottom of an acanthus leaf 'eye'.

therefore best to use the frosting tool with discretion and a lightness of touch. Overlap the edges of the indentations to provide a smooth transition across the

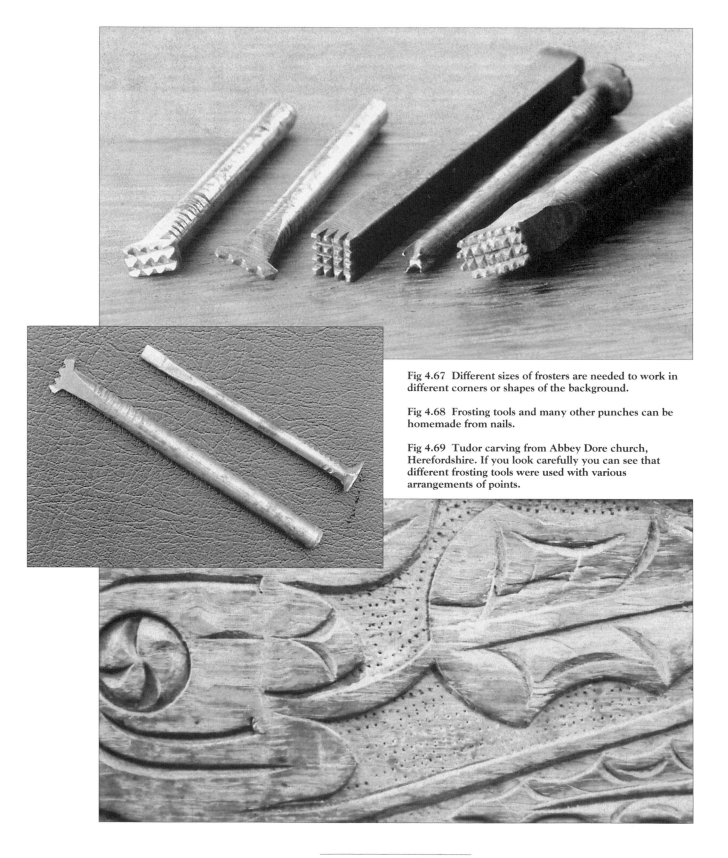

Fig 4.67 Different sizes of frosters are needed to work in different corners or shapes of the background.

Fig 4.68 Frosting tools and many other punches can be homemade from nails.

Fig 4.69 Tudor carving from Abbey Dore church, Herefordshire. If you look carefully you can see that different frosting tools were used with various arrangements of points.

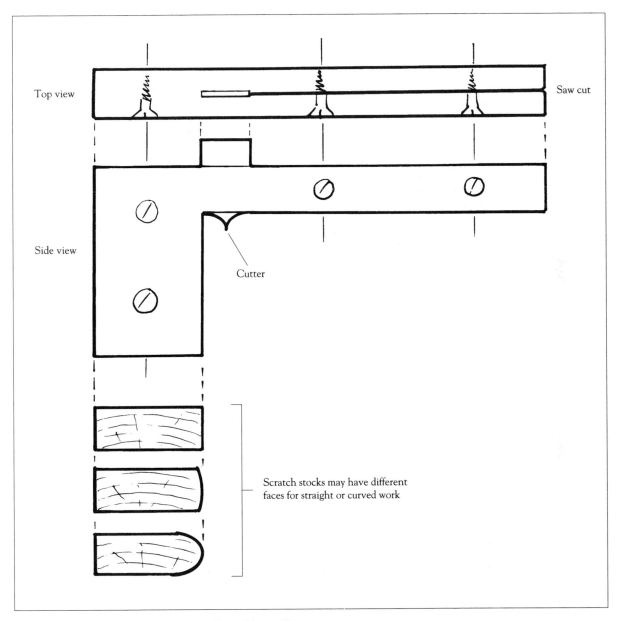

Top view

Saw cut

Side view

Cutter

Scratch stocks may have different
faces for straight or curved work

**Fig 4.70 A scratch stock for running small mouldings. The
cutter can be shaped to a specific need.**

frosting and work either to an even pattern or
randomly, but not mixing the two.

SCRATCH STOCKS AND SCRAPERS

Scratch stocks will run lengths of small mouldings –
particularly in furniture carving – which are then

carved or left unadorned. Although the idea and
construction of a scratch stock are simple – a blade is
clamped between two L-shaped pieces of wood (*see* Fig
4.70) – surprisingly accurate and detailed work can be
carried out. Mouldings wider than about 1in (25mm)
are not so easy to work this way, however, and
different shapes of blade may be needed to create a
larger, more complicated, profile in the wood.

The blade of a scratch stock can be made from an

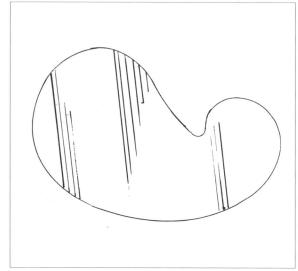

Fig 4.72 A goose-necked scraper, available commercially.

Fig 4.71 Scratch stocks are quickly made and can produce a wide range of moulded edges.

Fig 4.73 Different shapes of scrapers, with the goose-necked scraper on the right. They can be ground to specific shapes.

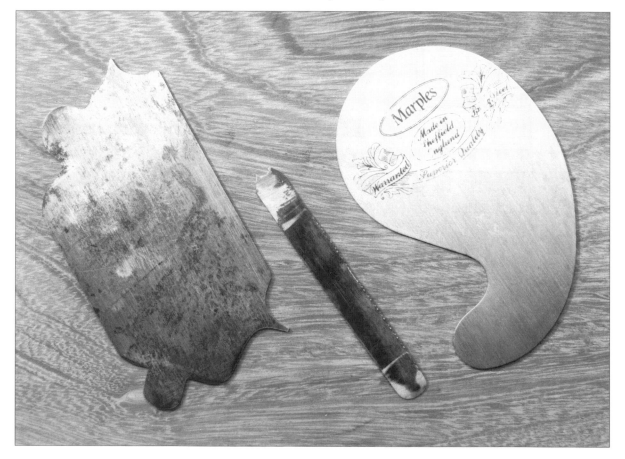

Fig 4.74 Sharpening a scraper involves burring over the edge ('ticketting') – you can use the side of an old chisel. This edge, if actually sharpened correctly ('ticketted'), will remove a proper shaving and so must cut, rather than scrape.

old hacksaw blade, shaped sharply square with a grinder and a file, and finished with slipstones. Do not blue the metal on the grinder. The shape is a 'negative' or reverse of the moulding shape that is actually wanted. Check the profile on waste wood.

An exact amount of the scratch blade protrudes from the stock, which is kept butted against the edge of the wood to act as a guide or fence. Be sure to fix the blade tightly in the stock; if it loosens the chances are you will not notice until too late and the work will be spoiled. The metal shape is worked backwards and forwards, stopping once the depth of cut is reached. Start with light strokes, tilting the stock forwards. Do not try to take off too much wood at once, but proceed gradually and methodically. If the moulding is to be carved, avoid sanding – the grit will take off the edge of the carving tool.

Scrapers are pieces of hardened sheet steel used to flatten surfaces such as backgrounds, or clean particular carved shapes. They are worked by hand, rather than in a jig like a scratch stock. Make them from old saw or hacksaw blades, shaping as for scratch stock blades and 'ticketted' – that is raising a wire edge which cuts, by rubbing an even harder piece of metal along the edge at a slight angle.

Scrapers can be indispensable in some work and surprisingly versatile. They are used mainly in furniture which is to be polished, prior to fine sanding (for example in cleaning up flutes in chair legs or bedposts), or for the backgrounds of low relief carving (such as is found in chair splats), or for cleaning up awkward grains.

SANDPAPER

Whether a carving is sandpapered or not depends both on the carver's intentions as well as the nature of the work. As sanding can be a tedious, unpleasant business, it is best to use other tools to get as close to the final surface as possible. Shaped scrapers used over the surface will flatten the surface, removing carving tool and rasp marks.

Sandpaper comes in a variety of abrasives, backing papers and qualities. Flexible backing cloth is probably the most useful for carvers. The abrasive is graded between very coarse and extremely fine. In its manufacture the abrasive grit is sieved to get a uniform particle size. The more holes in the sieve, the finer the grit. So the higher the number (i.e. the number of holes in the sieve) designated to a particular grade of sandpaper, the finer the abrasive.

You need to work through the grades of paper to get the best result (*see* Fig 4.75). The finer grades remove the scratch marks of the coarser grades. Always work *with* the grain, as working across the grain produces scratch marks, the smallest of which will show up when the work is stained, oiled or waxed. It is better to sand with the fingers, sensitive to the surface beneath, rather than sanding blocks. *Never* blow the dust away as it may get in your eyes – a vacuum cleaner is a help here. After each sanding, dampen the wood slightly and, when it has dried, sand again.

MARKING-OUT EQUIPMENT

Carvers often make measurements, for example for symmetry, and occasionally need to work accurately to a design. Calipers, dividers, compasses and rulers, as well as set-squares, marking gauges, carbon and tracing paper, and chalk, thick pencils or charcoal, all come in handy at different times.

ELECTRIC TOOLS

Overview

There are some carvers who take a purist attitude to carving and shun any electrical and mechanical aids. But it is a free choice. When we use a tool, it is both a means to an end and part of the creative process in which we are engaged – a sort of end in itself. *All* tools have advantages and limitations, whether they are hand tools or power-driven; all engage with the user in their own way; and all leave their particular marks on the outcome. We are free to choose the way and speed of working that best suits us, and the result we seek.

Electric tools can save a great deal of time by removing waste wood from carvings prior to working

Fig 4.75 Finishing such a barley-twist spindle involves working conscientiously with the shape, using the whole range of grits.

with gouges and chisels. Such tools include **power drills**, **power sanders**, and **power files**; **jigsaws**, **chainsaws** and **sabre saws**; and **pillar drills** and **pillar routers**. Exactly what use can be made of these tools depends on the nature of the work. Some electric tools can be made to finish work in their own right. Nowadays, many power tools are possessed and used as standard kit by large numbers of people; they need not be bought specifically for carving.

There is not the space in this book to go into the detailed use of these tools, but *do* read and observe the safety and operating instructions provided by the manufacturers.

Remember that electric tools are designed to be fast and events happen quickly – and sometimes suddenly. It is very easy to remove more wood than you originally intended, with possibly disastrous consequences to a design. Work out your intentions carefully first and proceed a step at a time. Check what is happening and then go on a bit further: 'Check twice and cut once'.

One very useful, almost indispensable, piece of equipment for a carver is the **bandsaw**. Versatile, safe, precise, simple and friendly, a bandsaw will rough out carvings and save a lot of time and effort in a variety of ways. After looking at this piece of equipment, two other electric carving tools gaining in popularity will be discussed: the **Arbortech** and the **high-speed flexible shaft**.

Bandsaws

Bandsaws range in size from small, bench-mounted models to large floor-mounted ones (*see* Fig 4.76). They are principally designed to make curved cuts – the actual amount of curve possible depends on the width of the blade – but they should be able to cut reasonably straight lines. The blade is a continuous band passing over two or three wheels, with one section open for use and fitted with guides and safety guards. The blades eventually wear out or break – usually at the join – and need to be replaced.

When buying a bandsaw, the two important dimensions to consider are the *throat* (from blade to machine body) and the *depth* of cut, both of which affect what you can achieve.

Blades will break as the flexing of the metal produces 'fatigue'. This fatigue is greatest with:

▪ Smaller wheels on the bandsaw

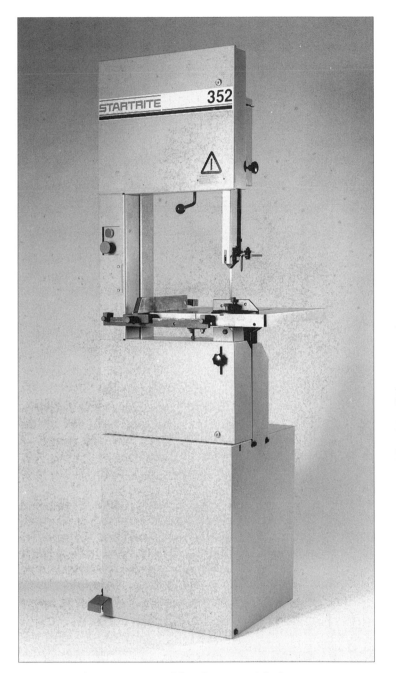

Fig 4.76 Bandsaws are very useful to the carver. A basic floor-standing bandsaw such as this will deal with a large range of work.

▪ Three rather than two wheels
▪ Faster speeds
▪ Higher blade tension.

These points should be borne in mind when buying or using a bandsaw.

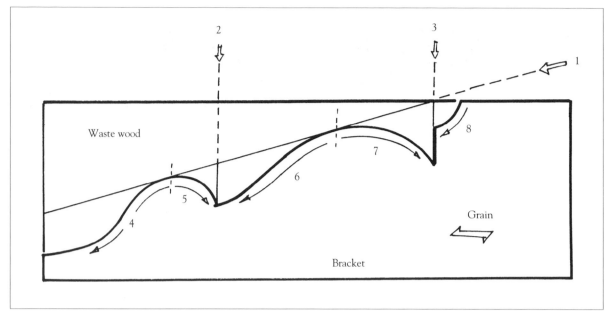

Fig 4.77 Work out the order of bandsaw cuts before you start so that the blade does not get trapped as it tries to reverse from a cut.

USING BANDSAWS

■ Always set the blade guides properly and accurately.

■ Feed the wood into the saw lightly and let the machine do the work. Never direct the pressure of your hands towards the blade; keep them as far away from it as is practicable. Use a push-stick for small work.

■ It is difficult, sometimes impossible, to reverse a bandsaw blade out of its cut as it tends to be pulled forwards out of its guides by the fibres of the wood. Try to work out the best approach before starting to cut (*see* Fig 4.77). Make stop cuts where necessary or work away the waste in smaller pieces – rather than getting the blade stuck in a position from which it cannot extract itself.

■ If a blade does get stuck, stop and disconnect the machine. Raise the blade guides enough to place a batten of wood across the blade teeth above the work. Use this batten to hold the blade in its guides while drawing the work forwards.

■ Curves are cut better if you think of working from the *back* of the blade rather than just the teeth.

■ The closer you can get to your original design, the less wood that subsequently needs to be removed – but the less freedom there is to alter and change. Therefore you must be sure of your design if you are adopting the close-shave approach.

SAFETY

■ Always follow the manufacturer's instructions and recommendations; ensure the correct width of blade is being used for the curves to be cut, with the appropriate tension.

■ Always set the safety guards correctly, within ¼in (6mm) of the wood surface, and only adjust them with the machine stopped.

■ Take care when coiling or uncoiling the blades – gloves are recommended.

Double check everything, including the locking of the table and any fence, before starting the machine.

The Arbortech

The Arbortech is a patented circular blade that fits on a 4–4½in (100–115mm) angle grinder. The blade itself has the appearance of a chainsaw blade, but with the teeth designed to cut on one side as well as the edge (*see* Fig 4.79). There are other versions of the same concept that actually use chains. The blade itself is reasonably priced so the main outlay is in the angle grinder.

USING THE ARBORTECH

The Arbortech is essentially a wasting device – cutting trenches, hollows and removing unwanted material

Fig 4.78 The Arbortech blade fits to an angle grinder and wastes wood at an impressive rate. Safety guards are available and recommended.

Fig 4.79 close-up of the cutting teeth of the Arbortech. These can be resharpened quite easily; instructions come with the blade.

rapidly. Both the edge and free side of the wheel can be used. The blade is sharpened with a chainsaw file or a special sharpening stick which is like a long slipstone.

If the grinder is held in both hands, quite delicate control is possible. Light pressure should be used with the blade doing the work. Adopt a light stroking action, stroking the blade towards you against its rotation and nibbling away, rather than making deep, heavy cuts.

Used with thought, the Arbortech can speed up the initial roughing out of sculptures (see Fig 4.80), perhaps after they leave the bandsaw.

SAFETY
Although a safe and effective way of removing wood, the Arbortech does have its drawbacks. The grinders

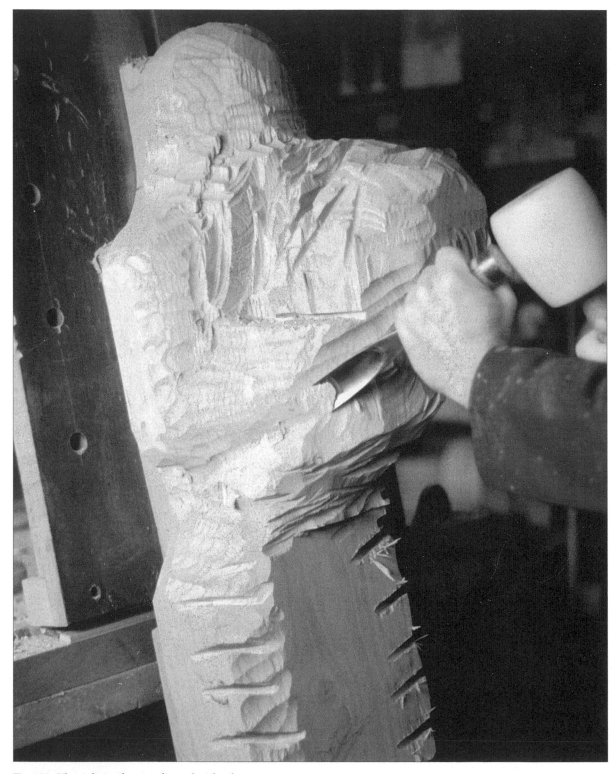

Fig 4.80 The Arbortech, co-ordinated with a large gouge and mallet, soon removed wood in the initial rough stages of this figure carving.

to which the Arbortech is fitted have a no-load speed of around 11 000 rpm so dust and chips are flung quite violently from the blade. There are guards available to reduce the effect, but face masks and eye and ear protection, as well as tight sleeve cuffs, are all necessary. This may make the user feel a little disconnected from reality, to say the least.

To some people, the noise and speed are aesthetically and otherwise unacceptable. It is preferable to use an Arbortech before buying it, if you can.

Both the Arbortech and the grinder come with important instructions for use and safety. Always follow these and *always* sharpen or adjust the blade with the machine isolated.

High-speed flexible shafts

These machines consist of a drive motor, hanging from a bracket (often on the wall), which rotates a flexible shaft at a high speed. The shaft ends in a handpiece which can be fitted with a large range of cutters, burrs, drills, sanding pads and other accessories (*see* Fig 4.81). There may be a foot-operated pedal varying the speed between 500 and 20 000 rpm depending on the machine. Despite the speed, the operation is surprisingly quiet.

The size of the motor and handpiece varies. If such a tool is only to be used occasionally, a smaller motor

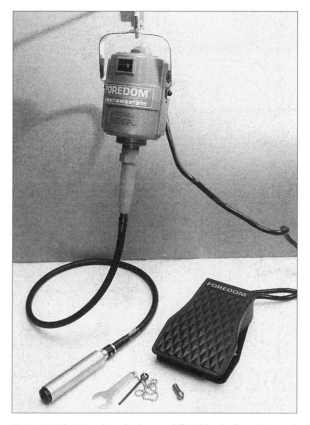

Fig 4.81 The Foredom high-speed flexible shaft, motor and foot pedal.

Fig 4.82 The 'business end' of a high-speed flexible shaft. Cutters come in a whole range of sizes and shapes.

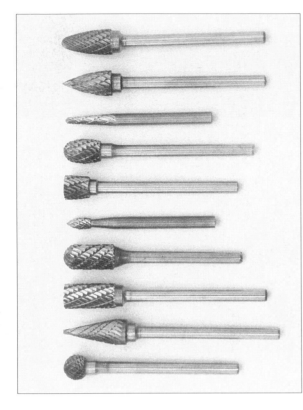

Fig 4.83 A range of solid carbide, high-speed burrs.

Fig 4.84 Tungsten-carbide-coated rotary burrs for the high-speed flexible shaft.

will be a satisfactory, cheaper option. If heavy work is contemplated, a larger, more 'professional' unit should be used. Although there are many makes on the market to be considered, one make that can be recommended is the Foredom range, both for the quality of the machine as well as the accessories available.

The burrs, cutters and so on that fit the handpieces are made in a very wide range of sizes and shapes (*see* Figs 4.82–4.84) – a manufacturer's catalogue needs to be consulted. Burrs and cutters can be made of tungsten-carbide or vanadium steel, and can have ruby- or diamond-grit coatings. They will cut other materials besides wood. Start with a few assorted ones to get a feel of what they can do and increase your stock as needs arise. Accessories are not cheap and it is easy to start building up large numbers.

USING HIGH-SPEED SHAFTS

High-speed shafts are primarily shaping and texturing tools, although very delicate work is possible too. Small burrs will clean up awkward corners and grain in normal carving. They cut slowly and a stroking action – as if using a paintbrush – is best. As with all electric tools, allow the tool to do the work – that is what you have paid for.

This equipment may be used as a complement to carving tools or on its own. It is largely a decision of temperament rather than need. Apart from texturing, they cannot do anything that the right carving tool can do. Using a high-speed flexible shaft is a different experience from using carving tools and comparisons are fairly worthless.

SAFETY

■ The cutters, burrs and sanding discs create a very fine dust when used, especially on hard wood, so a face mask is necessary.

■ Chips of wood can fly off and it is possible for a cutter or burr to break, so eye protection is essential.

■ Always use a cutter or other accessory at, or below, its maximum rated speed. Used above this speed and the cutter could fly apart, bend, or otherwise be damaged.

■ Never use a bent or damaged cutter or burr – or one that vibrates or chatters – throw these away. Never force or pressure the accessories.

MODIFYING TOOLS

Aims

To describe some simple ways of changing the existing shapes of woodcarving tools to make them suitable for particular carving situations

To indicate the possibilities for making entirely new tools

To look at some methods and equipment

To promote confidence with woodcarving tools

It must be said at the outset that this chapter is not a treatise on tool making. Based on my own understanding, experience and efforts, it is not without its limitations. However, my attempts to modify tools, or to make new ones when I have had the need, are worth sharing. The information and understanding that follows is gathered from simple processes that have worked well for me. Read through all the information before attempting these techniques.

INTRODUCTION

With the huge numbers of woodcarving tools on the market, it may be thought that carvers must be hard customers to satisfy if they cannot find what they need. But the truth is that the shapes and sizes available (for example the Sheffield List) were, and are, standardized through decisions relating to commercial production. Reasonably, manufacturers need to sell tools to be in business – and the more obscure a carving tool, the less financial contribution it will make. The shapes and sizes available today will be those that sell best – being the most useful to most carvers.

Carving, however, can involve very complicated three-dimensional shapes and the carver may find that

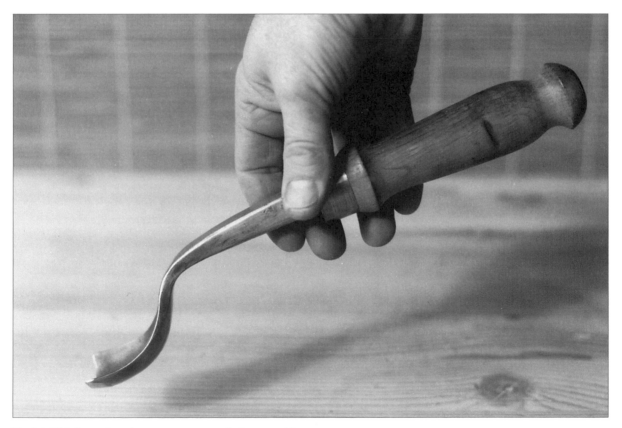

Fig 5.1 This large, front bent gouge was made from an old caulking chisel using a blacksmith's forge. Smaller work is possible with a much leaner set up.

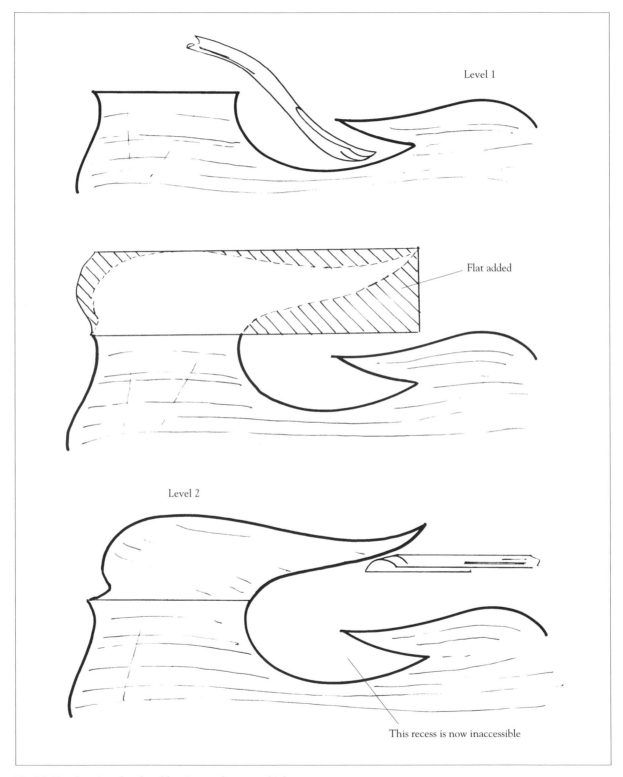

Level 1

Flat added

Level 2

This recess is now inaccessible

Fig 5.2 By planning ahead and leaving surfaces to which wood may be added, deep carving effects can be achieved by using 'flats'.

access to difficult corners or recesses will exploit his or her carving tools to the limit. In these circumstances carvers, tending to be adaptable, will work with what they have and make one tool do the work of several others, even if this means using the tool in an unorthodox way. And, within the range of tools produced by different firms, there will usually be something which will do the necessary work.

Failing these options, there is the possibility of changing the design of the carving. One approach is to incorporate 'flats', or areas where an additional piece of wood is added to increase the depth of carving at some point (*see* Fig 5.2). The deeper layers of carving are finished first, then the next layer of wood is added and carved. In this way a great depth of carving can be achieved using ordinary woodcarving tools – when the deepest layers would ordinarily have been impossible to carve. This has long been a carving practice, used, for instance, by medieval carvers, or Grinling Gibbons.

Sometimes, however, neither versatility nor re-designing solves a particular problem of access and, unless a new carving tool can be made, that part of the carving may be inaccessible. Rather than creating an entirely new tool, it is more usual to modify one already in use, perhaps a spare one. Perhaps you have been using a bent gouge which is not quite bent enough, or needs to be bent in a more appropriate direction; or perhaps a skew is not quite skewed

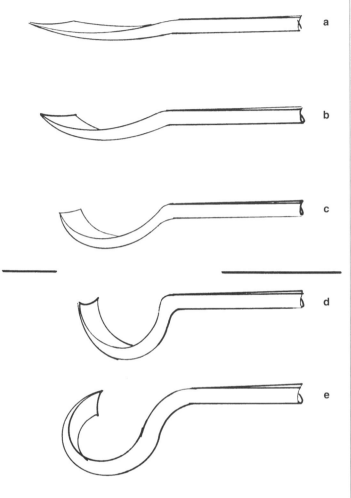

Fig 5.3 How much bend you get in a tool varies between manufacturers (**a–c**). But, for a particular job, you may need something which is not made (**d–e**).

Fig 5.4 Old and unused tools can be remade or changed into something much more useful.

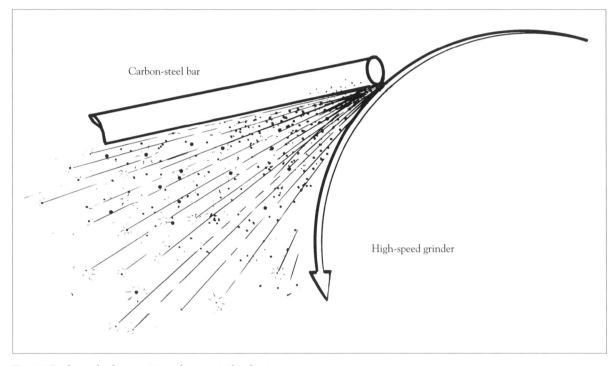

Carbon-steel bar

High-speed grinder

Fig 5.5 Such sparks from a piece of scrap steel indicate that it is made of high-carbon steel and can be made into a woodcarving tool.

enough. This level of modification is well within the capabilities of most carvers.

Repairing and reclaiming broken or worn-out carving tools is an offshoot of the ability to modify their shape. The same processes apply to these tools and include re-tempering a blade that has been over-heated or poorly tempered; and re-shaping a tool that has one of the faults mentioned in Chapter 2.

Gibbons was also thought to have made special tools to cope with certain carved work; this allows the possibility of designing carvings outside the compass of normal carving tools. If, to execute work, the availability of tools is not a problem, then there is one less barrier to a carver designing outrageously.

Some carvers, who enjoy smithing, make carving tools from scratch – which means finding the appropriate high-carbon steel, forging it to shape and then rendering the edge hard and strong enough to cut. Huge quantities of high-carbon steel are to be found in bars and rods (for example in the form of leaf and coil springs) in scrap yards, where rust is only superficial. The high-carbon nature of the steel reveals itself in the bright showers of spark that come from contact with a fast grinding wheel (*see* Fig 5.5). Such

metal can be made into perfectly serviceable woodcarving tools.

But, while the process is simpler than most people think, it involves more of a commitment to the idea – more expenditure and time to set up – than most woodcarvers wish to make, and cannot be dealt with here. A firm such as Henry Taylor Tools will make a tool to a carver's specification if it falls outside the range of tools they produce (see the Reference Section, page 346).

SCOPE OF MODIFYING TOOLS

Having said that this chapter is not a treatise on tool making, and that carvers, being practical by nature, should have no problems with the techniques and suggestions being offered here: what can someone reasonably expect to achieve in the way of modifying tools?

Perhaps the most useful area is creating a new bend – forwards, backwards or to the sides – or indeed straightening a blade. This is relatively straightforward if the bending is actually re-shaping an existing tool of the right width and sweep.

Hardening and tempering, or re-tempering, carving tools is again relatively straightforward, although it involves some means of generating the necessary heat. Hardening and tempering refer to heat-treating metal so as to render it hard enough, and resilient enough, to carve with. Bending a tool usually involves upsetting or destroying its temper so the tool then needs re-tempering – so this process supplements the previous one.

Lengthening, broadening or forming a new sweep are more skilled procedures and are more akin to the smithy work needed for new tools. Such curves are forged around suitable formers (*see* Figs 5.8, 5.9). Given time, care and some experimentation, these skills can be acquired to give further scope to the simple modifications that follow.

BASIC PROCEDURES

The shape of carving tools can be modified while they are cold, while being heated, or through a combination of both, depending on what is needed.

Cold procedures

Other than a small amount of bending to the soft parts of a tool – such as the tang – working with a cold tool involves *removing metal*.

Fig 5.6 All these tools were bent from the original shape for a particular purpose, using the basic techniques discussed in this chapter.

Fig 5.7 A short, wide old tool has enough metal to be forged into a longer narrower one.

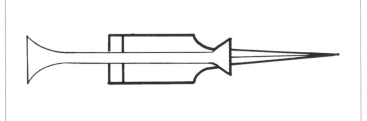

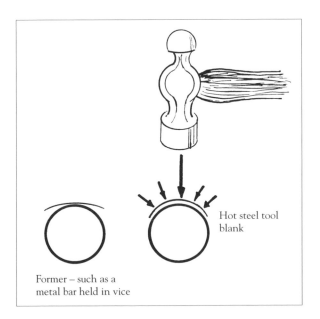

Former – such as a metal bar held in vice

Hot steel tool blank

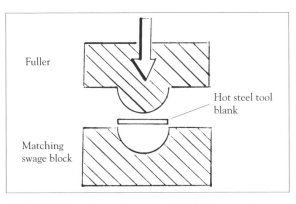

Fuller

Hot steel tool blank

Matching swage block

Fig 5.8 Tools are shaped commercially by hammering a 'fuller' into a matching 'swage block'.

Fig 5.9 It is not too difficult to change the sweep of a blade using a suitable former. Any roughness in the former will be transferred to the hot metal, so make sure the former surface is smooth.

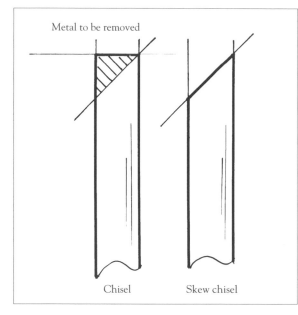

Fig 5.10 **Making a new skew chisel from an old firmer is an example of a simple cold procedure.**

Fig 5.11 **Even rasps and files can be re-shaped successfully. They are tempered harder, brittler, than carving tools.**

Removing metal is a limited, but valuable, process; grinding the bevel and even sharpening are instances of it. Another example is re-setting the angle of a skew chisel to increase its working point. As removing metal always results in something smaller, a larger tool, or amount of metal, is necessary to start with (*see* Fig 5.10).

Grinding wheels and sharpening stones do take time to remove metal from a blade as the steel has already been hardened. There is also the danger of blueing when a high-speed wheel is used. But if the tool has been **annealed** – that is, the hardness taken out – grinding and so on becomes a lot quicker. It make no odds if the steel turns blue, and files can be used for sensitive shaping. But to carve with the tool, it must be re-hardened.

Hot procedures

Removing cold steel may be a limited procedure, but when combined with heat, new possibilities are opened up. As the metal temperature rises, it becomes

ductile, plastic and eventually liquid.

At the ductile temperatures it can be bent and forged. **Forging** involves shaping the steel by hammering it: shorter, longer and so on. This procedure is more appropriate to a discussion of entirely new tools, and from the point of this chapter will only be touched on.

Probably the simplest source of heat for most carvers is a propane torch which is available with different sizes of nozzles or jets to produce corresponding flames. Such torches, working from a cylinder of gas, will generate the necessary heat for most tools. Woodstoves and fireplaces can also be acceptable.

After heating and shaping, further refinements of a carving tool can be made with the metal cold, before returning the necessary hardness and temper.

Details of heat sources are given later in this chapter (*see* page 241).

HARDENING, TEMPERING AND ANNEALING

The steel that is used in woodcarving tools is known as a 'high-carbon' steel; this has a certain amount of carbon in it (over 0.2%) as well as other trace elements. Put simply, the iron atoms in the steel form a lattice work; this crystal lattice expands as the steel is heated above a certain temperature and the carbon atoms enter. If the steel is cooled quickly ('quenched') the lattices contract, trapping the carbon atoms within their framework. Tension is created which appears as hardness. This process of heating to a high temperature and quenching is known as **hardening**. The degree of hardness depends on how rapidly the tool is cooled – how much carbon is trapped in the lattices.

Dark red
Blood red (dark cherry red)
Medium cherry red
Light (bright) cherry red
Dark yellow
Light yellow
HEAT White

Table 5.1 Heat colour changes in steel

When the steel is gradually heated – with the intention of hardening it – the metal will begin to show a dark red colour, the first visible glow of heat. The steel changes colour as it gets hotter: to a blood red, then to a dark cherry red, then a medium cherry red and then a light

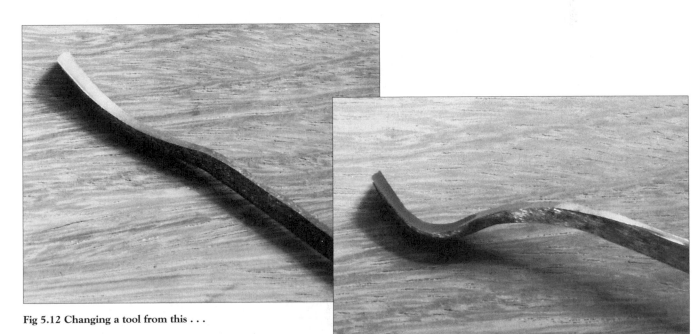

Fig 5.12 Changing a tool from this . . .

Fig 5.13 . . . to this, is a simply a matter of bending hot enough metal. A little more skill is needed to refine the shape, yet more to harden and finally temper it.

cherry colour (*see* Table 5.1). It is at this medium to light cherry red colour, sometimes called 'bright cherry' (about 1375°C), that the tool is quenched. Toolmakers in the past would have learned to judge the temperature solely by the colour of the metal.

These heat colours are best seen in a semi-dark room. If you have never seen them before, experiment on an old chisel or screwdriver. Try always to observe these colours in the same quality of light so that your assessment is consistent. Heat the steel evenly with the torch, moving the flame around as necessary.

Beyond the light cherry colour, the steel becomes gradually more yellow, light yellow, and then white. When a white colour is reached, sparks will start to fly from the metal – this is carbon leaving the steel or being burnt out. Heating the tool to white hot will probably ruin it.

From the first visible heat glow the metal starts to become malleable, becoming more so as the temperature rises (*see* Figs 5.12, 5.13).

If the steel is heated to a cherry red colour and then allowed to cool slowly (rather than quenching), all the carbon atoms leave the lattices of iron and the result is

the softest, most flexible condition that the steel can be in. The metal is said to be **annealed**. Annealed steel can be filed and worked much more easily than when it is in its hardened state.

A degree of annealed, softer metal is desirable behind the cutting edge – in the shank – of a woodcarving blade, to give a carving tool resilience to mallet impact and general use without the metal cracking. However, this tense hardness that arises from heating and quenching is *brittle* and carving with a tool in this state would probably lead to a fracturing of the metal. Re-heating to a much lower, but still precise, temperature causes some of the carbon atoms to escape the lattices of iron, so relieving the tension. This second process is known as **tempering** and seeks a balance between hardness and brittleness.

When steel is heated, but long before the malleable temperatures are reached, oxides are formed with the air on the surface of the metal. These oxides vary in colour according to the temperature of the metal. A distinct range of colours appear which can be used as a guide to the temperature of the blade at any particular point. Again, in the past these colours would

Fig 5.14 Polishing the surface of the tool before heating means that the tempering colours can easily be seen.

have been the only measure available to the toolmaker, who would have been sensitive to their gradations and what they signified. Different colours indicate a certain amount of softening of the steel from its original hardness, making it suitable for particular purposes.

To temper a blade, it *must* be hardened first. After hardening, you need to polish the surface in order to see easily the colours of the oxidation spectrum as the temperature of the metal is raised (see page 4 of the colour section between pages 340 and 341).

To get an idea of what these tempering colours look like, polish a bar of high-carbon steel or the flat face of an old chisel with emery paper (*see* Fig 5.14). The colours reveal themselves best in daylight. Gently and *slowly* apply heat to an area of the metal. The first colour to appear is a faint straw colour, starting the sequence given in Table 5.2.

Faint straw
Light straw (about 230°C)
Straw
Bronze (brown)
Peacock (bronze/brown)
Purple
Dark purple
HEAT Blue (about 300°C)

Table 5.2 Oxide colour changes in steel

The range between the first and last colours is only about 70°C, so care and stealth are needed in the heating. It is not always easy to see or separate out the colours as each colour merges with the next like a rainbow. With a little practice the colours become familiar and can be made to appear as bands with enough distinction to use them as indicators of hardness.

The colours themselves are entirely superficial and rub off easily with fine emery paper.

The colour at which a woodcarving tool should be set or fixed by a second **quenching** is that of *light straw*. A straw colour would be acceptable, perhaps even a slightly dark straw colour, particularly for sculpture tools taking a lot of hard work. However, heating to further along the colour range results in a softer metal which is no longer able to hold its edge.

The blue colour is seen when an edge is 'blued' on a fast grinding wheel. At this temperature hardness has been removed sufficiently from the edge to make it too soft to use for woodcarving.

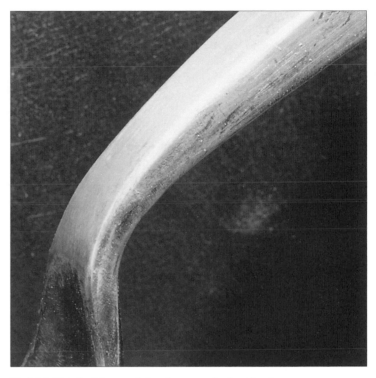

Fig 5.15 Detail of the crank in a homemade short bent gouge.

If you quench to fix a temper colour, but find you have gone beyond what you intended, the tool can be re-hardened and another attempt at tempering made – this will do the tool no harm.

If you heat the centre section of a polished metal bar, the spectrum of colours appear to *either side* of the blue as heat is conducted both ways (see Fig 5.16). Stop heating and the bands of colour still travel along the metal for some time, with the straw colours moving in front. The blue area can be used as a *reservoir of heat*, and with deft use of the propane torch, the required colours can be 'floated' along the metal of a blade and into required positions (see Fig 5.17). Try doing this. You can cool the metal between attempts and polish off the oxidation colours.

In the tempering process, when the exact colour is reached, the blade is quenched by rapidly dipping into water. This fixes the degree of hardness represented by the colour. Try quenching at particular colours.

It is not necessary to render a large amount of the blade light straw colour. In specialized woodcarving tools, only a good working amount behind the cutting edge is needed. However, different parts of the blade do need different degrees of hardness. Softer, more

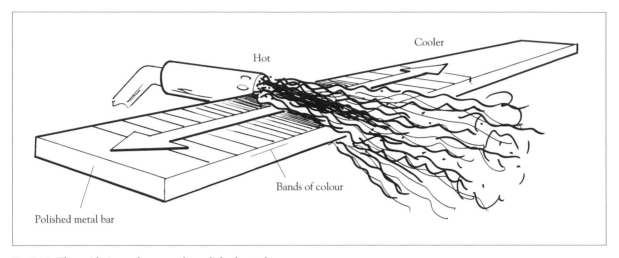

Fig 5.16 The oxidation colours on the polished metal surface move away from the source of heat and vary according to the temperature.

resilient and stronger metal is necessary behind the harder, but more brittle, cutting edge (*see* Fig 5.18). For example, the edge of a short bent tool should be tempered to a light straw colour, but the bend is rendered gradually darker, becoming blue at the shank.

Points were made earlier, in the discussion on bench grinders, about the relationship between mass and temperature (*see* page 138) – that information is relevant here. As heat is deliberately applied to a blade to temper it:

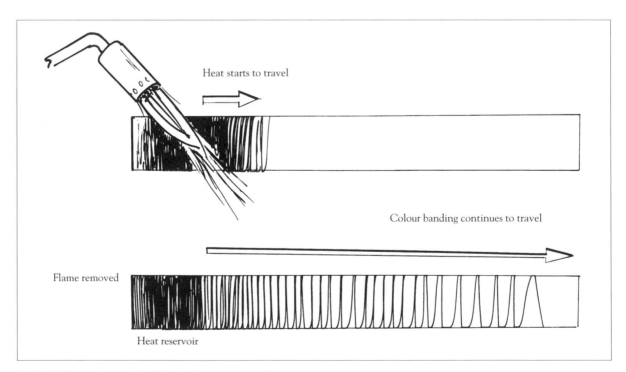

Fig 5.17 Using the metal itself to hold a reservoir of heat, which can be subtly floated along by deft application of its source, is an important tempering technique.

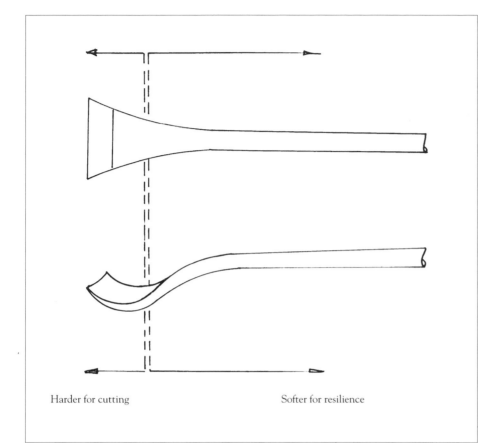

Harder for cutting   Softer for resilience

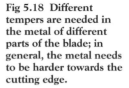

Fig 5.18 Different tempers are needed in the metal of different parts of the blade; in general, the metal needs to be harder towards the cutting edge.

Fig 5.19 The speed of oxidation colour change depends on how fast the temperature rises; this in turn depends on the thickness of the metal.

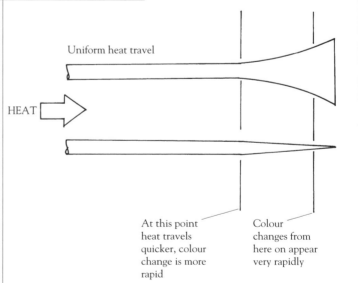

Uniform heat travel

HEAT

At this point heat travels quicker, colour change is more rapid

Colour changes from here on appear very rapidly

■ The thinnest parts of the carving blade, being of least mass, will rise in temperature the quickest;
■ The heat will travel slowest in the thicker parts, moving *more quickly* as the blade becomes thinner.

So the colour changes to light straw *can appear very quickly* as the heat approaches the thin cutting edge and corners (*see* Fig 5.19). A close eye must be kept on the movement and appearance of the colour banding – reacting quickly and dipping the tool into the water prevents further change to the colours.

Although this method of tempering by eye may seem a little casual, it has a long tradition (*see* Fig 5.20). Long before computer-regulated furnaces, toolmakers using such methods were producing the fine qualities of tempering seen in many old tools. My experience is that by learning to trust your eye – and with a little practice – not only can hardening and tempering be successful, but you may actually be able to improve on the temper of the original tool.

Experience is, of course, necessary, but correctly tempering a tool is far easier than usually thought. But,

at the end of the day, the proof is in the cutting of the wood. If the resulting tool seems a little soft, or is still not quite the right shape, there is no harm in repeating the process or experimenting further.

boils at about three times the temperature of water and cools the steel more slowly and with less shock. The resulting blade is slightly softer than if it were quenched in water, but this is not effectively a problem. Some toolmakers plunge really fine tools into tallow; others use brine (saturated salt solution) as a midway between water and oil – so increasing their options.

It is important to be aware that when a large, cherry-red hot piece of metal is plunged into a small amount of oil there is a danger of the oil igniting. The blade should be *dipped completely*; if part of the red hot blade is left above the oil, it may ignite the fumes.

So for safety when quenching in oil:

- Keep the oil in a lidded, metal can.
- Use at least 1 litre (1.8 pints) of oil.
- Keep a cover or safety blanket to hand.
- Dip the blade completely under the oil.
- Work in a well-ventilated area – unpleasant fumes will result from the quenching, the amount depending on the size of the blade being quenched.
- Wear eye protection at least, or better still a face shield.

Water, when used to quench red-hot metal, should be kept in a metal container close to where you are working. Obviously there is no danger of it igniting, but the heated water may well 'spit' when the tool plunges in.

Hardening in oil gives rise to a harmless, black patina on the metal; even water will leave the blade dirty and discoloured. The patina needs cleaning off in order to see the tempering colours of the subsequent stage better. 'Wet and dry' abrasive paper, made from emery or Carborundum, is available in various grits and will polish the surface.

The final quenching of the much lower tempering colours should be done in clean water. Plunge the blade straight in and swirl it around. On emerging, the polished surface is normally clean, and the beautiful tempering colours clearly visible for inspection.

Fig 5.20 Tools are being forged today in a manner that goes back generations.

QUENCHING

In practice, when the metal has been heated to a cherry red colour, you must maintain this colour evenly for a little while, soaking the metal in the heat to maximize the movement of the carbon. The tool is then quenched or dipped into a cooling liquid and moved up, down and around, to dissipate the heat rapidly and fix the crystal lattices.

The main liquids used for such cooling are:

- Oil (old car oil is adequate)
- Water (fresh).

Both should start at room temperatures.

Water is used for large tools – plunging the tool vertically in, edge first. There is quite a shock to the metal when it is cooled rapidly in this way, and with smaller or more delicate tools there is a danger of the blade warping or cracking. For these tools oil is safer. Oil

EQUIPMENT

The three main procedures at our disposal are:

- Removing metal
- Bending and shaping
- Hardening and tempering.

Most of the necessary tools for these procedures are to be found in the average workshop, and any further equipment need be inexpensive.

Fig 5.21 Sievert propane torches with different sizes of interchangeable nozzle.

Fig 5.22 A large fixed vice, small portable vice and bench top anvil.

Heat source

The blacksmith's forge contains special coal, which is said to create a carbon atmosphere around the hot metal and improve the quality of the steel. In practice I have found a good propane torch – such as plumbers use – adequate (*see* Fig 5.21). The direction and amount of the heat is accurate, and does not seem to affect the steel adversely. A large nozzle will give a good overall heat for larger tools and hardening; switch to a smaller one for more delicate tempering.

Fix the torch securely in position, in a vice or clamp. Alternatively, you can hold the torch in one hand while the tool is held, with tongs or Mole grips, in the other. As a naked flame is being used, work away from the wood area of the workshop; always work carefully and safely, and preferably outside if possible.

Start heating the metal slowly so as not to shock the blade. Water or oil coolants should be in metal containers and placed to hand *before* heat treatment is started.

Vice

A small, metalworking vice – designed to be roughly handled – is useful in a carving workshop, for example for gripping blades to fit or remove handles. A portable vice which clamps to the bench top will probably be quite satisfactory.

If you need to work on your woodcarving bench, try and keep the surface clean – metalwork tends to be a grubby business. Black slate-like roof tiles make a good protective surface.

Bear in mind that a metalworking vice (or clamp) may act as a 'heat drain' – absorbing the heat away from the blade (*see* Fig 5.23). As a consequence, the blade may conduct heat unexpectedly, need more heating up and may cool down quicker.

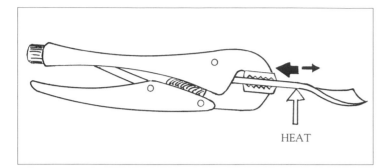

Fig 5.23 The means whereby a tool is held may itself act as a heat drain; the effect of applying the heat may then be unpredictable.

Small anvil

A solid, and reliably flat, surface is sometimes needed to true up part of a blade using a hammer. Small anvils are available, but there are also anvil-like surfaces on metalworking vices. Suitable lumps of metal can be found in scrap yards.

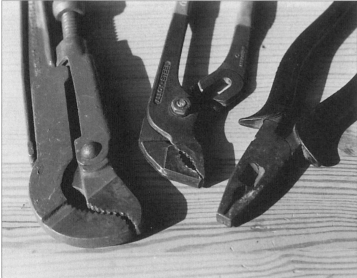

Fig 5.24 Three types of (non-locking) pliers or grips. Choose one which grips the particular tool you are working on most securely and suitably.

Fig 5.25 Mole (locking) grips lock securely onto the tool on which you are working.

General tools

How you are going to grip the hot carving tool, safely and securely, needs to be thought out *before* you start heating the metal. Tongs, locking grips (Mole grips) or different sizes of pliers are all possible devices (*see* Figs 5.24, 5.25). A vice, for instance, is no good for holding a blade that must be quickly dipped.

Hammers, pliers (for bending) and a hacksaw are tools which will be needed according to the work. There is plenty of scope for improvising but, again, try and work out what you might need *before* starting. It is quite frustrating to have to stop in the middle because you do not have the right tool.

Metal files of different sizes, shapes and roughness will be needed for removing metal more accurately than the grinding wheel. Use them when the metal is annealed.

Pliers with sharp jaws may mark the hot, softer metal during the bending. These marks can usually be filed off when the metal is cold. Pliers that are round in section, smooth-jawed or without sharp corners, mark soft metal far less. It is quite useful to have different sorts available.

Slipstones and 'wet and dry' abrasive paper will finely shape and polish the metal surface. Ordinary woodworking sandpaper will abrade annealed metal too.

Bench grinder

Details about grinders are given in Chapter 3 (*see* page 135).

SAFETY

Safety, as ever, lies in being in control, being aware of the dangers and not being distracted. Modifying tools in the ways we are discussing need give no problems – especially if the following basic points are observed.

■ The woodcarver's environment tends to be dry and contain inflammable wood chips, finishing agents, etc. – work *away* from these.

■ Never leave a naked flame unattended. Keep water nearby, if not a fire extinguisher or fire blanket.

■ Make sure a source of heat is safe before using it. For example if the torch is to be clamped or held in a vice, work out the arrangement before lighting it, rather than wandering around with a naked flame, looking for a home. Do not clamp the hot torch to a wooden surface.

■ Have good ventilation – fumes arise from the use of torches and other heat sources, as well as from quenching blades in oil.

■ Remove the wooden handle completely *before* heating up a blade. Even if it does not burn the handle, an expanding tang may loosen the hole.

■ Sharp tools left clamped in vices with their tangs and edges exposed are very dangerous.

■ Eye protection, if not a whole face shield, should be worn.

OVERVIEW OF THE PROCESS

In general terms, the procedure for modifying a woodcarving tool, using heat, is as follows.

First heating

■ Heat the tool to cherry red,
■ cooling slowly to *anneal*.

Second heating

■ *Shaping*: heat above the red colour to bend, shape, hammer, etc.
■ *Cooling*: slowly to room temperature for cold working.
■ Grind and file accurately to shape. Finish surface well.

Third heating

■ *Hardening*: in semi-dark light. Heat to bright cherry red, holding the colour for a little while.

■ *Quenching*: in water or oil.
■ Clean and polish the metal.

Fourth heating

■ *Tempering*: in daylight. Heat between light and dark straw in the region of the cutting edge; darker for the supporting, more resilient parts.
■ *Quenching*: in water.
■ Check blade colours. Hardening and tempering can be repeated if necessary.

WORKING WITH THE BLADE

The following notes describe some of the possibilities of using heat.

Bending

Work out the amount and position of the bend – forwards, backwards or to the side – before you start. Heat the part of the blade to be bent at least to red hot. It is always best to anneal the metal first to safeguard against cracking. Do not try to bend the metal when it is less than a dull red colour. To do so can result in the metal fracturing.

While the metal is still cold, decide on your plan for gripping and bending it. For example, part of the blade may be held in a metalworking vice – using a pair of pliers for bending in one hand and the torch in the other. Or you may fix the torch safely and use both hands to work the blade, in which case position the torch to point safely away from where you are working.

Bending the hot part over a corner of metal (or round metal bar) by hammering is another option, especially suitable for larger tools. Be careful not to damage the sweep.

If the bend is not quite what is wanted the first time, the metal can be re-heated and re-worked.

Forging

Forging refers more to hammering the metal to shape: shortening or lengthening the form; creating the internal curve (or sweep) by hammering the cutting edge over suitable metal formers or bending and forging tangs, shoulders and specific sweeps. All this is possible with enough practice.

At a simpler level, forging will augment bending. For

Fig 5.26 In the absence of swage blocks, a simple fishtail shape can be forged by hammering the hot end on an anvil. The shape can then be further refined over a round bar, filed and shaped.

Fig 5.27 A cold procedure: grinding the back edge of a skew chisel to emphasize the point and so gain access to tight corners.

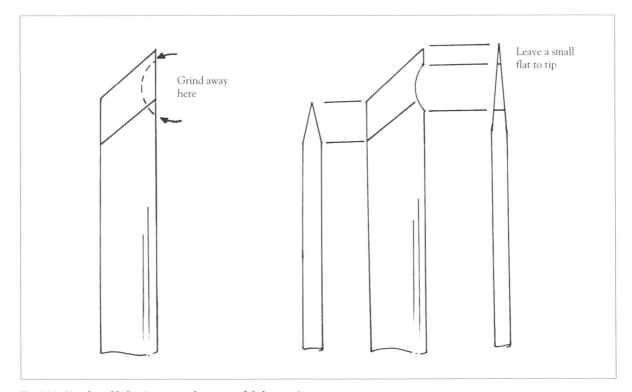

Fig 5.28 Simple cold shaping to produce a useful skew point.

example you can straighten, lengthen or flatten part of a blade using the anvil (*see* Fig 5.26). For this sort of work both hands are needed – with the heat source safely to one side. Again, re-heating may be necessary.

After bending (or other shaping), allow the metal to cool slowly, do not quench it. Refine the shape with files, emery paper glued to wood strips, slipstones and so on. Smoothing the surface at this stage makes post-hardening polishing easier.

SOME EXAMPLES OF MODIFYING TOOLS

The following examples of tool modifying follow from the information given so far in this chapter and illustrate just some of the possibilities. If you wish to attempt these projects, read through everything first.

Cold shaping

SKEW CHISEL

To emphasize the working point of a skew chisel grind metal from the back of the long corner (*see* Figs 5.27, 5.28). The point becomes very useful for delicate work and getting into tight corners – a specialized tool, not the everyday working skew. As it is weakened, take care not to rock the tool from side to side for fear of breaking it; store with a cork on the tip.

As the point itself is susceptible to over-heating, a *light* touch on the grinding wheel is necessary, with

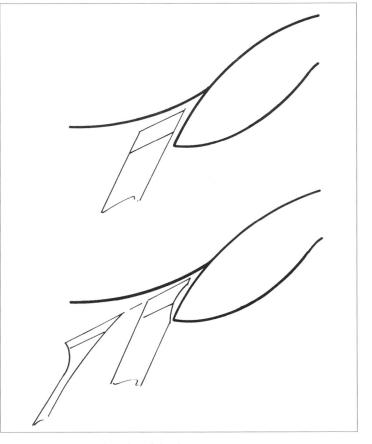

Fig 5.29 Sometimes the sides of the skew prevent it making a clean cut in a tight recess. In these cases a tool with an even more pronounced point may gain access.

Fig 5.30 Skewed fishtail chisel: again useful for getting into tight corners.

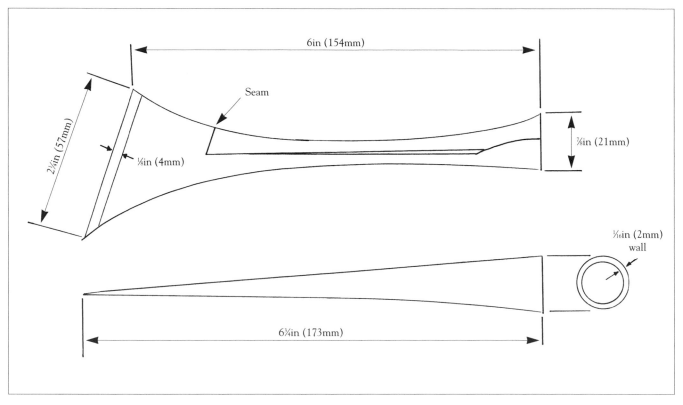

6in (154mm)

Seam

2¼in (57mm)

⅛in (4mm)

⅞in (21mm)

1/16in (2mm) wall

6¾in (173mm)

Fig 5.31 A socketed skew chisel, common in China around 1850, from the Science Museum, South Kensington, London (inventory no. 1873–53). The basic 'plate' was turned and seamed to form the socket, and surplus metal dressed forward to form the blade itself.

Fig 5.32 One way of making a skewed fishtail chisel using hot and cold procedures.

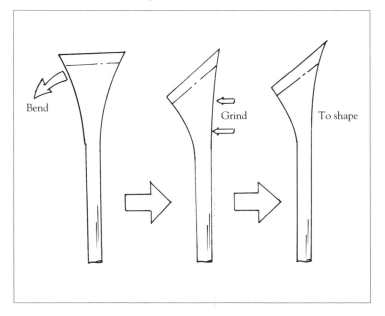

Bend

Grind

To shape

frequent cooling. Stop the grinding a little before the cutting edge and finish the ground surface with slipstones.

SKEWED FISHTAIL CHISEL

A skewed fishtail chisel is another tool that helps the carver to get into awkward recesses (*see* Figs 5.29, 5.30). It is also useful for cutting the flat ends of serifs in lettering and for finishing lightly convex surfaces. The shape itself goes back a long way and can be seen in woodcuts of medieval carvers at work. A socketed version from China, dated around 1850, is to be found in the Science Museum in Kensington (inventory no. 1875–53) (*see* Fig 5.31).

There are three different ways of making this shape:

■ Bend a normal fishtail chisel sideways; the shank then has to be hammered straight and the edge lined up again.
■ A simpler way is to take an oversize fishtail chisel, anneal it and grind away the surplus metal (*see* Fig 5.33). As described for a skew chisel in Chapter 3 (*see* page 173), set the angle first – try about 30° to begin with – then the bevels. Sharpen as normal and retain the corners. If the grinding is kept light and the blade

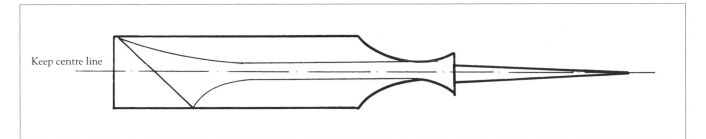

**Fig 5.33 Once annealed, surplus metal can be ground
away quickly, without blueing mattering.**

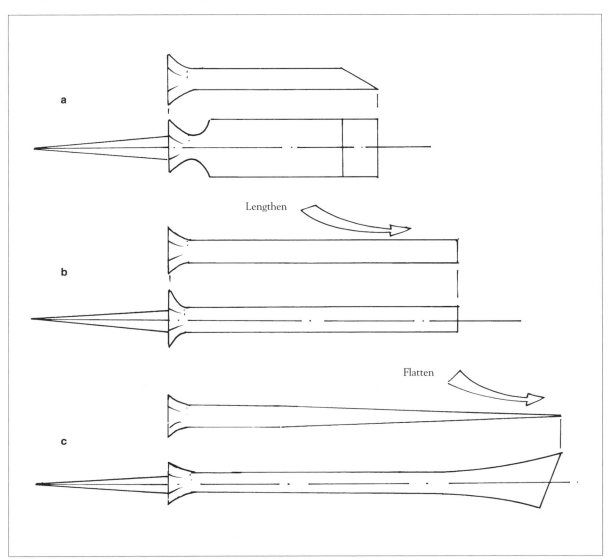

**Fig 5.34 A true forging would lengthen the red hot metal
by beating and turning it over (b), and then flattening the
end and forming it to the required shape (c) – which may
also be a fishtail gouge. Keep the centre line as the guide.
Some cold finishing may be needed before hardening.**

Fig 5.35 Such a knuckle gouge may enter a recess and remove wood by cutting *with* the grain for a clean finish, where other gouges would be cutting against it.

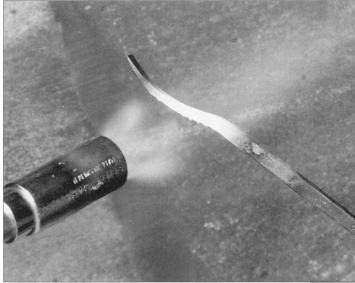

Fig 5.36 Heat the part of the blade to be bent to an adequate temperature.

Fig 5.37 Starting the bend.

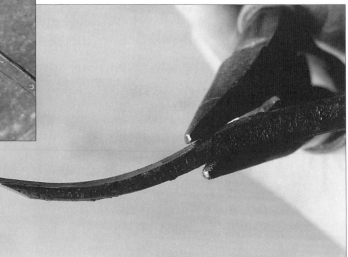

cool, the temper will be undisturbed.

■ The shape can also be made, more satisfyingly, by heating an old, short, fat chisel and drawing out the shape on a small anvil (*see* Fig 5.34). The tang and shoulder remain from the original chisel and the hammering improves the grain of the metal.

Hot shaping

KNUCKLE GOUGE

A knuckle gouge is a tighter, short bent (or spoonbit) gouge. It can cut within awkward recesses denied to normal short bent tools (*see* Fig 5.35). Knuckle **V**-tools and back bent gouges can be created in a similar way

Start with a short bent gouge that has the width and sweep that you want, but inadequate longitudinal curve.

Method

1 Heat the blade to cherry red; allow to anneal by slowly cooling in the air.
2 Re-heat the part to be bent (*see* Fig 5.36) to a blood red and bend using round-section pliers (*see* Fig 5.37). If you grip the blade too tightly across the width, you may flatten the sweep so work lightly. Re-heat as necessary to get the bend just right.
3 When the shape is correct, allow the metal to cool slowly and clean up the blade with fine files, slipstones, emery paper, etc.
4 Heat the bend to a bright cherry colour, soaking the heat for a little while, then quench in oil by plunging the blade and moving it around.
5 Clean off the oily residue and re-polish the metal. At

this stage the gouge is hardened but too brittle to use.

6 Temper the gouge using a fine torch nozzle or flame in one hand, and tongs in the other to hold the gouge. Lightly start the heat along the *shank*, turning the polished metal blue. Use the torch deftly to extend the colour spectrum so that the purple–bronze–straw colours start to separate and creep along the steel away from the blue (hottest) colour. Try to float the colours along the blade so that as the light straw colour reaches the cutting edge, more bronze colour appears in the first crank of the bend, turning to purple-blue at the shank.

7 At this point quench rapidly in water.

Dry the blade and the colours should be plainly visible, showing the range of hardening. These oxidation colours may be left or polished off. The tool can now be sharpened ready for use.

BENT V-TOOL

If a short bent original is not available, a different type of operation to the one described above will produce

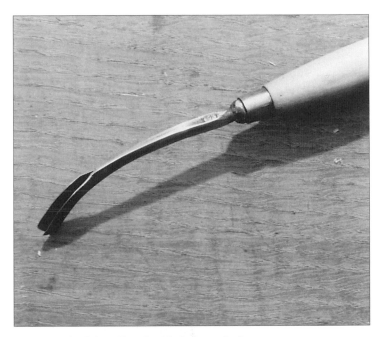

Fig 5.38 A back bent V-tool made for a particular purpose.

Fig 5.39 An example of the hot welding technique, where the sides of the V-tool are fused into one.

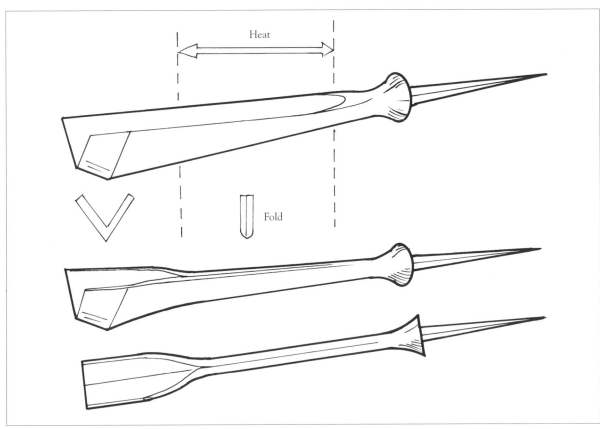

Fig 5.40 The weld in this tool is a fusion of the two sides into one shank of metal.

various bent V-tools from a spare straight one of the right width. A long, back bent V-tool is described here.

Method

1 After annealing by heating the whole blade blood red to the shoulder and slowly cooling, clean the inside cannel of the V-tool well.

2 Re-heat the centre part of the blade blood red from the shoulder to about 1in (25mm) towards the cutting edge, or say about one-quarter of the blade length. When this metal has become light cherry red *verging on yellow*, hammer the sides of the V-tool together on an anvil, without spreading them, and leaving the part towards the cutting edge untouched. The hammering will heat-weld the two sides of the tool together, effectively making them a single piece of metal – a shank (*see* Figs 5.39, 5.40).

3 Keeping the blade hotter than dark red, tidy the blade on the anvil and then bend it, using pliers, to the shape you want.

4 Refine the shape with the metal cold, using files, grinder, etc.

Once the shape is right, continue as for the knuckle gouge – hardening, tempering and sharpening in a similar fashion. You can go straight to bending without welding, but this is an interesting technique.

SMALL V-TOOL

A worn-out spoon bit or short bent gouge can be reborn as a very useful parting tool for delicate and accurate work.

Method

1 Anneal as described on page 235.

2 Grind or cut off any remaining spoon profile, but keep the bend in the shank to work on.

3 Re-heat and establish a 30° crank at the first 1in (25mm) of the shank towards the cutting end. Cool slowly.

4 Grip the shank in a metalworking vice and file a **V**-groove using a fine triangular file – such as a needle file – in the bent part of the blade. Finish with slipstones. Work the outside of the **V**-groove with flat files, making the walls a uniform thickness.

5 Re-heat and bend the blade into the shape you want: straight, spoonbit or back bend. Check over the cannel and finally refine the shape.

6 The end can now be hardened and tempered to a light straw colour, with a bronze colour at the junction of angle and shank.

Sharpen the tool and see how it cuts the wood.

SUMMARY

People are often surprised at how easy it is to modify carving tools – bending, hardening, tempering etc. There is something alchemical about using fire to create a new tool – a process far removed from woodcarving. These are useful skills to have or know about and you never know when they may be needed. The day they are, may be a day of great satisfaction. There is a great pleasure to be had in making or modifying such a tool yourself, and using it to overcome a particular problem.

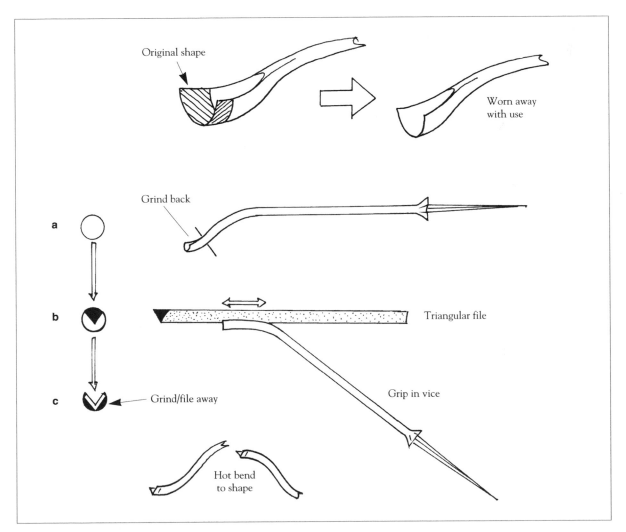

Fig 5.41 An old short bent gouge turned into a useful fine V-tool. Clean off the end (a); anneal and shape the inside (b); then the outside (c); and then hot bend to shape. A final cold finish to shape, then harden and temper.

HOLDING DEVICES

Aims

To consider the important aspects of holding carved work

To discuss a repertoire of techniques and possibilities

To encourage improvisation

To increase confidence

The means of holding a woodcarving is given only a passing mention in many woodcarving books. There are probably two reasons for this. The first is that as the methods are fairly simple and straightforward it may be supposed that little can be said about the matter. And secondly, as work is so varied – flat, round, abstractly shaped; from large sculpture to small, delicate netsuke; horizontally or vertically placed – there is often more of a need for the beginner to be a good improviser, which is something not so easily taught.

With experience, carvers build up a pool of techniques to hold the piece they are working on –

Waste wood to be held in vice

Fig 6.1 Holding work by a waste element, to be removed later, is often a convenient approach.

Fig 6.2 To carve this box, spigots were left in the turning with which to hold it; these will be cleaned off when the work is finished.

even going so far as to design their carving with the means of holding it in mind, so important is this aspect to carving. For example, waste wood, used to clamp the work to the bench or to grip it in a vice, can be left until the last moment before being removed (*see* Figs 6.1, 6.2); or separate pieces can be carved and then assembled before finishing (*see* Fig 6.3). Carvers tend to have favoured methods, just as they have favourite carving gouges.

For the beginner, holding the carving so as to get safely to the part they want can be quite a conundrum – and may remain so until a repertoire of methods has been built up. As with so much to be learned, this repertoire will come through problems being solved and possibilities explored. It is only fair to say, however, that even experienced carvers are sometimes at a loss for a while when trying to work out how to hold something exactly as they want.

The correct holding of a piece in order to carve it cannot be over-emphasized. This chapter will look at the reasons why this is so important, as well as the range of possibilities that exist.

First, however, we need to look at the workbench – the centrepiece of carving activity. It may be true that in Bali carvers sit on the floor and hold the carving between their feet; or that Japanese carvers sit cross-legged and use a simple plank – but in the West most work is gripped by one means or another to a carving bench. The bench, for us, is the indispensable starting point to holding work properly.

WORKBENCH

Workbenches vary enormously between carvers, not only because the size and weight of work that is undertaken varies so much, or because of workspace constraints, but also because the size, shape and preferences of carvers themselves vary. Some carvers like to work outside on a summer's evening. Others have to make do with a kitchen or spare corner of the house. Others again may have infirmities that make standing in the usual way difficult.

While there is no such thing as a 'standard carving bench', there may be an ideal one for a particular individual: a bench which works well, supporting and helping the carver achieve his or her ends. Most carvers make their own benches, or at least have them made to their own, specific needs. These benches become like old friends in whose company many hours will be spent. This is perhaps the only

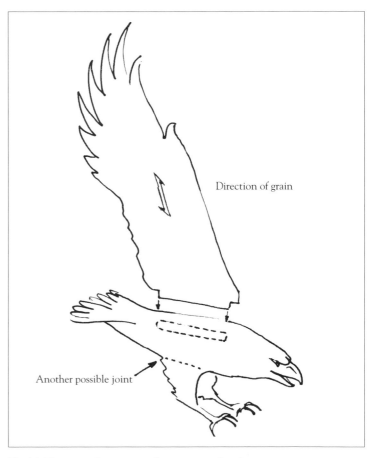

occasion when an old friend can be designed by yourself.

Despite their individuality, all carving benches have certain attributes which make them useful. The following general features need to be borne in mind while thinking and planning out a bench to your requirements.

Fig 6.3 Parts may be more easily part-carved, prior to assembly, than trying to work on the whole piece from the start.

Features of a woodcarving bench

HEIGHT

It is usual for carvers to stand at their work, and this should be done wherever possible as it gives the greatest freedom of movement around the piece that is being carved. A workbench for a carver is higher than that for a carpenter or joiner to allow a good standing posture to be maintained – too low a bench is bad news for the

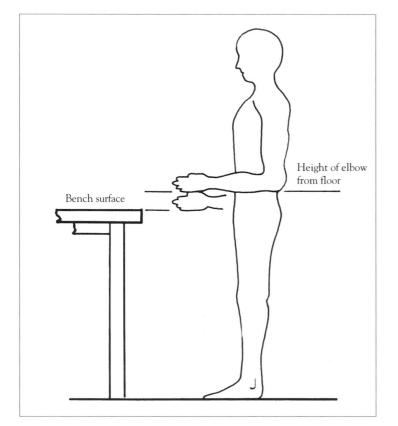

Fig 6.4 A well-tried guide to a bench height appropriate for carving.

Fig 6.5 Such blocks, of varying thicknesses and stored by the bench, give a ready means of altering the height of your working surface.

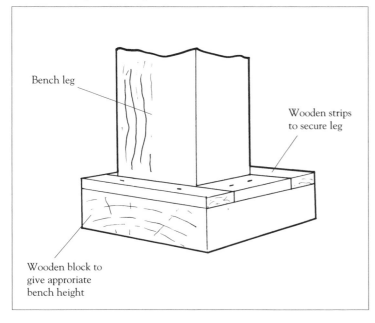

back. Lower benches suit carpenters because they position themselves *over* the work to plane it and so on.

Some books recommend a particular height for a carving bench, but in fact the appropriate height varies with the heights of different carvers. Someone over 6 feet tall will obviously need to work on a bench higher than that of someone 5 feet tall.

Finding the height

The best guide to the height is the traditional one: stand comfortably upright, raise your forearm horizontally and measure the height from the floor to the elbow (*see* Fig 6.4). The bench height is this measurement *less* the width of one of your hands.

You may need an accomplice to do the measuring, but the result should give a good, useful working height for the bench surface. Problems may still arise with particularly tall or large carvings, but for average work this height will be appropriate.

Carvers who need to sit will have to experiment to get a comfortable height and position – one that allows them to work for a long time without strain or discomfort. And this is really the point: carving can go on for many hours and, without the correct 'ergonomics', tiredness, backache and so on can spoil an otherwise enjoyable experience. Try, for example, raising the back legs of the chair about 1in (25mm), which tilts the seat a little towards the bench.

If a carpentry bench is the only one available, then you can either raise the height or make a false top.

◆ **Raise the height.**

Use glued-up plywood blocks of wood under the feet. Make the blocks *wider* than the feet of the bench, with strips of wood around the edge to keep the blocks in position (*see* Fig 6.5). This is a good method for a carving class using the woodworking room of a school. The blocks can be placed under the benches quickly with a team effort and easily stored away afterwards.

◆ **Make a false bench top.**

The false top clamps to the bench – this is dealt with on page 257 (*see* Fig 6.10).

STRENGTH AND WEIGHTING

For the average carver, a good workbench will last a lifetime, even though it may have been subject to considerable battering – but it does need to be strongly constructed.

In practice this means a working surface of at least 2in (50mm) thick and legs at least 3 x 3in (75 x

Fig 6.6 Plywood fillets between laminated sections makes this an extremely strong bench surface.

75mm). The best joints are mortise and tenons, to which cross-bracing may be added.

It is preferable to make the legs and framework from hardwood, such as beech, glued and pinned – although softwood is acceptable.

Pine or another softwood is best for the top as it has good gripping and deadening qualities, absorbs impacts and minimizes 'bounce'. It is also easily nailed or screwed into. Hardwood can be a bit bouncy for the top but is still preferred by some. Of manufactured materials, MDF (medium-density fibreboard) has a slippy surface and plywood can be dusty.

The idea is that the bench should be solid (in the sense of immovable) but with a certain amount of resilience. Various devices can hold the work steady, but beneath this the bench must be solid. The size and strength of a carving bench depends not only on the height of the carver and the size of work, but also on the amount of violence that is intended. Good advice for beginners is to build the bench stronger than they think they need. A bench can never be too strong – but it can be too weak.

As well as being strong in itself, a bench can still be made to 'walk' around a room under the jerking actions of heavy carving, especially mallet work. Two options to counter this are:

■ Screw or bolt the bench to the floor or wall, using angle irons or brackets.
■ Weight the *lowest* part of the bench, which may mean building in rails to the base. Compacted concrete blocks, such as are used for paving slabs, make excellent weights in manageable sizes; a sand box (which can be dampened) also works well.

PROPORTIONS

In addition to the height, the surface area of the bench is important. It was common practice for professional carvers to use a bench made from planks 3–4in (75–100mm) thick, running the whole length of the workshop. Too big is better than too small.

The surface of the bench should be *flat* and have enough room for:

■ The workpiece
■ Laying out carving tools, other tools and bits and pieces – some out of the way and towards the back when not being used
■ Changing the orientation of the carving or position

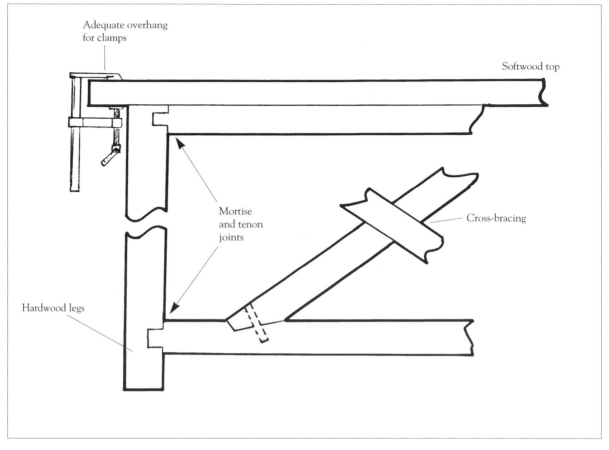

Fig 6.7 Some construction details for a carver's bench.

of the tools and generally being able to shunt things around.

This also has to be seen in the context of available space in the workroom.

As a guide for those starting with no idea of what sort of bench they will need, a working surface of 3 x 2 feet (1m x 60cm) is a useful working area. If you can imagine dealing with a whole range of shapes and sizes, then increase these dimensions. Benches of 6 x 2 feet 6in (2m x 75cm) are not uncommon. Do not make the bench deeper than you can comfortably reach.

There are many different sorts of carving bench – some of which appear later in this section – suitable for different types of work. You may, for example, like to change the proportions to give yourself a tall bench with more of the appearance of a modelling stand. Such a bench would be suitable for small figure work, raising the piece nearer to eye level.

FITTINGS

A bench not only holds the carving off the floor at a comfortable working height, it also has features which help hold the carving, thus making the work of the carver easier.

The working surface of the bench should overhang the under-framework by at least 2½–3in (65–75mm) as this allows versatile clamps to be used. An ordinary woodworker's vice might be fitted; there may be bench stops and pegs; and there may be holes for holdfasts, carver's screws, bolts, etc. You can make most changes to the bench as the need arises.

Drawers, cupboards and shelves are useful additions for the tools and equipment which relate to the bench (*see* Figs 6.8, 6.9). Make sure drawers and doors will not be obstructed by clamps and so on – it is quite irritating to have to undo a carefully arranged clamp in order to get at a drawer or cupboard. Position them lower down, or to one side at least.

The strongest part of the bench is over the legs so

Fig 6.8 Shelves and cupboards make use of the prime storage space beneath the bench.

Fig 6.9 Drawers incorporated into the bench for storing carving tools.

this is the best place for heavy thumping. Keep the ends of the bench clear as these are good parts for working around.

A toolrack at the back of the bench is useful; so is a lip at the back to stop small items rolling off. A step, perhaps forming part of a low shelf, can also make a very good foot rest.

You should see the carving bench as a focus of the working area – almost an operating table. Large amounts of time may be spent at the bench, so make it as comfortable, efficient and friendly as possible. It is not unusual for beginners to start with such a nice bench that they are afraid of marking it. By all means care for your bench, but remember that a bench is primarily a work station, contributing to the carving – a means to an end.

ALTERNATIVES

The bench described so far is probably the most common sort of working arrangement that carvers use. What follows are some variations and different ideas for benches and work stations that might suggest possibilities, or suit the needs of different carvers.

Tables

Sometimes a table in the kitchen or bedroom is all that is available to someone carving in their spare time. This arrangement can work well for small pieces, provided it is strong and stable enough, but there is usually a problem with the height, as most tables are designed for sitting at.

A working surface can be clamped to the table top to give extra height, and this surface that can be marked with impunity (*see* Fig 6.10). Line the underside with cork tiles to give a good grip and protect the table top. Unless the table can be fixed to the floor or wall, it may still only be suitable for light work.

Portable work centres

A portable work centre is a collapsible system that doubles as a bench and a saw-horse. It is designed for mobile carpentry and there are several varieties on the market. The best known is probably the Black & Decker Workmate, but there are several other types available. They tend to be small, low and light-weight. Nevertheless, if this is all that is available, try weighting the base and clamping on a table-type bench as described above (*see* Fig 6.10) to increase the height. It may be necessary to sit while carving to prevent backache.

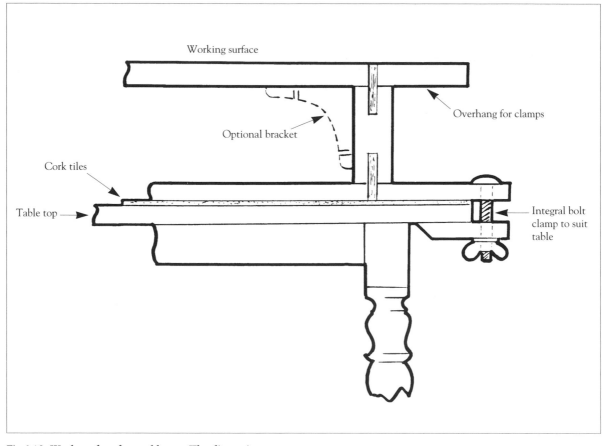

Fig 6.10 Work surface for a table top. The dimensions should suit the table's height, etc.; the top can be made of plywood.

Fig 6.11 Sculpture troughs may be floor- or bench-standing.

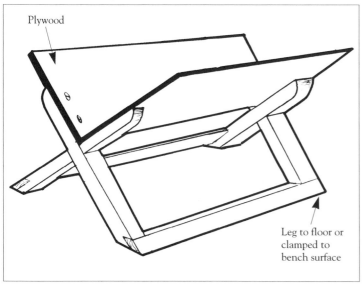

Sculpture troughs

For very awkward shapes, a trough such as shown in Fig 6.11 may be useful. The trough should be lined with an offcut of old, hessian-backed carpet – reversed with the hessian outside. The **V**-groove will easily jam and grip many odd shapes. Various sizes of sandbag packed around a carving will hold a large sculpture in a similar way. There is a tendency for the sand dust to leak out, but otherwise this can be a simple way of holding a difficult shape especially if you want the work horizontal for carving.

Collapsible benches

Perhaps even before the kitchen table, amateur carvers were consigned to the garage to make their noise and wood chips. If this puts the carver in competition with the car over space – and the car is winning – fit a collapsible bench. The car in turn can be consigned to the outdoors for the duration. The back edge of the working surface hinges to the wall and, when not in use, drops away vertically (*see* Fig 6.12). Strength can

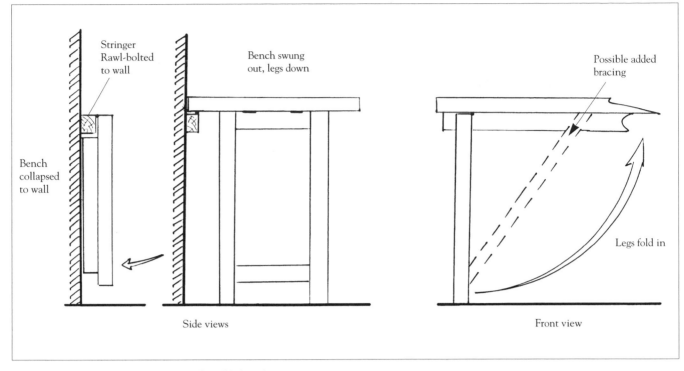

Stringer
Rawl-bolted
to wall

Bench swung
out, legs down

Possible added
bracing

Bench
collapsed
to wall

Legs fold in

Side views

Front view

**Fig 6.12 One way of constructing a collapsible bench
where space has to be shared.**

**Fig 6.13 Crosspieces A and B are wider than the tilting
surface and are clamped to the bench. As crosspiece B is
moved along the bench, so the working surface tilts.**

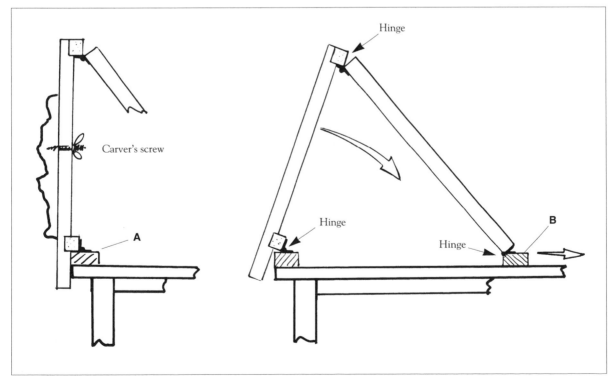

Carver's screw

A

Hinge

Hinge

Hinge

B

come from diagonal cross-bracing to the wall and floor corner, and through using substantial hinges.

Such a bench can make a substantial work surface, while collapsing to quite a narrow intrusion on the garage space. Racks and shelves can be fixed to the walls to store tools and equipment – if the garage is dry. Check the wall fastenings regularly and arrange the cross-bracing to minimize 'bounce' in the surface.

Tilting surfaces

Sometimes it is better to hold the workpiece at an angle or even vertically, for example a panel or something that will naturally be wall-mounted. Simply clamping or screwing of the work to a piece of wood, gripped upright in the vice, may be sufficient. It is not difficult to make a simple portable frame that clamps to the bench, with a central slot through which a carving is mounted using a carver's screw (see Fig 6.13). Be sure to construct such tilting surfaces strongly and use robust hinges.

An idea for a portable bench design by Gino Masero doubles as a horizontal and vertical working surface (see Figs 6.14, 6.15). The arcing metal brackets can be cut by most engineering firms.

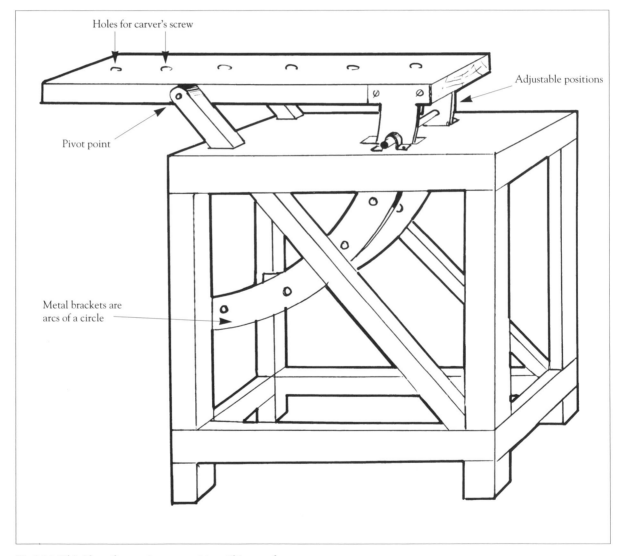

Holes for carver's screw

Adjustable positions

Pivot point

Metal brackets are arcs of a circle

Fig 6.14 This idea of an arcing support to a tilting surface can be adapted for many purposes. The important consideration is the placing of the pivot point.

Metal benches

Although wood is the traditional material for carving benches, excellent sub-frames can be welded up quite cheaply from lengths of metal found in scrap yards. The actual working surface must always be wood, but the sub-frame can be either all metal, using say 2 x 2in (50 x 50mm) square-section welded tube; or a wood and metal mix, for instance angle iron bolted between wooden legs, acting as stringers and bracing.

Sitting horses

Standing is the best position to carve in, but for some people there may be a choice between sitting to carve, or not carving at all. A carving horse is an option here. The carver sits astride something similar to a saw-horse, part of which is designed to take a vice or clamp (*see* Fig 6.17). The weight of the carver keeps everything stable, while padding and a backrest add to comfort. Make sure the timber and joints are strong

Fig 6.15 A sketch drawing of a multi-purpose, portable bench using metal arc stays.

Fig 6.16 View from beneath of a metal-frame bench. The wooden top is held with sturdy screws through welded metal lugs.

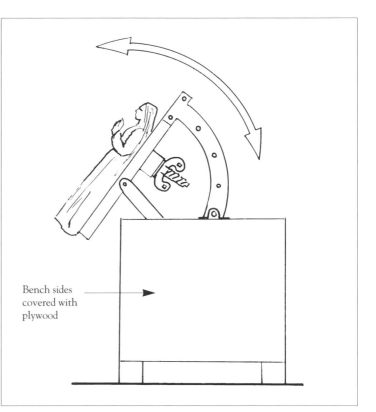

Bench sides covered with plywood

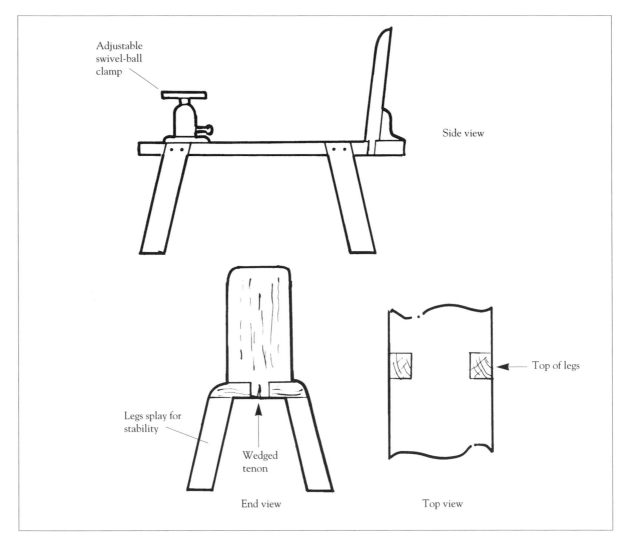

Adjustable swivel-ball clamp

Side view

Legs splay for stability

Wedged tenon

End view

Top of legs

Top view

Fig 6.17 In a sitting horse, the weight of the carver gives stability. Splay the legs so that the horse will not tip, especially when you lean backwards to view your work.

enough – use a hardwood and wedged through-tenons, with the legs splayed. For small carvings, there should be little problem with such an arrangement.

Tall stands

As with modelling stands, tall carving benches raise smaller pieces of work nearer to the eye (*see* Fig 6.18). The working surface itself is usually small. They can be a useful addition to a larger bench in the workshop – perhaps even clamping to its surface.

Panel peg boards

For carving panels, house signs and so on, a board like the one shown in Fig 6.19 can be useful, clamped to the main bench. The 1in (25mm) holes are set at 2–3in (50–75mm) intervals and staggered. Dowels are dropped into a few appropriate holes and the work itself caught with wedges. Easily knocked apart and re-positioned, a carved panel can be shuffled around as required.

Medieval carving frames

Nowadays figures tend to be carved vertically, but in the past figures seem to have been carved horizontally, held in a frame between ends. Fixed with large carver's screws, the work could be rotated to get at all parts conveniently. This is still the practice in some places, for example southern Germany.

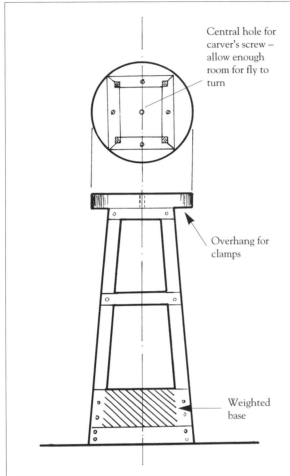

Central hole for carver's screw – allow enough room for fly to turn

Overhang for clamps

Weighted base

Fig 6.18 A tall bench for smaller carvings. Tools must be laid on a separate surface to one side, but the extra height can make working a lot easier.

Such a floor- or bench-standing framework, which is both adjustable and collapsible is shown in Fig 6.20. Taken from a medieval etching, the principle of the design is simple and quite elegant. Etchings of the time show very large pieces of work held this way, and it is an idea worth remembering – possibly as an adjustable way of carving turned work. Waste wood in the carving is allowed at each end where it meets the frame to take the screws. Without this, small plugs may be needed when the screws are removed.

Summary and construction notes

The sort of bench needed by a carver varies with the size and type of work; the size and type of the carver; and the size of the workshop.

It is always best to make the bench to personal requirements, or at least have one made to your specifications. The possibilities described above are by no means exhaustive, but constructing any carving bench will need consideration of the following points:

■ The appropriate *height*
■ An adequate, *flat* working surface
■ *Strength*: it is best to use mortise and tenon joints, with possible cross-bracing; 3in (75mm) square

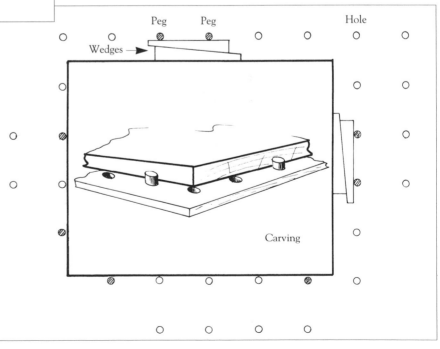

Peg Peg Hole

Wedges →

Carving

Fig 6.19 A peg board with wedges for small panels avoids the need for clamps, which may get in the way.

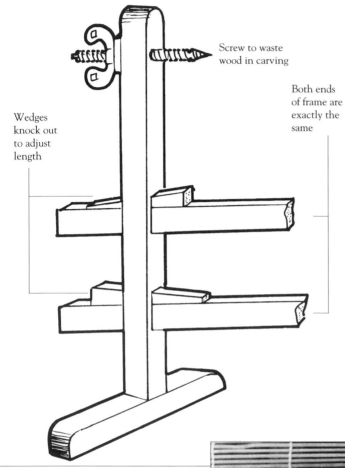

Screw to waste wood in carving

Both ends of frame are exactly the same

Wedges knock out to adjust length

Fig 6.20 Such 'medieval' carving frames were used to hold quite large and heavy carvings, rotating the work for access from all sides.

hardwood legs and a 2in (50mm) thick softwood top

■ *Stability*: consider the weighting and method of anchoring to the floor

■ *Projecting edges*: a projection of 2½–3in (65–75mm) at the least is needed to the front and sides

■ *Drawers, shelves*, etc.: these need to be out of the way of clamps, etc. Keep the ends of the bench free for working around and have a toolrack to the rear.

Bench discipline

The idea of 'discipline' has arisen in various parts of this book. Disciplines are working practices and habits that contribute to a more satisfying experience of carving; they help the carving proceed towards the best possible result. Such practices also protect tools from damage, and yourself from accidents. With the proviso that those people who love chaos may care to skip the following list, here are some particularly good habits that are centred on the carving bench and worth cultivating.

◆ **Keep the working area uncluttered as far as possible.**

This means bringing forward those tools in immediate use and keeping others out of the way, if not actually putting them away. Consciously arrange things, rather

Fig 6.21 Two useful brushes to keep by the bench: a stiff brush for cleaning carvings (actually an ex-horse brush); and a soft one for the bench (ex-wallpaper brush).

than just let them happen.

◆ **Have regular clearing up sessions.**

Clear up the bench between different stages of the carving, or at a natural break such as the end of the day. Keep a bench brush and pan handy to remove wood chips and shavings.

◆ **Line up carving tools.**

Arrange the carving tools neatly with their blades towards you – they are more easily distinguished and are far less likely to have their edges damaged. Putting gouges to one end, or bent tools to the other, also speeds their selection.

◆ **Always pick up and put down carving tools carefully.**

Beware of metal objects such as clamp heads against which edges may knock.

◆ **Attach work securely.**

Make sure the work is properly and securely held to the workbench, leaving both hands free to use the carving tools. When moving or adjusting the work, avoid crashing it into – or putting it onto – the carving tools.

◆ **Never try to catch a falling gouge or chisel.**

With the best will in the world, a tool may fall or get knocked from the bench. If you have a concrete floor, an old hessian-backed carpet, upside down and in front of the bench, may well save the edge – as well as being easier on the feet.

◆ **Use the different parts of the bench appropriately.**

The strongest parts of the bench are over the legs towards the corners, so use these parts for heavy thumping. Keep the corners clear as these are the areas that allow the greatest freedom of movement.

INDIVIDUAL HOLDING DEVICES

Fundamentals

The carving bench is the centre of the workshop – where the carving actually happens. How the work is held to the carving bench is equally as important. There are several criteria that an appropriate holding device will fulfil; these are discussed in order of importance.

EFFICIENCY

Holding a woodcarving in the right way at the right time increases working efficiency. This is true to the extent that if a piece of work is going slowly or laboriously, holding the carving in a different way (or even just changing its position) may well get the flow going again, and more quickly.

CONTROL

You need to be able to get to any part of your work at will, even if this means adjusting the way the carving is held. The more adjustable a holding device, the greater facility you have, the more control you have, and the more confidence that the piece can be carved.

INDEPENDENCE

The means of holding the work should not damage it. This may be an obvious point, but we are not just talking about forgetting to pad a metal clamp – the holding device should not dictate or interfere with the design either. In effect, the device should remain independent of the carving: enabling it to happen and working with the process, but making as few dictates on the design as possible.

CONVENIENCE

The means of holding a carving should not obstruct the act of carving itself. This can become unavoidable – clamps, for example, can become awkwardly positioned and a hazard to tool edges. At this point some adjustment may be necessary, or a new device for holding the carving used. There is also the need for wood to be placed so that the carver can work comfortably and without strain.

SAFETY

A carving must be held securely so that the carver need never worry about it coming loose, or springing out, from the holding device, even under the jolts and pressures of cutting.

The woodcarving should remain perfectly still – it is the tools that move. If the workpiece suddenly, or unpredictably, moves and control is lost, not only can the carving and the carving tools get damaged, but the carver can be hurt as well. Whatever the method of holding the work, check for safety *before* starting to carve, as well as at regular intervals while working.

Alternatives

Any holding device will have advantages and disadvantages, making it suitable for some situations and not for others. This is why a repertoire of methods and devices is needed. Within the development of a

Fig 6.22 Quick-action (above and left) and conventional (right) screw G-clamps. The one at the top with the swivel handle is particularly good.

particular carving, several different approaches may be needed.

As with all carving tools and equipment, it is best to acquire things as they are needed – or as you know what direction your carving is taking. A good vice and a few **G**-clamps will be enough to start with if no specific needs are obvious.

The following options are well-established methods for holding carving work. Although they have been divided into devices for holding panels and others for holding three-dimensional forms, their uses will often overlap.

PANELS

Very large panels present their own problems and may need a special structure to hold them, but smaller work done on the bench can normally be contained by the following devices.

Clamps

The principal clamp used by the carver is the **G-clamp** (or **cramp**). The term is used here to describe both the well-known clamp that looks like a letter **G**, as well as the quick-action version which slides on a bar – looking in some ways like a sash clamp (*see* Fig 6.22). Sash clamps themselves are of principal use to the carver who needs to glue up work, especially panels, but it is possible to use them for holding the carved panels themselves.

The words clamp and cramp are synonymous in this context, deriving from the Old High German *krampf*, meaning bent – a clamp or cramp being a metal bar bent at both ends. From the same root comes the sense of cramp as a violent contraction of the muscles, and the word 'crimp'.

G-clamps come in sizes that increase by 2in (50mm) increments: 6in (150mm), 8in (200mm), 10in (250mm) and so on. This measurement is the

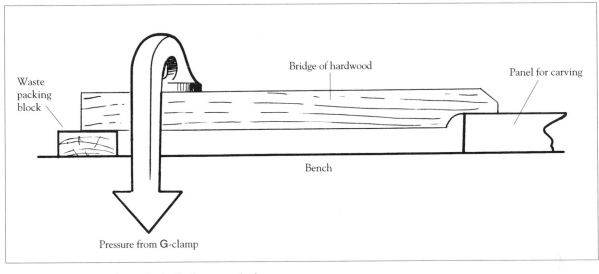

Fig 6.23 The bulk, and metal, of a G-clamp can be kept out of the way by a bridge of hardwood.

maximum open span; remember to allow for the bench top thickness. The most useful sizes of clamp to start with are probably the 8in (200mm) and 10in (250mm).

Clamps work from the front edge of the bench; usually the **pad** or **foot** is uppermost and the tightening bar, or **fly**, beneath. A piece of waste wood is placed between the metal pad and the work to stop

bruising or other damage. Make up a few special packing pieces from cork-lined plywood and keep them by the bench and always ready to hand.

The part of the clamp above the bench can get in the way of working and be a danger to cutting edges. One way round this is to use clamps in conjunction with 'bridges' of scrap wood to exert pressure on the panel (*see* Fig 6.23).

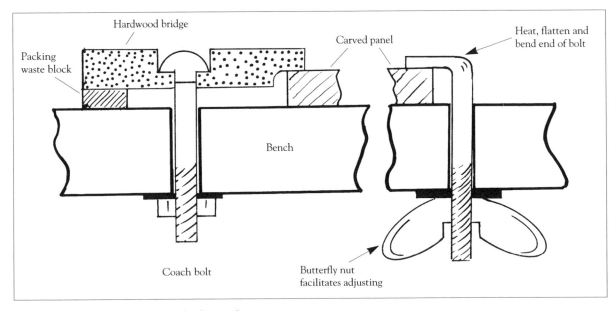

Fig 6.24 Coach bolts with wooden bridges and screw clamps are cheap ways of holding panels.

A **screw clamp**, a variation on the carver's screw (*see* page 275), can be made from a bolt, the head of which is removed and the end flattened and bent (*see* Fig 6.24). Ideally, wings can be welded to the nut to make a fly which can be tightened by hand.

G-clamps will hold work 'in the round' as well. In this case, waste wood is left on the bottom of the carving in which recesses are cut to take the clamp pad (*see* Fig 6.25). Slope the recesses downwards into the wood to get a good purchase. The work is held towards the end of the bench so that it can be clamped from two sides.

Holdfasts

The original **holdfast** was an L-shaped dog of metal thumped through a hole in the bench, which gripped the work by dint of friction (*see* Fig 6.26). Later models, still available, and in two sizes, have a screw thread which exerts considerable leverage. They grip very well and are as effective as a G-clamp, but work from the back of the bench to hold the panel. These two forms of bench clamp complement each other.

A holdfast needs an appropriately sized hole in the bench surface and can only reach as a 'radius' from this hole (*see* Fig 6.27). It is best not to bore large numbers of holes in the bench top in the hope of using holdfasts, but to start with a hole at each end of the bench and one in the middle, boring other holes as they are needed.

Metal collars come with some holdfasts, and these

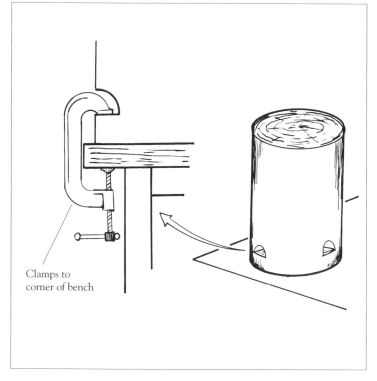

Clamps to
corner of bench

Fig 6.25 **Cutting slots into the waste part of a carving enables it to be gripped by G-clamps to the corner of a bench, over the leg.**

Fig 6.26 **(a) The original holdfast, probably deriving from a bench dog (*see* Fig 6.29), was jammed into position and relied on friction inside the bench hole. (b) More recent versions of the holdfast can be adjusted and released more easily because of the screw.**

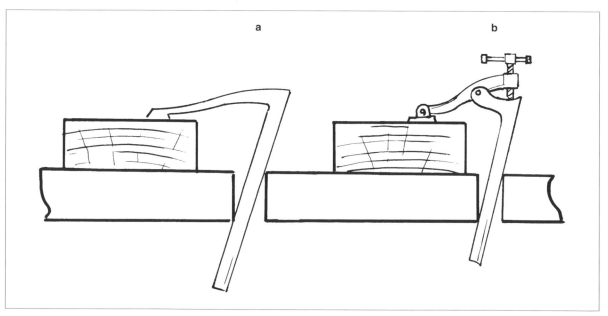

a

b

fit into the bench top to reinforce the holes. As these collars themselves can cause damage to the carving tools, sink them below the surface a little and keep them covered with a thin plywood or perspex disc when not in use (*see* Fig 6.28).

As with **G**-clamps, holdfasts need some padding beneath their **foot** (**shoe** or **pad**) and can project awkwardly where you want to work. A bridge of wood used with the holdfast can also help here.

Dogs, snibs and fences

These ways of holding a carving use the working surface of the bench directly and will mark it.

Dogs are metal staples, hammered across the bench top and the workpiece (*see* Fig 6.29). They are not particularly versatile as the work is effectively fixed – although this might be entirely appropriate. If the wood does not need to be moved during the carving, then screwing or nailing it down through a waste part is also a very simple and quick approach.

Snibs, sometimes also called dogs or **buttons**, are wooden pieces screwed to the bench top and projecting over the edge of the panel to hold it (*see* Fig 6.30). They need to be unscrewed to adjust the work, but represent a quick, makeshift way of holding a carving. Even a washer with a screw through it can be useful at times.

Fences are strips of wood, nailed or screwed to the bench, that simply wall-in a panel (*see* Fig 6.31). The strips of wood, being lower than the panel, do not obstruct the work and are not a hazard to tool edges. In

Fig 6.27 **The bench holdfast reaches through a radius from its hole.**

Fig 6.28 **Details of the holdfast hole in the bench, with collar and cover plate.**

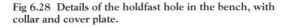

Plywood insert

Bench surface

Holdfast plate

Holdfast collar

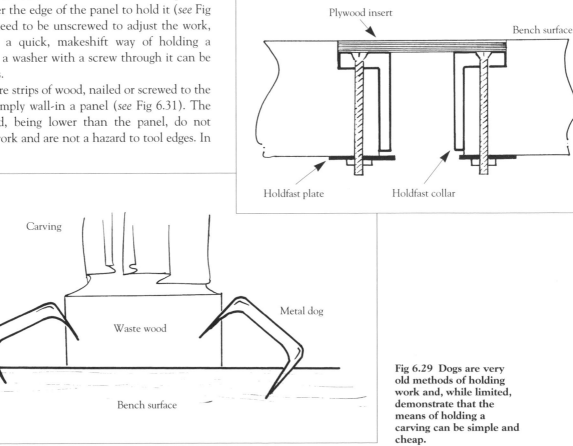

Carving

Metal dog

Waste wood

Bench surface

Fig 6.29 **Dogs are very old methods of holding work and, while limited, demonstrate that the means of holding a carving can be simple and cheap.**

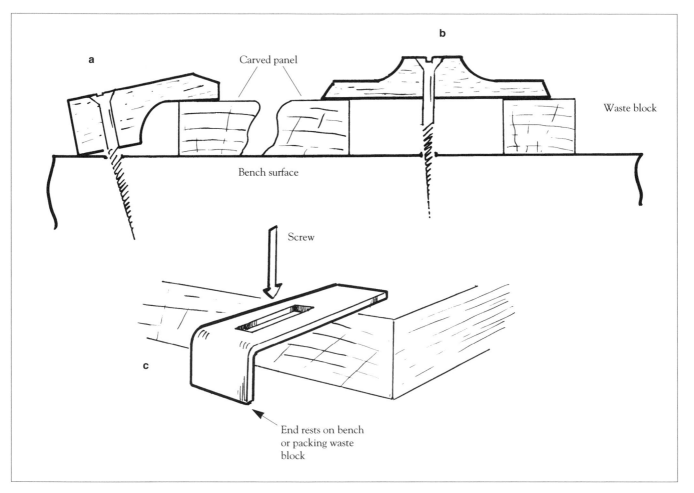

Carved panel

Waste block

Bench surface

Screw

c

End rests on bench
or packing waste
block

**Fig 6.30 Two wooden snibs (a and b) and a metal
version (c).**

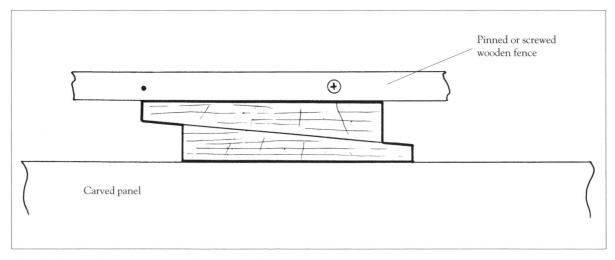

Pinned or screwed
wooden fence

Carved panel

**Fig 6.31 Fences, although they mark the bench surface,
are simple and effective options for panel carvings.**

this arrangement the panel cannot be moved; however, if you use wedges in the arrangement it allows the work to be quickly removed from the bench.

Paper and glue

This is an old method for holding thin panels – ones that are too thin, or have not enough room, for conventional cramping. For example patera or swags which are fretted out first and then applied to a fireplace surround. Bear in mind the possibility of designing ties or other waste pieces to be cut away at the last moment.

The idea is to glue the more fragile piece of wood to be carved to a larger piece that can be clamped or fixed to the bench. A piece of newspaper or brown wrapping paper is sandwiched in the join. A spatula, decorator's filling knife, or other thin knife will easily divide the paper and separate the joint, while the joint itself is strong enough to hold the piece as it is being carved (*see* Fig 6.32). Woodturners use this method to hold work taking considerable stress.

Brush white (PVA or polyvinyl acetate) glue that has been thinned a little with water on to the bench piece of wood. Lay on the paper, making sure that it is soaked in the glue. Brush glue onto the back of the carving wood and clamp the whole together. Make sure the glue is dry before starting work.

After slitting the join, any paper left on the reverse of the carving can be scraped off, soaked off,

Fig 6.32 A spatula releases a finished patera by slitting the newspaper to which it is glued.

sanded off (by rubbing the carving on sandpaper stuck to a flat board) or just left to disappear when the piece is glued into its final position.

IN THE ROUND

Vices

The common woodworking **vice** is a useful, if limited, addition to the carving bench. Vices with quick-release action are the most useful. The term 'vice',

Fig 6.33 On the right is a basic woodworking vice with lined jaws; to the left is the holding bolt for the carver's chops.

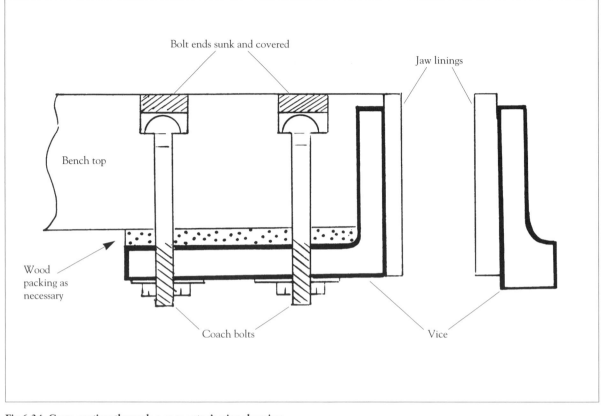

Fig 6.34 Cross-section through a carpenter's vice showing how all the metalwork that might damage the tools or the carvings is hidden or padded.

referring to jaws that open and close by means of a screw, first appears in the sixteenth century. The word itself comes from the Latin *vitis*, meaning a vine, or more exactly the stem with winding tendrils.

Exactly where the vice is fitted to the bench is a personal decision, but it is usual to have it more towards one side than the centre. Fig 6.34 shows a way of fitting such a vice to the bench so that no metal parts are exposed.

There is a fixed and a moving part to the vice; you will find a pin that, when removed, disengages the two. The fixed part is then easier to fit to the bench, housing its face flush with the bench edge, but a little below the surface wood. The underside of the vice will need packing to set the vice in its final bolted position. Make sure the face is at a dead right angle to the bench top. The underframe of the bench will need cutting to take the moving section of the vice – remove only the minimum amount of wood. Sink any fixing (coach) bolts below the bench surface and fill to hide the metal. Pad the jaws to prevent them bruising

whatever they are holding.

When using the vice a spigot or waste shoulder may be left on the workpiece; or the carving can be bolted (or screwed) to another block of wood which is then held in the jaws of the vice. Other holding devices can also be gripped by the vice – for example gripping a block of wood to which a swivel-ball system is fixed. Because the vice is stationary, re-positioning or adjusting work is limited

Engineer's vices are an alternative although, sitting on the bench surface as they do, the jaws are higher than the woodworking vice. It is therefore easy to knock tool edges against their metal bodies. Engineer's vices that swivel are the most useful; these can be quite small and fitted to the bench for a particular job. Again, the jaws need padding.

Woodcarver's chops

'**Chops**' is the name given to a particular wooden vice, like a set of jaws, that sits on the bench surface (*see* Fig 6.35). The vice is fixed with a bolt passing through the

Fig 6.35 Carver's chops. It is the back jaw which opens, sliding with the brass plate in a groove in the base. The jaws need re-lining now and then with cork and leather.

Fig 6.36 The holding bolt passes through a square hole in the base of the chops then along an internal rebate. The vice can be slid forwards and backwards as well as rotated.

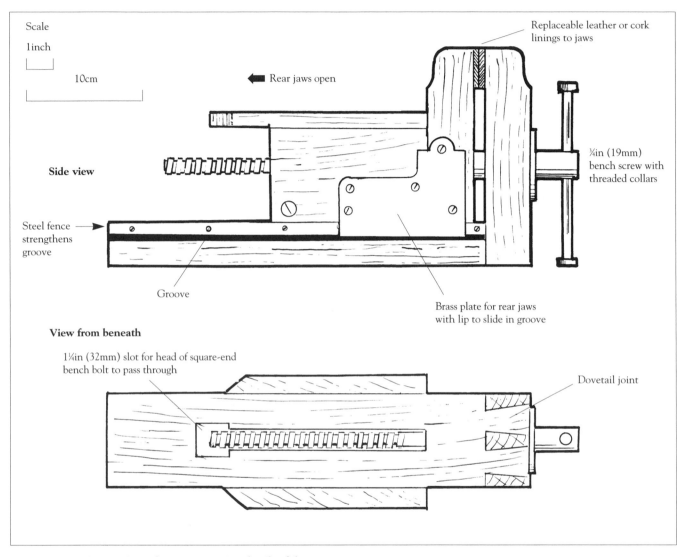

Scale

1inch

10cm

Side view

Steel fence
strengthens
groove

Groove

◄ Rear jaws open

Replaceable leather or cork
linings to jaws

¾in (19mm)
bench screw with
threaded collars

Brass plate for rear jaws
with lip to slide in groove

View from beneath

1¼in (32mm) slot for head of square-end
bench bolt to pass through

Dovetail joint

**Fig 6.37 Some basic construction details of the
woodcarver's chops.**

bench top to a butterfly nut underneath. When this bolt is loosened, the chops can be rotated to re-position the work, or it can be completely removed. The best chops are made of ash with leather and cork-lined jaws and brass runners. Being made of wood, carving tools are safe from damage.

Fitting carver's chops involves boring only one hole, but several may be arranged for different working positions on the bench. The jaws open towards the back, and the whole device can be moved horizontally (*see* Fig 6.36). These movements, together with the rotation of the vice, can push tools and equipment around the bench top if care is not taken. The vice

also sits rather high on the bench like an engineer's vice.

Carver's chops are certainly very useful means of holding some work on some occasions. For someone who has not used them before, it is probably best to see a set in action – perhaps even trying them out – in the first place, as they do not suit everyone.

Quality woodcarver's chops with an overall length of 18in (450mm) are available from Alec Tiranti Ltd (*see* the Reference Section, page 346), who have been making or supplying them for generations. Any other size will have to be custom-made and a scale working plan is shown in Figs 6.37, 6.38. The dovetail joints

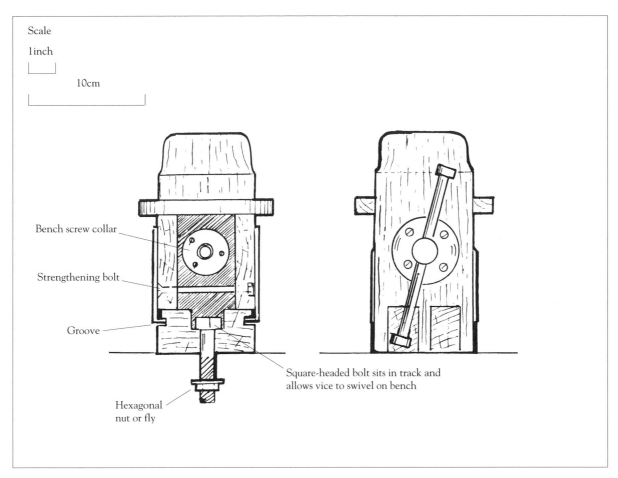

Scale

1inch

10cm

Bench screw collar

Strengthening bolt

Groove

Square-headed bolt sits in track and
allows vice to swivel on bench

Hexagonal
nut or fly

Fig 6.38 Front and back view of Fig 6.37.

and metal side cheeks give strength. Use ash for the
woodwork and a square-threaded screw.

Woodcarver's screws

These are a very elegant way of holding some types of
work. The tapered part of the screw is wound into a
pre-drilled hole in the base or back of the carving, and
tightened using the square hole in the **fly** as a spanner
(*see* Fig 6.40). The rest of the screw is then passed
through a hole in the bench; when the fly is tightened,
the work is gripped. Loosen the fly and the work can
be rotated.

As the main thread of the woodcarver's screw is
normally a strong, square type, a lot of pressure can be
exerted by tightening the fly. There is a tendency for the
screw to loosen in the carving so it will need re-
tightening periodically. Be careful not to over-tighten it.

If the screw is inserted into a carving with the
grain running vertically, the screw tends to *cut* the

**Fig 6.39 Collection of carver's screws, from the left: the
mighty Stubai screw; large and small Marples screws; small
brass Veritas screw; and a carver's clamp. None are
supplied with a washer (shown) but one is advisable.**

Fig 6.40 A square hole in the fly engages a spigot in the end of the screw with which to tighten it into the workpiece.

Fig 6.41 The working ends of carver's screws differ in taper and thread according to what the manufacturer thinks will give the best grip.

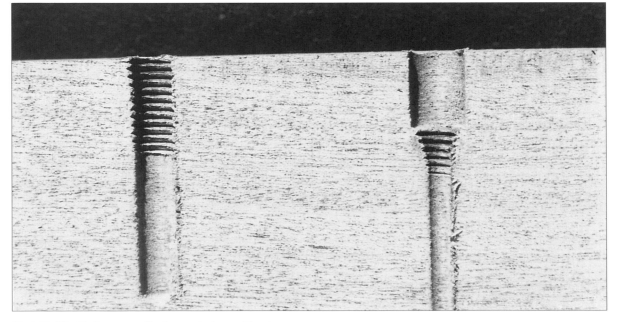

Fig 6.42 The Veritas screw fits the workpiece with a taper of about 5°(left); the Marples about 35°. The difference in the amount of grip they can get on the wood is obvious.

fibres rather than wrapping round them in the way it would if the grain was running across the thread. Screwing anything into end-grain is the weakest fixing; and into cross-grain the strongest fixing. To help support the screw when it is inserted into the base end-grain of a carving, a hole may first be bored a little way into the work the diameter of the parallel thread. A drop of wood glue to the end point of the screw helps to bind the wood fibres together and give a surer grip. Sometimes two screws are used, although then the workpiece cannot be rotated.

Instead of holding the carving to a horizontal bench, the woodcarver's screw can be used to fix the work to a thick plank, angled or vertically placed, and perhaps held in the bench vice (*see* Figs 6.43, 6.44). This arrangement is especially suitable for pieces intended for wall mounting.

One drawback carver's screws have – as do expanding bolts, coach screws and similar holding devices – is the resulting hole in the back or base of the carving. This may or may not be acceptable. It is sometimes possible to design around the hole, for example by allowing waste wood in the preliminary stages, or by using a mounting base, or a neat plug.

Carver's screws come in various sizes, some of the larger ones being made in continental Europe.

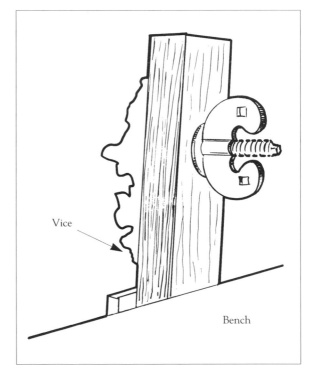

Fig 6.43 A carver's screw holding work through a vertical post; the screw will also work well in conjunction with the tilting surfaces mentioned earlier.

Fig 6.44 A screw post, or board, held in a vice allows work to be held vertically.

Fig 6.45 A carver's clamp: a simple sort of holdfast needing smaller but more precise holes in the bench. It can be usefully used with wooden bridges to hold the back of panels.

Fig 6.46 The excellent Spencer Franklin Hydraclamp with a special (non-standard) plate, custom-made to hold a small vice. The swivel-ball vices come in several sizes.

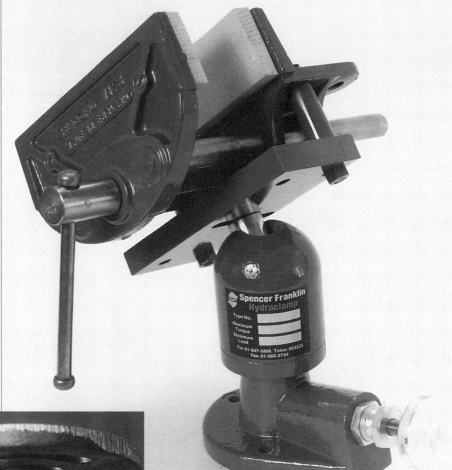

Fig 6.47 The standard plate with slots to take bolts in the base of the carving. The swivel ball is easily seen.

Swivel-ball systems

Most of the holding devices mentioned so far have limitations to their movement and the adjustability of the work they hold – at best two-dimensional re-positioning is possible. Fixing the carving to a ball which can rotate, swivel and be locked, moves the holding ability into three dimensions. There are several such clamps on the market, some crudely mechanical – but still very effective – and some based on hydraulic systems with amazing locking ability.

These **swivel-ball** holding devices are becoming increasingly popular, and this is not surprising because they represent in many ways the carver's dream come true: the work can be rotated in any direction and locked horizontally or at an angle. They are worth serious consideration and investigation.

The Spencer Franklin Hydraclamp (*see* the Reference Section, page 346), which has been well established and proven over many years, is a hydraulic system in which a plate is attached to a spigot extending from the ball (*see* Fig 6.46). The plate has many slots and holes allowing a range of adaptations (*see* Fig 6.47). The carving can be fixed directly to the plate using bolts or screws; or a woodworking vice can be improvised; or the spigot modified to meet a carver's individual needs. Although a little ingenuity may be required, once fitted the carving can be positioned so that any part can be got at easily. The work can be locked and moved safely. The clamp itself may be bolted directly to the carving bench, or mounted to a block of wood clamped to the bench top, or held in a vice (*see* Fig 6.48).

The Hydraclamp 1400, for example, will support 100lb (45kg), held at 45° and 12in (300mm) away from the centre of the ball, and there are larger and smaller versions available. In fact this tremendous holding ability creates a particular problem: the strength and weight of the bench may not be up to taking the weight of the carving, under what can become conditions of considerable leverage, and may 'walk'. A free-standing, floor-mounted metal stanchion or stand is one answer.

The Koch clamping system has a vice to hold the work rather than a face plate; it locks mechanically and is adjustable, but not quite to the same extent (*see* Figs 6.49, 6.50). Bench-mounted, the angled metal

Fig 6.48 If the clamp is fixed to a wooden base, this in turn can be simply fitted and removed from a bench.

Fig 6.49 The Koch clamping system.

Fig 6.50 The swivelling vice in the Koch system is mechanically held.

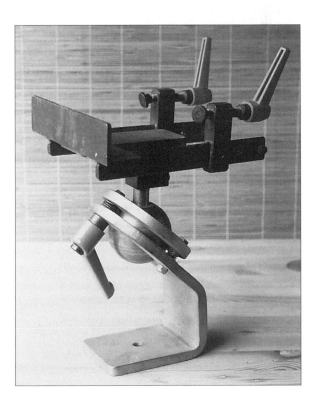

Fig 6.51 The Record adjustable carver's clamp fits like a sash clamp to the edge of the bench to take small work.

bracket from bench to ball makes it feel lighter and springier. The carving will vibrate and bounce when struck even lightly with a mallet.

The Record Marples carver's vice which clamps to the bench surface is, in terms of the above sophisticated systems, relatively cheap. It is a simple design that is suitable for small work which can be screwed to it (*see* Fig 6.51).

As all these metal swivel-ball systems fit to the bench top, there *is* a danger to the tool edges. Using a bench vice to hold them keeps their metal bodies out of the way, lowers the working height and makes them easily removable.

TURNED WORK

The application of carving disciplines to woodturning has a long history – you only have to look at such furniture as four-poster beds for an example. This sort of work would have been undertaken by two separate tradesmen: a turner and a carver. Today, however, many turners will have a go at carving their own work and vice versa.

Essentially, no turning is of a more complicated shape than can be found in carving; and most of the problems with holding turned work are the same as those for carved work.

Spindle turnings are often best left on the lathe – locking the mandrel, or using an indexing plate, to adjust the position of the work. Arrange a board, with a fence around, under the turning and on the bed of the lathe. This will act as a bench and the carving tools can be placed normally. With delicate spindles, extend a wooden supporting trough from the tool rest or saddle – such spindles can be quite flexible, if not fragile. The work may need reversing to get at the other side, or to work with the grain.

Face-plate work may, again, be best left on whatever device was used to hold it when it was being turned – though not necessarily *on* the lathe – and many of the holding methods described above can be used.

A bowl may be gripped between two bars of wood, bolted across, for lettering purposes. If the edge is not strong, grip it in a similar way but using a packing block to the centre. This arrangement is then clamped to the bench surface.

Carving should be done before any sanding to prevent the grit damaging the keen edge of the carving tools.

SUMMARY

This chapter cannot hope to cover all the ingenious ways that carvers find to hold their work. And that really is the crux of the matter. Often ingenuity, adaptability and foresight are needed unless a limited range of predictable work is undertaken.

Although holding a particular piece of work efficiently, conveniently, safely and securely, may be a problem, there will always be some way to achieve it – found from within a repertoire of techniques. Part of the challenge and joy of carving comes from successfully finding a creative response to these sorts of problems.

THE WORKPLACE

Aims

To advise on what makes a suitable and pleasant
working environment for carving

To encourage, in newcomers, the right balance
between tools and carving

To look at safety in the workplace

The type of workplace *needed* by a carver varies
with the nature of the carving work. Small and
intricate netsuke, for example, can be carved
with a tray on the carver's lap, sitting in an armchair.
Huge log sculptures, at the other extreme, may need a
block and tackle to handle them. In these cases the
workplace is adapted to the carving work.

On the other hand, many carvers have to fit the
carving to the workplace. They work on kitchen
tables, on benches attached to garage walls and in
garden sheds. Some are lucky, but most do not have
purpose-built workshops and the available space
dictates the size of work that can be undertaken.

If the size of the workplace is one factor
influencing the type of carving work, whether the
workplace is large or small, purpose-built or
improvised, there are other physical requirements that
matter. There are also non-physical factors to be
considered.

A carver needs to feel comfortable and at ease,
even 'at home', in the workplace. This applies as much
to those carving only an hour or two a week as to
those carvers spending more of their waking hours
inside a workshop than they do outside it.

A workplace must feel safe, secure, comfortable
and attractive to the user, supporting the mental states
that will express themselves in their work. It is really
worth the trouble to make the workplace as supportive
as possible, rather than a makeshift environment that
is continually unsatisfying or annoying.

I would like to include a plea for woodlice, spiders
and the like who love to dwell among wood and
behind benches. They are completely harmless (unless
you live in Sydney or somewhere similar) and are only
being what they are. Carving can be an isolated
occupation and these creatures are always there to talk
to – you only need to worry when they answer back!
So, please treat them kindly and allow them to share
your space.

**Fig 7.1 Despite the size of this book, it does not take much
to make a woodcarver happy.**

Fig 7.2 The foot of a metal bench, sitting on a concrete floor. The angle iron around the base has a wooded infill; this is weighted and the whole structure is immensely stable. The concrete itself can be sealed.

FEATURES OF A WORKPLACE

The following thoughts concern some of the physical qualities which help to make the workplace function well and support the carving process. One other useful facility to the workplace is running water.

Position of the bench

See the workbench as the hub of carving activity, whatever its shape or size. It is here that the actual carving takes place. Give your bench prime consideration and fit, arrange or orientate everything else around it – and not just around the tea-making facilities.

Floor

The floor must be solid enough for the bench to stand firmly on it. A bench will 'walk' on a springy wooden floor, especially when an amount of force is used. On the other hand, concrete floors are hard and cold on the feet and can damage any tools that happen to fall from the bench.

A wooden floor laid over a concrete one is an ideal compromise: firm but friendly. Alternatively 'duckboards', or a section of chipboard, or a reverse piece of hessian-backed carpet laid on the concrete in front of the bench will make standing a lot more comfortable.

Lighting

The bench cannot properly be arranged without careful consideration of the lighting. Carving or sculpture is essentially about light and shadow. The quality of the workplace lighting affects the carving and the final result enormously. Complete all-round lighting will produce no shadows and it becomes difficult to see what is happening to the carving.

Ideally the workplace lighting should reproduce that in which the finished carving will reside. To produce a working pattern of light and shadow, a variety of adjustable sources is needed. Many workplaces have single fixed windows to which the carving must be continually orientated – this can be

Fig 7.3 A window like this may be blocking a third of its potential lighting ability in the thick cross members, security bars, frosted pane and cobwebs.

Fig 7.4 Better, but cleaning would make a significant difference!

entirely satisfactory. Daylight is considered by most to be by far the best light to work in and workplaces that have no windows at all and depend entirely on artificial light are at a disadvantage.

There are some options to increase the quality and flexibility of the lighting. The best illumination is like that used for photographing objects: a main source of light (from above or to the side) and secondary lights 'filling in' from right angles to the first. But the important thing is to control what is going on.

NATURAL LIGHTING

Being able to adjust the amount of sunlight with venetian or roller blinds is a good start. The most useful light for carving comes in the lower half of a tall window, so blocking off the top half is an advantage. This is not the same as an overhead skylight or transparent panel in the middle of the room, which gives a good light for three-dimensional work.

Northern light in Britain is the most constant and mild, whereas southern windows give the maximum but most variable quality of light. Of the two, northern light is preferable.

Painting the walls and ceilings of the workplace bright white will increase the amount of ambient light; as

Fig 7.5 An adjustable light that fixes to the ceiling above the bench, out of the way of the work area itself.

will the large acrylo-plastic mirrors which are available – throwing light back from dingy corners of a room.

ARTIFICIAL LIGHTING

Normal light bulbs give a yellow tinge which affects the colours of the wood, but need not be a problem if you are considering only the relative light and shadow of a form. Fluorescent tubes are harder on the eyes and shadows, and in general are a bit insensitive. Daylight tubes and bulbs are better.

Adjustable angle lamps in various places help control the light direction greatly (*see* Fig 7.5). They can be turned on or off, swung here or there, closer or further away to the work, thus allowing changes to be made quickly.

Tool and equipment storage

Some carvers like to work in chaos with tools scattered everywhere. But if you are not like this, then its a case of the old adage 'a place for everything and everything in its place', as far as is practical. Use shelves, cupboards, hooks and so on.

Fig 7.6 Do not forget security.

It is helpful to divide tools and equipment into two categories:

■ Those which are stored for a long length of time
■ Those which are used often and only put away in the short term.

Keep the most frequently used tools nearer the work area – that is in, on, or by the bench. Relegate the others to less useful areas of the workplace.

Heating

It is said that carvers, in the main, are a long-lived lot. This may be because – in Darwinian manner – they have a habit of working in cold workshops and the weaker members of the species are weeded out early on. This habit may be due to stoicism or meanness. However, having a warm enough workplace does make a lot of difference to the well-being of the carver.

Temperature often goes with humidity: too hot an environment makes work hard and sluggish; too cold and the hands feel lumpy and insensitive. Too dry an atmosphere can lead to wood splitting; too moist and rust and mould thrive. A balance needs to be found within these variations.

First of all you need to look at the workshop.

■ Check the insulation: perhaps consider double-glazing the windows and soft-boarding (or fibre-boarding) the walls. Look for draughts.
■ A wooden floor is much warmer than a concrete one. If you place a wooden floor over concrete, insulate the space between.
■ Heating a workshop that is divided into smaller areas of use is more manageable.

Much less heat is needed to heat a workshop where these points have been applied.

Wood-burning stoves have always been popular if a little hazardous. Do check any insurance policy, as many insurers will not allow any naked flame – such as in these stoves, or bottled-gas fires – in the workplace.

Remember that paraffin (kerosene) and bottled-gas fires give off both fumes and water vapour – in fact, when one gallon of paraffin is burnt it produces one gallon of water vapour. Both types of fire need good ventilation; if they can be used in an indirect form of heating – ducting the fumes externally – so much the better.

Electric heating is probably the cheapest form to install, if not the cheapest to run. Both installation and running costs need to be considered when working out overheads. Electric convector heaters with thermostats, and infra-red heaters, work well, as do night-storage heaters on cheap electricity.

Wood storage

It is worth thinking about where and how wood is to be stored when setting up a workplace initially. Will it be kept in the workshop or separately? How soon will the wood be needed? How much space is available? Are racks necessary? Can the wood be got at easily? Is there woodworm in the place? Where is the source of heating to be and where will you be wanting to move or work?

Keep wood dry and aired, and stored in such a way that you can see exactly what you have got.

Cleaning

Although some carvers thrive on chaos, it does have its drawbacks for most of us: tools get lost, damaged or broken; dirt gets onto carvings, etc. Carving is a disciplined craft and generally keeping the workshop tidy and clean is good practice.

Having found places for tools, it is a matter of putting them away when not in use. The best habit is one of 'policing the area' – for example, if you are crossing the workshop anyway, take something with you that can be put away. This saves on intensive clearing up sessions.

An 'industrial' vacuum cleaner is a definite asset in a workshop for clearing up. A bench brush and soft floor brush are useful but tend to raise the dust. Wood chips and shavings from carving are fairly large and easily cleared up; dust on the other hand floats around in the air for a long time. Routing or power-sanding in a small workshop can soon cover everything in fine dust.

It is a good idea to keep carvings covered between sessions.

BEGINNER'S SYNDROME

This book is mainly about the tools and equipment used for carving; notes about woodcarving itself are only made as they apply in context. There is, however, a real danger for newcomers to carving, one that may be reinforced by the nature of this book, and which needs to be considered.

Someone coming new to carving will buy their carving tools; sharpen them; build up a bench; set up a

Fig 7.7 St Michael, southern Germany, about 1490. The great confidence the unknown carver has in his ability to use his tools has given rise to this mixture of easy posture and tense lines. Even such a master must have started somewhere, as a beginner.

Fig 7.8 Detail of Fig 7.7. Tool cuts are visible all over: in the precision of the mouth, the eyes as well as the hair and armour. Certainly there must be natural talent, but carving is also the result of hard work and constantly seeking to improve. We, too, must put steel to wood if we want to make headway in the craft.

Fig 7.9 Detail of Fig 7.7. It is easy to overlook the effort that is required, the deep and deft use of tools that have liberated this hand, so loose and relaxed, from a solid block of wood. Rather than be intimidated by such work, we can be inspired and challenged to do better.

workplace; hunt around for wood; read many books . . . all of which can be very exciting, interesting, and enjoyable – and make them feel as if they are getting somewhere. But none of this is *actually carving*.

These activities are very important and contribute to the carving process, but there are many would-be carvers who actually never get round to carving, or carve very little, because they spend all their time and effort on the tools, equipment and other paraphernalia. If only they had *this* clamp, or *those* tools, a better place to work, a nicer bench or whatever – then they can get on with it. But it never seems to happen, or rarely. A student carves in a class for a couple of hours a week and is always planning to carve at home, but years later they have never managed to get the conditions right. This state of affairs is common enough to need discussing.

One of the main reasons for this 'beginner's syndrome' is that carving itself is very demanding and challenging, especially when you are beginning. There is a lot to learn and initial efforts can be disappointing. There is also the well-known 'blank canvas', which can phase even experienced carvers. Tools and equipment are much less threatening and a ready diversion. They represent a definite, and understandable, Siren-call to the unwary beginner. The reply involves a sort of strapping of yourself to the bench – in a friendly way.

The first thing is to notice the prevarication. If you recognize the condition I have described, in whole or part, you have to ask yourself whether you *really* want to carve. If you do, then the following approach may get things moving:

■ Having acknowledged and accepted where you are, strongly try to visualize yourself carving.

■ Decide what sort of carving is within your grasp and that you are really capable of. It does not matter whether this is just a few decorative strokes to the surface of a chopping board. Assess what is the 'bottom line' of your vision, what you could actually achieve as a project. Beginners often set their sights too high.

■ Decide that for the moment you have enough tools; that you will just finish this one simple project and not concern yourself with others right now. Decide to enjoy the carving, no matter how 'good' or 'bad' the end result. 'Practice makes perfect' and you are starting to practice.

■ Allocate an amount of time within which to start the carving – write this down – and a period of time to finish it.

■ Start the carving. If you do not manage to start and finish within the time frames, then you must try to understand the reasons.

■ Enjoy the carving and the result; carving at *any* level is no mean achievement. Assess your carving – not by comparing it with other carvers, but by deciding what you might have done to make it better, a happier result for yourself. Consider keeping a journal for these thoughts and others related to your carving.

■ Try and make bench time a regular pattern or habit.

■ Decide on a second project. See how much carving you can do before buying any new tools, working out your needs from actually carving before buying them.

The attitude to establish in your heart and mind is that you are a carver – no matter at what level. Which means that you carve – *by definition*; not collect tools.

SAFETY IN THE WORKPLACE

Good advice about safety in the workplace is to stand at the entrance with a notepad and challenge yourself to think of all the ways you could be hurt in the space in front of you, once you start using it, the tools and the equipment.

The following specific notes should be read together with the other safety notes in this book.

■ Make sure that where you walk is free from the danger of sharp edges and corners, things to bump into and wires to trip over. See that you can easily and safely work around your bench.

■ All electric wires should be installed, earthed and protected properly (*see* Fig 7.10).

■ Bag up and remove dust and debris regularly – especially rags that are used for finishing.

■ Install a smoke alarm and extinguisher.

First aid box

There are notes on safety practices in the Reference Section (*see* page 343), as well as interspersed where appropriate throughout this book. Despite care, accidents are always possible – mostly unpredictable and sudden. A fully equipped first aid box should be present in every workplace.

Carving is a solitary occupation and therefore carvers may well be on their own when an accident happens. The first aid box should be readily accessible.

Fig 7.10 Safety in the workshop requires being vigilant for possible dangers – such as this worn flex.

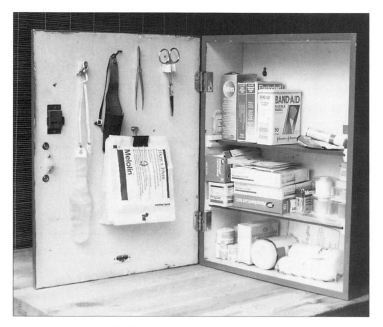

Fig 7.11 Keep a fully stocked first aid box, and make sure you know how to use the contents.

The most common accident is a clean cut to the hand or finger by the razor-sharp carving tools. Nicks are more annoying for getting blood on the carving – sweat and tears are enough – than for the personal injury. But remember that you may have to deal with this, or a larger cut, dexterously, using only one hand. Do be aware of this and make sure that you can get at, and open, things easily – as well as knowing how to use them.

Carvers should always be up to date on their tetanus jabs.

Some useful items to be included in the first aid box are:

- Plaster strips, Steri-Strips and individual plasters
- Lint and cotton wool
- Crêpe and cotton bandages in assorted sizes
- Scissors
- Antiseptic
- Needle for removing splinters
- Eye-bath and wash.

Always replace items in the first aid box as soon as they are used and keep it stocked. When you want an item, you want it straight away.

WOOD

Aims

To show how the growth of a tree produces and affects the wood within it

To describe those properties of wood which carvers need to understand and work

To help choose the material to suit a specific project or design

To give some general advice on the selection, seasoning, storage, glueing up and care of wood

To clarify some of the terms used in talking about trees and wood

To help beginners feel more at ease with the material they are working in, so adding to their general confidence

E ach of the aims will be considered in a little more detail in turn.

How the growth of a tree produces and affects the wood within it

Unlike the material of stonecarvers, which is relatively fixed and unchanging, the material woodcarvers work with has changed and unfolded as it grew – and continues to change as it is worked. The massive 400-year-old oak tree started as a single acorn, lost in the dark soil one autumn day.

As the leaves of a tree are lifted higher and higher to catch the sunlight, rising further away from the roots, so the connecting food and water channels grow longer and longer. These hollow channels are the fibres which are bound together in bundles and masses,

Fig 8.1 The seedling – it is hard to grasp that all great woodcarvings start from both physical and mental seedlings.

Fig 8.2 From seed to tree, tree to timber, to carving. This oak carving on a door at Berkeley Castle, Gloucestershire, shows a fine understanding of grain in the layout of the design.

Fig 8.3 Some trees, such as this yew tree grow quite wildly . . .

Fig 8.4 . . . and this is reflected in the fibrous structure within.

tighter or looser, thinner or thicker – depending on the species. It is this fibrous material that is carved. A woodcarver may be cutting into what was once the very heart of a great tree.

Once planted, and the seed having sent its roots deep into the soil, the tree can never leave that spot. It constantly absorbs the changing environment: the rainfall, the sunlight; the wind, frost and lightning; the warmth of summer and the cold of winter that makes for a temperate climate. Trees of the same species on the south side of a valley will grow quicker than those on the north. And even the north side of a tree is different from the south side. Each tree grows according to its individual experience.

Woodcarvers not only work with a fibrous material – a tree – but with different species of trees; with unique examples of a particular species; and with singular parts of any one tree – with knots and burls, wany grain and unusually thick sections. The starting material of a carver is often of a size and composition that workers in any other wood craft would not use.

Wood can be treated as a passive material on which a design will be imposed, whether it likes it or not. But this would be to miss one of the rich veins of joy available to a woodcarver – the wood itself. Each piece of wood is unique, and carvers need to be alert to

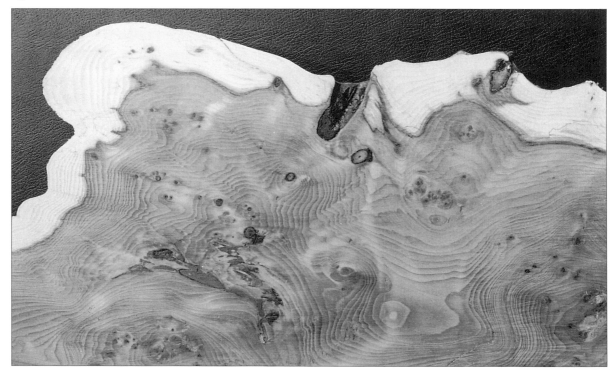

get the most out of the material in front of them. This should not be done in a dewy-eyed, romantic way, but with the realism born of true intimacy.

The properties of wood with which carvers in particular need to understand and work

Tilman Riemenschneider used great lumps of limewood; the carver of the Winchester Misericords used oak; Henry Moore used the boles of elm trees; and in the Victoria and Albert Museum, in London, there is exquisitely detailed work in boxwood. Why is it that these carvers chose these particular timbers – and not others – for their designs?

Undoubtedly availability and cost were, and always have been, factors. In the days when transporting anything was a fairly major undertaking, artisans tended to live nearer the source of their materials and woodcarvers would naturally work in the woods available locally.

Often overlooked in appreciating the history of sculpture is the circumscribing effect that the attributes and limits of any material has on the sculptor who works it. The designs that can be expressed through one particular species of wood can be very difficult, if not physically impossible, to express in another. Looking at carvings in the past, the designs that particular schools and styles of carvers used always seem, at their best, to fit perfectly with the type of wood used. The designs do not appear to have come before the material or vice versa; it is as if they arose naturally together. Sometimes the link is strikingly obvious: in the case of the limewood carvers of Renaissance Germany it can be said that without limewood, with its unique characteristics, being available locally, the whole phenomenon could not have taken place.

Suiting the material to a specific project or design

An understanding of wood grows with experience. So carvers who have been working in the medium for some time will have at least an adequate understanding, if not a very good understanding, of their material – they will know what they can expect from it.

This chapter is aimed mainly at beginners who perhaps have never worked with wood before; consequently they may have little knowledge or experience of the material. There is a lot of knowledge, relating to wood, that is shared between the different woodworking crafts. But what do *woodcarvers* – as

Fig 8.5 Self-portrait of the master, Tilman Riemenschneider (1460–1531), whose woodcarvings are almost exclusively in the limewood of the region in which he worked.

opposed to, say, carpenters – need to know about wood?

It is not possible to know too much about the material you are working with – but it *is* possible to know too little. And the consequences of knowing too little are quite likely to be some adverse effect such as the wood splitting, reacting badly to a stain, or lacking strength in a part where the design calls for it.

Some general advice on the selection, seasoning, storage, gluing up and care of wood

Husbanding wood is a concern of all woodcarvers – without the wood what are they? Husbanding can

Fig 8.6 Part of the 'Altar of the Holy Blood', St Jacob's Church, Rothenburg, by Riemenschneider. The clarity and intense detail of all the carving in the altar are possible only because of the material qualities of limewood.

involve the relatively minor exercise of choosing a piece of wood from a timber yard specializing in the needs of carvers; or it may involve a large-scale operation such as buying and converting whole trees.

Whatever need a carver has, the final carving will rarely look anything like the original tree, and only a small amount of the original tree will have been used by all those woodworkers interested in it. The rest will have been burned on site, removed in the timber yard, succumbed to the weather or other defects, or will have been swept up from the workshop floor and thrown away.

Time, effort and financial outlay are needed to obtain the wood, so thought must be given to the material in order to make the most of it – from the tree to the finished piece.

From the point of view of the planet, nobody in the West can now claim to be unaware that resources can no longer be taken for granted. Carvers are working with woods from all over the world and from all levels of forest and woodland management. In the long term, carvers have a responsibility to trees over and above their being vehicles for short-term creative achievements. Indeed, it should not just be a matter of 'responsibility' for trees, but a love of them.

Clarifying some of the terms used in talking about trees and wood

Being able to name what concerns us is tantamount to acquiring a language with which to understand and share our experiences. For those who have arrived at woodcarving with little or no experience of wood, this chapter will clarify terms that are commonly used and help them find their way around.

Feeling more at ease with the material being worked and so adding to general confidence

It is not just the terms themselves that need to be understood by the beginner, but the substance these terms describe, and this involves time, exploration and experience.

A carver works *with* wood, not against it. Newcomers to carving not only have to gain the skills of sharpening, using their carving tools, working out the designs they want to carve, but also how to bring all this to bear on the material. This combination of challenges is what makes woodcarving and wood sculpture such a stimulating occupation.

The wood itself may suggest an idea and actually form the design in your mind. Or you can find a piece of wood to fit the idea. Either way, as a feeling for working wood grows – how to cut it and shape it well – the carver becomes more free. Carving becomes more of a lovers' dance – even if at times dancing with an old piece of oak feels more of a tussle – where both dancers must contribute to the final display. There is no need to think in terms of fighting or subduing the material. You have to seduce and cajole, read and listen, direct with affection and be prepared to be directed. The material is a means of expression, not something that keeps getting in the way.

GROWTH OF A TREE
A brief biology

Trees dwell in two worlds: growing their trunks, branches and leaves into the sunlit air; and their roots into the dark earth. The ancient Chinese believed that trees held heaven and earth together and that without trees, heaven and earth would separate.

The root system can be deep and extensive, or surprisingly shallow – as in the trees from tropical rainforests. Roots seek out water and food elements such as sodium, potassium and iron which ascend the tree to the leaves as a crude, watery sap (Fig 8.7). Sunlight and carbon dioxide act to transform the inorganic salts into chemicals which go into the life processes of the tree, including its growth (Fig 8.8). This much heavier sap passes to buds and branches, and back down the trunk to the roots. If you burn a piece of wood, the ash represents all the solid material which has been taken from the soil by the tree; the smoke will be some of these chemicals, as well as carbon dioxide absorbed by the leaves; the

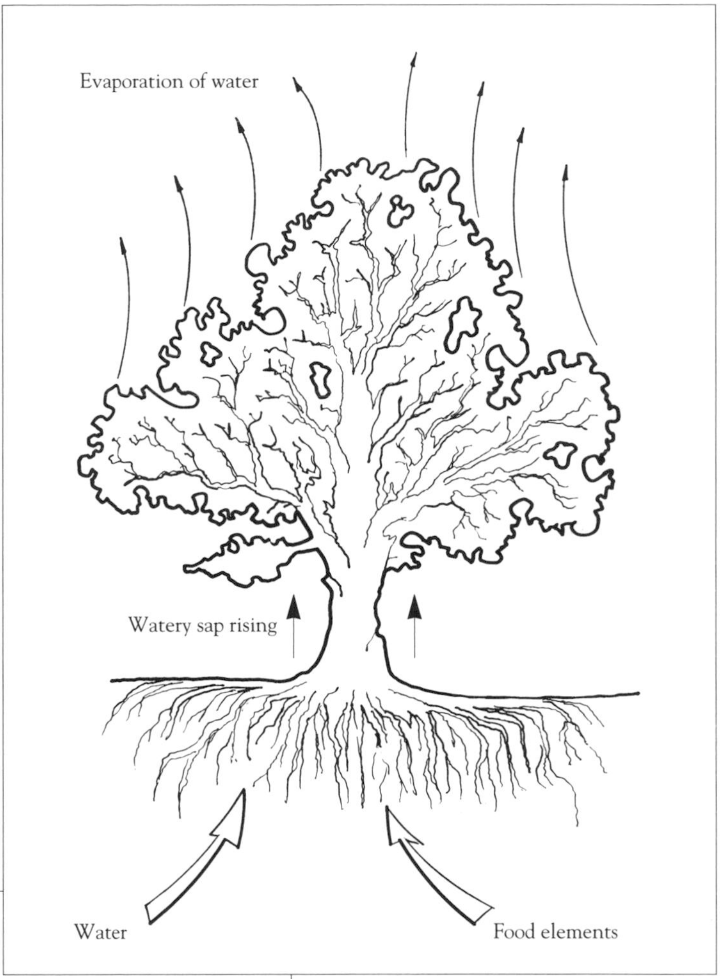

Fig 8.7 Water, with dissolved nutrients, is drawn right up the tree by the considerable force exerted by evaporation from the leaves, far above.

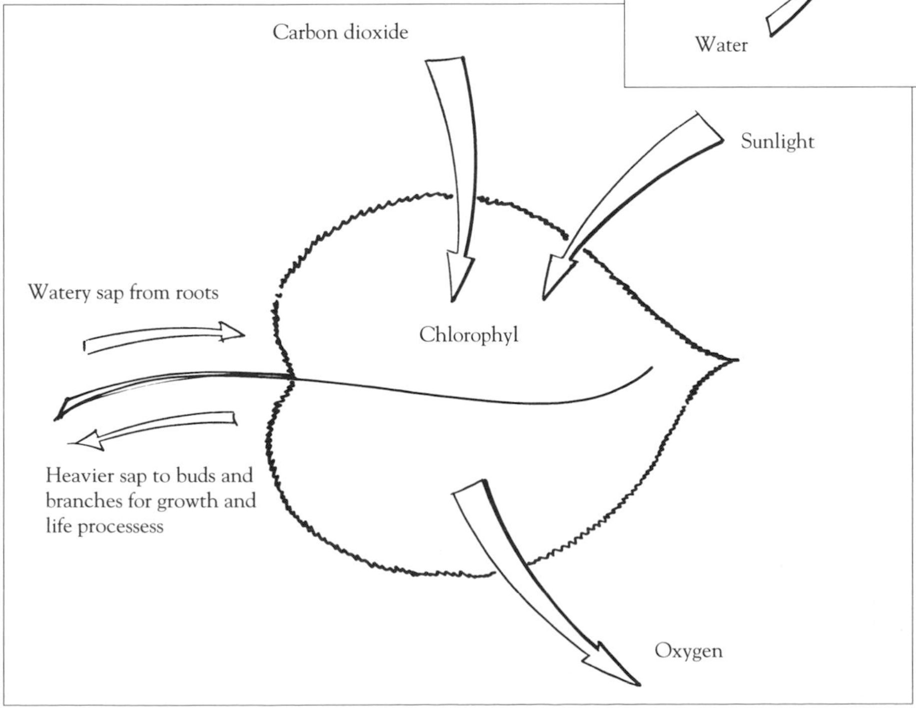

Fig 8.8 The metabolism of a tree depends on trapping the energy of sunlight.

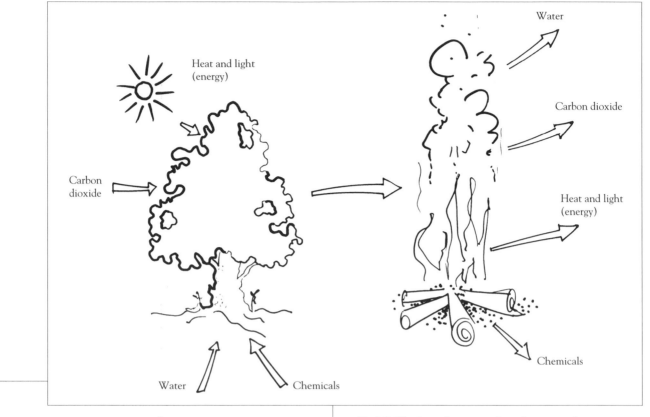

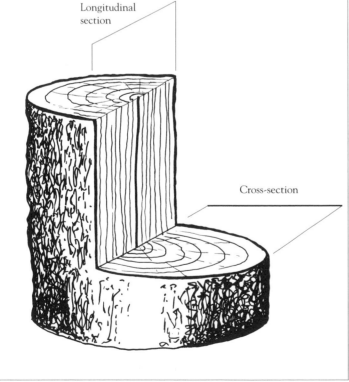

Longitudinal section

Cross-section

Fig 8.9 The law of conservation of energy: what you get out is what went in.

Fig 8.10 Examining cross- and longitudinal sections through a tree stump will show how the features described in the text interconnect.

heat from the burning is trapped sunlight – the fire in the grate is heat from the sun (Fig 8.9).

Trees are products of their immediate environment: the amount of sunlight, its direction, the availability of water, the chemicals in the soil and seasonal changes. All these factors will affect its growth.

We are all familiar with logs or felled tree stumps. In such a cross-section of a tree, the places where the growth and life processes take place can be seen (Fig 8.11). Starting on the outside, the **bark** protects against the weather, insects and animals. It is almost completely impervious to water, but pervious to air.

Just inside the bark is the **bast**, a spongy layer in which most of the sap travels as it returns from the leaves. If a tree is bark-ringed (Fig 8.12), this layer is destroyed and nourishment is denied to the roots of the tree which subsequently die, terminating the tree itself.

Inside the bast, but before the wood proper, is a

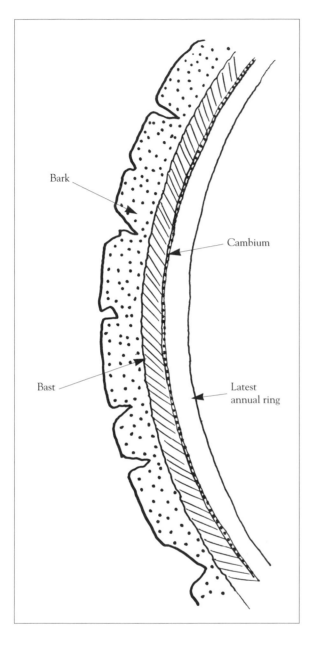

Fig 8.11 A magnified cross-section of the outer part of a tree.

Fig 8.12 The effect of 'ringing' a tree.

Bark

Cambium

Bast

Latest annual ring

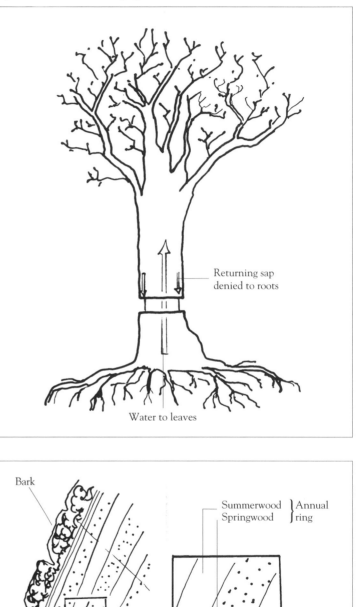

Returning sap denied to roots

Water to leaves

Bark

Summerwood } Annual
Springwood } ring

Fig 8.13 The exact form of the annual rings depends both on the species and the individual history of the tree.

microscopic layer of cells extending throughout the whole tree; it is sometimes just visible to the naked eye. This is the **cambium**, a protoplasmic layer of cells which creates the bast and bark to the outside, and the wood itself on the inside. Wood has a fibrous structure with hollow channels (like veins) and sheets of fibres which conduct food and water and act as a mechanical support. It is these fibres which form the **grain** with which woodcarvers work. The cambium is the growing part of the tree, the most alive and active part – rather

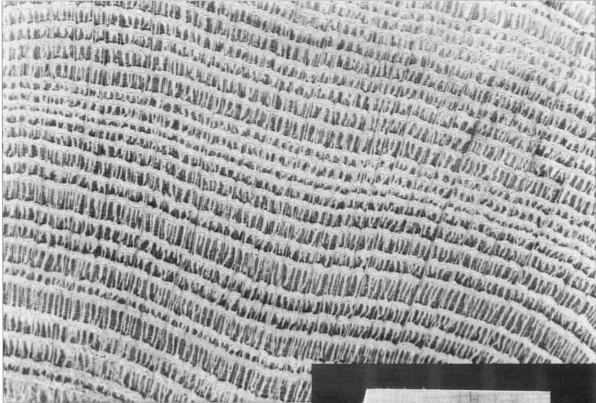

Fig 8.14 Section through English oak: the end-grain clearly shows light springwood and dark sapwood that make up the annual rings; medullary rays are also visible.

Fig 8.15 (Right) Wider annual rings in the same species indicate faster growth and softer timber.

like a skin draped over a skeleton of wood.

A tree grows both in girth and height as the cambium adds layers of fibrous tissue everywhere, including the veins of leaves. This fibrous tissue is correctly known as **wood**. An amount of *usable* wood is technically called **timber**. In practice, however, these two terms are loosely used to mean the same thing, i.e. the material that is being worked.

In temperate zones, spring is the occasion for a great eruption of activity. Warmth evaporates water from the leaves and more is drawn in from the roots. The cambium quickly responds, laying down a layer of **springwood** – wood that is light in both weight and colour, and carries large amounts of water and mineral salts upwards. As the season moves on, the activity of the cambium slows down, producing a darker, heavier, and stronger layer of fibres – **summerwood**. Summerwood is more skeletal than conductive. In

Fig 8.16 **The block of wood on the left shows a regular faster pattern of growth; that in the centre a more irregular pattern; and that on the right a slow-growing regular growth.**

winter the cambium is virtually dormant. This pattern is repeated every year with the inner springwood and outer summerwood, together, forming an **annual ring** (*see* Fig 8.13, and Table 8.1).

Springwood	Summerwood
Grows first in the year	Grows later in the year
In the annual ring: nearer the centre of the tree	In the annual ring: nearer the outside of the tree
Conductive	Skeletal
More porous	Less porous
Lighter colour	Darker colour
Lighter weight	Heavier weight

Table 8.1 **General differences between springwood and summerwood of a tree.**

The annual rings represent the story or history of the tree. They can be wider or tighter depending on how well the tree grew in a particular year (for instance growing faster with more sunlight), or varying in width across the trunk depending on whether the tree grew bent or straight. Annual rings only appear circular in a cross-section, cut them any other way and intricate patterns are produced, called the **figure** of the timber. As young trees grow quickly, the rings towards the centre of the tree tend to be broader, growing tighter and narrower towards the outside as the tree reaches maturity.

In tropical climates, with no seasons, there may be no – or few visible – rings at all, with trees growing continuously the whole year round.

The base of a tree is thicker because it has been growing for a longer time than the higher parts. As it grows, low branches that were part of the original sapling – having fallen or broken off – will be incorporated into the body of the trunk, becoming **knots**. Wood laid down later tends to be clear or free of knots, although later branch growth will affect the pattern of the grain. 'Knotty heart' in a tree is an instance of a sapling having a large number of small branches early on.

The cross-section shows a few more features worth noting (*see* Fig 8.17). The very centre of the tree is the pith or **medulla** of the original seedling. This is mechanically always a weak point and often the source

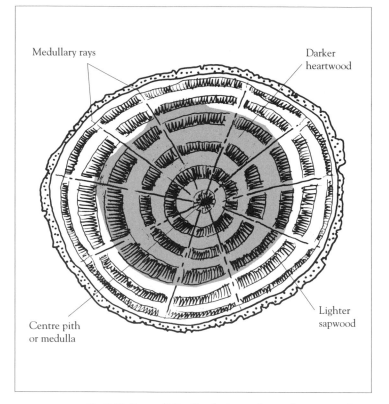

Fig 8.17 Some distinctive features of a tree's cross-section.

Fig 8.18 The medullary rays, often contributing much to the figure, are apparent in this piece of oak fencing; note how the colour has been bleached grey by the sunshine.

of rot in the middle of a tree.

From the centre – though not necessarily reaching it – radiate the **medullary rays** (*see* Fig 8.19). These are sheets of tissue that store and conduct food and water across (in and out of) the tree. It is the medullary rays that produce the 'silver ray' figuring in English oak. Again, they are a weak point; when a tree starts splitting, it is almost always along the lines of these rays.

As the tree grows, the central parts take on more of a skeletal role, rather than one of conducting sap, and become the **heartwood**. The fibres towards the middle of the tree – but only roughly following the lines of the annual rings – clog through chemical changes. Heartwood is darker, denser, more stable and generally more disease resistant (*see* Table 8.2) and as such it is the wood of choice for carvers. Sometimes though the heart of a tree is completely absent, leaving a surprisingly healthy tree, consisting only of a ring of sapwood.

This **sapwood**, situated outside the heartwood, has the original qualities of the fibres laid down by the cambium. It is softer, lighter in weight and colour, still porous and contains moisture or resins; it is more 'living' and subject to disease, especially when the tree is dead. In most cases these qualities make sapwood unattractive, if not useless, to the carver.

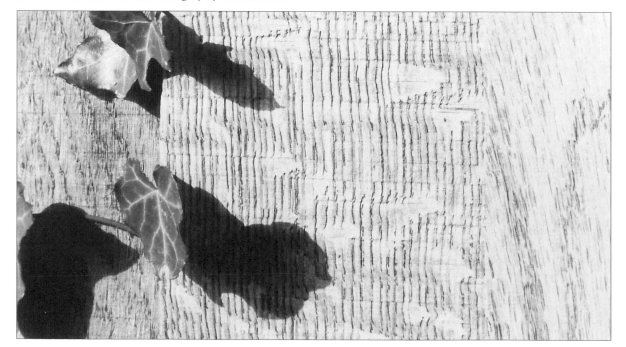

Quality	Heartwood	Sapwood
Moisture	–	+
Weight	+	–
Density	+	–
Porosity	–	+
Stability	+	–
Disease resistance	+	–
Darkness	+	–

+ proportionally higher
– proportionally lower

Table 8.2 General proportional characteristics of (inner) heartwood and (outer) sapwood.

Hardwoods and softwoods

There are two broad categories of tree: **hardwoods** and **softwoods**. These terms should not be confused with 'hard' wood and 'soft' wood, which are much looser terms to do with the actual physical density of the material.

Hardwoods

Such trees might more properly be called deciduous or broadleaf trees and include oak, walnut, box or maple. They have broad leaves, mostly changing colour and being shed in the winter. The timber is close-grained with fine pores, making it harder, heavier and more durable than most softwoods.

Softwoods

These trees might more properly be called evergreen, conifer or needle-leaf trees. Species include pines and firs, but also hemlock, yew and holly. The internal structure is recognizably different to that of the broadleaf trees, with large open fibres called tracheids, and a grain that is usually easy to split. Most splinter easily and are less durable than the hardwoods, although some species such as redwood, hemlock and yew are very durable.

WOOD AS A MATERIAL

Although there are some sculptors who carve trees *in situ*, normally wood or timber is changed so drastically in making it fit for carving that it is easy to forget it once grew as a tree.

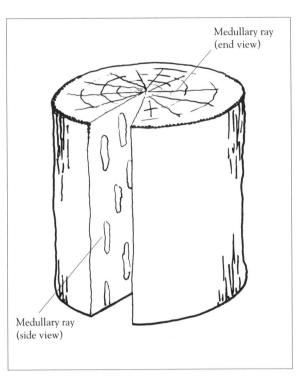

Fig 8.19 The medullary rays, although they appear as lines in a cross-section, are actually sheets of tissue, conducting food and water across the tree.

Conversion

This is the term used for reducing a whole tree into various useful pieces of wood. This is usually undertaken by timber yards, although carvers may do the work themselves. There are two reasons for converting trees into timber:

▦ To make the most economic and best use of the material
▦ To **season** or dry the wood (*see* page 301).

Both converting and seasoning wood produce different qualities in the timber from those present in the original tree. These are qualities needed by carvers.

When trees are converted into timber, they can be sawn up in many ways. When wood is bought, any **nominal size** quoted will be the dimensions arising from the original sawing – rough and unplaned. Some allowance is usually left for shrinkage when the wood was cut. If you take a 2in (50mm) nominal board, it should be exactly this measurement – but may only finish 1¾in (45mm) after planing. If you want to end up with a **finished** 2in (50mm) board you must start with a larger nominal size; this may be 2½in (65mm)

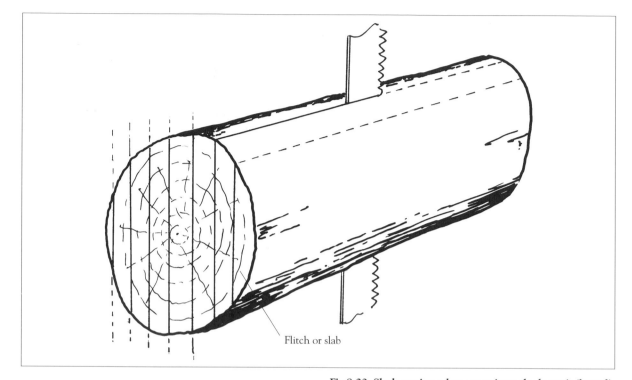

Flitch or slab

Fig 8.20 Slash-sawing a log; sometimes the heart is 'boxed' or removed.

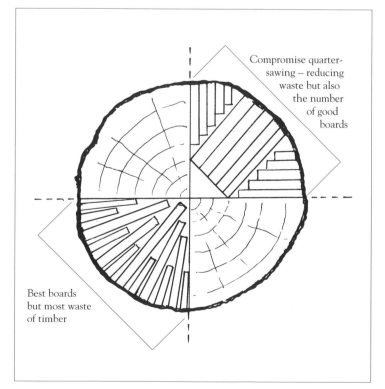

Compromise quarter-sawing – reducing waste but also the number of good boards

Best boards but most waste of timber

Fig 8.21 There are several ways of quarter cutting a log – all aim to reveal the figure of the medullary rays in the most economic way.

and therefore less economical. **Finish**, or **finished** means the surfaces have been planed.

Sawing itself can be straight **through and through** (also called **plain-sawn** or **slash-sawn**) where the tree is moved across a huge bandsaw blade which rips it into parallel boards. There is little wastage and wide boards result so the wood tends to be cheaper. However, the figure is less interesting and the wood is less stable the further it is cut towards the sides of the tree, tending to move and warp.

Quarter-sawing is an alternative method, but is comparatively rare and costly. The tree is rotated in its presentation to the saw, producing radially cut planks, i.e. sawn roughly in the direction of the medullary rays (*see* Fig 8.21). This method is more wasteful and time-consuming, which is why it is more expensive. Cutting along the sheet-like medullary rays yields wood with the best figure and greatest stability; it shrinks less and more uniformly, tending to split and warp less.

A **flitch** or **slab** is timber, usually thick, which has the rounded sides of the tree still clearly visible.

After sawing, the wood will be sorted for quality and seasoned – an extremely important procedure for any woodworker.

Seasoning

The fibres of a living tree are full of water, especially the sapwood. The water is continually drawn through the fibres from the soil as the sun evaporates it from the leaves above. Once a tree is dead – whether still standing or cut as a log or as boards – the water will start to leave the wood by evaporation. If left long enough, an equilibrium will be reached: the amount of moisture in the wood balances the amount of water vapour in the surrounding air.

The effect of moisture in wood is a matter of everyday experience. In the winter, with damper atmospheres, wooden doors swell and stick and frames warp. In a dry summer gaps appear where once there was a neat fit, surfaces start to check or crack and joints loosen. The shrinking and expanding of wood fibres according to their water content is the phenomenon that makes it appear 'alive', or to breathe.

Immediately a log or board is cut from a tree it starts to lose water from the cut ends of the fibres (*see* Fig 8.23) – to be replaced by air. Water is lost first and most quickly from between the cellular fibres, then more slowly from within the cells themselves. As the wood dries out it shrinks.

Fig 8.22 Seasoning their own flitches is one way for carvers to obtain bulky pieces of wood.

Fig 8.23 Relative water loss from a newly cut log.

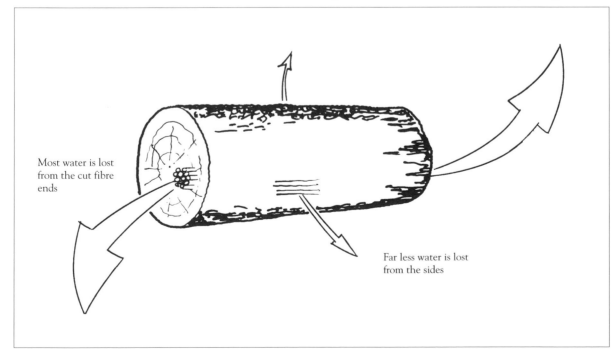

Most water is lost from the cut fibre ends

Far less water is lost from the sides

Fig 8.24 Boards are often marked to record their passage through timber yards. The ends of this one show light shakes which are common; a woodworker would normally be expected to make allowance in the length when calculating requirements.

The outer sapwood has a much higher water content than the inner heartwood and so shrinks more. This sets up stresses which are released as cracking or checking at the surface – at times quite severe splits arise as the medullary rays are torn apart. Terms like 'shake', 'split' and 'check' are freely used to mean the same event, that is the opening up of fibres to varying degrees through water loss and shrinkage stresses. Distortion and warping can also result from the different shrinking of heartwood and sapwood.

Water leaves the cut ends of the fibres far more quickly than from the sides, which may still be covered in bark, so the ends of planks and logs shrink and split more than the more internal parts of the wood.

Eventually, as the wood dries, the stresses reach a new equilibrium and the wood settles down to a new shape. **Seasoning** is the attempt to control the drying process of wood so that the stresses are minimized, a level of moisture content equal to that of the surrounding air is arrived at, and the wood is as free from shakes as possible.

The **moisture content** is the weight of water in a piece of wood, measured as a percentage of the weight of the same wood completely dried. The moisture content needed by woodworkers will vary according to the average relative humidity in which they are working, and the dryness of where the wood will eventually reside. The level can vary between about 9% and 14%.

Seasoning used always to be done in the air, '**air drying**', which has a measure of unpredictability. '**Kiln drying**' in special ovens allows more predictable behaviour in the wood.

Seasoned or dried wood has several advantages over 'green' or wet wood. Seasoned wood is lighter in weight and harder than wet wood; it is more resistant to infection or woodworm; and it has arrived at a balance of internal stress and is not only more stable, but a predictable size (*see* Table 8.3).

Seasoned	Unseasoned
Low moisture content	High moisture content
Lighter	Heavier
More stable	Less stable
More predictable	Less predictable
More disease resistant	Less disease resistant

Table 8.3 Comparison of seasoned and unseasoned timber.

Kiln-dried wood, through the treatment itself, sometimes has different working properties to air-dried wood of the same species. For example, beech tends to become pinker in colour and more brittle to work if kiln dried in a steam kiln.

The idea of balanced forces within a piece of timber is important. It is a mistake to think that because a lump of wood has been seasoned or has been lying around for years that it is completely inert. Removing further material from the lump, or bringing it into a dry, heated workshop, will create new stresses. This is especially likely where there are both thick and thin parts in the same carving, or where both sapwood and heartwood are present. The balancing of these internal forces, or stresses, may well lead to checks appearing in the surface – or even outright splitting of the wood. Any joiner's shop will tell of beautiful, wide, seasoned boards that rip down the middle to produce two useless, banana-shaped pieces.

If a piece of wood splits it is, to say the least, very frustrating. All that can be done is to minimize the risk right from the start. Kiln drying is normally the task of specialized firms as it is a fairly exact process involving specialized equipment. Air drying wet wood is undertaken by many carvers, especially those given

free wood. The main requirement is the correct storage conditions – features necessary for correct storage of wood anyway.

To air dry wood, the process of drying must be slowed down and made more even, giving a chance for the fibres to mould into a new shape. The following measures all help towards this end.

■ It is best to fell a tree in the winter when it contains least water. For some species, such as oak, elm, ash or chestnut, if the tree is dead, leaving it in the ground a while with the bark on allows a little more water to slowly leave. But some other species, such as sycamore and beech, start to rot immediately.

■ Leaving wood to cure as a whole log creates the most drying problems. The figuring in a *whole* log is always the best, but the different shrinking of the heartwood and sapwood create more stress than most wood can stand without splitting. Elm is a wood that has an interlocking grain and is therefore often successfully dried as a whole log.

■ Logs are best halved or quartered to relieve the stress between the heartwood and the sapwood. Cut away the immediate pith and heartwood. Medieval carvers used to carve wood wet, but halved and

Fig 8.25 This piece of olive ash was flat when in the whole board, but warped when released.

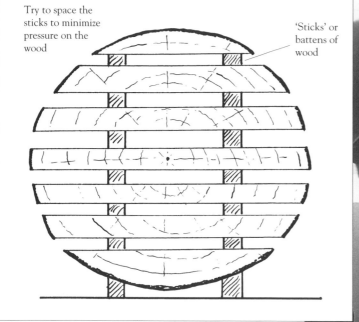

Try to space the sticks to minimize pressure on the wood

'Sticks' or battens of wood

Fig 8.26 A whole log stored 'in stick'; the same principles apply to storing wood, as well as to drying it.

Fig 8.27 Wood adjusts to new stresses as it is carved. With large pieces and those from a single log, it is a good idea to cover them in polythene between sessions to prevent sudden moisture loss from the newly exposed parts.

hollowed out at the back. This minimized and sometimes avoided splitting, and also accounts for the large numbers of wall-mounted, three-quarter view carvings made in this period. Boards should be cut in uniform thickness.

■ Leave the bark on, so slowing water loss from the side.

■ Seal the ends with melted paraffin wax, shellac, varnish or commercial end-sealer. Keep an eye on the ends – water is lost quickly here and splitting can happen rapidly. Re-seal the ends if any signs of splitting occur.

■ Store the wood off the ground 'in stick' with spacing battens to allow good air circulation (*see* Fig 8.26). Keep covered from rain, wind, frost, sunlight and dry atmospheres (such as central heating). Mechanical restraint such as binding or weighting can also be used to 'coax' a board into shape.

■ Some people like to store smaller pieces inside plastic bags.

■ It is always a good strategy to have the seasoned wood in the workshop for a while before use; or, ideally, left in the place where the carving will eventually reside. This gives it a chance to adjust and settle down. The dry atmosphere of central heating must be taken into account by carvers working at home.

The rule of thumb is that hardwoods need at least 1 year of drying for every inch (25mm) of thickness. So a 4in (100mm) slab or flitch really needs 4 years; but as the rate of drying varies between species a little sampling at an earlier stage will help assess how the drying is coming along. If you are going to air dry your own wood from scratch, you have to see the process as having a time pattern rather like making wine: laying down stocks at intervals for use in the future, with a little 'tasting' now and then.

Using green or wet wood is a hazard that some carvers risk in order to achieve the size they want without having to laminate smaller pieces of wood. These gains are offset by the threat of splitting. Hollowing out has already been mentioned, as well as selecting woods such as elm where possible. Carving should be done as quickly as you can, with the wood still fresh from the tree and sealed, or kept under plastic wraps, at all other times. The more uniform the distribution of mass, the more evenly the wood will dry – so mixing a large bulk with thin sections is the most risky.

A chemical called polyethylglycol (PEG) is available which replaces the water in timber. It is a messy process which involves vats to soak the pieces of wood in, and makes the wood subsequently unpleasant to work. It is used by some sculptors wanting to work in large single pieces of otherwise unstable material, but even this chemical is not a guarantee of complete success.

Movement

The seasonal movement of wood (seen in doors and windows) must be taken into account and to a large extent follows a predictable pattern. The movement can be estimated from where in the tree the original piece of wood came from (*see* Fig 8.29). As a general rule, a log shrinks:

- The least along its length
- The greatest around its circumference (i.e. tangentially)
- Somewhere in between in a radial direction.

Fig 8.28 Whole logs are used for sculpture to take advantage of the figuring.

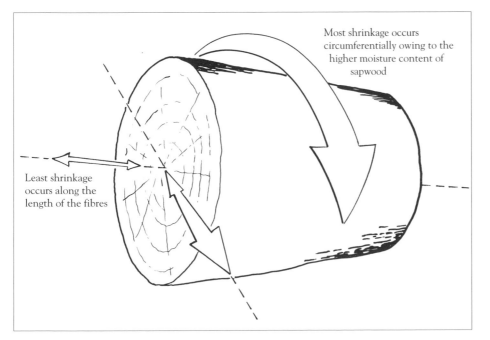

Most shrinkage occurs circumferentially owing to the higher moisture content of sapwood

Least shrinkage occurs along the length of the fibres

Fig 8.29 Relative amounts of shrinkage in a newly cut log.

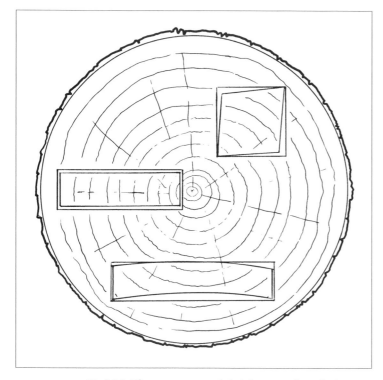

Fig 8.30 The outer sapwood shrinks more than the inner heartwood, and boards taken from different parts of a tree will change shape according to their relative position.

Fig 8.31 Take care with a flat panel not to keep it clamped to a bench for too long without allowing the underside to 'breathe'.

So, depending on the lie of the grain in a piece of wood – how the fibres relate to the tree – will the wood move. Combinations of these movements create the stresses which cause warping and twisting.

Figure 8.30 shows how these principles work in practice, with pieces of wood taken from different parts of a tree.

As long as seasoned wood is free to 'breathe' or to expand and shrink freely, there is little problem. But when wood is glued up and no longer able to move independently, various stresses are again brought into play. Gluing up will be dealt with on page 327.

A similar problem arises when a large, flat panel is clamped to the bench for carving. Even though seasoned wood may be glued up in a way to minimize warping, the side of the panel that is clamped to the bench is shut off from the atmosphere and no longer able to breathe. In dry air, the free surface can lose water and shrink quite quickly and when, after a few days, the work is unclamped, the panel can spring up at the ends (*see* Fig 8.31). The side to the bench has a higher moisture content and is, by comparison, swollen. Wetting the drier surface and clamping the opposite side down may be tried, but sometimes the panel will not return to its original shape. When such a panel is not being carved, unclamp it and stand it up,

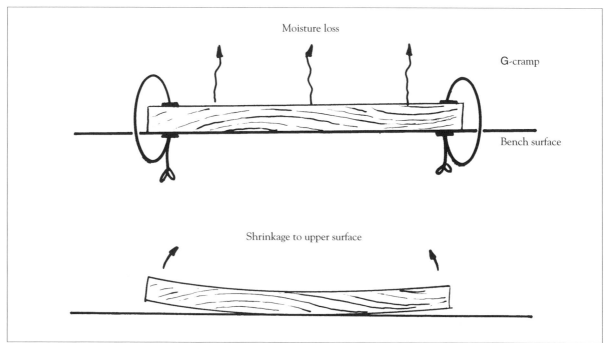

Fig 8.32 A particular pattern of shakes might be considered an interesting feature of some sculptures, rather than a 'fault'.

Fig 8.33 With a split like this you have to accept that you now own two boards, not one.

perhaps even turn it over, so that air can circulate freely around it.

Defects

What carvers and sculptors want – or put up with – from their material is an individual matter. One carver's sense of defect is another's sense of strength or character. There are some sculptors who accept splits, knots, sappy wood or even woodworm as in some way the 'truth' of the material, although a consensus of most carvers would find these characteristics unacceptable and interfering with their vision.

The idea of a defect implies some state of perfection against which the qualities of any single piece of wood can be measured. But as no such ideal exists, perhaps the best way of describing a defect is to say that it is some characteristic in a particular piece of wood that interferes with the intended design or execution of a work. Such a problem may not be present in another sample of the same species.

In this sense almost *any* quality may be a defect at some time or other. But in practice there are some defects which most carvers avoid if at all possible. Sometimes defects reveal themselves as carving progresses; for example what appears to be a small knot on the surface can become a large hole full of decayed wood. The best that can be done is to learn to read the wood as accurately as possible and minimize the risks.

The two principal defects relate to splitting and knots.

SPLITTING

This is a principal category of defect and a bane of *all* workers in wood. **Splits** can render a piece of wood useless. Although all precautions with seasoning may be taken, once carving has started, a new balancing of stresses may impinge on a weakness in the fibres and result in them opening up.

Other terms for the lengthwise parting of wood fibres are **cracks**, **checks** or **shakes**, all of which can be any size from a hairline surface check to splits right through from the outside to the heartwood (*see* Fig 8.34). Although these terms are often used to mean the same thing, checks tend to be more surface phenomena (*see* Fig 8.35) whereas shakes tend to be deeper, and splits disastrous.

Ring shakes involve separation between annual rings and will usually be seen in the primary log (*see* Figs 8.36, 8.37). Ring shakes may result from the impact of the tree on the ground as it is felled, or excess bending of the tree in high winds. Substantial amounts of useful wood may still be available from a log with a ring shake, depending on its position and extent.

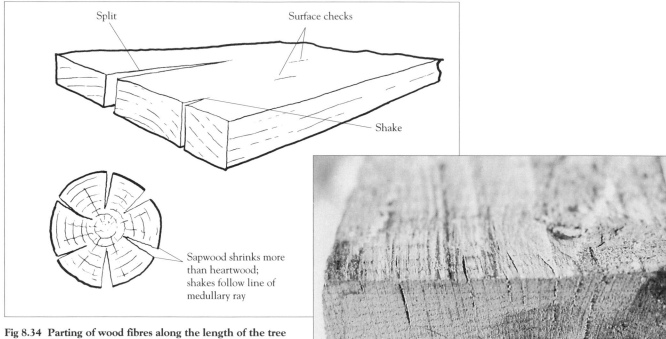

Fig 8.34 **Parting of wood fibres along the length of the tree due to shrinkage stresses.**

Fig 8.35 **Surface checking, following the medullary rays, may not penetrate very deeply.**

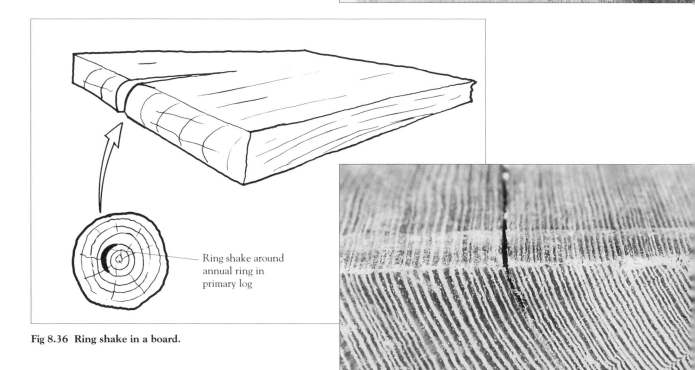

Fig 8.36 **Ring shake in a board.**

Fig 8.37 **Ring shake following an annual ring.**

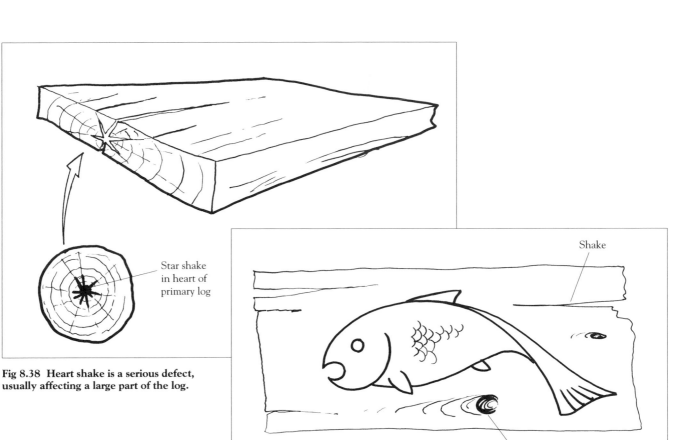

Fig 8.38 Heart shake is a serious defect, usually affecting a large part of the log.

Fig 8.39 Placing a design within a board to eliminate the unwanted defective wood may involve altering the design to fit.

Heart shakes are splits radiating from the centre, often right across to the outside. Where the number of radiating splits is extensive, it is known as a **star shake** (*see* Fig 8.38). Both heart and star shakes are thought to arise from the very heart of the tree as it starts to decay after reaching maturity, but probably high winds and sudden changes in temperature may be factors. Such defects can make a log unusable.

Splitting as the result of drying always starts from the outside of a log – or the equivalent in a board – as the sapwood shrinks more than the heartwood.

If a split is present in the wood *before* the carving starts, it is often possible to re-design the carving around it. Some of the elements can be shuffled around so as to cut out the split with the waste wood (*see* Fig 8.39). There is great satisfaction to be had when you can do this – taking what looked like a forsaken piece of wood and redeeming it.

If a split occurs *after* carving there are a few options, depending on the extent of the damage.

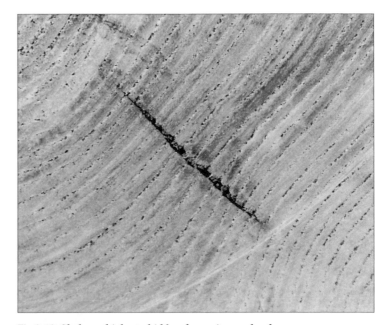

Fig 8.40 Shakes which are hidden from view and only reveal themselves later in the carving leave less scope for adapting the design.

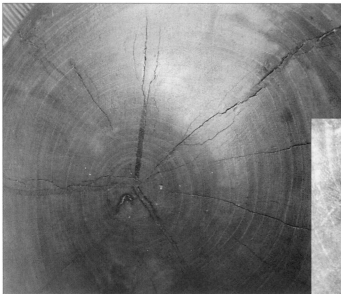

Fig 8.41 Surface checks in a whole-log elm sculpture. The smaller ones are filled with wax, which squeezes out or fails to fill, as the wood expands and contracts with the changing humidity of the seasons.

Fig 8.42 Larger cracks filled with wedges. Even though the wood was carefully matched some 10 years previously, colour changes have made them more obvious; nevertheless they help the feel of the work when it is touched.

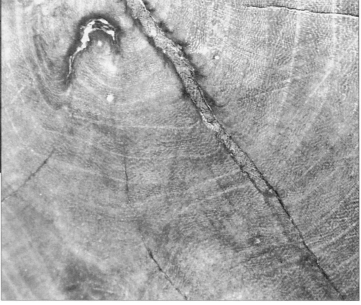

▨ Ignore it and use the 'well-it's-wood-isn't-it' ploy as you come to sell the carving, which may involve using the 'truth to the materials' argument mentioned above. It may indeed be best to leave small surface checks, perhaps filling them with wax, along with the waxing of the rest of the carving (see Fig 8.41). With large splits though, no amount of idealism can prevent the gaping truth ruining the work.

▨ See if there is yet scope for judicious fiddling with the design.

▨ A small element of the carving can be deliberately broken off at the split. This should leave a perfectly matching pair of surfaces to re-glue, virtually invisible if carefully done and re-carved over. Spring wire C-clamps, made from old bed springs, can help with the gluing.

▨ Filling may be possible either with slivers of matching wood (see Fig 8.42), commercial filler, glue-and-sawdust or wax (see Fig 8.43). Using wood to fill may be a problem if the carving swells with a change in ambient moisture. The splits, originally releasing particular stresses, may want to close, thus exerting pressure on the inserts with new tensions and splits appearing elsewhere. Wood inserts *can* be a successful repair if the splits are small, but allow the wood to settle down adequately first. Wax and other fillers will be similarly squeezed out and drawn in as the wood swells and contracts.

Fig 8.43 A collection of waxes in different colours, used for filling small defects in the wood surface.

Fig 8.44 Not a knot but a hollow resin channel in a piece of jelutong. Many tropical hardwoods have such channels running deeply through them and not necessarily apparent on the surface.

Fig 8.45 A typical 'dead' knot.

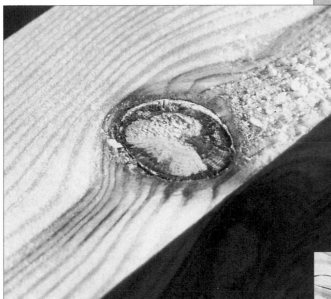

Filling, like other repairs, can help a piece by preventing the eye from being continuously distracted by an obvious defect, but careful judgement is needed. If possible, assess the cause of splitting – perhaps the stock of wood is less dry than you thought it was.

Keeping carvings covered in plastic between carving sessions will prevent rapid drying and changes in stress.

KNOTS

Knots can be a source of great beauty in work where the natural qualities of wood are being exploited. However, they can also be a distraction when the carving is more figurative – an awkwardly placed knot in a face, for example, may look like a disfigurement. As with splits, it is often possible to design around knots or place them in wasted areas.

Knots can be exploited in ways that splits never can, and may be live or dead. **Live knots** are still integrated with the surrounding wood fibres and arise from twigs of branches which were alive when the tree was felled. They sometimes mark a change in grain direction (as do crotches and other natural formations), allowing a weak part in some designs to

Fig 8.46 If you look carefully at the right-hand side of this carving, a small repair is visible where a black hole appeared at the point where it was hoped only a tiny knot would be.

acquire strength. Sometimes the grain is just awkward, but this can usually be dealt with by taking shallow cuts and working *across* the grain of the knot.

Dead knots are often loose in the timber and surrounded by an unsightly black or chalky ring (*see*

Fig 8.47 Close up of the repair. The rotten dead knot was bored out, and a 'live knot' inserted; the leaves were then adjusted to camouflage the circular pattern as best as possible.

Fig 8.48 The back of the carving shows the other end of the knot. By hiding the main bulk of the knot at the back, what proved to be an otherwise lovely piece of wood was redeemed.

Fig 8.45). These knots are much older, being from branches that were dead before the tree was brought down. Such knots can often be knocked out and glued firmly back in again, but the different colour makes them very prominent.

One option may be to replace the dead knot with a live one, removed from another piece of the same timber by means of a plug-cutter (*see* Figs 8.46, 8.47). It may be impossible to get the visible insert not to look too geometrical. A 'dutchman' is another possibility: a more lozenge-shaped insert, orientated along the grain and using carefully matched wood. The insert need not be very deep, depending on how much over-carving needs to be done. Cut the insert with square walls first and match the hole to it. A tighter fit is got if the dutchman is well dried first, expanding to tighten the joint. This sort of repair can be very effective, especially if the carving is worked over it.

Decay

The natural cycle for a dead tree is to rot down under the onslaught of weather, insects and fungi, gradually returning its constituents to the soil.

Foxing, a yellow-brown discolouration in timber, is one of the first signs of decay and is caused by fungus infestation. **Spalting** is a mottling and lining of the wood, and can be desirable in sculptures working with an interesting figure. Spalting also represents early decay and may contain sapwood which has become spongy. The black lines themselves seem to be a damage limitation response by the tree to the fungal infection.

Wood decays most readily when:

- It is wetter than the surrounding air
- It is in contact with the soil
- It contains sapwood.

This means that, as with seasoning, wood is best stored in the dry and away from soil.

It is the chemical properties in timber which make it resistant to decay, as much as the physical ones. The chemical-rich heartwood is much more resistant to decay than sapwood. It is even, in some species, poisonous to insects and fungi. It is best not to use sapwood if it can be avoided.

Storage

The best way of keeping wood is as if it were being air dried (*see* page 304). The points mentioned in that context also apply to the general storing of wood and should be referred to.

It is worth having timber in the workshop for some time before using it, whether it has been air or kiln dried, so as to allow it to acclimatize and settle down. Ideally the wood should be stored for a while where the carving will eventually reside – but this is not normally possible.

Beware of dry atmospheres such as those in centrally heated houses, where a lot of leisure carvers work. Keeping wood in a damp outhouse or garage, and then bringing it into a warm, very dry house is asking for trouble. Try to introduce what you need gradually – perhaps initially in a plastic bag – some time before you need it and keep a close eye on it. Keep work covered in plastic between working sessions.

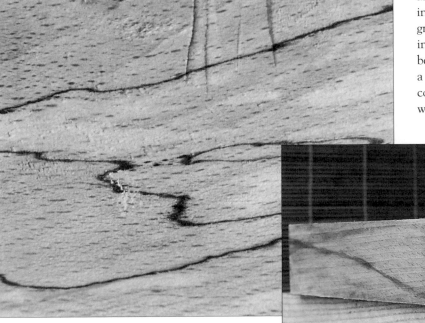

Fig 8.49 Spalted beech.

Fig 8.50 Remember that spalting, when visible in the end-grain, usually reaches irregularly through the whole length of the piece of wood.

Woodworm

If you see the familiar hole, with a little sawdust plug, it means that the beetle has emerged from its pupa, strolled along the surface of the wood and probably laid its eggs close by. One hole represents lots of tunnels which were created when the previously laid eggs hatched into larvae – the 'worm' – and voraciously fed. Normally, like most insects, woodworm activity is seasonal, but with more and more uniformity of temperature in houses, they can be active all the year round.

There are several species of woodworm, some worse than others. From the biologist's point of view they are only doing their job of re-cycling dead wood; but from the carver's point of view, none of them is welcome.

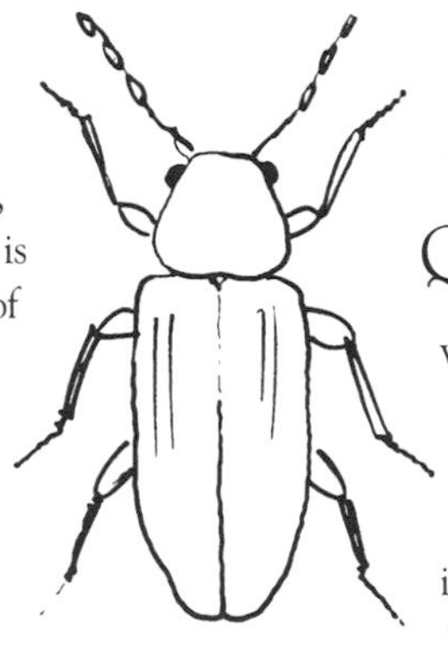

Most woodworm prefer sapwood to heartwood (*see* Fig 8.53), and moist wood to dry. So properly seasoned, good quality timber is a good start to avoiding them. Also avoid leaving sapwood around the workshop.

Active woodworm holes have sawdust in them, old holes are dirty and empty. There are many colourless, proprietary agents available which can be used in a preventative way – always following the manufacturer's safety recommendations.

Treat a finished piece of carving as a matter of course, before final polishing. Also treat the workshop.

QUALITIES OF WOOD

Wood may be simply a vehicle to display the carving, as in the work of Grinling Gibbons where a figureless limewood supports the virtuosity of the designs. Or the wood itself may be the source of a carver's inspiration – the sculpture a result of the carver's exploration of the material. Or there may be a point in between where a type of wood is sought for qualities which work with a preconceived idea.

Whichever approach is taken, wood exhibits many properties that need to be considered in the carving design or as the carving is evolving. Not only

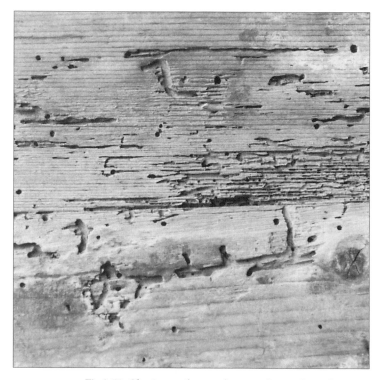

Fig 8.52 Classic woodworm damage: the single surface holes lead to extensive tunnelling beneath. Sawdust in the exit holes is a sure sign of activity.

Fig 8.51 Above *Anobium punctatum*: the common furniture beetle varies in length from ⅒ to ¼in (2.5 to 6mm) and accounts for 75% of all woodworm damage in Britain. Larvae may bore around in the wood for up to 2 years, and infestation only becomes apparent when the beetle emerges, leaving a ⅟₁₆in (2mm) hole. After only 2 weeks as a beetle, a further 30 eggs may be laid.

Fig 8.53 A piece of laburnum showing that the sapwood is usually the preferred restaurant for woodworm.

do species differ in their characteristics, but individual trees and parts of the same tree differ as well. The qualities in any particular piece of wood depend on how the tree has grown. This is the same as saying it depends on how the fibres were laid down, or the nature of the grain.

Grain

Grain refers to the hollow fibres in the tree. Originally, as annual rings, they conducted sap or water; later, clogged with chemicals, they performed a skeletal role. Grain fibres run the length of the tree and may be straight or twisted; bent or interlocking; or spiralling around the tree in a direction which changes every year.

Beginners find grain a little confusing at first – a little difficult to 'read'. One way to understand wood grain is by imagining how you sharpen a pencil: the fibres in the pencil run parallel along its length. As you sharpen it with a knife, slicing off the end, you are **working with the grain** – the wood fibres are pushed together and support each other resulting in easy, clean cuts (*see* Fig 8.55).

If you try to sharpen a pencil in the opposite direction to normal, the fibres catch and tear up, failing to support each other. This would be trying to cut **against the grain** (*see* Fig 8.56). The expression 'against the grain' itself has the sense of going against the natural inclination of a thing. It *can* be done with a very sharp blade and taking shallow cuts; but the surface is never as good, and carvers only attempt this

Fig 8.54 A tight joint with matched grain in the abdomen of this carved butterfly makes full use of the figuring available in lacewood.

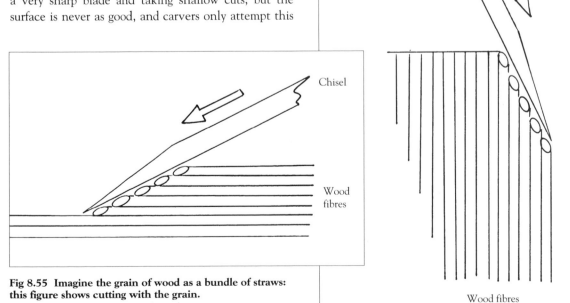

Fig 8.55 Imagine the grain of wood as a bundle of straws: this figure shows cutting with the grain.

Fig 8.56 Cutting against the grain.

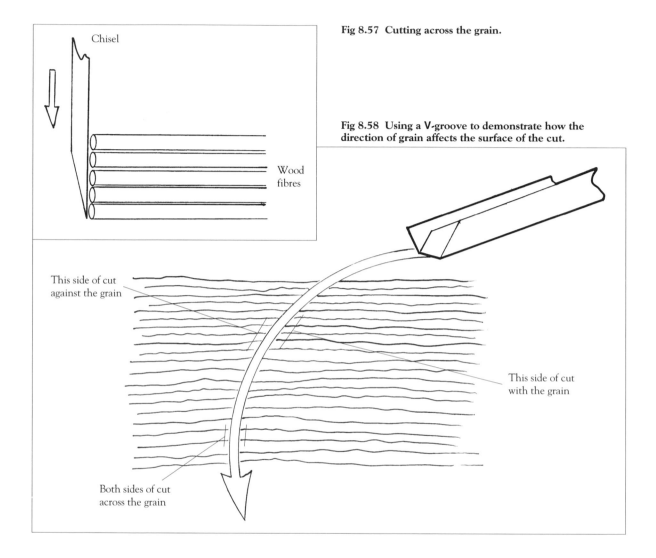

Fig 8.57 Cutting across the grain.

Chisel

Wood
fibres

Fig 8.58 Using a V-groove to demonstrate how the direction of grain affects the surface of the cut.

This side of cut
against the grain

This side of cut
with the grain

Both sides of cut
across the grain

way if there is no alternative.

Cutting at right angles to the fibres is cutting **across the grain** (*see* Fig 8.57). With sharp tools in some woods, this can be as clean as cutting with the grain.

The grain, then, is the arrangement of fibres in a piece of wood, its direction in three dimensions. Recognizing the way the wood is modified by the lie of the grain – either visually in advance, or by reacting to how the wood is cutting – is a necessary skill of the carver; one only properly acquired through experience.

Carving with the grain gives the sweetest, cleanest cut; against the grain the roughest. An experiment will further help beginners get used to the idea of grain. Using a V-tool or U-shaped gouge, cut an arcing groove in the surface of a small panel of wood,

making the curve run through at least 90°. Examine the edges of the cut (*see* Fig 8.58). At any point one side of the groove will be shiny and the other rough as the cut has been simultaneously with and against the lie of the fibres or the grain. Try with a sharp blade to clean the side of the groove *against* the grain. You may be successful, but not as successful as reversing the direction of the cut and taking a thin shaving *with* the grain.

A related term is **end-grain**. Cutting across the grain reveals the hollow ends of the tube-like fibres: this is end-grain. It is seen for example in the cross-section of the log, but always appears throughout any carving. By capillary action, end-grain will soak up any finishing liquids (stains, oils, varnishes, etc.) far more than **side-grain**, the walls of the fibres. Liquids pass between the fibres of side-grain, but not so much into them. This different reaction to liquids results in the end-grain tending to have a darker, more matt appearance compared with side-grain, because of the differing ways they reflect light. This can be a problem, about which a little more will be said in Chapter 9 (*see* page 334).

Besides the need to take grain into account while actually carving and in the finishing of a piece, grain must be considered in the design stage before any carving actually starts.

The maximum strength of wood is along the length of the fibres (**long grain**), and weakest where the fibres are shortest (**short grain**). So where possible this feature should be used to make any potentially weak element in a carving as strong as possible, for example by running the grain down the legs of a carved horse, or along fingers. If the grain ran in the opposite direction – across the legs – they would be

Fig 8.59 A detail of St Joseph the Elder by Hans Leinberger, about 1523. The depth to which wood was removed around the book was at least 15in (380mm). This no doubt involved boring away at least some of the waste first and a lot of cutting across the grain. The fingers are casually 'tied' to the book – beautifully supporting the otherwise weak cross-grain.

Fig 8.60 End- and side-grain. On the upper surface, the large arrows indicate cuts that would be *with* the grain.

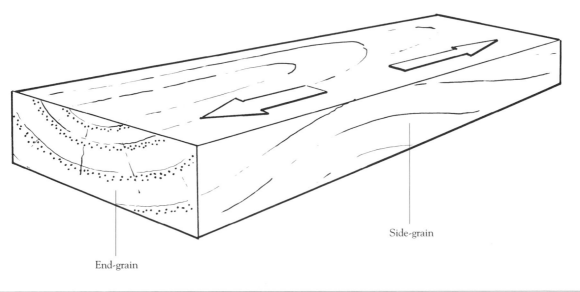

Side-grain

End-grain

Short grain across leg is weak

Long grain, or wood fibres, along the leg, is strong

Fig 8.61 A T'ang dynasty horse such as this illustrates the problems of suiting the grain, with its longitudinal strength, to the carving.

significantly weaker. The short grain might not even survive the trauma of being carved.

Sometimes, if the grain can be used to strengthen one element in a carving, it is running in the wrong direction for another (*see* Fig 8.61). Some options to deal with this problem are:

■ Re-design the piece rather than risking breakage.
■ Find some compromise in presenting the design to the wood, so lessening strength in one area to gain it in another.
■ Find a crotched piece of wood, or a piece with an

unusual running grain.
■ Strengthen the design by 'tying' some other element to it. For example a bird may be placed so as to touch a leaf or twig in a nonchalant way which effectively acts as a support or brace. Some cunning is necessary to make such an artifice look unaffected.
■ Glueing on another piece of wood with grain going in the direction that is wanted. One very common place where this solution has been adopted, for centuries, is in the outstretched arms of a crucified Christ (or corpus). In such a body position, the grain

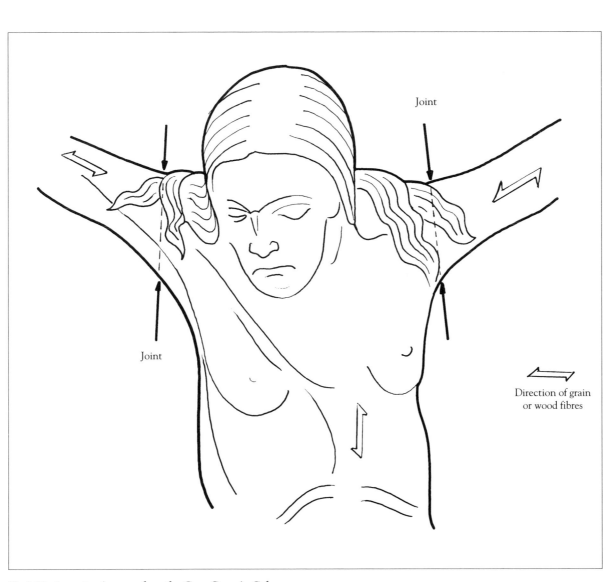

Joint

Joint

Direction of grain
or wood fibres

Fig 8.62 A masterpiece, such as the Gero Cross in Cologne Cathedral (970 CE) which is nearly 6 foot 2in (185cm) high, must have separate arms. This is partly because no tree would match the size needed, partly for economy of material and partly for the strength gained by running the wood fibres *along* the arms. Careful jointing with dowels or a tenon is further obscured by the hair.

of the arms is always at right angles to that of the body: one way long, the other short. The solution is to carve the arms, with lengthwise grain, separately from the body, joining them at the natural crease between the deltoid and biceps muscles, thus making the joint almost invisible (*see* Fig 8.62).

■ Using secret dowels and pinning from behind.

■ Accepting the risk but going carefully. The final piece will probably need some protection from handling or being touched. Viewers of carvings have strong tendencies to wiggle delicate bits to see how strong they are.

Hardness

Hardness depends on the relative air and chemical content of a piece of wood after it has been seasoned. Conductive sapwood has a lot of air, but while it is easy to cut in most species, it can be spongy and not take an edge. Heartwood, with a high chemical content is much harder and denser. Some tropical woods, such as lignum, are as hard as some stone.

Hardness also depends on the bonding of the wood fibres, giving rise to variations in flexibility, strength and the ease with which the piece will split.

Figure

A cross-section through a tree shows the cut ends of wood fibres laid down in annual rings. If the tree is cut in any other direction the grain of the annual rings forms a pattern – this is the **figuring** or **figure** of the wood.

Some woods, such as ebony, may have little or no visible figure at all; some, such as maple, have a slight regular pattern; and yet others, like lacewood, are highly figured. English oak is prized for its silvery medullary rays; in bird's-eye maple it is the tiny knots which are the attraction.

The figure is affected by how the tree has grown, from which part the wood has come, the presence of knots or burrs and so on – making each piece unique.

Burrs or **burls** are the wart-like outgrowths seen in some species of tree, such as elm. They are like a benign tumour, with an excessive growth of numerous small twigs, possibly caused by viruses or trauma. The grain is completely haphazard within the burr which can make for difficult shaping, although the final figuring is usually extraordinary.

Along with figure there is the colour. This can vary greatly between heartwood and sapwood, as for example in yew; or there can be very little variation, as in ash. Colouring in wood ranges from black to white, red to yellow, and more or less any other colour as well.

How much figure or colour is wanted depends on the carver's design and intentions. Colour and figure need to match the subject of the carving. A face, normally of a uniform colour, would look strange if mottled by the use of a highly figured wood;   or an

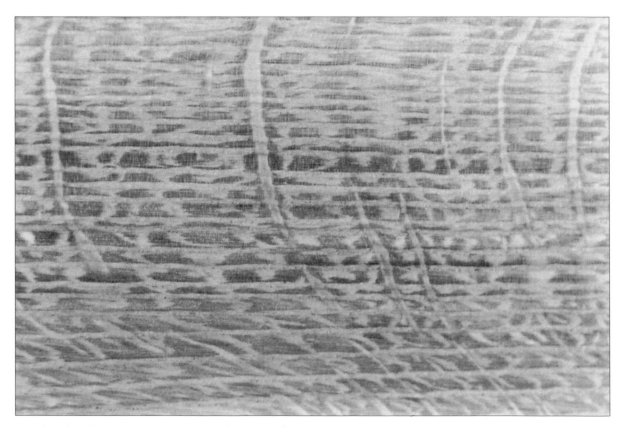

Fig 8.63 The 'silver rays' in quarter-sawn oak are prized figuring.

Fig 8.64 Bland limewood, often being likened to cheese, will take finely detailed carving and not camouflage it with strong grain.

Fig 8.65 Details such as the ring in the magpie's beak are suitable for limewood but would be much weaker in a more open-grained wood.

otter may look best in brown or brown/red wood, rather than pale yellow.

Texture

Wood is a very tactile material, attractive to the hand and feeling warm because of the insulating air within it. Woods with a more open grain, such as oak or ash, feel different from those such as box, with its tight grain and silky smooth surface.

The openness of the grain is important when considering the amount of detail that is required in a particular carving. The more open the grain, the bolder and simpler the carving needs to be. The finest details need the tightest grain of wood (*see* Figs 8.64, 8.65). Comparing carvings from different periods in history will demonstrate this principle nicely. Different styles of carving are suited to different openness of wood grain – usually from a locally available timber. Compare carvings in, say, oak, lime or boxwood.

Durability

Seasoned wood, kept dry and at an even temperature, will last far longer than most people believe is possible – witness woodcarvings found in Egyptian tombs. But this sort of case is the exception. Left to its own devices, wood follows the natural pattern of decaying, especially if left in damp conditions or in contact with the earth.

There are few woods which survive well outside. Frost for one thing will freeze the internal moisture and cause splitting. English oak has always been considered a very durable wood, and teak is selected for its natural protective oils – but even these will succumb to frost.

Decay can be delayed by treating outdoor woodcarvings – such as sign-boards – with one of the proprietary preservatives on the market and by protecting the wood from direct confrontation with the elements. Linseed oil is a traditional preservative; thinned a little with turpentine and brushed on regularly, it tends to considerably darken the wood.

SUITABILITY OF DESIGN AND MATERIAL

Points have been made several times in this chapter about matching the material to the carving and design. Gathering these points together as a series of questions, but not in any order of importance, will produce some helpful considerations and guidelines.

▪ How big will the work be? Will the wood need glueing up, or will the design fit into an available piece of timber?

▪ Does the carving depend on the light and shadow of a detailed design, with the wood primarily as a vehicle for this; or is the wood figuring of primary importance, with a broader, more shaped approach to the carving?

▪ What is the relative cost and availability of the timber?

▪ Are you designing within your own capabilities as a carver?

▪ How appropriate is the figuring and colour of the wood to the design? Does the wood relate to the subject?

▪ How much detail needs to be held by the wood?

▪ How much strength is needed, and where? Is the

work to be handled or not?

▪ Is a highly polished finish wanted or some rougher texture?

▪ Is the carving to be eaten from? (A tight-grained, flavourless wood, such as sycamore, is needed here.)

▪ Is the finished work to reside outside or inside?

▪ Will the wood have any effect on your carving tools? (Some tropical woods contain calcium deposits.)

A few woods, such as the rosewoods and cocobolo, are allergenic and the dust of others, such as iroko, affects some people adversely.

In the past, generations of carvers would evolve designs that worked well with the local woods they, of necessity, had to use. They would select from among a few species which were known to 'work'. The wood itself was often painted or gilded; a 'natural' surface would be considered unfinished. The idea of 'wood for wood's sake' is a new one.

Your own opinions about the use of any tropical hardwoods need to be considered, and perhaps enquiries made into the origins of the wood you want to use. Today the world, like the number of trees in it, is shrinking and many more woods are available and consumed by carvers. Never forget that wood is only a 'renewable resource' if it is re-planted or encouraged to regenerate naturally.

CHOICE OF WOOD

There is very little wood that cannot be carved; it is doubtful if there is a timber out there that someone, at some time or other, has not had a go at carving.

Most trade carvers use a limited range of wood, perhaps half a dozen species. Instrument-makers may only ever want to carve one species for one part of the instrument. Some sculptors make a point of working with as wide a range of wood as possible.

Although established carvers will know what woods they want, the approach taken here is from working with newcomers and based on how we all acquire knowledge: from others and from our own experience. Some books on carving give great lists of woods, with statistical columns of comparable qualities. My view is that newcomers to carving have never found this approach particularly helpful. For a start there is too much material (what does an 'average density of X' really mean anyway?). Even, within a species, there are trees and parts of trees deviating from the general characteristics. This is not to say that

Fig 8.66 Simple bold lines and planes are well suited to a wood such as elm.

knowledge of general characteristics are not important or helpful.

Rather than give such lists of wood, another approach may be found more helpful to those starting woodcarving, and unsure about which wood to choose.

■ Begin by not worrying too much; see yourself exploring wood in the same way you are exploring everything else: the carving tools, the designs and the techniques.

■ In the beginning, when you are finding your way around tools, how they work and so on, find one or two species of famously carver-friendly wood. Use well-seasoned wood, with little figure; not too hard, nor too soft; clean and knot free, on which to practise and experiment with the tools. Limewood, fruitwood such as pear, basswood and walnut are examples. Avoid the pines and the oaks – extremes of soft and hard – to begin with.

■ As you start becoming familiar with tools and handling them, and start to design and widen your ideas – *look*. Look at carvings in books and magazines with a magnifying glass. Best of all, examine carvings *in situ*. Look at old and contemporary work: both the design and the wood, and how the two aspects work together. Store up this information in your heart and mind. So many carvers have gone before you and have left an enormous resource of visible information for you to mull over. Meet other carvers, possibly in local carving clubs and exchange ideas.

■ Using what has been said in this chapter as a guide, and your increasing knowledge, start exploring species of wood, one by one, as you feel the need. Start collecting bits of wood wherever you find them until you have a small stock readily available for designs as they arise. Explore defects and problems.

In this way knowledge grows slowly but surely into a natural appreciation of wood and its suitability for particular designs and uses.

Fig 8.67 Some carvers only ever work with free 'natural' wood.

SOURCES OF WOOD

Wood is technically the fibrous 'woody' matter which constitutes the bole, trunk, branches, twigs and even leaf veins of a tree. **Timber** is the term for this woody material in usable quantities, especially after conversion.

If you are not 'growing your own', there are two sources of wood for the carver.

'Free' wood

It is not unusual for carvers to be given wood, as many people prefer to give it away rather than burn it. Logs will have to be converted and seasoned.

The wood in old and second-hand furniture tends to be dried out and more brittle than it was originally. Scrape off the varnish rather than sanding the wood.

For those inclined to sculpture, woodlands and driftwood from beaches need be their only source. All found wood should be washed with warm water and a soft brush used to remove the dirt and salt first. Be careful to dry the wood as slowly as possible.

Other sources include beams from demolition sites, reclamation yards, railway sleepers and so on.

Buying wood

Wood is often bought by a carver to suit a particular design. Wood that is bought can be seen and inspected, some aspects of its quality are guaranteed and there should be an assurance about its seasoning and moisture content.

Carving is labour-intensive and the cost of the wood is usually only a small part of the overall cost of a project. Carvers, probably more than most woodworkers, can therefore afford to spend money on the right wood for a particular job. It is always a great shame to lose a carving – not to mention the time – by using inferior wood as a cheaper expedient.

Fig 8.68 A carefully selected stack of timber for a large carved panel.

Fig 8.69 You may choose to make the change of grain, or figure, at a join a feature, rather than disguise it.

There are quite a few timber yards today that advertise in woodworking magazines. Some timber yards make a point of serving the woodcarver or turner and sell smaller, selected stuff – often the manager has a personal interest in the craft as well. A list of some such yards is given in the Reference Section (see page 347). Such firms often produce catalogues.

Check out all the local timber yards too. They vary tremendously in how helpful they are and what they stock. Most timber yards are reluctant to sell less than whole boards, nevertheless, as the definition of a 'board' can vary considerably, it is always worth asking what they have in stock. Clubbing together with other woodcarvers can be a useful approach.

Selecting the wood

It is always best to select the wood yourself, even if you are a newcomer to the job – you can see shakes and knots as well as the next person. Take along a block plane or spokeshave as you will normally be allowed to clean a small area of a selected board for closer inspection. Do not leave the selection to someone who has no interest in what you are doing, but is only interested in selling you a lump of wood quickly, before their tea-break. Try to find out their least busy time of day and enlist their help or interest.

Hardwoods in Britain are sold in *cubic feet*, with allowances made for the wany edge, bark and splits. This is a comparative measure to which all the odd sizes are converted for pricing. Although softwoods are sold in metric sizes, metric hardwoods are some way off as yet.

A cubic foot could be a board in any of the following shapes:

■ 1in (25mm) thick x 12 feet (3.6m) long x 12in (300mm) wide
■ 2in (50mm) thick x 6 feet (1.8m) long x 12in (300mm) wide
■ 3in (75mm) thick x 3 feet (0.9m) long x 12in (300mm) wide
■ 4in (100mm) thick x 1½ feet (0.45m) long x 12in (300mm) wide.

Remember that you may be dealing with nominal sizes, as sawn from the tree. Shrinkage should have been allowed for, but this needs checking, especially if an accurate planed dimension is needed. Wood may be warped, bent, etc. – another reason for seeing what you are buying.

As a last point, buy wood from properly managed, sustained sources. It can no longer be thought of as simply 'growing on trees'.

GLUING UP

Fundamentals

You might want to glue wood together for a variety of reasons.

■ To arrive at the size of wood you need for a particular carving
■ To get an appropriate direction of grain
■ To economize on time and waste
■ To avoid the instability inherent in a single, large

piece of wood, which may contain too much of a mixture of heartwood and sapwood.

So gluing gives control over the following aspects of wood:

■ Size
■ Stability
■ Grain direction
■ Waste.

Plain glued joints – joints which rely on the glue for strength with no mechanical advantage from the shape of the joint – are usually all that is needed by carvers. It is these that this section deals with.

There are many excellent woodworking glues available today, often stronger than the wood itself and easy to use. PVA (polyvinyl acetate) or 'white' glues are the most suitable for carvers, giving permanent and strong joints. Some of these glues are suitable for both external and internal use.

Urea formaldehyde-based glues (e.g. Cascamite) are excellent for outside use. To some degree they are

Fig 8.70 The two immaculate glue lines on the right are barely visible; the one on the left is given away by the change of grain at this point.

space-filling, but their brittle, crystal nature does tend to take the edge off carving tools and so should be used with caution.

There are specialized glues which will stick wet wood with up to 25% moisture content. An example would be Balcotan which is used in boat building – it actually reacts with the water in the wood. This sort of glue is more expensive than white glue and can be used if there is ever any doubt about the dryness of the timber.

All glues have an 'open time' when the joint can be adjusted. They then pass through a curing stage during which time the joint should be clamped and rendered immovable. At some point the jointed wood can be handled, with the final, fully cured strength occurring later. Details of these times and stages, the optimum drying conditions, and the shelf-life of the glue, will appear on specific containers.

Glues work in two ways:

■ Their chemicals actually bond to the fibres of the wood.
■ They soak between the fibres and set around them.

The following points should be considered before gluing.

■ With the exception of the specialist glue mentioned above, glues are susceptible to the surrounding temperature and moisture. Always read the information on the bottle or pack.
■ Gluing fibres *end to end* is a very weak joint that needs dowelling or strengthening in some way. Fibres glued *side to side* produces the strongest bond.
■ The closer fitting the two surfaces to be glued, the stronger the joint. It is worth taking that extra bit of trouble over preparing the surfaces. Once carved, a joint which has 'sprung' can be very difficult to re-glue or clamp up.

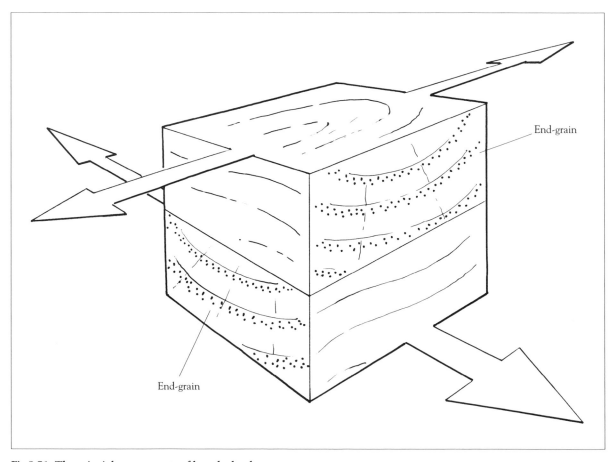

Fig 8.71 The principle movements of boards that have been glued with fibres running in contrary directions will be antagonistic.

■ The harder or more dense the wood, the greater the pressure of clamping that is needed to get the glue to penetrate the fibres.

■ Glue will not penetrate naturally oily woods (such as teak or pitch pine) particularly well as most glues are water-based. The surfaces to be glued need washing several times with methanol (methylated spirits) first, and the raising of small 'keys' of grain with the corner of a chisel.

When two pieces of wood are glued together, either face to face or edge to edge, they still move as separate items. It is important to consider how any piece of wood will perform in the context of the whole: minimizing the movement or making one movement compensate for another.

Movement is minimized by using quarter-sawn boards, but these are not necessarily available. Problems may arise in the following situations:

■ When different species of wood are used which shrink and expand by differing amounts

■ When grain runs in different directions, so movements are working against each other (*see* Fig 8.71)

■ When different cuts from the same tree are used, for example mixing slash-sawn with quarter-sawn wood (*see* Fig 8.72)

■ When the moisture content differs between the pieces of wood, with one being less seasoned than the other.

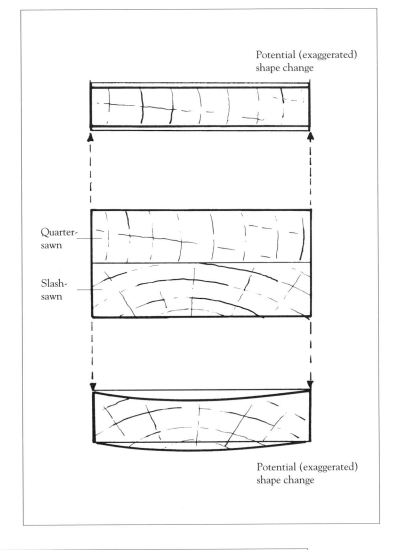

Potential (exaggerated) shape change

Quarter-sawn

Slash-sawn

Potential (exaggerated) shape change

Fig 8.72 (Right) A joint with wood from different cuts from the tree may give rise to stress problems; the individual pieces move differently.

Fig 8.73 Gluing boards edge to edge for compensatory movements.

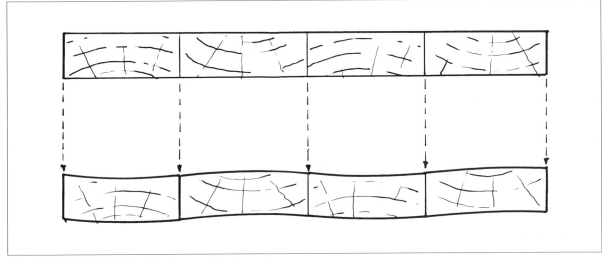

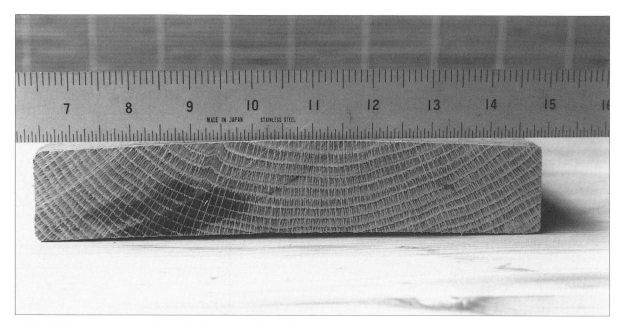

Fig 8.74 It is important to estimate in what way a piece of wood will change shape in order to glue up the most stable structure.

Types of joint

The plain glued joints that carvers use take the following forms.

EDGE TO EDGE

This sort of joint is used in panels. It may be 'rubbed', that is one piece left perched neatly on the other, or 'clamped', in which case sash cramps are used to tighten the joint. 'Rubbing' is literally that: air and excess glue are squeezed out by rubbing one piece of wood against another until the joint is felt to stick, which is when the glue starts to be absorbed.

Arrange the grain so that each plank warps or moves in the opposite direction to the one next to it (*see* Fig 8.73). The movement between boards is

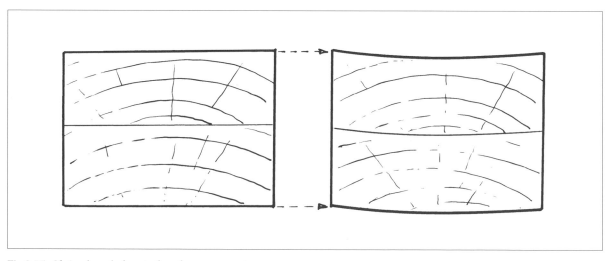

Fig 8.75 Gluing boards face to face for compensatory movements.

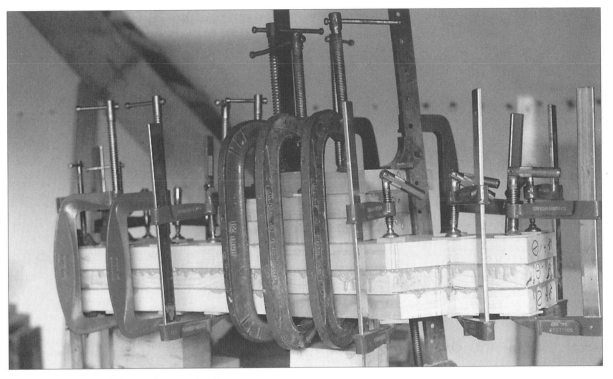

Fig 8.76 Gluing boards face to face requires large pressures to ensure that the glue penetrates the wood fibres sufficiently.

mutually compensating. Sometimes a wide plank is split into narrow ones to avoid excess movement and give the panel greater overall stability.

FACE TO FACE

This sort of joint is used to create a bulk of wood. For example a 10in (250mm) thick block can be laminated from five 2in (50mm) boards. Again, allow for movement but this time the movement needs to be complementary (*see* Fig 8.75). The clamping pressure needed is much greater than that for edge joints as it is spread over a wider surface and a certain amount of pressure is always needed to force the glue between fibres (*see* Fig 8.76). The more open the grain, the easier the glue will penetrate. In this sort of clamping, with wide surfaces, it is more common to use too few clamps than too many.

FLATS

Flats are small surfaces on a carving to which a carver sticks extra pieces of wood, building out a certain section for an effect. In these cases, off-cuts from the original wood are kept and the grain closely matched. A rubbed joint may be all that is necessary. Small C-clamps made from bed spring coils are also helpful.

END-GRAIN

Where end-grain needs to be fixed to side-grain, for example in a crucifix or bird's wing, dowels, dowel screws or some type of mortise joint is needed to get mechanical strength into the joint.

Basic procedures

◼ Always do a 'dry run' to check the equipment, the set up, and order of doing things.

◼ Check the matching of grain, not only for movement but also colour, figure, etc. Unless it is a feature, the joint should be as neat and invisible as possible. Take enough time over this as gluing is difficult to undo. A thicker glue line is a weaker one – the more the fibres are in contact between pieces the better.

◼ Design the carving to put the glue line where it is least noticeable: in a shadow or groove, and not, for example, down the centre of a face.

◼ Remember that a glue line cut at right angles only shows as a hair line; whereas if the glue line is cut along its length to any extent, a thicker line appears.

◼ Enough even pressure is needed to squeeze the glue out all around the glue line, but excessive pressure will squeeze out too much glue, leaving the joint dry.

■ Wipe away excess glue with a damp cloth to allow the glue line full access to the air.

■ Store the glue in the right conditions according to the maker's recommendations. Some glues have a shelf life.

SUMMARY

This chapter sets down some basic information that carvers need to know about their material. But how much do carvers *really* need to know about wood?

One answer to this question is that it is not possible to know too much about the material you are working in – but it *is* possible to know too little. The consequences of knowing too little will be some adverse effect on a carving: the wood splitting through inadequate seasoning; a disastrous result from staining; the wood failing to meet the needs of the design, and breaking; or the shadows of the form being camouflaged by an uncontrolled grain.

Knowledge will reduce the risk of meeting these hazards. And knowledge best comes with the natural flow of experience, which hopefully is enjoyable and the result of exploration and challenge.

Fig 8.77 A small seated figure, from the back, made up of five smaller pieces glued together. Already much time has been saved in roughing out . . .

Fig 8.78 . . . but what will matter is how invisible the glue lines are. And the test of this is often only in the carving.

FINISHING

Aims

To look at why surface applications are used, and at some of their effects

To describe some basic, straightforward and reliable finishes, applicable to most carvings

To suggest some alternative areas for experimentation

In this context 'finishing' refers to the surface treatment of a carving, after all toolwork or sanding has been completed. There is not the space in this book to deal with finishing in detail – this would need a book in itself. For example, gilding – a traditional complement to carved work – is a craft in its own right.

As a preliminary point, *experimentation* is very important. The final appearance of a carving will depend on a combination of:

- The surface texture of the carving
- The colour and quality of the wood itself
- The type of finish that has been applied.

Leaving the wood surface straight from the chisel or sanding it are only two options open to the experimenting carver or sculptor. Before applying a finish consider using the following: texturing with wire brushes; burning and brushing; frosting or using rotary burrs; inlaying other materials. There are many possibilities to be consciously explored.

The natural colours of some species of wood will combine with that of the applied finish to affect the final colour of the carving. There are many different finishes that can be used to achieve the effect the carver wants, from simple waxes to chemicals and

Fig 9.1 The lion's mane from 'Death Astride a Lion' carved for a bell tower in southern Germany in about 1400. Vigorous gouge and V-tool use can be seen; a split to the side of the mouth has been repaired with wooden inserts and overcarved; a plugged knot hole has been filled poorly at a later date.

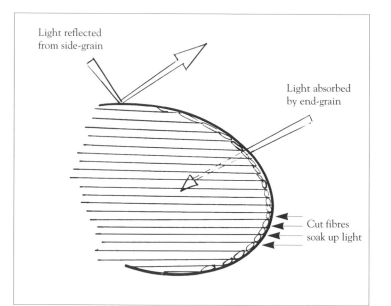

Light reflected from side-grain

Light absorbed by end-grain

Cut fibres soak up light

Fig 9.2 The cut of the fibres in the wood affect the absorption of finishes and how the carving appears after their application.

colours. Always try the finish out on some hidden part first to avoid unexpected results.

The surface of the wood reflects light (*see* Fig 9.2), so whatever effect the wood surface has been given *prior* to the finish will affect how the light is reflected. This in turn will alter the appearance of the finish. For example, all woods tend to darken when oils and polishes are applied, and rough end-grain will darken more than smooth side-grain. The final cut of a sharp chisel closes the pores and smooths the surface of the wood; this has a different effect on finishes, compared with sanding.

REASONS FOR FINISHING

Woodcarvings from the earliest known onwards were 'polychromed', that is coloured or painted to look life-like. The wood itself was only a supporting medium for the coloured skin of 'reality'. Even Greek marble sculpture was polychromed in this way.

During the Middle Ages, woodcarvers began to

Fig 9.3 A detail of 'The Banquet at Simon's' by Riemenschneider (1490–92). Note the stained background in the windows which, together with the sketchlines of the V-tool around the outside, adds to the depth of relief. It is not known to what extent the equivalent of sandpaper was available, but it is thought that materials such as sharkskin might have been used to smooth over already well-flattened surfaces.

leave their work uncoloured, perhaps only burnished with a handful of shavings or a tool handle, sometimes sharkskin was used. Both Grinling Gibbons and Tilman Riemenschneider of Würzburg used simple varnishes to seal what was otherwise the natural appearance of wood. The woods were plain and a foil for decorative and detailed carving. Since that time, carvings were frequently thought to need no more additional polish than that coming from use and handling. And, indeed, one way of finishing is not to 'finish' at all.

Today, there is a further change of taste and appreciation, with a greater variety of interesting and exotic woods available to be carved, particularly for their beauty and figuring, as well as an abundance of new finishing agents. Many carvings are enhanced or even 'made' by the finish. It is rare now not to find a carving that has not been treated in some way.

There are three principal reasons for finishing.

Protection

By filling the pores between the wood fibres, the wood is protected from picking up dirt and grease, especially that acquired through handling. The patina left from either of these sources may leave naked wood looking dull and grubby. Often the same areas of a carving are fingered, so that the colour begins to appear irregular

in a way that detracts from the overall appearance.

Protection may include a prophylactic anti-woodworm treatment (*see* Fig 9.4).

Sealing

Sealing wood inhibits or slows down the transfer of moisture between its surface and the air. Centrally heated houses can be very dry, and workshops damp. The woodcarving, if sealed, remains in a fairly well-controlled environment and is not so subject to ambient moisture changes.

Enhancing

Whether the finish is a simple application of a sealer or the sandblasting, burning and colour-staining of some sculptures, the finish itself *must* enhance the work. To put it the other way: if the finish detracts from the appearance of the carving,

Fig 9.4 Woodworm fluid can be applied with a brush or a fine spray – such as this one used for misting flowers. Be sure to mark the container carefully and keep it where it cannot accidently be used for any other purpose.

Fig 9.5 A typical collection of oils and shellac polishes.

there is no point in using it.

A carving which has taken days, weeks, even months to complete may be ruined in a few minutes by applying the wrong finish. Many a carver, who has been impatient to finish a job, has regretted not making a few experiments on similar waste wood first.

SOME SIMPLE FINISHES

The following basic treatments, while not particularly adventurous, have been used successfully by myself for many years. They may be all that your carvings ever need.

Lacquers or varnishes that produce a synthetic, glossy appearance cannot be recommended for woodcarvings.

Remember that all tool work or sanding needs to be completed *thoroughly* before finishing. Oils and (especially) stains will make any torn grain, sanding scratches, cutting faults, tool or file marks stand out.

Shellac

Shellac is made from *lac*, a resinous substance exuded by an insect (*Coccus lacca*) in the course of laying its eggs. It is collected, crushed, melted, filtered and sold in flakes. The shellac is then dissolved in denatured alcohol to make the usable liquid. Shellac can be bought already made up. **Button polish**, **white polish** and **sanding sealer** are all based on shellac. It is used in the French polishing of furniture – which is not our concern here.

Shellac dries quickly on the wood as the alcohol evaporates, without raising the grain fibres. Working with it needs an efficient speed. There is a choice between natural shellac, which is orange or brown, and clear transparent shellac which has been bleached. The choice will depend on the lightness or darkness of the wood. Brown shellac will enrich darker woods.

Method of application

1 Make sure the wood is completely dry before applying the shellac.
2 Apply the liquid with a brush (which has to be cleaned with methylated spirits). As shellac dries quickly, work systematically with the grain, keeping a 'live edge' into which subsequent brush strokes can be worked.
3 Several thin coats are better than one thick one, leaving 30–60min between coats. When dry, the shellac can be lightly cut back with the finest wirewool (no. 0000). Brush or vacuum the dust off carefully; do not blow.

Shellac will seal wood after oiling or prior to waxing. It cannot be mixed with water, nor is it waterproof; water will stain it.

Oil

Oil finishes look best on hardwoods. Linseed oil is the most common oil used in this context. It dries in contact with the air in the wood to form a skin; it may also react with the chemicals in the wood as well – usually to the benefit of the appearance. Oils will not raise the wood grain.

Linseed oil comes in a **raw** or **boiled** state. The boiled oil is thicker, penetrates more slowly and dries faster than raw linseed oil. To make the application of these oils easier and to get them to penetrate the wood quicker they need diluting with pure turpentine. Dilute three parts raw linseed oil with about one part turpentine; dilute boiled linseed oil with equal parts of turpentine. Keep these drying oils in sealed jars to prevent them forming a skin.

Method of application

1 Apply the diluted oil – fairly warm if possible – with a soft brush onto the clean, dry, bare wood and allow it to soak in.
2 Keep brushing on the oil until it starts to remain on the surface. Leave for 10min and wipe off the excess with a cloth. Do not allow oil to stand in pools.
3 After several coats the oil will penetrate less and less as the wood becomes saturated. Wipe off the excess and, taking a clothes brush, vigorously brush the surface. As the oil dries, brush regularly to bring up the polished sheen. Keep a brush especially for burnishing oiled finishes.

One method used by some carvers is to submerge the carving completely in linseed oil, which may then be heated up slowly to assist the oil's penetration into the wood. When bubbles no longer arise from the carving it is considered saturated and should be removed and thoroughly wiped off. This is perhaps useful for smaller carvings.

It is worth mentioning a few other oils:

■ **Tung (China wood) oil** A natural oil, more expensive than linseed oil but it is more water- and

Fig 9.6 'Working' tins of commercial waxes. Avoid the ones with silicon in them as these may react with oils and other finishes.

Fig 9.7 Pure beeswax made to a desired consistency – keep it sealed from the air to prevent the turpentine evaporating.

heat-resistant; it can be used instead of linseed oil.

■ **Teak oil** A blend of natural oils and solvents developed originally for teakwood and light brown in colour. It dries quicker than linseed oil but added pigments will affect the end-grain of lighter woods, making them look grubby and oily.

■ **Danish oil** This contains resin-based hardeners that make the oil go off quickly to form a hard shell that is resistant to wear. It cannot be applied to a waxed surface, as can linseed oil, to freshen it up. In a similar way to teak oil, the end-grain of lighter woods is affected.

■ **Walnut oil** This is used for carved vessels and other food containers, as it is an edible oil that dries with a nutty aroma.

OIL, SHELLAC AND WAXES

After oiling as described above, a coat or two of shellac will seal the surface further, prior to waxing. Shellac is not affected by oil in the way it is by water. The advantage of sealing in the oil is that the carving can then be handled and the surface kept clean. The oil continues to dry and 'cure' with the air in the wood itself.

Waxes

There are three sorts of waxes, depending on their origin:

■ **Mineral** e.g. benzine or paraffin wax

■ **Vegetable** e.g. carnauba wax

■ **Animal** e.g. beeswax.

White paraffin wax can be used where a completely bland or clear finish is needed, although beeswax is also available in a bleached form. Mineral wax brushed on to the ends of timber will inhibit the drying process, in which case it can be dissolved in white spirit. A little mineral wax added to beeswax will make the beeswax harder.

Silicon waxes, made into commercial polishes with all sorts of additives, cannot be recommended.

Carnauba wax comes from a Brazilian palm. It

dries to a very hard finish and, again, a little added to beeswax will give a tougher finish. Carnauba is too hard and brittle to use on its own.

Beeswax is a well-tried finish for carvings, although it is maintained by some museums that this wax (and its vehicle, turpentine) oxidizes with air over time to the actual detriment of the wood. It is the principal wax for finishing carvings and can also be used to repair small surface checks. It is a soft yellow wax which melts at a low temperature, it does not seal the pores well and tends to pick up dirt and show water marks. Bare wood should always be sealed before waxing and the wax left to dry thoroughly before handling.

Beeswax needs to be dissolved in pure turpentine to make it soft enough to apply; as the turpentine evaporates, so the wax is left to harden.

MAKING BEESWAX POLISH

Heat is needed to properly dissolve the wax and, as turpentine is very flammable, wax polish must always be made up in a double-boiler – not over direct heat or a naked flame. A double-boiler consists of a container with the inflammable substances to be warmed or mixed placed inside another container with heated

water (*see* Fig 9.8). Although called a 'boiler', the water will not necessarily be boiling; with beeswax it need only be hot to very hot. The outside, heated container will obviously be a pan, but the inner vessel can be polythene or plastic. This system of heating insures that the turpentine never rises to a flash temperature and is safely placed to warm up and mix with the beeswax.

Method

1 Grate up the beeswax and spread it out evenly on the bottom of the inner container. Adding about 5% carnauba wax to the beeswax greatly increases its hardness and resistance to dirt.

2 Pour in the pure turpentine until the wax is just submerged.

3 Warm up the mixture in the double-boiler on the stove, with the windows open. Stir as the wax melts to a creamy paste.

4 Take a little out and allow it to cool; examine the consistency. Add more turpentine for a thinner consistency, more wax for a thicker consistency.

5 If the source of beeswax is from a beekeeper, unrefined (the wax, not the beekeeper!), pass the melted wax through muslin to remove impurities.

6 Store in an airtight container.

APPLYING BEESWAX POLISH

1 Apply the creamy wax to the carving with a soft brush, after sealing with oil or shellac. Work it well into the corners but prevent them filling or clogging – once the wax is dry these are difficult to clean out. A

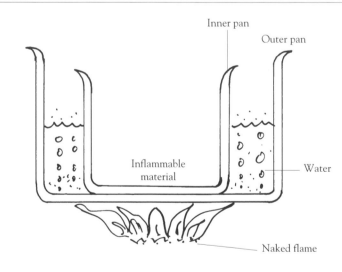

Fig 9.8 A double-boiler prevents inflammable substances overheating and igniting on a naked flame.

Fig 9.9 Beeswax from a local beekeeper and an ex-cheese grater. The small block is hard carnauba wax; a small percentage is added to the beeswax to toughen it.

Fig 9.10 A small meths stove, primarily designed for camping, is ideal for the low temperatures required to melt beeswax.

Fig 9.11 It is a good idea to keep separate brushes for polishing oil or wax finishes. Keep another brush entirely for brushing bare wood.

toothbrush is useful for small details.

2 Use a soft brush, such as a clothes brush, to burnish the surface vigorously – it is a good idea to keep a brush especially for this purpose. The waxed wood will remain sticky for some time and should not be handled.

3 After 24 hours a second coat can be applied with clean, fine (no. 0000) wirewool which cuts back the first coat.

4 After another 24 hours, brush the carving again and allow the wax to dry. The carving can then be polished with a cotton cloth.

COLOUR

The use of pigments in the form of stains and dyes to add colour to all, or part, of a carving, and such a practice as fuming oak (see Fig 9.12) are subjects that need more space to cover than is available here. However, a few notes may be a helpful start to an exploration of stains or dyes.

The terms 'stains' and 'dyes' are to all intents synonymous for carvers. Stains can be bought ready made up or in powder form, in a huge variety of colours. Clothes dyes, watercolours and oil paints also work on wood.

There are three main types of stain, depending on the medium which carries the pigment: water-based, oil based and spirit-based stains. This medium is also used for any further dilution.

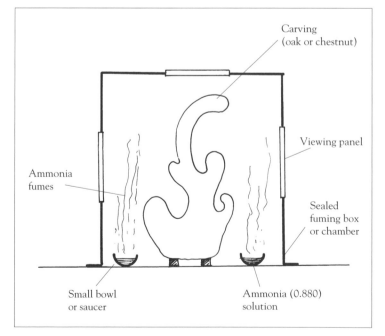

Fig 9.12 A fuming cupboard controls the ammonia vapours in contact with the carving.

Fig 9.13 A collection of water-based stains and a 'two-part' bleach. When colouring wood, an initial decision to make is whether to work with the existing colour, or to remove it and start afresh.

WATER-BASED STAINS

Water-based stains have the pigments dissolved in water; their characteristics include:

■ Good penetration into the wood
■ Quick drying by evaporation, so it is easy to get tide marks or overlap marks
■ Taking further finishes, but they need sealing first
■ Raising the wood grain – therefore they are most suitable for sanded carvings, which need dampening first with clean water, then drying and re-sanding.

OIL-BASED STAINS

Oil-based stains have the pigments dissolved in linseed oil and turpentine; their characteristics include:

■ Poorer penetration into the wood – not as good as water-based stains
■ Slow drying, so there is no danger of tide marks or overlap marks
■ Needing shellac or wax for sealing, but not all finishes are accepted, so some trials are needed
■ Not raising the wood grain – therefore they are suitable for carvings that are not sanded.

SPIRIT-BASED STAINS

Spirit-based stains have the pigments dissolved in methanol; their characteristics include:

■ Poor penetration
■ Very quick drying so overlap marks are easily created; the drying can be slowed by adding a little shellac-based polish
■ Taking further finishes, but need sealing
■ Not raising the grain – therefore they are suitable for carvings left from the chisel.

The colour of the wood itself will affect the final colour of the stain: stains appear darker:

■ When wet
■ On a rough surface
■ On end-grain.

So work the colour in thin coats, allowing the wood to dry in between, to see what is happening. Do test some spare wood first as stains are very difficult to remove.

Wood can be bleached before colouring to remove natural colour and strong figuring. The 'two-part' bleaches are strongest but need great care in use.

Staining some parts of a carving only – for example backgrounds – while leaving other parts natural wood, can look very interesting.

SAFETY

The shellac, oil and wax finishes and stains discussed above are safe if care is taken. Use commonsense and proceed conscientiously.

■ Follow all instructions and advice on packages, especially with bleaches and other caustic finishes. Some firms produce leaflets and guidelines for using products.
■ Use and store turpentine, spirit- and oil-based stains, as well as all other finishes, in well-ventilated areas.
■ Keep containers closed when not in use; keep them away from children, and away from heat and naked flames.
■ All brushes should be cleaned properly, and used rags sealed in plastic bags and disposed of away from the workshop. It is not unknown for rags in some circumstances to spontaneously combust.
■ Avoid inhaling the vapours, or allowing vapours to contact skin and eyes. If contact is made with the eyes, irrigate them fully with lots of fresh water and seek medical advice if necessary.

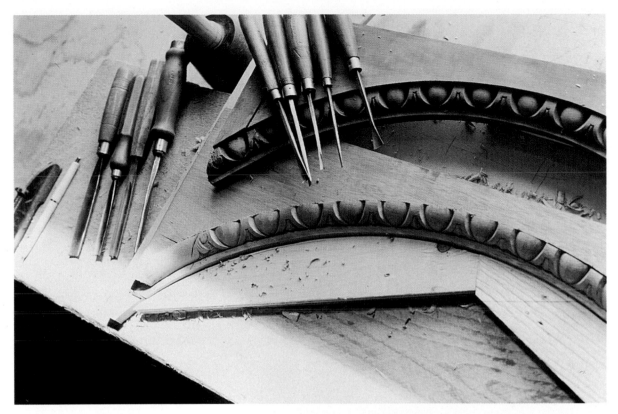

To reproduce a section of 'egg and dart' moulding, the work is held by contoured fences to a board which is in turn clamped to the carving bench.

Life-sized skull in yew wood and lectern in reclaimed oak, courtesy of the Bristol Buddhist Centre. Tool marks on the skull are clearly visible.

Section of a headboard in limewood. In this sort of work,
where a smooth, polished finish is needed, sandpaper is
used to remove tool marks from the surface.

Detail from a Green
Man, elmwood.

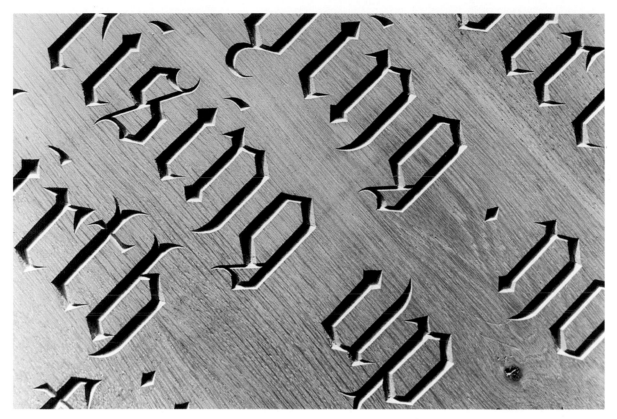

Detail of an Old English text. Originally, this style of letter resulted from penwork; the letters here were designed to be simply cut with chisels.

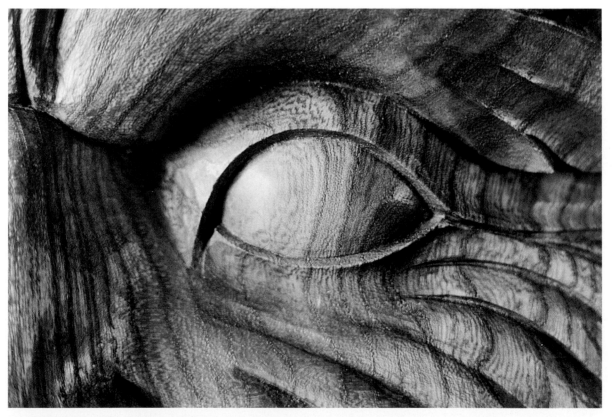

Detail of a 'grotesque' in limewood. Toolmarks on the surface add to the vigour of the lines.

Photograph © Ken Day

Two wide-spreading oak trees growing in what is now pasture land. Woodcarvers should neither forget, nor take for granted, the source of their material.

A typical oxidation spectrum produced by heating a polished steel surface. Normally the lighter colours are 'floated' into position from a hotter, annealed part of the blade - the colour representing the highest temperature being blue. From left to right: blue; dark purple; purple; peacock (bronze/brown); bronze (brown); straw; light straw; faint straw.

REFERENCE SECTION

T his chapter starts with some activities which, although not acts of carving in themselves, are very important to the carver. They will help anyone aspiring to work better in the craft.

This chapter also gathers together safety considerations. Please do not skip or dismiss this section – or the other safety advice appearing elsewhere in the book. Statistically, *somebody* has these accidents!

The chapter then contains a brief list of suppliers of tools, equipment and materials that I can recommend personally, with a few pointers as to where to look further. Finally imperial/metric conversion tables are given.

BACKGROUND STUDIES

Research

When carving something intended to represent something else, adequate research is essential: partly for the belief and appreciation of the viewer, but also to help the process of carving itself. It is difficult to carve wood already carved away.

Say for instance the carving is to be of a squirrel. Few people can sit down and draw a convincing squirrel in three dimensions – so how could they carve one? Our brains recognize the real world by the smallest of clues, a bushy tail may be all you need to recognize a squirrel as it disappears up a tree – but much more information is needed to carve one (or even catch one). And how much more information is needed for a complicated subject such as 'The Death of the Great Northumbrian Hero, Siward'?

Research means looking at squirrels – or whatever – as closely as possible. Look at them in life, in books; handle a squirrel if possible; look at how other artists and carvers have dealt with this and similar subjects; draw them and model them. Anything to understand the subject better. This is particularly important in wildlife carvings – what may be an interesting line to the carver may be a shootable condition to a horse fancier.

Drawing

One of the best ways to develop the hand and eye is to draw. Not that there is a need to become an artist with a pencil, but drawing develops the mind's eye for carving, as well as being a useful skill for studying and recording subjects. Draw, but learn to be truthful in what you see and to free up the lines and curves.

These days drawings are easy to enlarge using

Fig 10.1 Detail from the Marienaltar in Creglingen, southern Germany, carved between 1505 and 1510 by Riemenschneider. Onlookers who have never tried to carve wood often fail to appreciate the background of draughtsmanship and, usually, modelling that makes such work exude confidence.

photocopiers; however, the older method of square-to-square scaling up should not be forgotten, nor that wondrous instrument, the pantograph.

Photography

Photographing a subject, or model, as the basis for a carving is a quick way of rendering an exact pose. It is helpful with problems of foreshortening and for those who really cannot make headway with their drawing. If possible, though, use it in conjunction with active sketching.

A photocopy of the print can be enlarged and transferred to the wood ready for bandsawing. A slide can be enlarged and projected straight onto a panel surface or onto drawing paper hung on the wall.

Photograph the many carvings and sculptures that appear all over our cities. These architectural

Fig 10.2 A simple record taken in plaster.

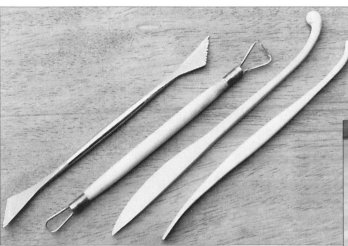

Fig 10.3 From the left: a metal modelling tool; a tool for scooping away modelling material; and two homemade modelling tools. Quite a lot of modelling tools can be made by yourself as you see what you need.

Fig 10.4 Modelling material such as this is reusable and will last a long time; modelling can be as much a three-dimensional scribbling as producing accurate measurements to work from.

decorations and patterns will develop your eye for form, interest and beauty. Do not forget to build up a portfolio of your own work as well.

The 'morgue'

This is a graphic designer's term for reference collections of cuttings, pictures and information filed in scrapbooks, folders or drawers.

Built up over years, the morgue is browsed through for inspiration, and studied when a problem needs solving. For example – and this is probably where the term originated – if a carver is interested in the human body then gathering pictures from magazines, photographs, *anything* that depicts heads, hands, eyes, poses, action, old and young, male and female, will soon build up into an invaluable source of reference.

Plaster casts

Sometimes it is possible to take a simple plaster cast of a carving, or part of a carving – to record it, study it and perhaps even copy it. Low relief carving works best as there are problems taking a cast from undercut work.

Push malleable Plasticine on to the wood, allow it to cool and lift it off. Being oil-based, it usually comes away cleanly without leaving a residue on finished work. Carefully make up the sides so that the Plasticine forms a container, and pour in plaster of Paris. When this has cooled, the Plasticine should again peel away easily. Care needs to be taken to prevent distortion. Dry the plaster well in a warm place and varnish it.

Different plasters are worth investigating. Some, like dental plaster, will take fine details; some new types dry extremely hard.

Modelling

Modelling is useful in several ways. Firstly, while drawing can strive to be three-dimensional and help clarify ideas, it is still actually two-dimensional. The image cannot be rotated, the lighting changed and so on. To get a real feel for what you want to achieve, and to solve many of the problems of design, modelling in clay or Plasticine is better than drawing for the carver.

The second use of modelling is in helping to develop, as does drawing, a three-dimensional sense. Modelling pins down the imagination quickly, putting together the details in your mind.

Another advantage is that a model – which need only be a preliminary sketch – gives you a chance for measuring up from all directions and deciding on the most economic use of the wood.

Modelling can allow a carving to be started with confidence, the carver knowing where the main masses are so as not to make some initial and irretrievable blunder. Details are not usually needed as they can be worked out in the wood as the carving proceeds. It is important to realize that modelled work looks different to carving – it has its own techniques and approach – and should not be just copied. Rather, use a model like a drawing, to start the journey into the carving in the right direction. As soon as your confidence in the work is established, discard the model and concentrate on the carving in front of you.

Transferring work to the solid

Tracing paper and carbon paper are well-tried methods for transferring drawings. Standing a sheet of plate glass in front of a clay model and drawing the profile with a chinagraph pencil – while moving the eye-line to avoid distortion – is a way of capturing an outline for small three-dimensional work; an outline that can be subsequently bandsawn.

SAFETY

Notes on safety are found throughout this book. They are gathered together here for reference, with no apology for repetition. No claim is made for

Fig 10.5 Surrounded by sharp edges – small nicks like this are easily done and more of a nuisance. Carvers need to be aware of dangers all the time.

completeness as full, or particular, circumstances cannot be accounted for.

The best safeguard against accidents is mindfulness. *It is lack of concentration and forethought that causes most accidents.* For example, putting your hand on the edge of a projecting gouge: what actually caused the accident was not the gouge, but the attitude that placed it dangerously in the first place. Lack of experience is also important. An effort should be made to understand and familiarize yourself with all tools and equipment before using them in earnest.

Safety lies in:

▪ Being in control
▪ Being aware of the dangers
▪ Not being distracted
▪ Not being over-confident
▪ Gaining experience.

General safety precautions

IN THE WORKSHOP

▪ Stand at the entrance of the workplace with a notepad and challenge yourself to think of all the ways you could be hurt in the space in front of you, including the tools and equipment.
▪ Keep a fully stocked first aid box easily accessible.
▪ There are even more possibilities for accidents when children and visitors enter the workplace.
▪ All electric wires should be installed, earthed and covered properly.

■ Store and arrange tools and equipment safely, securely and conveniently.

■ A fire alarm and extinguisher should always be installed.

■ The carver's environment tends to be dry and contain inflammable wood chips, finishing agents, etc. Never leave a naked flame unattended. No smoking is the best advice. If you need to use one, make sure a source of heat is safe *before* using it.

■ Bag up and remove dust and debris regularly, especially any rags used for finishing.

■ Use and store solvents, glues, turpentine, spirit- and oil-based stains, as well as all other finishes, in well-ventilated areas. Keep containers closed when not in use; and keep them away from children, heat and naked flames.

■ Make sure that where you walk is free from the danger of sharp edges and corners, things to bump into and wires to trip over. See that you can easily and safely work around your bench, and that wood chips and dust on the floor do not make it slippy.

■ Sharp tools left clamped in vices with their tangs or edges exposed, or projecting in the air on the bench, are dangerous.

■ Long hair, etc. should be tied back and loose clothing (cuffs and ties) and jewellery (necklaces and rings) should be kept away from the moving parts of machines – and in general out of the sphere of activity.

ELECTRIC TOOLS AND EQUIPMENT

■ Always follow the manufacturer's instructions and recommendations.

■ Familiarize yourself with any tool or piece of equipment *before* using it.

■ Guards, rests, etc. should be properly adjusted and *used*.

■ Keep hands and fingers well clear of moving parts – remember that accidents happen quickly, sometimes before you have noticed it. Never reach over or across machines.

■ Double check everything, including the locking of chucks, the table, or any fence before starting the machine.

■ Face or eye protection is often necessary. Grit and sparks are quite capable of penetrating the eyeball; chips of wood can fly off; and it is possible for a cutter or burr to break.

■ Keep face masks and eye and ear protection easily to hand – and put them on *before* using the equipment.

■ Fix work securely before drilling, power shaping, and so on.

■ Keep wiring from machines and electrical hand tools neatly out of the way, not trailing over the floor or work surfaces.

■ Always sharpen, or change, a blade or cutter with the machine isolated, that is with the plug pulled out.

■ Do not drip water from the cooling jar over motors, electrical connections or plugs.

■ Use a cutter or other accessories for a high-speed shaft at – or below – its maximum rated speed. Used *above* the speed for which they are designed, the cutter could fly apart, bend or otherwise be damaged.

■ Never use a bent or damaged cutter or burr in a high-speed flexible shaft; or one that vibrates or chatters – throw these away. Never force or pressure these accessories.

SAFETY PRECAUTIONS FOR WOODCARVERS

Again many of these points occur in context in this book and should be studied there.

■ Always hold work securely to a *stable* bench or surface.

■ Do not lay carving tools down with edges projecting, or close to where your hands are working.

■ Blunt tools require more force – sharp ones are less dangerous. Keep your tools sharp and clean.

■ Keep both hands, and fingers, *behind* the cutting edge at all times.

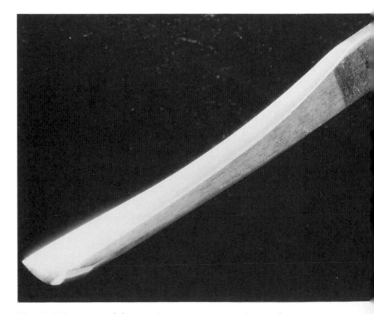

Fig 10.6 Beauty *and* danger; in some ways carving tools can be said to be 'double-edged'.

■ Never cut, or exert pressure, towards any part of the body.

■ A tough glove is recommended when rasps are being used. A fingerless glove will protect the heels of the hands when working on sharply cut wood.

■ Take particular care when using the benchstrop, especially with the forward stroke.

■ *Both* hands should be on the carving tool, with the blade-hand resting on the wood. The only exceptions to this are during mallet work and specific, one-handed carving techniques.

■ If using one hand to hold the work and the other to manipulate the chisel, use the thumb of the work-holding hand as a pivot or guide to control the cutting – *never* cut towards the work-holding hand.

■ In vigorous mallet work, especially with very hard, brittle or old and dry woods, eye protection is advisable.

■ Never try to catch a falling carving tool. Carve in footwear strong enough to protect the feet from such an event.

■ When sanding use a dust mask; *never* blow; and protect your eyes.

There are two other conditions which can affect carvers besides the obvious family of accidents.

Hand and wrist damage

Hand and wrist damage from thumping handles with the palm of the hand has been mentioned in the section about using mallets (*see* pages 202–4).

Repetitive strain injury

Repetitive strain injury is felt as a burning sensation in the wrist or elbow joints of those carvers prone to it, possibly with redness and swelling. The condition is caused by mechanical stress on a tendon attachment, especially through holding or repeating the same, tense position of the joint for long periods of time. The condition is commonly known as 'tennis elbow' or 'condylitis'. Seek medical advice early. This is important for reasons of health insurance. It can be a slow condition to clear up and may be incapacitating in the long term. On the other hand, there are forearm straps which can remove strain from the elbow and help full recovery. Do not think the problem has gone because you have taken pain killers. Besides removing the strain from the joint you will need to find new techniques of working which eliminate, or reduce, strain. Luckily there is plenty of scope for this in carving.

RESOURCES
Suppliers of tools and equipment

The following firms, in alphabetical order, are ones that I have dealt with personally and can recommend – not only for the excellent quality of the tools and equipment that they stock, but also the personal care with which they supply them. The fact that a firm is not included is in no way an adverse reflection on them. A lot of information is set out in this book on selecting tools and equipment, and more help will come from firms whose staff are interested, knowledgeable and friendly.

Some of the firms charge for what is often a substantial and very useful catalogue – phoning them may be the best approach. Most supply far more than the basic items that are listed and may be able to give the name of a local supplier of their own makes of tools.

UK

Avery Knight and Bowlers
James Street West
Bath
Avon BA1 2BT
Tel: (0225) 425894
■ Supply the French Auriou woodcarving tools; hand-cut rasps and rifflers; adzes and rotary rasps.

Axminster Power Tool Centre
Chard Street
Axminster
Devon EX13 5DZ
Tel: (0297) 33656
■ Supply Ashley Iles and Kirschen carving tools; knives, mallets, rifflers, carver's screws, scorps, adzes; full range of sharpening equipment; large range of other hand and power tools.

John Boddy Ltd
Riverside Sawmills
Boroughbridge
North Yorks YO5 9IJ
Tel: (0423) 322370
■ Supply Henry Taylor, Ashley Iles and Robert Sorby brands of woodcarving tools; knives, rifflers, punches, carver's screws and holdfasts; full range of sharpening equipment; Arbortech and guard; finishing products.

Bristol Design (Tools) Ltd:
14 Perry Road
Bristol BS1 5BG
Tel: (0272) 291740
▧ Supply their own make of carving tools; second-hand carving tools and other woodworking equipment; sharpening products; brass ferrules; tungsten carbide coated rifflers; adzes.

Craft Supplies Ltd
The Mill
Millers Dale
Buxton
Derbys SK17 8SN
Tel: (0298) 871636
▧ Supply many items for woodturners that may be useful to carvers: from glass domes to clock faces and mechanisms; brass ferrules; Stubai carver's screws; Pfeil and Sorby carving tools as well as other carving, sharpening and finishing products; PEG, native and some exotic woods.

Ashley Iles (Edge Tools) Ltd
Works: East Kirkby
Spilsby
Lincs PE23 4DD
Tel: (0790) 763372
▧ Supply their own make of carving tools; carver's screws; bench holdfasts; sharpening products.

Henry Taylor (Tools) Ltd
The Forge
Lowther Road
Sheffield S6 2DR
Tel: (0742) 340282/340321
▧ Supply their own make of carving tools; sharpening products; punches; rifflers, knives and adzes.

J. R. Simbles & Sons
The Broadway
Queens Road
Watford
Herts WD1 2LD
Tel: (0923) 226052
▧ Supply spindles, plummer blocks, wheels and all the parts needed to make a slow-speed grinder; very large selection of accessory bits and pieces useful to the carver; some carving tools, sharpening and finishing products, rifflers and high-speed cutters.

HTF Tools
16 Badgers Croft
Eccleshall
Stafford ST21 6DS
Tel: (0785) 850539
▧ Supply Lignostone mallets.

Record Tools Ltd
Parkway Works
Sheffield S9 3BL
Tel: (0742) 449066
▧ Supply Record adjustable carver's vice; carver's screws, bench vices.

Robert Sorby Ltd
Athol Road
Sheffield S8 0PA
Tel: (0742) 554231
▧ Supply their own make of carving tools.

Spencer Franklin Engineering
Windrush Industrial Park
Witney
Oxon OX8 5EZ
Tel: (0993) 776401
▧ Make and supply the range of Hydraclamp swivel-ball holding devices.

Tilgear
Bridge House
69 Station Road
Cuffley
Herts EN6 4BR
Tel: (0707) 873545
▧ Supply Pfeil woodcarving tools and knives; rifflers; full range of sharpening products; Tormek (wet) grinders; Foredom high-speed flexible shafts and full range of burrs and cutters; Spencer Franklin Hydraclamps; carver's screws, bench vices and holdfasts; finishing products.

Alec Tiranti Ltd
70 High Street
Theale
Berks. RG7 5AR
Tel: (0734) 302775
▧ Supply Henry Taylor woodcarving tools; full range of sharpening products; carver's screws, chops, mallets, adzes, rasps and rifflers; name and decorative punches; other sculpture material – Plasticine, modelling clay, plaster; high-speed burrs and cutters.

USA

Wayne Barton
Alpine School of Carving
225 Vine Avenue
Park Ridge
IL 60068
Tel: 708 692-2822

Gottlieb Brandli
Swiss Cabinetry
1609 13th Avenue
Monroe
WN 53566
Tel: 608 325-6681

Rick & Ellen Butz
PO Box 151
Blue Mountain Lake
NY 12812
Tel: 518 352-7737

Woodcraft Supply Corp
210 Wood County Industrial Park
PO Box 1686
Parkerburg
WV 26102
Tel: 304 464-5286

Suppliers of wood

The best place to start a search for local wood suppliers or timber yards is in woodcarving, woodturning and woodworking magazines. Follow this by asking other carvers and interested parties in your area. Then try the Yellow Pages and local papers.

John Boddy Ltd
Riverside Sawmills
Boroughbridge
North Yorks YO5 9LJ
Tel: (0423) 322370

Craft Supplies Ltd
The Mill
Millers Dale
Buxton
Derbys SK17 8SN
Tel: (0298) 871636

English Timbers
1a Main Street
Kirkburn
Driffield
East Yorks YO25 9DU
Tel: (0377) 89301

B. & P.L. Goodrum
Laindon Barn
Dunton Road
Laindon
Essex SS15 4BD
Tel: (0268) 419432

R. & L. Keenleyside
16–19 Station Road
Bedlington Station
Northumberland NE22 7JN
Tel: (0670) 823133

Lothian Tree Services
Whitehill Sawmill
Thornton Farm
Rosewell
Midlothian EH24 9EF
Tel: (031) 440 4175

North Higham Sawmills
Paddock Street
Norwich
Norfolk NR2 4TW
Tel: (0603) 622978

Wessex Timber
Longney
Gloucester GL2 6SJ
Tel: (0452) 740610

Working Tree
Milland
Nr Liphook
Hants GU30 7JS
Tel: (0428) 741505

Yandle and Sons
Hurst Works
Martock
Somerset TA12 6JU
Tel: (0935) 822207

Miscellaneous suppliers

LEATHER

Association of Designer–Leatherworkers
c/o MacGregor and Michael
37 Silver Street
Tetbury
Glos. GL8 8DL
If any woodcarver writes to the ADL (with an SAE) they will be happy to put them in touch with a local leatherworker.

TURNING TOOLS AND EQUIPMENT

Craft Supplies Ltd
The Mill
Millers Dale
Buxton
Derbys SK17 8SN
Tel: (0298) 871636

BOOKS

GMC Publications
166 High Street
Lewes
East Sussex BN7 1XU
Tel: 0273 477374

Stobart Davies Ltd
Priory House
Priory Street
Hertford SG14 1RN
Tel: (0992) 501518

CONVERSION TABLES

Use the following ratios to convert between imperial and metric measurements:

1 foot	=	0.30 metres
1 metre	=	3.28 feet
1lb	=	0.45 kg
1kg	=	2.20 lb
1 UK pint	=	0.57 litres
1 litre	=	1.76 UK pints

Tool catalogues often use the following approximations between imperial and metric size.

INCHES	MM	INCHES	MM
$\frac{1}{16}$	2	$\frac{7}{8}$	22
$\frac{1}{8}$	3	1	25
$\frac{3}{16}$	5	$1\frac{1}{8}$	30
$\frac{1}{4}$	6	$1\frac{1}{4}$	32
$\frac{5}{16}$	8	$1\frac{3}{8}$	36
$\frac{3}{8}$	10	$1\frac{1}{2}$	38
$\frac{7}{16}$	11	$1\frac{3}{4}$	44
$\frac{1}{2}$	13	2	51
$\frac{5}{8}$	16	$2\frac{1}{2}$	64
$\frac{3}{4}$	19	3	76

INDEX

ABOUT THE AUTHOR

Chris Pye has been both a professional woodcarver and woodturner for nearly 20 years. He started with carving, owing his formative introduction to the master woodcarver Gino Masero. A little later he added woodturning, learning from many individuals. His first love has always been carving but he considers himself equally at home in both crafts, often combining them.

His carved work, which is mainly commissioned, covers a broad spectrum and ranges from lettering to heraldry; large bedheads and organ screens to small butterflies; figurework and personal sculpture to the restoration of old carvings and decorative work on furniture. He is also skilled at making and altering his own carving tools.

In the turning field his work varies from 10ft (3m) newel posts and stair parts to table legs, lamps and knobs for the trade; as well as individual bowls and boxes. Turning and carving are combined in four-poster bedposts, barley twists, lettered bowls, columns and various one-off pieces. In 1991 he demonstrated at the Association of Woodturners of Great Britain's International Seminar in Loughborough.

Chris Pye has several years of experience teaching adult education classes in woodcarving as well as private students in both turning and carving. He runs regular courses from his home in the Golden Valley on the edge of the Black Mountains. Presently he is undertaking a Post-Graduate Certificate in Education at Hereford Technical College, concentrating on the teaching of these subjects.

A regular contributor to *Woodcarving*, *Woodturning* and other magazines, this is his first book – the first of a series of books on carving – with others in line on turning, and combining the two crafts.

Chris Pye was born in Co. Durham but has lived a large part of his life in the south west of England. A Buddhist for over 25 years, when not carving, turning or writing, he likes painting and enjoys spending time with his wife and two sons, Daniel and Finian.

Chris Pye
The Poplars
Ewyas Harold
Herefordshire HR2 0HU